WINDOWS™ 3
COMPANION

WINDOWS™ 3
COMPANION

Lori L. Lorenz
R. Michael O'Mara

With:

Mark W. Crane
Jeff Yocom
Linda Baughman

Edited by:

Clyde Zellers

Louisville, Kentucky

PUBLISHED BY
Microsoft Press
A Division of Microsoft Corporation
One Microsoft Way, Redmond, Washington 98052-6399

Copyright © 1990 by Lori L. Lorenz and R. Michael O'Mara

Library of Congress Cataloging-in-Publication Data

Lorenz, Lori L., 1962-
      Windows 3 companion / Lori L. Lorenz, R. Michael O'Mara.
         p.   cm.
      ISBN 0-936767-19-7 : $27.95
      1. Microsoft Windows (Computer programs) I. O'Mara, R. Michael,
1951- . II. Title. III. Title: Windows three companion.
QA76.76.W56L67   1990
005.4'3- -dc20
                                   90-5920
                                   CIP

Printed and bound in the United States of America.

4 5 6 7 8 9 R A R A 4 3 2 1 0

Distributed to the book trade in Canada by General Publishing Company, Ltd.

Distributed to the book trade outside the United States and Canada by Penguin Books Ltd.

Penguin Books Ltd., Harmondsworth, Middlesex, England
Penguin Books Australia Ltd., Ringwood, Victoria, Australia
Penguin Books N.Z. Ltd., 182-190 Wairau Road, Auckland 10, New Zealand

British Cataloging in Publication Data available   ———

TABLE OF CONTENTS

SECTION 1: USING MICROSOFT WINDOWS

SECTION 2: USING PROGRAM MANAGER APPLICATIONS

11 Using Paintbrush

12 Using Terminal

13 Using Recorder

14 Using Desktop Accessories

15 Playing Games

SECTION 3: BEYOND THE BASICS

SECTION 4: APPENDICES

SECTION 5: REFERENCE

Dedication

To Danielle Aldebaran, another first—LLL
To Mrs. Helen Scott, for inspiration, even now—RMO
To my mother and all-time MVP, Wanda Gail Crane—MWC
To Greg Zoeller, my friend whom I don't see enough—JPY
To the memory of Rose L. Fairfax, editor and friend—LYB

Acknowledgments

We are indebted to many people for their assistance with this book:

Clyde Zellers, for verifying the technical accuracy and for coordinating the editing with good judgment, tact, and a sense of humor.

Maureen Pawley, for coordinating the production, typesetting, and assembly, and for experimenting with methods for capturing figures.

Linda Watkins, Pamela Moore, Toni Bowers, Jim Welp, Jody Gilbert, Duane Spurlock, Martha Clayton, and Mary Welp for conscientious editing despite a harrowing schedule.

Karl Feige, for the color figures, Paintbrush figures, and section breaks and Julie Tirpak, for the cover design.

Tim Landgrave and Blake Ragsdell, for technical assistance with networks and on-line communications and Joe Pierce, for technical assistance with the memory section.

Doug Cobb and Tom Cottingham, for initiating the book project and for resources, direction, and a pleasant working environment. Lou Armstrong and Tracy Smith, for getting another modem line quickly. Allan McGuffey, for photos for the color poster in Paintbrush. Gena Cobb, for help with the index. Shalana Hampton, Alex Baughman, and Ann Rockers, for copying and helping with corrections.

Dave and Jo-Ann Parks at Printer's Type Service, for outstanding service once again.

Mike Tonegawa for the picture on the back cover.

Lori Sills at Microsoft, for quick response to our requests and questions.

Danny Castleman at The Computer Shop, for technical assistance with new products and a chance to work with an HP ScanJet Plus.

Our families and loved ones, for their encouragement and patience when our work disrupted their lives.

Finally, to the rest of The Cobb Group—Gary Barnhart, Lisa Beebe, Doug Been, Julia Bennett, Tara Billinger, Jenny Camacho, Katherine Chesky, Steve Cobb, Teresa Codey, Gordon Colby, Luanne Flynn, Laura Heuser, Rebecca Hodge, Godwin Ighodaro, Lori Junkins, Ginger Kepple, Kathleen Lane, Janice Marks, Marco Mason, Elayne Noltemeyer, Beth Ording, Jonathan Pyles, Beth Riggle, Raven Sexton, Brent Shean, Patricia Shields, Gina Sledge, Kim Spalding, Tirri Totten, Elaine Van Horn, Jeff Warner, Kellie Woods, and Peggy Zeillmann—for sharing our experiences and goals.

Preface

*T*he most exciting of Windows 3's many new features is its advanced memory-management capabilities. With Windows 3, you can unleash the power of your 286 or 386 computer's protected mode. Unlike earlier releases that made you purchase separate versions of Windows for different hardware, Windows 3 integrates in one package three operating modes to derive maximum speed and functionality from your computer. Its new Setup routine will detect which hardware you have and configure your computer and Windows to work together. Once installed, Windows automatically starts in the appropriate mode. Developers can now include more features in their Windows applications, while users can run more applications simultaneously and manipulate larger quantities of data.

If you want to use a mix of DOS and Windows applications, you can load several applications, then switch between them without returning to the DOS prompt. In fact, if you're using a 386-based computer, Windows will let DOS applications execute *simultaneously* with your Windows applications. Windows' new program execution shell—Program Manager—presents your applications as icons you can run with a click of your mouse and allows you to set up additional icons to run DOS, as well as Windows, applications.

Valuable new applications and extended features of familiar ones provide welcome additions to Windows 3. File Manager replaces the cumbersome MS-DOS Executive with file and directory icons you can manipulate in the Directory Tree. Print Manager lets you queue your printing tasks so you can work in another application while you print. With Windows' expanded Control Panel, you can customize your system without manually editing the WIN.INI. The new PIF Editor includes options to access the powerful new multitasking features of the 386 enhanced mode. Windows 3 provides Recorder for recording and playing back macros, an enhanced Terminal with new file transfer protocols, and many helpful tools for accessing network resources. If your time permits, you'll enjoy the challenge of Windows' version of Solitaire with multiple scoring options.

Windows 3 helps PC users work in a more natural, intuitive fashion. Its attractive "3-D" graphical user interface makes all Windows applications easy to learn and fun to use. In short, Windows 3 is *the* operating environment to go with for the 1990s. All of its power is not without a price, however—Windows is a very complex environment. Even with its user-friendly features, learning Windows is a big job.

ABOUT THIS BOOK

We wrote *Windows 3 Companion* to help make Microsoft Windows 3 easier to learn and use. If you are new to the Windows operating environment, you can use this book as a tutorial to help you get started. If you're already familiar with Windows, you can use this book as a reference guide to help you fully utilize the new capabilities of Windows 3.

We had two goals in mind as we created this book. First, we wanted to help you learn to use Windows efficiently—after all, one of Windows' strongest selling points is that it saves time. Second, we wanted to provide Windows information in a format that you can return to time and time again, whether you're a Windows novice or an expert. We think we've achieved both goals.

Organization

We designed the five sections of *Windows 3 Companion* to help you quickly find the information you need. Even if you've worked with earlier releases of Windows, you'll want to skim the chapters in Section 1 to learn how to use the new options. You should read the chapters on File Manager and Print Manager so you can take advantage of these time-saving additions to Windows. In Section 2, we show you how to work with applications such as Write, Paintbrush, Terminal, and Recorder. We also explain the features of the Desktop accessories and provide tips for improving your Reversi and Solitaire skills. Section 3 eliminates the mystery of Windows' three operating modes and explains which mode is compatible with various hardware configurations. If you plan to work with both Windows and non-Windows applications, you'll need to pay careful attention to the chapter on PIFs. Appendix 1 in Section 4 discusses installation procedures. Since Windows relies heavily on color to communicate, in Appendix 2, we provide a color version of selected figures. The Reference section includes a glossary of Windows terms and a thoroughly cross-referenced index. The menu maps will help you track down elusive dialog boxes, and the detachable quick reference pages list keyboard shortcuts.

Throughout the book, we added icons to many side headings to help you find information about specific applications, functions, and tools. Each Windows application and Control Panel setting is represented by a unique icon, which we present with the introduction to the application or setting. All Paintbrush tool icons appear with headings that identify their functions.

A graduate of Carleton College in Minnesota, Lori L. Lorenz worked as an information center consultant at Westinghouse Materials Company and Honeywell, Inc., before joining The Cobb Group as an author. Lori is an assistant editor of *Inside Microsoft Windows*, The Cobb Group's new monthly publication for Windows users.

R. Michael O'Mara wrote technical manuals and served as vice president of presentation services for Kinetic Corporation before joining The Cobb Group as an author. His background includes specialties in computer graphics, business communications, and design. Mike is a graduate of Morehead State University in Kentucky.

Mark W. Crane is the author of *Word for Windows Companion* and is the co-author of several Cobb Group books, including *LaserJet Companion, Quattro Companion*, and *HyperPAD Companion*. He is also editor-in-chief of three Cobb Group journals: *Inside Microsoft Windows, Inside Word for Windows*, and *Inside MS-DOS*. Mark holds a B.S. from Purdue University and served as a PC specialist with Citizens Fidelity Corporation before joining The Cobb Group.

Jeff Yocom co-authored the books *Word for Windows Companion, Douglas Cobb's Paradox 3 Handbook, Hands-On Paradox 3*, and *LaserJet Companion*. He is also editor-in-chief of *Inside WordPerfect* and the *Paradox User's Journal*. A graduate of the University of Louisville, Jeff was a writer and software specialist at U of L's Office of News and Public Information before joining The Cobb Group.

Linda Baughman is manager of training at The Cobb Group. A graduate of the University of Kentucky and the University of Louisville, Linda taught business and technical writing at the University of Louisville before joining The Cobb Group as an editor.

ABOUT THE AUTHORS

During our months of research in preparation for *Windows 3 Companion*, we explored every feature of Windows. The result was more material than we could conceivably include in one book. Our continuing work with Windows has garnered additional tips, techniques, and shortcuts that we'd like to tell you about.

If you're interested in learning more about Microsoft Windows, we urge you to subscribe to The Cobb Group's monthly journal for Windows users—*Inside Microsoft Windows*. Each month, this journal explains tips and techniques that will help you become more proficient with this powerful operating environment. It allows us to pass along to you all the exciting new capabilities and techniques we uncover as we continue to explore Windows. To receive a free issue of *Inside Microsoft Windows*, just fill out and return the card located at the back of this book.

THERE'S MORE!

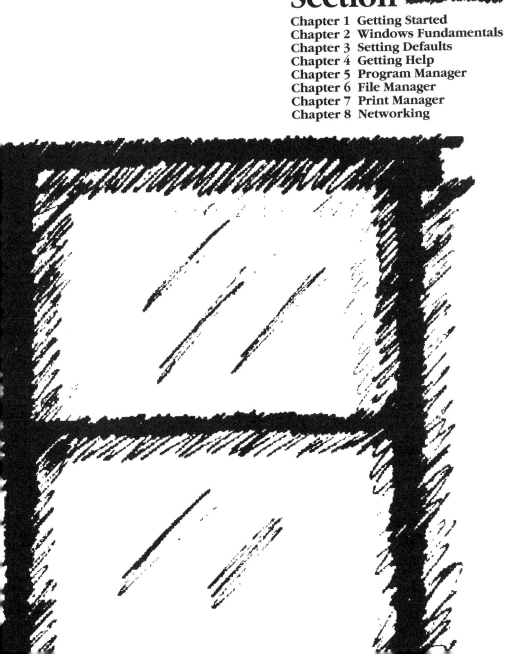

Section 1

Using Microsoft Windows

In this chapter

Getting Started 1

*I*n this chapter, we'll review the key features of Microsoft Windows 3 and go over what you'll need to install and run it. (If you are installing Windows yourself, you'll want to refer to the complete installation procedure outlined in Appendix 1.) We'll explain how to start Windows in each of its operating modes, and how to exit Windows and return to the DOS prompt. Then, we'll list your options for tailoring Windows to suit your needs and explain where to find more information on customizing Windows.

WHY SHOULD I DO WINDOWS?

Microsoft Windows replaces the sparse and often intimidating DOS command line with a visually pleasing and richly featured graphical user interface. You interact with the computer by selecting commands from intuitive, easy-to-use menus or by pointing at icons instead of typing terse instructions at the *C:>* prompt. Your mouse replaces the keyboard as your primary means of communication with the computer. Windows offers the advantages of a consistent, predictable interface for all Windows-based applications. Whether you are using a spreadsheet, a word processor, or a desktop publishing application, you always open a file or print a document the same way. Each application appears in a rectangular window on your screen. You can see the contents of several windows at a time, move information between them, and switch from one application to another with a click of a mouse—without exiting one application and loading another. Windows-based applications not only share a common user interface that makes learning to use several applications easy, Windows provides common access to your display, printers, and other system peripherials for all your Windows-based applications.

Windows has a completely redesigned look with new colors, fonts, 3D buttons, and other new or improved applications. Windows' new program execution shell—Program Manager—presents your applications as icons, organized into groups, ready for you to select and run with a click of your mouse. With the new File Manager, you can copy a file by simply dragging its file icon to the symbol for a different drive. The Task Manager makes it easier than ever before to switch between applications; and the new, expanded Control Panel allows you to control your Windows environment with unprecedented ease.

With the introduction of Windows 3, your 80286- or 80386-based computer is released from the confines of the DOS 640Kb barrier. Windows 3 can now use the full potential of your 286- or 386-based computer's protected mode to bring advanced memory management and true multitasking to all your Windows applications. DOS and conventional DOS-based applications can't exploit the potential of your 286 or 386 computer, but Windows can! With a 386 computer, you can even run DOS applications and Windows applications simultaneously.

**Windows'
operating modes**

Windows has three operating modes. Real mode is the previous standard and is compatible with essentially all MS-DOS computers and the previous versions of Windows. The two new operating modes—standard and 386 enhanced—take advantage of the protected modes of 286 and 386 chips to add extended memory management and improved multitasking capabilities to Windows 3. Windows no longer comes in different versions for different computers. All three operating modes are integrated into a single package, and Windows will even sense automatically which mode is appropriate for your hardware.

Real mode simulates the operation of an 8088 computer and does not address extended memory (even if it is available). You'll be confined to the 640Kb of conventional memory, which strictly limits the size and number of tasks you can run. Real mode sacrifices most of the advanced memory management capabilities of Windows 3. You will, however, be able to use expanded memory if you have memory that meets the LIM EMS 4.0 standard installed on your system.

In standard mode, Windows can access the full 16Mb of extended memory addressable by the 80286 chip, and can multitask Windows-based applications. But DOS applications will be suspended while you are working in the Windows environment, and Windows applications will be suspended while a DOS application is active. You'll need this mode to avoid conflicts with applications such as Lotus 1-2-3 release 3 that use DOS extenders.

Windows' most powerful operating mode is 386 enhanced mode, which uses the protected mode of the 80386 processor to maximize your computer's memory management and multitasking capabilities. On an 80386-based computer, Windows can address the maximum amount of extended memory and reallocate memory to the various tasks it runs. It can even create virtual 8088 machines in memory so that each application thinks that it is running on its own computer. In 386 enhanced mode, and with the appropriate PIF file settings, Windows can implement multitasking for some of your DOS applications so that they can continue to run in the background, even while you work with another application in the foreground.

To install and run Windows, your computer system must meet certain specifications that we will detail in this chapter. We will assume that you are familiar with the concepts and terms involved in software installation. If you are a novice, we suggest you consult your local PC guru or vendor to obtain a clearer understanding of these concepts.

SYSTEM SPECIFICATIONS

Windows requires at least an MS-DOS-based computer with a minimum of 640Kb of RAM, a hard drive, and a monitor. In addition, you'll want a mouse and a printer, plus a modem if you want to use Windows' Terminal application. These are the minimum requirements for Windows to run in real mode—its least powerful, and least demanding, configuration. You'll need a 386 computer and extended memory to use all the features of Windows 3. You'll see a noticeable difference in Windows' performance on faster machines.

Hardware

- 286/386-based computer—Although Windows will run on almost any MS-DOS computer with 640Kb of RAM, you'll need a computer based on the Intel 80286 or 80386 chips (such as an IBM PC AT, IBM PS/2, or a compatible) to take advantage of many of Windows' important features. Windows uses the protected mode available on these chips to facilitate multitasking and extended memory management in its standard mode. Of course, Windows' 386 enhanced mode is available only if you have a 386 computer with extended memory. Computers based on the Intel 8088 or 8086 chips (such as the IBM PC and XT and their compatibles) can operate only in real mode. They will be confined by the 640Kb of conventional memory, which severely limits Windows. And that, in the world of Windows, leaves you on the outside looking in. In addition, performance may be frustratingly slow on older, typically slower, machines.

- 1+Mb RAM—Microsoft recommends that your computer have at least 1Mb of total memory (640Kb conventional, plus 384Kb extended). You should configure any memory above 1Mb as extended memory for the best performance from Windows. You'll want 2 Mb (or more) of extended memory if you plan to use Windows' multitasking capabilities with large applications. Windows 386 enhanced mode requires at least 2 Mb of memory. Windows will run in real mode if you have less than 1 Mb of memory. However, in this memory configuration, Windows will limit the functions you can use.

- A hard drive—You need a hard drive with 6-8 Mb free, and at least one floppy drive for the installation disks.

- Monitor and graphic display adapter—Windows will work with many of the common video graphics adapters and monitors. If your specific display is not on Windows' list of supported devices, consult the manufacturer of your equipment. Many will have special drivers available to allow you to use their equipment with Windows 3. Your other option is to select one of Windows' generic drivers which, although it probably won't make optimal use of your display, will probably allow you to use Windows on your equipment. A graphical user interface really comes into its own on a high resolution display. As such, we strongly recommend a VGA (or at least an EGA) display—preferably in color.

- Mouse—You can operate Windows solely with the keyboard, but you need a mouse to realize the full benefit of the graphical user interface.

- Optional hardware—You'll need a Hayes-compatible modem if you plan to use Windows' Terminal application for communications. For printing, you'll need one of the printers Windows supports. As with displays, the manufacturer of your printer may have a driver available to allow you to use your printer with Windows 3, even if it does not appear on Windows' standard list of supported devices.

DOS

Windows needs MS-DOS or PC-DOS versions 3.1 or higher installed on your computer. Although Windows' environment may seem to be a separate operating system, it is not! Windows adds to and expands—but does not replace—the DOS operating system. You need them both.

Compatible software

To get the maximum benefit from your Windows environment, you'll need to use applications created specifically for Windows, such as Microsoft Excel, Microsoft Word for Windows, and Aldus PageMaker. Windows-based applications will have a consistent user interface and the ability to smoothly integrate with the other applications on your desktop. They will all share the same printers and other system resources under Windows' direction, and pass information back and forth through Windows' Clipboard.

Initially, a few older Windows applications may not be fully compatible with the new memory management and fonts of Windows 3. If you get an error message when you try to run an older Windows application in Windows 3, you need to check with the software manufacturer to see if an update is available. Until you receive the update, you can operate Windows in real mode for compatibility with older applications.

However, you aren't limited to Windows-based applications. You can launch many of your favorite DOS applications from within Windows. Some DOS applications will run in a window on your desktop along side your Windows applications and retain at least some of the advantages of the Windows environment. Others must run full screen.

A few applications and system utility programs are incompatible with Windows 3. The first form of incompatibility concerns system enhancement software such as 386MAX, DESQview, and other programs that use the protected mode of your 286 or 386 processor to offer memory management or multitasking services not available in DOS. Windows 3 now includes protected mode control in its standard and 386 enhanced modes; and, in general, you can't expect two programs that attempt to control your 286 or 386 processor's protected mode to co-exist on your computer.

Incompatibilities

Applications that use "DOS extenders" to address memory beyond the 640Kb of conventional memory may conflict with Windows 3 in some operating modes. Lotus 1-2-3 release 3 and dBase IV are examples of large, complex applications that use this technology. As this book goes to press, we expect most major applications using DOS extenders to run in Windows real or standard modes, but not under 386 enhanced mode. The situation may improve as software developers work to resolve the conflicts.

A more common form of incompatibility is a "pop-up" or TSR (Terminate-and-Stay-Resident) program. Although some TSRs—such as most networks—will work just fine with Windows, many pop-up utilities won't be available while you are operating in the Windows environment.

An outstanding Setup utility program is included to install Windows on your computer. Windows is a complex product, and installing it can be a lengthy process; but the Setup utility program leads you painlessly through the entire installation procedure. Of course, we've learned to expect an installation program to automatically copy files from the installation disks to your hard drive. But Setup doesn't stop there! It examines your system and configures Windows to work with the hardware it finds installed, modifies your AUTOEXEC.BAT and CONFIG.SYS files, allows you to install and configure your printer, and searches your hard drive for existing applications and installs them in Windows' Program Manager. The Setup utility program allows you the option of controlling each step of your Windows installation, and it even has its own Help system. After running the Setup utility program and rebooting your computer, Windows will be ready to run. See Appendix 1 for more complete information on installing Windows.

INSTALLING WINDOWS

If you have a previous version of Windows installed on your computer, Setup (Windows' installation utility) will automatically save some of your preferences and system information for use in Windows 3. We've included a special section in Appendix 1 to help you make the transition from your old Windows environment to the new and improved version.

Upgrading to Windows 3

**STARTING
WINDOWS**

To start Windows, simply type *WIN* at the DOS prompt and press [Enter]. Windows will start in the default operating mode for your machine and immediately run the Program Manager, from which you'll be able to launch your applications. You can add switches to the basic Windows startup command to invoke a different operating mode, fine-tune Windows' use of expanded memory, or run a specified application immediately upon entering the Windows environment.

**The Windows
mode switch**

By default, Windows starts in the most powerful operating mode supported by your hardware. If you have an 80386-based computer with extended memory, Windows will start in 386 enhanced mode. If your computer is an 80286 (IBM AT, PS/2 30-50, or compatible) with extended memory, Windows will use its standard mode. Windows uses real mode as the default operating mode for other machines.

Occasionally, you may need to override Windows' default operating mode for your machine. You might need to run Windows in real mode for compatibility with older Windows applications, or you might want to run standard mode on a 386 machine. You can add a command line switch to the starting command to specify Windows' operating mode.

Standard mode

If you start Windows with the command *WIN/S,* you can force Windows into standard mode, even on a 386-based computer. You don't need to explicitly invoke standard mode on a 286-based computer, since Windows will recognize the 80286 processor and use that mode as the default when you start the program with the *WIN* command.

386 enhanced mode

On a 386 machine with at least 2Mb of RAM, 386 enhanced mode is the default, so you shouldn't need to use the *WIN /3* command to explicitly invoke 386 enhanced mode.

Real mode

You can instruct Windows to run in real mode by starting the program with the command: *WIN/R.* There are additional command line switches available to fine-tune how Windows uses your expanded memory in real mode.

Previous versions of Windows offered only real mode; consequently, you may need to use it for compatibility with some older Windows-based applications. Some non-Windows DOS applications may also run only in real mode.

The Run command

If you want to run an application as soon as you enter the Windows environment, you can specify its file name as part of the Windows startup command. For example, typing the command *WIN /S CALENDAR.EXE* will start Windows in standard mode and immediately run the Calendar application. The Program Manager will appear as an icon on your desktop instead of taking its usual place as the active window. If the application you want to run is in a different drive or directory that is not part of your DOS search path, you must supply a full path name in addition to the file name of the application you want to run.

You can go a step farther with the Run command by supplying the name of a document or data file for the application to open as soon as it begins running. Just add the file name to the Windows startup command line, after the file name for the application. For example, if you use the command line *WIN C:\EXCEL\ EXCEL.EXE B:\CHECKBK.XLS,* Windows will start in the default operating mode for your machine, automatically run Microsoft Excel, which is in the \EXCEL directory of the C drive, and then immediately open the CHECKBK.XLS spreadsheet file from the disk in the B drive.

EXITING WINDOWS

The safest way to end a Windows session and return to the DOS prompt is to select Exit Windows from the File menu in Program Manager. Close commands are available, and may seem equivalent; but always returning to Program Manager and using the Exit Windows command is the best way to ensure that Windows will close all open files and take care of other housekeeping chores before you leave the Windows environment. Refer to Chapter 6 for more information on the necessity for proper exit procedures.

TAILORING WINDOWS TO YOUR NEEDS

You can control the look and feel of Windows as you install printers, fonts, and applications. You can change all those choices, and many more, from within Windows—without reinstalling the software. The Control Panel and Windows Setup applications allow you to modify your Windows environment to accommodate changes in your computer equipment, your current needs, or your changing preferences.

The Control Panel options

The Control Panel application offers extensive opportunities to customize your Windows environment to fit your own needs and style. You can make most of the changes "on-the-fly" while you work with Windows. When you exit from Windows, you'll have the option to keep the changes you've made as the new defaults, or to discard them. Occasionally, you'll have to reboot Windows to implement a major change.

With Control Panel you can configure your computer's ports, and install, remove, configure, and select printers. You can control international settings like date or currency formats, and set your keyboard for foreign language characters. You will be able to delete, add, and size the fonts you employ for more appealing and effective communications. The Color and Desktop commands allow you to customize Windows' appearance to your own personal taste. The Mouse command can switch your mouse buttons and adjust tracking sensitivity. You also can change your system date and time, and disable the sound if you find the computer's beeps annoying. The Control Panel also includes special settings for the multitasking functions of 386 enhanced mode. We'll cover the Control Panel and its many options in Chapter 3.

Windows Setup

The Windows Setup application allows you to restructure Windows to reflect changes in your display, keyboard, mouse, network, or swap file. However, you probably won't need to change any of these settings unless you physically change your computer hardware.

The portion of Windows Setup that you are likely to use is its Set Up Applications... command. After you install new Windows-based applications on your computer, you can instruct Windows Setup to search your disk drives for the applications and install them in Program Manager. Refer to Chapter 6 for a full explanation of the Windows Setup application.

Adding applications another way

You also can add applications directly to the Program Manager. In fact, you can create and remove group windows and arrange your applications to appear any way you like. As soon as you finish installing Windows, you'll probably need to go to the Program Manager to add some of your non-Windows applications that Windows Setup didn't recognize. Chapter 5 will help you explore the power of the Program Manager.

Windows needs to know a number of technical details about the applications it runs. Windows-based applications are designed to automatically supply Windows with the information it needs. For non-Windows applications, the information goes into a separate PIF file. Often software developers will supply a PIF file to facilitate the use of their application with Windows. But, you may need to create or edit the PIF file to enable some of your non-Windows applications to run well in Windows. Chapter 17 explains the PIF editor.

WIN.INI and friends

The preferences and configuration information for Windows are stored in special files (WIN.INI, and SYSTEM.INI) on your hard drive. The Windows Setup and Control Panel applications give you the flexibility to change almost any aspect of the Windows environment easily and quickly and record those changes in the INI files. Previous versions of Windows required you to modify those files directly to control some features—a tedious and confusing procedure filled with the potential for mistakes. Although you can read and edit the information in these files with Notepad (or any ASCII text editor), it will seldom be necessary. Only program developers, or an occasional PC technician, will need to edit the INI files.

In this chapter

Windows Fundamentals 2

*W*indows offers something special for everyone who uses a personal computer. Perhaps its most powerful feature is its ability to address 16 megabytes (Mb) of memory or more for Windows applications, allowing them to run fast and implement a wide range of useful services. In addition to its advanced memory-management capabilities, Windows also sports an attractive graphical user interface that makes all Windows applications easy to learn and fun to use.

You may be surprised to know that Windows will let you load several DOS applications at once (even if your machine has only 1Mb of memory), and switch between them without returning to the DOS prompt. On a 386-based computer, Windows will even let you run multiple DOS applications simultaneously.

In this chapter, we'll introduce to you the feature you'll probably care about the most—Windows' graphical environment, which is also known as Windows' graphical user interface (GUI). If you're already familiar with the graphical environments of the Apple Macintosh or a previous version of Windows, we suggest you skim this chapter just to be sure you're familiar with our terminology. If you've worked only in a character-based environment, however, you'll want to read this chapter carefully—it lays the groundwork for everything to follow.

If you've never worked in a graphical environment before, you'll find that working in Windows is much easier (and more fun) than working in a character-based environment. One reason you'll enjoy Windows' graphical environment is because you can do much of your work with the mouse instead of the keyboard. By using the mouse to manipulate various elements on the screen directly, you can quickly and easily perform tasks that would otherwise require dozens of keystrokes. If you haven't installed a mouse on your computer (or if you're a keyboard fanatic), you'll be relieved to know that most Windows applications will let you use either the keyboard or the mouse.

UNDERSTANDING THE ENVIRONMENT

Windows' graphical environment also provides three key features you'll find in nearly all Windows applications: drop-down menus, dialog boxes, and icons. As you'll discover later in this chapter, these three elements are the primary reason Windows' applications are easy to learn and use. Once you've learned to use your first application, you can come up to speed on a new application quickly because these graphical elements give all Windows applications a similar look and feel.

Another benefit to working in Windows' graphical environment is that it allows you to easily exchange information between applications. In fact, you can either dynamically link applications so that data is automatically updated as it changes, or you can copy and paste data from one application to another without establishing a dynamic link.

Finally, Windows' graphical environment allows you to see on the screen an exact representation of an application's printed output. For example, if you're using a word processor to create a report that uses a variety of type styles, Windows will let you see on the screen how the report will appear when you print it. In addition, if you want to integrate both text and graphics on a single page, Windows will allow you to view both the text and graphics on the screen simultaneously. This ability to see on the screen what will appear in the printed output is referred to as WYSIWYG (What-You-See-Is-What-You-Get) capability.

Before we move on, keep in mind that there is a fundamental difference between the way you'll approach commands in a graphical environment as opposed to a character-based environment. Instead of selecting a command and indicating what you want that command to act upon, Windows applications require that you first indicate what material you want the command to affect, and then select the command. For example, to assign boldface to some text in a document, you would first highlight the text you want to make bold, then issue the command that assigns boldfacing. You'll see many examples of this type of syntax throughout this book.

USING THE POINTER

The pointer, a floating graphic on your screen that represents the actions of your mouse, will let you interact with Windows. The pointer will assume several shapes, depending on how its function changes. You'll see the pointer change into a different graphic when you start an application, move objects on the desktop, or use a Paintbrush tool.

The pointer's graphic is directly related to what you're doing with Windows. For example, if you start an application and are waiting for it to open, the pointer turns into an hourglass. Table 2-1 shows an assortment of the pointers you'll use in Windows. Because some pointers have an active area that does all the work, you must have the active area of the pointer on top of an item or pointing to a specific spot in order for the pointer to accomplish its task. For example, the I-beam pointer must be positioned on the text you want to manipulate.

Table 2-1

Pointer	Name	Definition
⯯	Arrow pointer	The "mouse" pointer for all Windows applications is used for selecting commands, activating applications, and moving windows.
⤢ ⇕ ⇔	Sizing pointers	These pointers adjust the size of a window on the desktop.
✥	Move pointer	This pointer allows you to move a window with the arrow keys to a new location on the desktop.
+	Crosshair pointer	Whenever you work with graphics, you'll see the crosshair pointer or a variation of it. This pointer is often found in Windows' drawing application, Paintbrush.
☞	Hand pointer	The Help application uses the hand pointer to jump between Help topics. You can read more about the hand pointer and Help topics in Chapter 4.
⌛	Hourglass pointer	The hourglass pointer indicates that Windows is working to complete the command you issued. While the hourglass is on the desktop, you can't issue any other commands or select desktop elements. When the pointer returns to its previous shape, you can go to the next task.
I	I-beam pointer	The default arrow pointer changes into an I-beam shape whenever you point to a desktop element that works with text. You'll also see a blinking vertical line, or cursor, in that desktop element. Although the cursor is sometimes called an insertion point marker, we'll use the term *cursor.*
⊘	Prevent pointer	The prevent pointer indicates that you can't relocate a desktop element where you're pointing. Later in this chapter and in Chapters 5 and 6, you'll see references to the prevent pointer.

You'll see these pointers throughout Windows.

Navigating

Pointer movements correspond to the movements you make with the mouse. If you move the mouse to the right, the pointer moves to the right. The mouse buttons enable you to perform Windows functions. The left mouse button is the primary button. The right mouse button is used for special functions, which we'll point out as we discuss Windows' applications. If you'd prefer to use the right mouse button as your primary button, use Windows' Control Panel to swap the function of the left and right mouse buttons. Chapter 3 explains this process.

When you're navigating with the keyboard, you'll use the direction keys ([Page Up], [Page Down], [Home], [End], ↑, ↓, ←, and →) to move through selections or text. You'll also use the [Tab] key to move between elements in a dialog box.

Selecting

When you want to run an application or choose a command, you use the mouse to issue your instructions. Windows uses three main mouse actions for selecting: clicking, double-clicking, and dragging. Clicking is a single press and release of the left mouse button. Double-clicking is pressing the left mouse button twice in quick succession. Dragging involves holding down the left mouse button and moving the mouse without releasing the button. After you select a series of items or text by dragging or move an item by dragging, you release the button to complete the action. We use the terms click and drag, and drag interchangeably.

Windows also uses some variations of the three main mouse actions. Later when we discuss the various Windows desktop accessories like Write, we'll introduce functions that require mouse and keyboard action. Tasks that use the mouse with specific keys are secondary functions just like the secondary functions you see on calculators or keyboards. For example, in order to select all the text in a Write document, you press the [Ctrl] key at the same time you click your mouse button. You'll perform other Windows functions with the mouse and the [Shift], [Alt], or [Ctrl] keys.

As you work with Windows' various applications, your desktop and its elements will change. Not only will your pointers change, but also other elements like icons or windows. After you select an item, it will be highlighted, or appear in inverse video (white becomes black and vice versa). Later, when you use tools in Paintbrush, you'll see guidelines (fine dashed lines) that outline the shape the pointer is creating. We'll point out these changes as you learn about the functions of Windows.

WORKING WITH ICONS

An icon is a graphic representation of an application, a document, or a program item. You can move icons to change their location, not their function. Icons are like the tip of an iceberg because they are a small part of a larger program that shows up on your desktop. When you activate the icon to run an application, the application shows up on your desktop as a window.

An icon is made up of two parts: a graphic, and a title. The graphic identifies the application with a schematic picture that represents its function. For example, the Write icon shown in Table 2-2 shows a pen writing an *A,* indicating that this application creates text. The title, *Write,* is the application's name.

Table 2-2

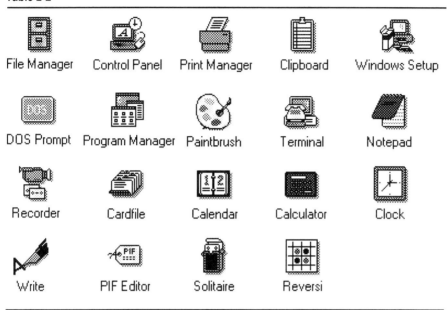

File Manager   Control Panel   Print Manager   Clipboard   Windows Setup

DOS Prompt   Program Manager   Paintbrush   Terminal   Notepad

Recorder   Cardfile   Calendar   Calculator   Clock

Write   PIF Editor   Solitaire   Reversi

You'll find these application icons in Windows.

Activating an icon

You can run, or activate, an application by double-clicking on its icon. After the first click, Windows will highlight the icon's title. After the second click, Windows will change the pointer into an hourglass, indicating you must wait, then Windows will set up the application's window on the desktop.

If you are using the keyboard instead of a mouse, you can use the Program Manager's menu to open or run an application. (Later in this chapter, we'll show you how to use menus.) First, use the arrow keys to move the highlight to an icon's title. Instead of a pointer moving on the screen, as you see when you use a mouse, the highlight on an icon's title moves when you use the arrow keys. After you highlight the icon, press [Alt]F to access the File menu. Next, press *O* to choose the Open command. Windows will then activate the icon and open the application's window.

Moving icons

If you want to move an icon, you need to click and drag it with the mouse. When you click on an icon, Windows will highlight the title. As you drag the icon, the pointer transforms into an untitled black-and-white version of the icon. When you release the mouse button, the icon will return to its normal appearance.

If you are using the keyboard, you can't move individual icons. But, there is an exception. You can move an icon when it's in a minimized window. We'll talk about minimizing windows later in this chapter.

WORKING WITH A WINDOW

A window is a framed area in which Windows runs an application, displays a document, or performs a task. When you start an application by double-clicking its icon, it will appear in an application window on the desktop. Windows provides several types of windows; primarily, application and document windows. In an application window, you can work with a specific application like Microsoft's word processor, Word for Windows. The application window furnishes menus of commands and a work area for your data. Your data can appear either in the work area or in another smaller window called a document window.

You can open several document windows as partitions of the work area when you're working with an application that that enables you to do this. The various document windows can each display one file. These files themselves often are referred to as documents, even though they may be spreadsheets or graphic images. However, not all Windows applications are designed to use document windows. Windows' desktop accessories, such as Write or Paintbrush, can't use document windows. Later in this chapter, we'll show you how to get around this limitation by using multiple application windows.

Windows also uses variations of application and document windows. A shell, which is a variation of an application window, does more than regular application functions; it actually controls the applications and devices of your PC. The shell, application windows, and document windows form a hierarchy similar to the hierarchy on a ship, where the admiral, captain, and crew form the various levels. The shell is like the admiral, who directs operations, since the shell starts an application when you have a job in mind. The application window is like the captain of a ship, who manipulates the crew, since the application window manipulates the data with a series of instructions. The document windows are like the crew stations where the work gets done.

A group window, a variant of a document window, groups icons inside shells like the Program Manager or the File Manager. We'll talk more about group windows when we discuss the Program Manager in Chapter 5 and the File Manager in Chapter 6.

Before you can work with a window, you need to know what's in it. Figure 2-1 shows a Write window with labeled parts. All windows have a frame, title bar, Control menu, and menu bar. The frame is the outside edge of the window that controls the size of the window. The title bar presents the name of the application and the file it's working with (if applicable). The color of the title bar tells you if the window is active (meaning it's the one you're working in) or inactive. By default, an active window has a blue title bar and an inactive one has a white title bar. You can have more than one inactive window at a time. However, only one window will be active at a time. The Control menu, the box containing the dash in the upper-left corner of the window, is used predominantly by keyboard users to do the same window manipulation as a mouse (for example, move or size the window). The menu bar, below the title bar, contains a series of menus listed by title (for example, the File menu).

Figure 2-1

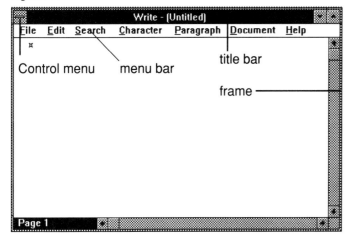

All windows contain a frame, title bar, Control menu, and menu bar.

Navigating in a window

Windows lets you navigate within a window by using the vertical and horizontal scroll bars located at the right and bottom of a window, respectively. The vertical scroll bar advances the work area one line at a time in the direction of the arrow if you click on one of the arrow boxes at the top or bottom of the scroll bar. For example, if you need to see one line above the top line in a Write window, you would click on the top arrow box on the vertical scroll bar to move up one line. In addition, you can use the horizontal scroll bar to shift the work area to the right or left.

If you want to move through your document at a faster rate, you can continuously select the arrow box by holding down the mouse button instead of just clicking on the arrow box. The document will keep scrolling until you release the mouse button. If you know the approximate location of the information you want to scroll to, you can drag the slider (the white box on the scroll bar) to quickly move to another part of the document. After you release the mouse button, Windows will display the new location. As you scroll between the pages of the document, the page status bar will change to reflect the new position.

Using the slider is fine if you know where the information appears in your document. However, if you don't know where it is, you may want to advance one screenful of information at a time. You can do this by clicking above or below the slider. If you want to bring the previous screenful of information into view, click in the vertical scroll bar above the slider. If you want to bring the following screenful of information into view, click below the slider.

To scroll through your document with the keyboard, you can use the direction keys and key combinations. You need to use the arrow keys to move up and down lines. To move a screenful at a time, use the [Page Up] and [Page Down] keys. You can quickly move to the top of the work area by pressing [Ctrl][Home]. If you want to move to the bottom of the work area, press [Ctrl][End].

Moving windows

Moving the window is necessary when you need more space or when you need to view more than one window on your desktop. To move a window, drag the title bar at the top of the window to the new location, then release the mouse button to place the window. As you drag the title bar, a guideline the shape and size of the window frame will appear so you can find a space that is the right size for your window. Since Windows doesn't reconstruct all the complex graphics with each movement of the mouse, the whole process of moving a window becomes much quicker.

If you're using the keyboard, you must use the Control menu to move a window. First, press [Alt][Spacebar] to access the Control menu. Next, press *M* to choose the Move command, then use the arrow keys to reposition the window. Press [Enter] to place the window.

If you want Windows to rearrange the windows on the desktop, you can use the commands on Task Manager and on the Control menu. We'll show you more about the Control menu and Task Manager later in this chapter. (For more about the Program Manager, read Chapter 5.)

Resizing a window

Resizing a window allows you to vary your workspace and make room for other windows. To size a window, move the pointer over any part of the frame. When you do, the pointer will change into a double-headed arrow called a sizing pointer. When you adjust the top or bottom of a window, you'll see this pointer ($\updownarrow$). When you adjust the sides, the pointer will look like this ($\leftrightarrow$). If you adjust a window from a corner, you'll see this pointer ($\nearrow$), indicating that you can change both the height and width simultaneously. After you point to any part of the window frame, click and drag to change the size. You'll see guidelines similar to the ones you see when you move a window. When the window is the right size, release the mouse button to lock in the new size. As an example, Figure 2-2 shows a Write window before and after sizing.

Figure 2-2

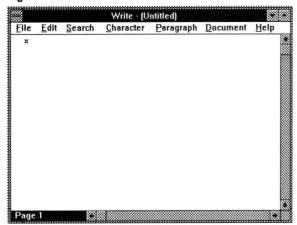 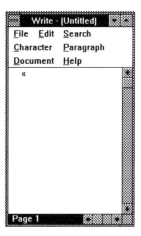

You click and drag a window frame to resize it.

If you are using the keyboard, you have to use a different method to resize a window. First, press [Alt][Spacebar] to access the Control menu. Next, press *S* to choose the Size command, then use the arrow keys to change the dimensions. Finally, press [Enter] to finish resizing the window.

Multiple windows offer an easy way to copy information between applications or documents. For example, if you are writing a report that involves statistics, you might use Word for Windows to create the report and Excel to create the statistics. If both windows are on the desktop, you can quickly move between them to calculate statistics and copy the numbers into your report.

Working with more than one window

Besides using more than one application on the desktop, you can have more than one copy of an application on the desktop. For example, for every Write document you want to open, you need a running copy of Write. Because Write has a simple application window that can have only one document in its work area at a time, you need multiple copies of Write running to have multiple documents on the desktop. Once you have multiple documents on the desktop, you can move between them by just clicking on the one you want to activate. We'll show you how to copy information between windows in Section 2 of this book, when we discuss Windows' built-in applications.

Using group windows

The Program Manager starts out with five standard group windows: Main, Accessories, Games, Windows Applications, and Non-Windows Applications. Group windows are variations of document windows since they are partitions of the Program Manager. Group windows don't have menu bars because they use the shell's menu bar commands. The various Windows application icons are sorted into groups when Windows is installed. You can add group windows to the Program Manager, and you can add application icons to these group windows. You'll learn how to do this in Chapter 5.

You can move and resize the group windows just as you do the application windows, but you are limited to the space of the Program Manager window. Likewise, if you minimize the group window into an icon, Windows will place the icon at the bottom of the Program Manager window. We'll show you how to minimize windows shortly.

In order to move or resize the group window with the keyboard, you have to access the group window's Control menu. To do this, press [Alt]- (hyphen). Now you can use the Control menu commands to manipulate the group window the same way you did for a regular window.

When you close a group window by double-clicking on its Control menu or issuing the Close command with the keyboard, it will minimize into an icon on the Program Manager window rather than disappear from the desktop.

Using the Minimize and Maximize boxes

In addition to resizing a window by moving its frame, you can resize a window with the Minimize, Maximize, and Restore boxes in the upper-right corner of the window. If you click on the Minimize box (the box with the down arrow), Windows will substitute an icon for the window and move the icon to the bottom of the desktop. The application still will be running, but won't consume as much space on the desktop. If you click the Maximize box (the box with the up arrow), Windows will enlarge the window to fill the entire desktop. After the window is maximized, Windows will replace the Maximize box with the Restore box (the box with a double arrow). If you click the Restore box, Windows will restore the window to its previous size.

To restore a minimized icon into a window, just double-click on the icon. If you click on the icon once, its Control menu will pop up, and you can choose the Restore command to accomplish the same task.

To minimize, maximize, or restore your window size with the keyboard, you can use the Control menu. First, press [Alt][Spacebar] to access the Control menu of the active window. Next, press the underlined letter of the command to minimize, maximize, or restore the window.

A minimized icon remembers its location. You can move the minimized icon by dragging it or using the Move command on its Control menu. If you move the icon on the desktop and then restore the application to its original size, the next time you minimize the icon during your Windows session, the icon will return to its initial location. For example, if you resize your Write document to fill all but the left edge of your screen, you can move any minimized icons to the left edge of the screen. Then, you can still access the other icons on the desktop since the application window won't cover them.

When you're working with group windows, you can use a shortcut to maximize the group window to fill the Program Manager workspace. To do this, double-click on the group's title bar. You can use the Restore box to return the group window to its previous size.

When you're finished working with an application window, you can store it by closing it or exiting the application. It's always better to exit with the Exit command on the File menu so the application's files are closed along with the data files. The Close command on the Control menu will remove the application from the desktop, but it won't clear the application from your PC's memory or, in some cases, save the file. For a shortcut, you can double-click on the Control menu box to close the window, although it's best to use the Exit command if you don't know whether the application will save your changes.

Closing versus exiting

If you just want to move a window out of the way to make more room on the desktop, you can minimize the window into an icon. This way, the application still will be in memory and you can restore it to a window more quickly than restarting it from the Program Manager. Minimizing an application into an icon also leaves the file open, which saves a step when you want to use the application. Otherwise, you'd have to open the file again after you restarted the application. Later in this chapter, we'll show you another safe way to exit an application with the Control menu Switch To... command.

The Program Manager launches all the applications that run in Windows. The Program Manager, the first application you see when you start Windows, uses a special window called a shell. A shell is a window that can start other programs. A shell always contains two active windows, itself and another window. For example, the Program Manager window and one of its interior windows, called a group window, can both be active. If all the windows inside the Program Manager window are minimized, however, an icon and the shell are active or selected. When the Program Manager window is inactive, the group window is inactive too. Figure 2-3 displays all the elements of the Program Manager, including the group windows and minimized group icons. In Chapter 5, we'll talk about the Program Manager in detail.

PROGRAM MANAGER

Figure 2-3

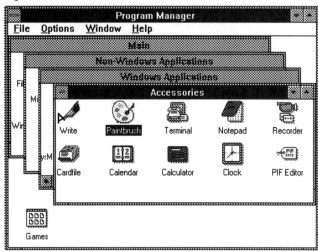

*A group window
is a Program
Manager element.*

FILE MANAGER

The File Manager, another shell, is true to its name—it manages files. It does all the things you used to do with DOS. You can find its icon in the Main group window. With File Manager, you can format disks, copy files, create directories, and rearrange the files in your directories.

All these DOS functions are implemented by the Directory Tree in File Manager. The Directory Tree works with directories. As you can see in Figure 2-4, each directory has an icon next to its name in the Directory Tree window. The Directory Tree window is like the group windows in the Program Manager. You can use more than one Directory window at a time, but like group windows, only one can be active at a time. We'll give you all the details about File Manager in Chapter 6.

**USING THE
MENU BAR**

Every application window has a menu bar that provides access to the application's commands. Each application's menu bar works the same way—the commands differ, but the way you access them doesn't.

The menu bar, which always appears directly below the title bar in the application window, lists the names of the drop-down menus. For example, the File menu is the first menu listed on Write's menu bar, shown in Figure 2-5.

Issuing commands

You can issue commands with the mouse, the keyboard, and the accelerator keys. We'll explain how to issue commands with a mouse first, then with a keyboard. You'll want to employ accelerator key shortcuts for the commands you use constantly.

When you click on the menu, a box with commands drops down. To issue a command, you just click on a command in the box. When you release the mouse button, the highlight moves to that line in the box and Windows issues that command. You can save yourself a step by just clicking on the menu and then dragging to the command you want. When you release the mouse button, the application will execute that command.

Figure 2-4

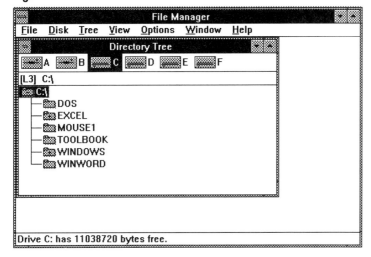

The Directory Tree is part of File Manager.

Figure 2-5

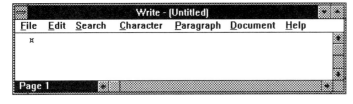

Write's menu bar contains seven menus.

If you're using a keyboard, you can access the menu bar by pressing the [Alt] key and the first letter of the menu name. Notice that the File menu has an underlined *F*. The underlined letter is the one you use with the [Alt] key to access that menu. If you then press [Alt] by itself, the menu will close. You can use the arrow keys to move between and within the menus. To issue a command from the keyboard, type the underlined letter in the command name. You can also use the arrow keys to move the highlight to the command you want. After the command is highlighted, press [Enter] to issue it.

The keystroke combinations you see next to some of the commands are accelerator keys. They offer a third and often faster way to issue a command. Only the commands used most often have accelerator keys. For example, you can issue the Undo command on Write's Edit menu by pressing [Alt][Backspace]. As we present the various applications, we will point out the accelerator keys.

Types of commands

Each menu groups its commands differently depending on the functions of the commands. For example, Write's Paragraph menu, shown in Figure 2-6, groups the reset (Normal) command separately from the alignment, spacing, and indenting commands.

Figure 2-6

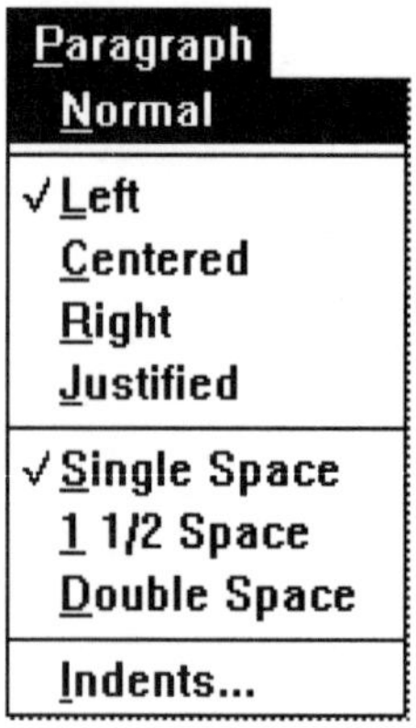

Paragraph
Normal
√ Left
Centered
Right
Justified
√ Single Space
1 1/2 Space
Double Space
Indents...

Write's Paragraph menu groups alignment commands.

Windows supplies many types of commands that can be divided into three categories: immediate, toggle, and user input. Immediate commands, of course, work as soon as you issue them without any request for user input. They perform a single operation. For example, in Write, the File menu's New command opens a new file. Toggle commands will keep an option on until you turn it off. An example is the Paragraph menu's Left command (left alignment) in Write. You can tell when a toggle command is on by the check mark next to its name. User input commands have an ellipsis (...) next to the command name to let you know that the application needs information from you before the command can work. The application requests this information by presenting a dialog box. For example, when you issue Write's Open... command, you'll see a File Open dialog box from which you can choose a file.

Sometimes a command name will change to fit the context of the last action you performed. The Undo command changes to let you know specifically what it will affect. For instance, if the last action you completed involved formatting, the Undo command will change to Undo Formatting on the menu. You'll find this change in a command name in special cases with most of the applications. We'll discuss more Undo commands later in our explanation of Windows applications.

Some menus, called cascading menus, let you access additional menus. On a regular menu will appear a command with a pointing triangle beside it, as shown in Figure 2-7. This lets you access another level of menus that will appear when you select the triangle beside the command. Highlight the command you want on the cascading menu and release the mouse button to select it. You'll see cascading menus in applications like Excel.

Figure 2-7

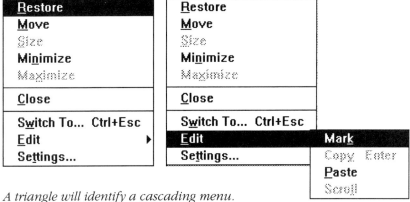

A triangle will identify a cascading menu.

USING THE CONTROL MENU

The Control menu provides keyboard users with the commands to move, size, and switch between windows. Press [Alt][Spacebar] to access the Control Menu of any application window. The menu normally has seven commands: Restore, Move, Size, Minimize, Maximize, Close, and Switch To.... After you highlight a command, press [Enter] to issue it. Let's briefly discuss each of these commands.

If you choose the Restore command, it will restore the window to its original size before it was minimized or maximized.

The Move command lets you use the arrow keys to move the window to a new location. When you choose the Move command, you'll see a four-headed arrow, called the move pointer, and guidelines the same shape as the window. Use the arrow keys to relocate the move pointer and the window. To complete the move, press [Enter].

The Size command operates like the Move command. When you choose the Size command, a guideline appears you can move with the arrow keys. To finalize the change, press [Enter].

The Minimize and Maximize commands work the same way the Minimize and Maximize boxes work. Choosing Minimize reduces a window into an icon. Choosing Maximize enlarges an application window to fill the desktop, or a group window to fill the Program Manager workspace.

The Close command closes the window. If you close an application window, Windows exits from the application and returns you to the Program Manager, but Windows may not save your work. If the application is written so an error message appears when you close the window without saving, you'll have a second chance to save your work.

When you select the Switch To... command, Windows will display the Task Manager's Task List dialog box.

Task Manager

The Task Manager is a built-in feature of Windows that allows you to switch between multiple, open applications, end tasks, and arrange the windows and icons on your desktop. Unlike the Program Manager or File Manager, the Task Manager is not a distinct application with its own icon; it is an integral feature of Windows and is always available.

When you call on the Task Manager, Windows will display the Task List dialog box shown in Figure 2-8. This dialog box lists the applications Windows is running on the desktop in their order of appearance. The active window is at the top of the list. The six buttons at the bottom of the dialog box allow you to switch between the different applications (Switch To), close an application window (End Task), exit the dialog box (Cancel), rearrange the windows on the desktop in a cascaded stack (Cascade), rearrange the open application windows so each one gets an equal portion of the desktop (Tile), and arrange the minimized icons on the desktop (Arrange Icons). To activate one of these buttons, just click on it.

Figure 2-8

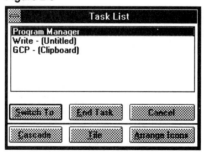

The Task List dialog box manipulates all the items on the desktop.

If you want to switch between the application windows, usually you'll just click on the one you want to use. However, you can't click on something you can't see on the desktop, so to activate a window that is covered, use the Switch To... command to bring the window to the top of the pile. If you use a keyboard instead of a mouse, the Switch To... command provides the only way to move between the windows.

To move to another window, select Switch To... from the Control menu or use the accelerator key [Ctrl][Esc] to display the Task List dialog box. Mouse users can take a shortcut to the Task List dialog box by double-clicking on any vacant part of the desktop. In the Task List dialog box, you can switch to the window whose title is highlighted in the list box by clicking on the Switch To button. If you're using the keyboard, simply press *S* to select the Switch To button.

The End Task button is a safe way to exit an application without losing any changes you made to your document. After you select one of the listed windows, choose the End Task button to exit that window. When you do, the next window on the list appears on the desktop as the active window.

When you've finished working with the Task Manager, you can close it by clicking Cancel or by clicking anywhere on the desktop. You can also close the dialog box by double-clicking on its Control menu or by pressing [Alt][F4].

If you have several windows open on the desktop, and you don't want to manually resize them so they fit on the desktop, you can let the Task Manager organize the desktop for you. The Cascade, Tile, and Arrange Icons buttons organize your desktop to work more efficiently by making the windows easier to find and move. The Cascade button stacks the windows diagonally so their title bars show. Figure 2-9 shows the desktop with cascading windows. The Tile button divides the space among all the windows so you can see the work area of each window. Figure 2-10 on the following page shows the effect of the Tile button. The Arrange Icons button is handy when you have several minimized icons that were moved but not tidied up. Figure 2-11 on the next page shows the desktop after we used the Arrange Icons button to rearrange our minimized icons.

Figure 2-9

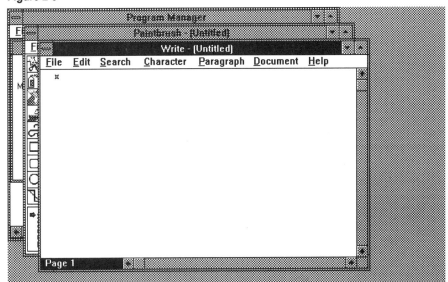

The Cascade button stacks the windows on the desktop with the title bars visible.

Figure 2-10

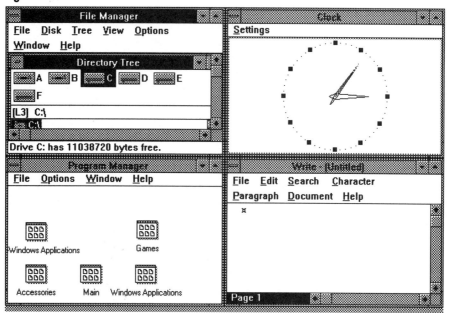

The Tile button divides the desktop among all the windows.

Figure 2-11

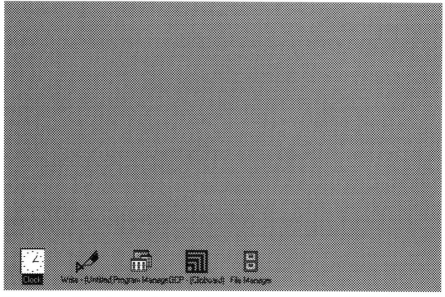

The Arrange Icons button places minimized icons in a row on the desktop.

Many command names on Windows' menus are followed by an ellipsis (...). The ellipsis indicates that a second level of options appears "below" that command. These options appear in a special window called a dialog box. Dialog boxes open automatically when you issue a command that's followed by an ellipsis. When you've completed your selections in a dialog box, you can click OK or press [Enter] to close the dialog box. To cancel your selections, click Cancel or press [Esc]. You can also close a dialog box by opening the Control menu and selecting Close, by pressing [Alt][F4], or by double-clicking the Control menu box.

Dialog boxes share some features with other windows. All dialog boxes have a Control menu that you can use to move and close the box. Most of them have OK and Cancel buttons. If you select the Open... command from the File menu in Write, you'll see the File Open dialog box shown in Figure 2-12.

WORKING WITH DIALOG BOXES

Figure 2-12

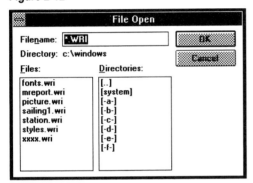

The File Open dialog box includes a Control menu, a title bar, an OK button, and a Cancel button.

Just as you can have only one application window active at a time, you can activate only one part of a dialog box at a time. An active dialog box element is either highlighted, outlined with a dashed line, or designated by a blinking cursor in its box. Active buttons are outlined in black.

To move to an element in a dialog box, just click on it. To navigate in a dialog box with the keyboard, press [Tab] to move forward or [Shift][Tab] to move backward. You can also move to another item by pressing [Alt] plus the underlined character in a dialog box element's name. For example, in the File Open dialog box, you would type [Alt]D to move to the Directories list box. Table 2-3 lists the keyboard shortcuts you can use in dialog boxes.

Navigating in a dialog box

Table 2-3

Keystroke	Function
[Tab]	Move to the next item.
[Shift][Tab]	Move to the previous item.
[Alt]*n*	Move to the item with a title that has *n* underlined.
↑,↓,←,→	Move between options in a group, or move the cursor up or down in a list or left or right in a text box.
[Home]	Move to the top item in a list box, or move to the first character in a text box.
[End]	Move to the last item in a list box, or move to the last character in a text box.
[Page Up] or [Page Down]	Scroll up or down one boxful of data at a time in a list box.
[Alt]↓	Open a drop-down list box.
[Alt]↓ or [Alt]↑	Select an item in a drop-down list box.
[Spacebar]	Select or cancel a highlighted item in a list box and select or clear a check box.
[Ctrl]/ (slash)	Select all items in a list box.
[Ctrl]\ (backslash)	Cancel all selections except the active item in a list box. The active item will have a dashed frame around it.
[Shift]↑,↓	Extend the list box highlight in the direction of the arrow.
[Shift][Home]	Extend the text box highlight to the first character.
[Shift][End]	Extend the text box highlight to the last character.
[Enter]	Execute the active command button, or select the highlighted item and simultaneously execute the active command button.
[Esc] or [Alt][F4]	Close or exit a dialog box without completing any commands.

You can use these keys to navigate in a dialog box.

Dialog box elements

    You can issue instructions from a dialog box in several ways. The elements of a dialog box are tools you can use to set options and make choices before executing the command. Dialog box elements range from simple check boxes to multiple-part scroll bars. Windows varies the basic dialog box elements to accommodate the needs of the individual commands. We'll explain basic check boxes, radio buttons, list boxes, drop-down list boxes, scroll bars, text boxes, increment boxes, display boxes, command buttons, and group boxes. As we present Windows' desktop applications, we'll point out the variations on these basic dialog box elements.

A group box organizes dialog box elements by function so an option is easier to find in a busy dialog box. The group box doesn't set an option itself but simply frames a number of different options under one main heading. Group boxes contain an assortment of dialog box elements, such as text boxes, drop-down list boxes, buttons, and check boxes. For example, the International-Date Format dialog box shown in Figure 2-13 has a Short Date Format group box. This group box in turn contains a combination of radio buttons for Order, a text box for Separator, and check boxes for other details, such as leading zeros. We'll often direct you to part of a dialog box by referring to a group box title.

Group boxes

Figure 2-13

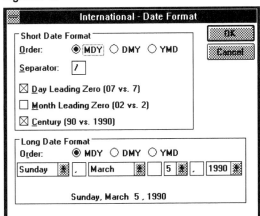

The International-Date Format dialog box has two group boxes: Short Date Format and Long Date Format.

A check box lets you turn a particular dialog box option on or off. To select a check box option with the mouse, simply click inside the check box or on the check box's name. As soon as you select a check box option, an *X* will appear inside the check box to indicate that you've turned that option on. To deselect a check box option, simply choose that option a second time. As you'd expect, deselecting a check box option causes the *X* to disappear, indicating that you've turned that option off.

Check boxes

To select or deselect a check box option with the keyboard, you can use either of two techniques. First, you can hold down the [Alt] key while you type the underlined letter in the check box option name. You also can use the [Tab] key to activate the check box inside the dialog box (a dotted line will frame the check box option to indicate that it is currently activated). Once you've activated the check box option, you can turn that option on or off by pressing the [Spacebar].

For example, Write's File Save As dialog box, shown in Figure 2-14, has three check boxes. If you want to create a backup copy of your work, you can use the Make Backup check box. When you click on this check box, an *X* will appear in it, indicating that you want to make a backup copy the next time you save a file. If you change your mind and don't want to use this option, you can turn it off by clicking on the box again.

Figure 2-14

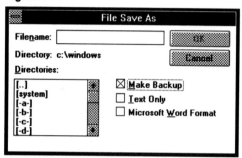

Write's File Save As dialog box has three check boxes.

Radio buttons

Radio buttons allow you to choose a single option from a group of options, much as you'd choose one answer to a question on a multiple-choice exam. For example, the Graphics Resolution section of the HP LaserJet on LPT1: dialog box in Figure 2-15 presents three radio buttons that let you choose among three levels of graphics resolution. As you can see, the 75 dots per inch (dpi) button—the default for this dialog box—is already selected. To select a different radio button with the mouse, click on either the button or the button's name. When you select a new radio button, the highlight will move from the old button to the new one.

Figure 2-15

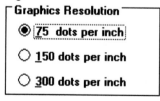

The Graphics Resolution section from a printer setup dialog box has three radio buttons.

To select a radio button with the keyboard, you can use either of two techniques. First, you can hold down the [Alt] key while you type the underlined character in the radio button's name. You can also use the [Tab] key to move to the group box, then use the arrow keys to change the selection.

You may be wondering why some options are represented by radio buttons and others by check boxes. Here's why: Radio buttons are used for options that are mutually exclusive. When you select an option from a group, the previously selected option will become deselected. Check box options, however, are independent of all other options in the dialog box. You can select or deselect any check box option without affecting any other options in a dialog box; that is, you can select more than one check box option at a time.

By the way, this button was named radio button because it's circular like old radio knobs. Sometimes we will refer to these buttons as option buttons.

Like radio buttons, list boxes let you choose a single option from a group of options. Windows uses list boxes instead of radio buttons when one of three conditions exist: when you must select an option from a large list, when the list of options is dynamic, or when Windows needs to save space in the dialog box.

List boxes

Consider the dialog box shown in Figure 2-16, which appears when you choose the Open... command from Write's File menu. As you can see, this dialog box lets you specify the file you want to open in either of two ways: with the Filename text box or with the Files and Directories list boxes. Later in this chapter, we'll show you how to work with text boxes in detail.

Figure 2-16

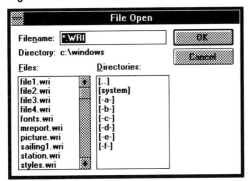

To open a File in Write, you can use the Files and Directories list boxes in the File Open dialog box.

To select an option from a list box with the mouse, simply click on the appropriate option. To make a selection with the keyboard, first press the [Tab] key repeatedly until you've activated the appropriate list box. At this point, a dotted line will frame either the selected entry or the first entry in the list. Now, you can use the ↑ and ↓ keys to highlight the appropriate option in the list.

Since list boxes can't always display the entire list of options at once, you'll occasionally need to use the scroll bars along the right side of the list box to find the option you want to choose. As we discussed earlier in this chapter, you can click on the scroll arrows or the scroll bar, or drag the slider to move through the list. To scroll with the keyboard, you can use the ↑ or ↓ keys to move one line at a time. Alternatively, you can use the [Page Up] and [Page Down] keys to scroll through the list a boxful at a time. To move to the top of the list, press the [Home] key. To move to the bottom of the list, press the [End] key.

Sometimes a dialog box will use a text box in conjunction with a list box. In these instances, you can change the dialog box's current setting by making a new entry in the text box or selecting a new item from the list box. In either case, the entry in the text box will change to reflect the dialog box's new setting.

Some dialog boxes allow you to select more than one option at once. If the original command can work with several options at once, you can also select more than one item from that command's dialog box. For example, if you want to add a number of applications to Windows with the Windows Setup application, you can select more than one application in the list box, as shown in Figure 2-17. You can select adjacent or non-adjacent items by simply clicking on the item. To select items with the keyboard, move the dotted-line frame to an application and then press [Spacebar]. To deselect an item, click on it (or press [Spacebar]) to toggle the highlight off.

Figure 2-17

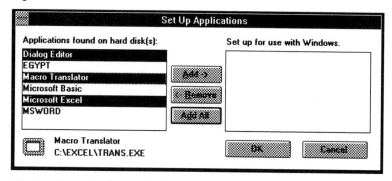

The Set Up Applications dialog box from Windows Setup allows multiple selections.

Drop-down list boxes

Drop-down list boxes serve the same purpose as standard list boxes. They allow you to choose a single option from a large, dynamic list. Unlike standard list boxes, however, a drop-down list box does not appear on the screen at all times. Instead, you'll see only a text box containing the list box's current setting, along with the special drop-down arrow (an underlined arrow). To display the options in a drop-down list box, you must "drop down" the list from within the dialog box.

The PCL/HP LaserJet on LPT1: dialog box, shown in Figure 2-18, contains four drop-down list boxes: Printer, Paper Source, Paper Size, and Memory. As you might expect, you can drop down any of these list boxes with the mouse simply by clicking on the appropriate drop-down arrow. For example, if you click on the arrow on the Printer drop-down list box, the list will drop down and show you the entire list, as shown in Figure 2-19.

Figure 2-18

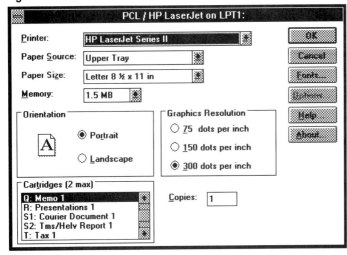

The PCL/HP LaserJet on LPT1: dialog box contains four drop-down list boxes.

Figure 2-19

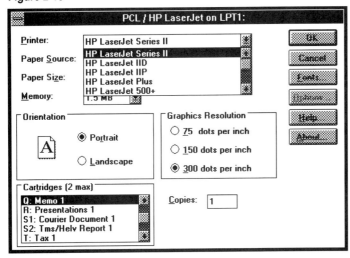

The Printer drop-down list box expands when you click on its drop-down arrow.

To expand a drop-down list box with the keyboard, first use the [Tab] key to move to the appropriate drop-down list box. Once you've activated the appropriate area, hold down the [Alt] key and press the ↓ key to see the entire list.

Once you've expanded a drop-down list box, you can use it exactly as you use a standard list box. When you make a selection from the list, the list box will disappear, and your new selection will appear in the text box portion of the drop-down list box. If you expand a list box by mistake, simply click on a different area of the dialog box. (With the keyboard, press [Tab].)

Scroll bars

So far, you've seen scroll bars that can help you navigate through windows and lists. In addition to its navigational capability, a scroll bar can control the value of an option. For example, if you want to increase the double-click speed of the mouse or the pace or time between clicks that Windows recognizes as a double-click, you need to use the scroll bar in the Mouse dialog box of the Control Panel to vary the speed. As you can see in Figure 2-20, the scroll bar in the Double-Click Speed box represents the range of double-click speeds. As you drag the slider along the gradient, the default double-click pace of the mouse changes. Windows uses this gradient type of scroll bar in other dialog boxes to control such options as custom colors (color gradient) or key repeat rates (another speed gradient).

Figure 2-20

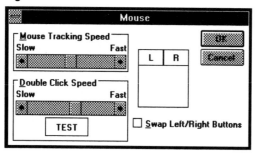

The Mouse dialog box from the Control Panel uses a scroll bar to control the double-click speed.

Windows doesn't highlight the scroll bar to show you it's active as it does with other dialog box elements. Instead, when the scroll bar is active, its slider will blink in alternating shades of gray.

To control a gradient scroll bar with the keyboard, simply use the ← or → keys to move the slider. Remember, you need to use either the [Tab] key or the [Alt] key plus the underlined letter in the scroll bar's name to activate the scroll bar so you can change the option's value.

Text boxes

Text boxes allow you to answer a dialog box's "fill in the blank" questions. You can enter file names, directories, or drives in text boxes, as well as text you want to locate. For instance, to find a particular phrase in a Write document, you issue the Find... command on the Search menu, then type the phrase you want to find in a Find What text box, such as the one in Figure 2-21.

Figure 2-21

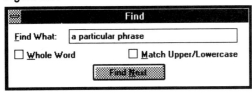

Write's Find dialog box contains a text box for the phrase you want to locate.

To make an entry into a text box with the keyboard, first press the [Tab] key repeatedly to move to the text box. When you use the keyboard to activate a text box that contains an entry, the text box's entry will appear in inverse type. At this point, you can type a new entry that will replace the existing entry. If, however, you use the keyboard to activate an empty text box, a blinking cursor will appear along the left edge of the text box. As you might imagine, any new characters you type will appear just to the left of the cursor inside the text box.

Activating a text box with a mouse is a little trickier than activating a text box with the keyboard. When you move the arrow pointer inside the boundaries of the text box, the pointer will change to an I-beam pointer (as we showed you at the beginning of this chapter). If you press the mouse button while the I-beam is inside the text box, a blinking cursor will appear at the I-beam's position. As you type, the characters will appear to the left of the cursor.

To highlight an existing entry in a text box with the mouse, first position the I-beam at the left edge of the text box. Next, click and drag the I-beam across the characters inside the text box. As you drag across the characters, their appearance will change from normal type to highlighted type (inverse video). After you've highlighted the appropriate characters, any new entry you type will replace the highlighted characters in that text box.

Increment boxes

An increment box is a text box that will accept only numbers. Windows adds a pair of arrows to the increment box that you can use with the mouse to scroll up and down the range of values for an option. For example, the Custom Color Selector on the Control Panel uses increment boxes to set values for hue, saturation, and luminosity, as shown in Figure 2-22 on the next page.

To change a value, simply click on one of the arrows to increment the value. If you hold down the mouse button on one of the arrows, the number will continue to change until you release the button. If you are confined to the keyboard or know the number you want to enter in the increment box, you can click on the increment box area and then type the new number.

Figure 2-22

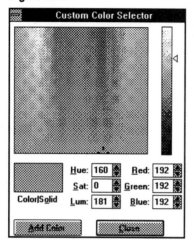

The Custom Color Selector uses increment boxes to set hue, saturation, and luminosity.

Display boxes

A display box or area provides a picture of the results from one or more options in the dialog box. For example, the PCL/HP LaserJet on LPT1: dialog box from the Control Panel has a display that shows you how the print will appear on a page. In the display area, a graphic of a page with the letter *A* on it changes depending on the orientation option you select. Figure 2-23 shows the graphics for both Portrait and Landscape orientation. Notice how the graphic changes as you change the option.

Figure 2-23

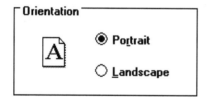 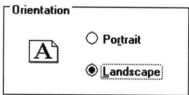

The display reflects the Orientation setting for the printer.

Command buttons

Command buttons are the large, gray, rectangular elements with words on them. Command buttons look like 3-D buttons with the command in black letters at the center of the button. If a command isn't available, then the letters change to gray. The dialog box in Figure 2-24 contains three command buttons: OK, Cancel, and Setup.... The OK and Cancel command buttons appear in nearly every dialog box. The OK command button closes the dialog box and carries out the selected command; the Cancel command button also closes the dialog box but without executing the command. To select the OK command button, use either the mouse to click on OK, or use the keyboard and press [Enter] or the [Spacebar]. (The heavy outline around the OK button indicates this default option will be selected when you press [Enter]. In other dialog boxes, buttons other than OK may be outlined.) To select the Cancel command button, use the mouse to click on Cancel or press [Esc].

Figure 2-24

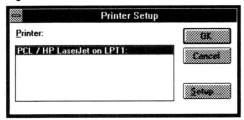

Write's Printer Setup dialog box has three command buttons.

Like the Setup... button in the Printer Setup dialog box in Figure 2-24, some command button names are followed by an ellipsis (...). Selecting these kinds of buttons will open another dialog box. Windows will keep the first dialog box open along with the second dialog box. Typically, when you close the second dialog box, you'll return to the first dialog box, where you can continue making selections. As you might expect, you can select a button of this type either by using the mouse to click on the button, or holding down the [Alt] key and typing the underlined letter in the button's name.

Sometimes two chevrons (>>) will follow a command button name. This type of command button is called a push button. When you choose a push button, the dialog box will expand to display additional options.

In our discussions throughout the book, we'll often refer to a push or command button simply as a button. For instance, we might instruct you to choose the Options >> button or the Cancel button. In addition, we'll typically instruct you to choose OK rather than to choose the OK command button. We think you'll find these conventions make our explanations more readable.

Identifying alert messages

Windows uses dialog boxes for its alert messages. For example, Windows will present a message if you attempt to exit a program before saving your work. These messages range from critical Windows system messages to information messages. Windows makes the importance of a message easy to recognize by using a color icon to tell you what type of message you're reading. Figure 2-25 displays the four icons Windows uses with alert messages: a red stop sign for critical messages, a yellow circle with an exclamation mark for warnings, a green circle with a question mark for a warning that requires user verification, and a purple circle with a lowercase *i* for information.

Figure 2-25

Windows identifies alert messages with four icons.

Alert messages appear in standard dialog boxes that have title bars, Control menus, and usually buttons for OK and Cancel. If you can attempt a command again, there is a Retry button. For example, in Figure 2-26, the critical message tells you that Windows cannot connect to a network drive. Since the action cannot be completed, you don't need a Cancel button. If you click on OK, you can return to the dialog box you were working with before the error occurred. To respond to a message with the keyboard, press [Tab] to move to the command button (OK or Cancel), then press [Enter] or the [Spacebar] to choose it.

Figure 2-26

This message indicates that Windows cannot complete a command.

Understanding system messages

Not all error messages appear in a standard dialog box. Some system messages that don't relate to a specific command also don't follow the dialog box standard. For example, if you try to read the files from drive A but there isn't a floppy disk in the drive, you'll see a system error message that explains the problem: *Cannot read from drive A:* and two buttons, Cancel and Retry, for your response. You can interpret this message as *Put a floppy disk in the drive, or cancel.* The error message is in a framed dialog box but doesn't have a title bar, icon, or Control menu.

Moving a dialog box

You can reposition a dialog box or a message box on your screen by dragging its title bar. When you click on the title bar, you'll see guidelines the shape and size of the dialog box. After you move the mouse to position the guidelines and release the mouse button, the dialog box will move to that spot.

If you're using the keyboard, you need to use the Control menu to move the dialog box. To move a dialog box, first press [Alt][Spacebar] to open the dialog box's Control menu. Next, press *M* to choose the Move command, and then use the arrow keys to move the dialog box. Finally, press [Enter] to complete the move.

You can click on one of the command buttons, such as OK or Cancel, to exit a dialog box. You can also double-click on the Control menu, press [Esc], or press [Alt][F4] to close the dialog box and not save any changes.

Exiting a dialog box

In this chapter

Setting Defaults 3

*H*ave you ever desired a new color combination on your screen? Did a warning beep ever annoy you so much you needed to turn it off? If so, you'll want to make Windows friendlier by changing some of the options, like screen colors or the warning beep. Control Panel is the application that lets you customize Windows by changing its default settings. Windows also lets you change the defaults that govern your hardware, such as the type of monitor, but you must use the Windows Setup application.

In this chapter, we'll take you on a tour of Control Panel and Windows Setup applications. We'll use Control Panel to change colors, fonts, ports, mouse capabilities, desktop patterns, 386 features, printers, international settings, the date, the time, and the warning beep. Since there are so many things to look at, first we'll discuss the settings that affect the look and feel of Windows, then talk about settings that affect printers or external devices. We'll also show you how to use the Windows Setup application to change your hardware configuration and how to add application icons to the Program Manager group windows. If you are part of a network, you'll want to refer to Chapter 8, in which we cover Control Panel's Network icon.

CONTROL PANEL

Before you can change Windows' default settings, you must start Control Panel. To do this, click on the Main group window to access the Control Panel icon, place your pointer on the icon, and double-click. If you're running Windows in 286 standard mode, you'll then see the Control Panel application window shown in Figure 3-1 on the next page. The 10 icons in this window will help you change any Windows setting. Your changes will be incorporated in your WIN.INI file so the next time you start Windows, the changes will still be active. To exit Control Panel, issue the Exit command on the Settings menu.

Starting Control Panel

Figure 3-1

*The Windows standard mode
Control Panel has 10 icons.*

If you are running Windows in 386 enhanced mode, you'll see a Control Panel with 11 icons, as shown in Figure 3-2. The extra icon controls 386 Enhanced settings. You'll find yet another icon on your Control Panel if you run a network version of Windows. Figure 3-3 shows a Control Panel with the Network icon.

Figure 3-2

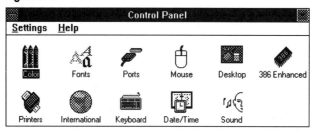

*The 386 Enhanced
icon on Control
Panel controls
the 386-based
functions.*

Figure 3-3

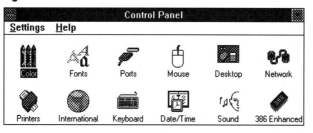

*The Network icon
on Control Panel
lets you issue
network commands
or change network
settings.*

**SETTING
ENVIRONMENT
OPTIONS**

Windows creates a pleasant working environment with color, sound, and a mouse. Control Panel gives you easy access to these and other Windows environment options.

To activate Control Panel icons with the mouse and use the specific function you want, just double-click on the function's icon. To activate icons with the keyboard, you'll use Control Panel's Settings menu. The Settings menu has one command for each of the 10 Control Panel icons. These commands provide access to all the Control Panel functions. If you have the 386 Enhanced or Network icon on your Control Panel, Windows adds a 386 Enhanced... or Network... command to your Settings menu. Just open the Settings menu and select the command that names the application you want to use, or use the arrow keys to move the highlight to the icon, then press [Enter].

To change screen colors, double-click on the Color icon to bring up the Color dialog box shown in Figure 3-4. Control Panel will highlight the current color scheme in the Color Schemes list box. When setting screen colors, you can use Windows' color schemes or choose your own combinations. In order to view the list of preformatted color schemes, click on the drop-down arrow of the Color Schemes drop-down list box. If you select one of the listed schemes, you can preview the result in the sample window in the Color dialog box.

Setting the screen colors

Figure 3-4

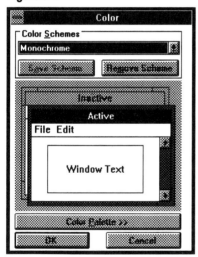

The Color dialog box will let you change the screen colors.

To add a color palette to the Color dialog box and to choose your own colors, select the Color Palette >> button. Control Panel will add two palettes—Basic Colors and Custom Colors—a Screen Element drop-down list box, and a Define Custom Colors... button. Figure 3-5 on the next page shows the expanded Color dialog box.

When changing screen colors, first choose the screen element whose color you want to change, then select a color. To select a screen element, you can either click on an area in the sample window or choose from the Screen Element drop-down list box in the upper-right corner of the expanded Color dialog box. For instance, if you click on the desktop area of the sample window, the high-lighted entry in the Screen Element list box will change to *Desktop*. At this point, you can select a color. When you click on one of the color boxes in the Basic Colors palette, a thick black border and a dotted outline will surround your selection; the selected screen element of the sample window will automatically change to your chosen color.

Figure 3-5

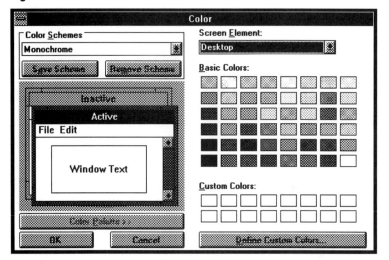

To choose your own colors, simply select the Color Palette >> button.

If you use the keyboard, you can press [Tab] to move forward through the Color dialog box and [Shift][Tab] to move backward. Once you have arrived at the Basic Colors palette, you can navigate between the color boxes by using the arrow keys. As you move through the Basic Colors palette with the arrow keys, the dotted outline will move to each color in succession. When you reach the color you want to use, press [Spacebar], and the black border will then frame your selection. When you choose a color with the [Spacebar], the selected screen element in the sample window will change automatically to that color. If we click on the hot pink color box, for example, the desktop element we selected earlier will become hot pink in the sample window.

After you make all your color choices, click on OK. Windows will implement your color changes and return you to Control Panel.

If you select a preformatted color scheme and modify it but don't save it, the Color Schemes list box will be blank when you return to the Color dialog box.

If the Basic Colors palette doesn't offer the color you want, you can create it with the Custom Colors palette. To do this, activate the Color dialog box, click on the Color Palette >> button to expand the dialog box, then click on the Define Custom Colors… button to bring up the Custom Color Selector dialog box shown in Figure 3-6. This dialog box has an interactive color grid (color refiner box) for mouse-controlled color selection, a color scroll bar (vertical luminosity bar), a Color/Solid display box, and a series of increment boxes for fine-tuning. To use the Custom Color Selector dialog box, move the pointer to a spot on the color grid and click. Note that a dashed crosshair (color refiner cursor) moves to that spot. The color you select will appear in the Color/Solid display box as both a color pattern and a solid. If you double-click on the solid color, Windows will select the pure color your monitor supports instead of a dot pattern simulation.

Defining and using custom colors

Figure 3-6

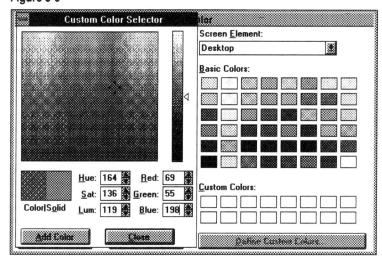

You can use the Custom Color Selector dialog box to define a new color scheme.

To the right of the color grid, you'll see a color scroll bar with a triangular slider. To change the brightness or intensity of the color, click and drag the triangular slider. Alternatively, you can point anywhere on the scroll bar and click to move the slider to that position. For finer detail, you can use the up and down arrows on the increment boxes below the color grid to increase or decrease the settings for Hue, Sat (saturation), Lum (luminosity or brightness), Red, Green, and Blue. These settings adjust automatically with the movement of the crosshair or slider.

If you are using the keyboard, press [Alt]O to select the solid color. To define custom colors with the keyboard, you must use the increment boxes. You can't access the color grid or the color scroll bar with the keyboard. To change the color, tab to one of the increment boxes, then type the new value. You will not be able to use the increment arrows.

When you choose colors, you should follow a specific order in defining hue, saturation, and luminosity. Hue controls the colors you choose across the horizontal axis of the color grid. Saturation controls the vertical axis that goes from gray to a pure color. The color bar to the right of the color grid controls the luminosity. For better control when you adjust colors, select hue first, then saturation and luminosity.

After you have found the right color, you can add it to the Custom Colors palette by selecting the Add Color button. You can add a color to each of the 16 selection boxes in the Custom Colors palette.

To remove a color from the Custom Colors palette, you actually have to replace it with another color. To do this, first click on the color you want to replace (note that you can use the Custom Color Selector dialog box simultaneously with the Custom Colors palette). Next, choose a custom color from the color grid and click on the Add Color button to replace the custom color.

If you want a Custom Colors selection box to appear blank, select that box and fill it with white. To select white, move the slider to the top of the color scroll bar and select the solid color by either double-clicking it or pressing [Alt]O. When you select the Add Color button, the designated box in the Custom Colors section will appear blank. After you've defined the custom colors, press the Close button to return to the Color dialog box.

Saving color schemes

You can save your new color scheme by selecting the Save Scheme button in the Color dialog box. A Save Scheme dialog box will appear, prompting you to name your color scheme. You can use any character, including spaces, in the color scheme's name.

To save your changes in the Color dialog box and return to Control Panel, click on OK. Choosing Cancel or double-clicking on the Control menu will close the dialog box without changing your screen.

Activating a scheme

You don't have to save and name a color scheme in order to use it. You can click on OK at the lower-left corner of the Color dialog box, and Windows will repaint the screen with the new colors. If the colors clash or aren't satisfactory, reselect the Color icon and create another scheme. As we indicated earlier, you can also choose one of the schemes in the Color Schemes drop-down list box and click on OK to activate that selection.

If you don't want to keep one of your custom color schemes, you can remove it from the Color Schemes list. You need only open the Color Schemes drop-down list box, highlight the named color scheme, and click the Remove Scheme button. The only color scheme you can't delete is the Windows Default scheme. If you remove a color scheme that came with Windows and want to retrieve it, you have to either reinstall Windows, or re-create the color scheme yourself.

Removing color schemes

If you use a PC with an LCD (liquid crystal display) overlay to give presentations, you may want to create a couple of color schemes especially for your presentations. Colors have varying brightness when translated into monochrome. The Palette Manager is Windows' way of adjusting program colors to hardware capabilities. Windows can translate a red program color to a monochrome gray if the hardware is monochrome. However, LCD overlays project your PC's screen in monochrome, not in color. The LCD overlay receives the EGA color image from your PC and translates it into monochrome. Sometimes, parts of the image, such as similar shades of gray, are not translated uniquely and blend together. Control Panel can help you keep your images intact by changing the troublesome colors into ones the LCD overlay can translate into a distinctive gray. A good way to find out which colors translate to which monochrome patterns is to bring up the Custom Color Selector dialog box and then turn on your LCD overlay. Note which colors are readable in the color grid, then make a special color scheme with just those colors.

A presentation tip

When you double-click on the Fonts icon, you'll see the dialog box shown in Figure 3-7 on the next page. With the Fonts dialog box, you can define the default fonts for the screen and printer and add fonts from floppy or hard disks. The Installed Fonts list box will highlight the current font, and the Sample of Font display box will list all the available sizes of that font and show the font in each size. If the font shows only one example size, it's probably a vector font that can be scaled to any size. Control Panel makes the installed list of fonts available to all Windows applications that can use them, such as Write.

Using fonts

If you want to add a font, click on the Add... button in the Fonts dialog box to bring up the Add Font Files dialog box shown in Figure 3-8 on the next page. Double-click on a drive ID, or type the drive ID and full path name in the Font Filename text box to access the font source, usually a floppy disk in drive A or B. Windows will look at the disk drive for any font file ending with the extension .FON and display in the Font Files list box the available font files it finds. You choose a font file either by clicking on the name in the Font Files list box or typing the file name in the Font Filename text box. Note that you can use DOS wildcard characters in the file name (*.FON) to install more than one font file at a time.

Adding fonts

Figure 3-7

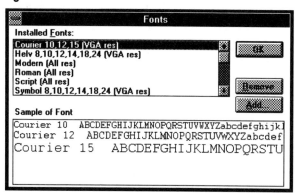

The Fonts dialog box displays a list of installed fonts.

Figure 3-8

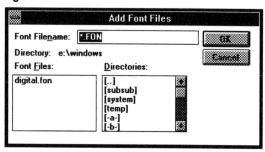

The Add Font Files dialog box provides a list of fonts you can install.

After you have selected the font files, click on OK. Windows will copy the files onto your hard disk. The dialog box will remain open so you can copy or remove other font files. Remember, fonts consume memory and hard drive space; if you are running out of memory, don't keep unnecessary fonts on your PC.

A quicker way

You can select font files more efficiently by using the keyboard simultaneously with your mouse. To highlight several font files at once, hold down the [Ctrl] key, and click the mouse button on each item you want to select from the Add Font Files dialog box. To select several fonts with the keyboard, hold down the [Ctrl] key, then use the arrow keys to highlight the files.

Installing from a floppy disk

To install fonts from a floppy disk, highlight the directory you want to use from the Directories list box in the Add Font Files dialog box. Then, Windows will display all the fonts available from the disk in the Font Files list box. You can make your selection using any of the techniques we've explained, then click on OK.

Since you will use some fonts more than others, you can delete those fonts you don't need or want. The Remove button in the Fonts dialog box deletes a selected font file in Windows' repertoire. To remove an unwanted font, highlight a selection from the Installed Fonts list box, then press the Remove button. A warning dialog box appears, requiring you to verify whether you want to remove the font. Click on Yes to continue or Cancel to return to the Fonts dialog box.

Removing font files

A word of advice: Since Windows uses Helvetica for its system font, removing it would make dialog boxes and windows difficult to read. Therefore, it would be very unwise to remove the Helvetica font.

Suppose you want to install the Gothic font from a floppy disk in drive A onto your hard disk. To do this, follow these steps:

Example

- In Control Panel, activate the Fonts icon.
- Select Add... in the Fonts dialog box.
- Double-click [-a-] in the Directories list box.
- Select all Gothic files in the Font Files list box by highlighting them or by typing *a:\Gothic *.FON* in the Font Filename text box.
- Click on OK or press [Enter].
- To verify the addition, highlight the Gothic font in the Installed Fonts list box. The font and its various sizes should be displayed.
- Finally, click on OK to close the Fonts dialog box and return to Control Panel.

The Mouse icon on Control Panel allows you to set the tracking speed, clicking speed, and primary button for your mouse. You can adjust these settings to match your skill level or preference. Let's activate the Mouse icon and explore the options available in the Mouse dialog box, shown in Figure 3-9.

Controlling the mouse

Figure 3-9

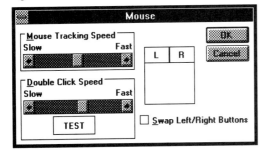

The Mouse dialog box lets you control tracking and clicking speeds, and the primary button on your mouse.

Setting the mouse tracking speed

The Mouse Tracking Speed section of the Mouse dialog box has a horizontal scroll bar with a flashing slider that controls the speed gradient of the mouse. Tracking speed refers to the pace of Windows' efforts to keep up with you when you drag the mouse. If you'd like to speed up the response time for dragging, drag the slider toward the fast end of the scroll bar.

Setting the double-click speed

The horizontal scroll bar in the Double Click Speed section of the Mouse dialog box controls the clicking speed of the mouse. The faster the setting, the faster you can double-click and initiate Windows' response to the action.

Choosing the primary mouse button

To the right of the Mouse Tracking Speed and Double Click Speed sections in the Mouse dialog box is a schematic representation of the mouse with left (L) and right (R) buttons. When you press your left or right mouse button, the corresponding button (L or R) on the mouse representation becomes highlighted. The schematic mouse will help you tell which button is designated as the primary (L) and which is the secondary (R) position. As we mentioned in Chapter 2, Windows uses the left mouse button as the default primary button. With the Swap Left/Right Buttons check box, you can change the primary mouse button from the left to right position. Go ahead and click on the check box, then try your buttons. Notice the change in the location of the letters L and R. The L is now on the right side of the schematic mouse. To change it back to its original state, you'll have to deselect the Swap Left/Right Buttons check box with the right mouse button (now the primary one). If you don't change it, remember to select with the right button since it is now the primary button.

Setting up the desktop

Some of the features of the Desktop dialog box, such as wallpaper, are decorative and allow you to alter the ambiance of your working environment. Other features, such as window frame size, are pragmatic and facilitate your work. As you gain confidence and skill working in Windows, you may want to create your own wallpaper and copy it onto your desktop. To do this, you can use the Paintbrush application to personalize your desktop. We will show you how to change the desktop pattern or select a wallpaper image for the desktop. You also can use the Desktop dialog box to change the cursor blink rate, size the icon-placement grid (granularity), and change the width of window borders. When you activate the Desktop icon, you'll see the Desktop dialog box, shown in Figure 3-10, which enables you to change some aspects of your desktop.

Picking a pattern

The Pattern section of the Desktop dialog box lets you choose a pattern for your desktop or even design your own. The Name drop-down list box provides a selection of patterns. Rather than choosing a pattern for your desktop sight unseen, you can preview the pattern by selecting the Edit Pattern... button. Your chosen pattern will appear in the Desktop-Edit Pattern dialog box. The background color of the pattern will be the Desktop color you selected in the Color dialog box; the pattern will be the Window Text color from your color scheme. As you can see in Figure 3-11, the Name drop-down list box, in the Desktop-Edit Pattern dialog box, allows you to continue previewing patterns. Table 3-1 on the following page shows the available patterns that come with Windows.

Figure 3-10

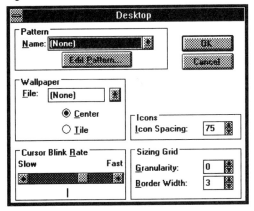

The Desktop dialog box can change the look of the desktop, the width of the window border, the cursor blink rate, and icon spacing.

Figure 3-11

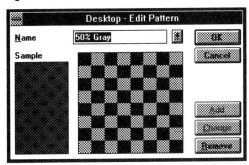

The Desktop-Edit Pattern dialog box will display the available patterns.

Table 3-1

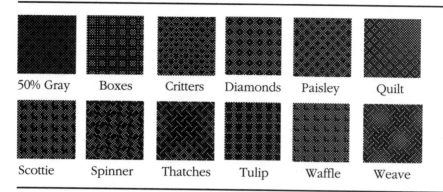

50% Gray	Boxes	Critters	Diamonds	Paisley	Quilt
Scottie	Spinner	Thatches	Tulip	Waffle	Weave

The installed patterns that you can use on the desktop are displayed here.

Creating new patterns

You may want to create your own desktop pattern. First, highlight (None) from the Name drop-down list box in the Pattern section of the Desktop dialog box, then click on the Edit Pattern... button to bring up the Desktop-Edit Pattern dialog box. Now you can type a name in the Name drop-down list box. When you type a name, the Add button is active, as shown in Figure 3-12. To change the pattern, move your pointer to the center box, and click anywhere. A black square will appear; it is a bit on a bit map. Click on that spot again, and the black square will go away. The bits toggle on and off. Note that the Sample display box to the left reflects the changes you make on the bit map. When you are satisfied with your new pattern, type a name in the Name text box, then click on the Add button. When you finished adding patterns, click on OK to return to the Desktop dialog box. If you are press Cancel instead of OK, the changes you made will be deleted and Windows will return you to the Desktop dialog box. To see how the new pattern looks on the desktop, choose OK in the Desktop dialog box.

Figure 3-12

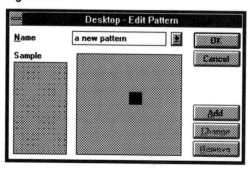

The Desktop-Edit Pattern dialog box displays a bit map that you can change.

You can save time by modifying an established wallpaper pattern instead of starting from scratch. Initially, you need to select the pattern from the Name drop-down list box in the Desktop-Edit Pattern dialog box. Then, change the bit map by toggling the bits on or off until you've altered the pattern to your satisfaction. Select the Change button to replace the existing desktop pattern, or type in a new name in the Name text box, then click on Add to add another pattern.

Changing patterns

If a pattern you create isn't what you had in mind, don't worry; you can remove it. Return to the Desktop dialog box and click on the Edit Pattern... button. Select the name of the pattern you want to remove in the Name drop-down list box, and click on the Remove button. Windows will then present a warning dialog box, asking you to verify the deletion. Click Yes to remove the pattern. Click on OK again in the Desktop-Edit Pattern dialog box to return to the Desktop dialog box.

Removing patterns

In addition to bit map patterns, you can use wallpaper to customize your desktop. The File drop-down list box in the Desktop dialog box contains several striking images whose colored graphics will be an impressive addition to your desktop. Tables 3-2a and 3-2b on the following pages provide a sample of each wallpaper pattern. Appendix 2 provides a color version of these tables. Wallpaper is a detailed Paintbrush image that can be centered on your screen for a large single image or tiled in a pattern of four smaller images. If you want to leave an *Out To Lunch* message or put your company logo on your Windows desktop, you can create your own wallpaper with the Paintbrush application. You'll need to save your Paintbrush file with a .BMP extension and make sure it's in the Windows directory so Windows can find it again. In Chapter 11, we will provide more information about creating wallpaper files. Remember, wallpaper will use more memory than a pattern, so if you have a memory shortage, you may want to avoid using wallpaper.

Putting up wallpaper

To select a wallpaper pattern, click on the File drop-down list box in the Wallpaper section, then click on a file. By default, Windows centers the wallpaper file. If you want the wallpaper to fill the desktop, you can click on the Tile radio button. Some wallpaper files already fill the desktop, such as the Chess wallpaper shown in Table 3-2b.

If you are using both a pattern and wallpaper, wallpaper will overlay the pattern. If you tile the wallpaper, the pattern will be completely covered up. If you use centered wallpaper, the pattern will be visible only if the wallpaper doesn't fill the screen.

If you don't want to use a wallpaper file anymore, or if your file was damaged and you can't use it, then you need to remove the file from your hard drive with the File Manager. You can learn how to delete files in Chapter 6.

Removing wallpaper

Table 3-2a

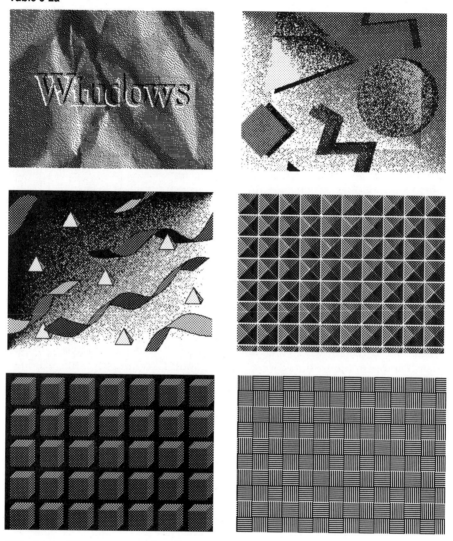

Windows offers a variety of wallpaper images.

Controlling the cursor blink rate

The Cursor Blink Rate section of the Desktop dialog box has a horizontal scroll bar. You can drag the slider toward the slow or fast end of the scroll bar to change the blink rate. Note that a blinking cursor under the scroll bar indicates the new blink rate you've selected.

Table 3-2b

The Chess wallpaper pattern fills the desktop.

The Desktop dialog box provides the Granularity increment box to create an invisible grid of guidelines on which Windows arranges your desktop elements. By default, granularity is set to 0—no grid. If you enter a value for granularity, Control Panel will set up the grid. Then, whenever you cascade the windows on your desktop with the Task Manager, the windows will line up using the grid.

What do the granularity values mean? Each value increases the space between guides by 8 pixels (your screen is 72 pixels per inch). The values range from 0 to 49. The larger the value, the farther apart the desktop elements will be and the larger the size of a cascaded window.

As you work with applications, you'll find situations in which the title of a minimized icon is wider than the icon. If this happens when you have several icons on your desktop, the titles will overlap. The granularity grid helps a little, but you need to use the Icon Spacing increment box to solve this problem. By increasing the value in this increment box to allot more space for each icon, you can position the icons farther apart. You allot space in increments of pixels. You'll see a difference in spacing if you change the Icon Spacing value in increments of 10 pixels. By default, spacing is a little over an inch, or 75 pixels.

Creating a placement grid for icons

Allotting space for an icon

Setting border width

If you have trouble sizing windows because the frame area is too narrow, you can increase the width of the frame. The Border Width setting varies the width of the window frame and ranges from 1 to 49. By default, the Border Width equals 3. The narrowest border has a width of 1. You can use the increment arrows to change the width value the same way you can change the granularity value.

Changing International settings

You can change basic formats, such as keyboard layout, date, and time, by using the International dialog box. To access this dialog box, double-click the International icon in the Control Panel window. As you can see in Figure 3-13, this dialog box contains four drop-down list boxes, a text box, four format boxes, and the default settings for the United States. The Country setting controls many of the other settings. If you change the Country setting, the other settings (except Language and Keyboard Layout) will follow suit. You can still make changes in any of those specific areas to override the global changes if you wish.

Figure 3-13

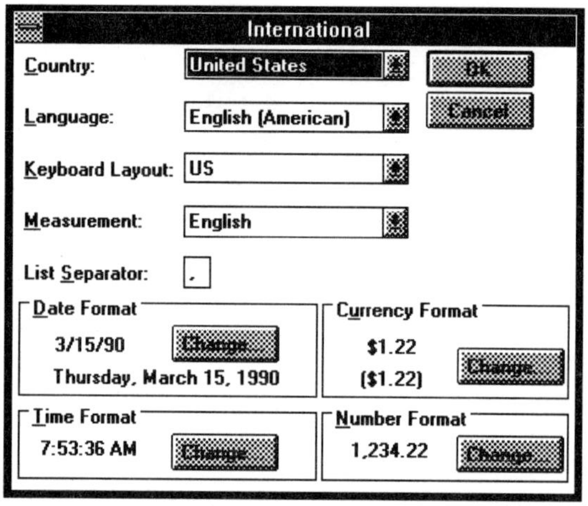

International
Country:	United States	OK
Language:	English (American)	Cancel
Keyboard Layout:	US	
Measurement:	English	
List Separator:	,	

Date Format
3/15/90   Change
Thursday, March 15, 1990

Currency Format
$1.22   Change
($1.22)

Time Format
7:53:36 AM   Change

Number Format
1,234.22   Change

The International dialog box will let you make changes to basic formats such as date and time.

Picking a country

The Country drop-down list box will let you choose a country on which to base your various formats. For instance, if you change the country from the United States to Italy, as shown in Figure 3-14, Windows will change the currency from dollars to lire. The Date Format will change from month-day-year to the European day-month-year format. The changes in the Country setting also will affect the Measurement setting and the List Separator. For example, Italians use commas for a decimal point and separate thousands with periods. As we mentioned earlier, the Country setting doesn't affect the Language or Keyboard Layout settings, which are separate considerations.

Figure 3-14

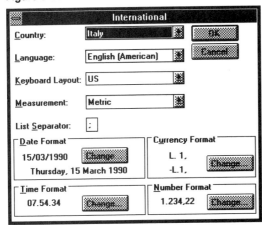

When you change the country to Italy, the Control Panel will automatically adjust other settings.

Windows comes with many language formats. You can use the Language drop-down list box in the International dialog box to choose among the available formats. By default, *English (American)* appears in the list box to match the default nation in the Country text box.

Choosing a language

The keyboard layout determines which characters use which keyboard keys. Windows provides several keyboard layouts. The default keyboard layout is US. Most languages have special characters, which require a unique layout.

Changing the keyboard layout

The Measurement option in the International dialog box lets you select the way Windows will display measurements. The Measurement drop-down list box offers two options: English and Metric. As you might expect, the default is the English system of measurement.

Metric vs. English

You can change the date format manually in the Date Format section of the International dialog box or automatically with the Country drop-down list box. The Date Format section displays the format currently in use. To alter the current date format, click on the Change... button. In the International-Date Format dialog box shown in Figure 3-15 on the next page, you can specify the short and long date formats.

Date format

You'll use the Short Date Format group box to determine the order of the month-day-year sequence and the type of character separator you want. When you select a date order from the Order options, you'll see a dotted border around the order pattern. If you want a different separator character, select the Separator text box, then type the new character. Notice that the pointer changes to an I-beam when it's in the text box. The three check boxes in the Short Date Format group box control the format of the numbers in a date. You can choose the number of digits for day, month, or year. Clicking in the check boxes will activate the first choice in the parentheses next to the box's name.

Figure 3-15

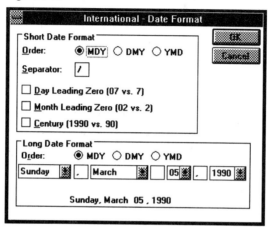

The International-Date Format dialog box sets the short and long date formats.

The Long Date Format group box sets the order and the format for a completely spelled-out date. First, establish the date order by selecting one of the Order radio buttons. Notice that both the displayed date and the list and text boxes above the date change their order to match your choice. Now you can format the date elements, like the day of the week, to a short or long version. For instance, Sunday can be displayed as *Sun* or *Sunday*. To display the list of choices, click on the drop-down arrow. You can also modify the punctuation and spacing of the date with the text boxes located between the date elements. Click in the text box to place a cursor inside it, then type in the punctuation you want or leave it blank for no punctuation.

Currency format

The Currency Format section of the International dialog box lets you change the way Windows displays currency. When you press the Change... button in this group box, you'll see the International-Currency Format dialog box shown in Figure 3-16. In the Symbol Placement and Negative drop-down list boxes, you can tell Windows where to place currency symbols and how to display negative values. You can change the currency denomination symbol by highlighting the current symbol in the Symbol text box and typing in a new one. The Decimal Digits box is a single character text box that allows you to change the number of decimal digits up to a value of nine.

Figure 3-16

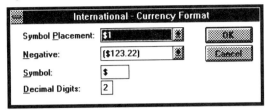

The International-Currency Format dialog box controls the appearance of symbols, negative numbers, and decimals.

You can change the time format by clicking on the Change... button in the Time Format section of the International dialog box. You can choose either the 12-hour or 24-hour time system in the International-Time Format dialog box shown in Figure 3-17. The Separator text box will let you type in the separator character of your choice. The Leading Zero radio buttons give you the option of placing a zero in front of the displayed time. The text boxes to the right of the hour system radio buttons allow you to set AM or PM notation.

Time format

Figure 3-17

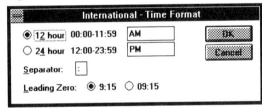

The International-Time Format dialog box will let you set the 12- or 24-hour system, the separator character, or the leading zero.

You can change the number format by pressing the Change... button in the Number Format section. In the International-Number Format dialog box, shown in Figure 3-18, you can enter a thousands separator, a decimal separator, or the number of decimal digits in the respective text boxes. You can also indicate whether to use a leading zero. The defaults for the number format are governed by the Country setting in the International dialog box. By default, Windows uses a comma for the thousands separator, a period for the decimal separator, two decimal digits, and a leading zero. To change one of the separator formats, double-click in the text box and enter the change. When you want to change the Leading Zero option, choose the radio button beside the format you desire.

Number format

Figure 3-18

The International-Number Format dialog box enables you to set the numerical formatting to reflect a particular nation's preferences.

Setting keyboard options

When you double-click on the Keyboard icon on Control Panel, you'll activate the Keyboard dialog box, shown in Figure 3-19. This dialog box lets you set and test the key repeat rate. You can increase or decrease the rate at which a key will type by moving the slider on the scroll bar toward the slow or fast end. The Test Typematic text box allows you to test the rate of change, first by clicking in the text box, and then holding down a character key. The box will display the characters you type at the rate you've set as you depress and hold a key.

Figure 3-19

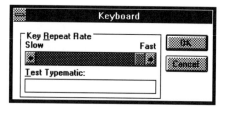

The Keyboard dialog box will let you set and test the key repeat rate.

Setting the date and time

In addition to changing the date and time format, you can change the actual date and time within your system. Any alterations you make to the date and time will affect the Clock and Calender as well as your system clock. To change the date or time, double-click on the Date/Time icon in the Control Panel window. When you do, you'll see the Date & Time dialog box shown in Figure 3-20, with sections for setting the date and time. You can set the numbers in each section by highlighting a portion of the date or time, then typing your entry.

If you double-click on the month portion of the Date section in the dialog box, the month will be highlighted, and you can enter new text. If you click on an increment arrow to change the number, the number will be highlighted. You can also change your date and time by first placing the cursor in any portion of the date or time. Then, when you click on an increment arrow, Windows automatically will highlight and change the section of the date or time you've chosen.

Figure 3-20

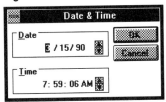

The Date & Time dialog box lets you change the date and time for your system.

The Sound icon on Control Panel accesses the Sound dialog box. As you can see in Figure 3-21, the Warning Beep check box is turned on by default. You can toggle the warning beep off by selecting the check box to remove the *X*.

Sound settings

Figure 3-21

The Sound dialog box lets you turn the warning beep on or off.

If you are running Windows with a 386 PC, you will see an additional icon on Control Panel that looks like a computer chip with the number 386 on top. Once you activate the 386 Enhanced icon, you'll see the 386 Enhanced dialog box shown in Figure 3-22. This dialog box lets you control access to a device, such as a printer, and determine which window gets more processor time. Only non-Windows based applications and earlier versions of Windows applications will need to use the settings in the 386 Enhanced dialog box. Windows 3.0-based applications already have these settings built in.

Using 386 enhanced settings

Figure 3-22

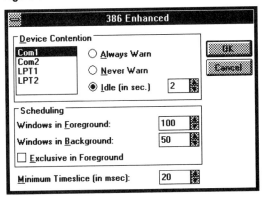

The 386 Enhanced dialog box controls access to devices and processing time.

Waiting for a device

All application windows on the desktop can access devices, and sometimes they will compete for the same device, such as a printer. If this happens, Windows can make the applications take turns. You can use the radio buttons in the Device Contention section to control when applications access a device or to warn you with a message box so you can manually set the access. To manually set the access, you specify in the message box which application receives control. For example, to set the option for COM1, you can click on Always Warn to warn you if two applications are trying to access the device simultaneously. A better way is to click on Idle so an application will wait a couple of seconds after COM1 is available again before trying to use it.

Sharing computer time

Not only do multiple application windows have to share devices, they also have to share the computer's processing time. A unit of the processing time is called a time slice, which is defined in milliseconds. An application gets to use the computer's processor for the duration of the time slice. All Windows applications share one time slice, but other non-Windows applications use a separate time slice. You can set the time slice in the Minimum Timeslice text box to a value between 1 and 1000 milliseconds. By default, the minimum time slice is 20 milliseconds.

Besides setting the duration of a time slice, establishing the priority for getting a time slice is also an important multitasking choice. An application can process information while it's active in the foreground or while it's inactive in the background. Normally, you give processing priority to a foreground application because you are currently interacting with it. However, if you have a communications program or major process working in the background, you should give the background application a higher priority than the foreground application so it won't be interrupted.

There is a fine distinction between foreground and background processing selections in the Scheduling group box. Note that the foreground selection says *Windows in Foreground* and the background selection says *Windows in Background*. These settings are used only if a non-Windows application is active, in other words, a non-Windows application in the foreground and a Windows application in the background.

You can weigh the priority given to foreground and background processes by changing the values in the increment text boxes. These numbers range from 1 to 1000 but do not have a specific value assigned to them. As you define your needs and your knowledge of Windows deepens, you can use a variety of scheduling ratios. By default, the foreground is 100 and the background is 50.

If you don't want non-Windows applications running when Windows applications are running, you can check the Exclusive in Foreground check box.

When this check box is selected, Control Panel will reserve 100% of the processing time for Windows applications when one application is active. This means Windows doesn't allow background processing.

You can provide Windows with more tools, such as printers and modems, but you must tell Windows what external devices are available. Typically, you'll report your hardware to Windows by configuring ports, installing drivers, and assigning ports to the installed devices.

CONTROLLING PRINTERS AND DEVICES

Your PC's communication ports, named COM1, COM2, COM3, and COM4, are serial ports. To configure these ports, you will probably need to refer to your printer manual to find out the default settings. You'll also need a manual if you want to set up a modem on your PC through Windows. You can perform the configuration with DOS, but it will be easier to use Windows.

Controlling ports

To configure a port, activate the Ports icon on Control Panel. You'll then see the Ports dialog box shown in Figure 3-23. The Ports dialog box contains four COM icons that represent the serial ports. If you want to specify a port, double-click on a COM icon to open the Ports-Settings dialog box, shown in Figure 3-24 on the following page. You also can open this dialog box by clicking on an icon and choosing the Settings... button. If all or some of the ports use the same settings, you can select them by pressing [Shift] and clicking to highlight them, and establish all the settings at once. For example, you can highlight COM1 and COM2, then click on Settings... to display the Ports-Settings dialog box. After you set the parameters, such as data bits and parity, select OK to return to the Ports dialog box. By default, the settings are Baud Rate 9600, Data Bits 8, Parity None, Stop Bits 1, and Flow Control None. Table 3-3 on the next page describes the settings and their alternatives. For further details on modems and communications settings, read Chapter 12.

Configuring a port

Figure 3-23

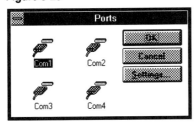

The Ports dialog box will let you set all four COM ports.

Figure 3-24

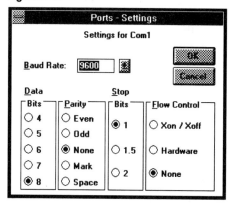

The Ports-Settings dialog box sets the parameters of a COM port.

Table 3-3

Parameter	Defined as...	Common Setting
Baud rate	the data transfer speed between a device and your PC.	9600 for printers 1200 or 2400 for modems
Data bits	the number of bits sent in a computer word.	7 or 8
Parity	the verification bit. It can be even, odd, not used, a mark or a space. If data bits are set at 7, parity is usually even. If data bits are set at 8, parity is not used.	Even or none
Stop bits	separators between computer words in number of bits.	1
Flow control	interaction between printer and computer. The hardware needs to tell the computer when it's ready for more data. *Xon/Xoff* is a message sent back to the computer telling it to send more data. *Hardware* refers to hardware handshaking that's conducted over one of the wires in the cable. *None* means handshaking isn't necessary.	Xon/Xoff

You'll use these communications settings to configure a port.

You can copy port settings only if you use a mouse with Windows. To copy a port setting, drag the COM icon you want to copy (the source) on top of the COM icon you want to change (the target). Notice that the pointer changes to a port socket when you copy the settings. A warning message dialog box like the one in Figure 3-25 will ask you to confirm your decision to copy port settings. Press OK to complete the copy.

Copying port settings

Figure 3-25

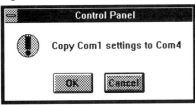

A warning message dialog box asks you to confirm the port copy.

The Control Panel will make choosing a printer an easy decision by providing a Printers dialog box when you activate the Printers icon. From a dialog box like the one shown in Figure 3-26, you can select, add, spool, or even install new printers. To select a printer listed in the Installed Printers list box, highlight the one you want. Windows will select only one printer at a time.

Controlling printers

Figure 3-26

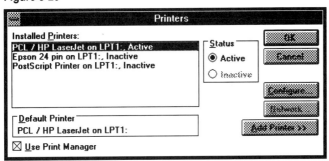

The Printers dialog box will help you select among several printers.

Windows recognizes printers connected to your PC as either active or inactive. Windows employs special software, called a printer driver, to run the active printer. If you attempt to print with an inactive printer, your printout will be inaccurate or unreadable because Windows is using the active printer's driver, which doesn't work with an incompatible printer. The Status section and the Installed Printers list box in the Printers dialog box will display the status of the selected printer. When you select another printer, the Status section will change to reflect the status of your new choice. If you want to use a new printer, you not only have to select it but also change the status to Active.

Changing printer status

Windows always has one printer active per port. You can change the status of an inactive printer to active by selecting it and then choosing the Active radio button. However, you can't make the default printer inactive, since Windows makes the Inactive radio button unavailable. Additionally, your printers must have a port assignment, or you won't be able to activate them.

Choosing a default printer

If you begin printing before you've chosen a printer, Windows will send the output to the printer listed in the Default Printer box. If you haven't chosen a default printer, Windows will warn you with a message. You can change the default printer by double-clicking on a different printer in the Installed Printers list or by making one of the other printers active. You can make a printer the default only if it has a port assignment. If it doesn't, you must assign a port to the selected printer before it will replace the current default printer. You can assign a port to a printer by configuring the printer.

Configuring a printer

The Printers-Configure dialog box, shown in Figure 3-27, will let you select a port. You can also use this dialog box to change the port assigned to a printer. To access this dialog box, select the Configure... button in the Printers dialog box. By default, the LPT1: port is selected in the Ports list box. You can, however, choose any port from the Ports list box.

Figure 3-27

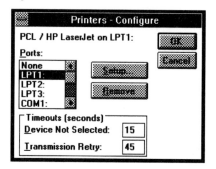

The Printers-Configure dialog box is useful primarily for arranging links between printers and ports.

In the Printers-Configure dialog box, the Timeouts [seconds] section sets time limits. Before Windows sends data to a printer, it asks for a ready signal. If Windows doesn't get the signal before the Device Not Selected time limit runs out, it sends you a message that the printer is not available. When Windows is able to send data to the printer, you may run into a different problem. The printer processes data in chunks, or batches. If it doesn't ask for the next batch of data before the Transmission Retry time runs out, Windows will send the data again. If that doesn't work, Windows will present an error message. The default values for the time limits in the Timeouts [seconds] section will work in most cases.

However, if you get many error messages, you may need to increase the time limit allotted. All you need to do is double-click in the Device Not Selected or the Transmission Retry text box, then type the desired time limit, which will replace the old setting automatically.

If you want to queue printing, that is, print a file while working on something else, you need to select the Use Print Manager check box located below the Default Printer section of the Printers dialog box. The Print Manager controls the queuing of your print jobs from an application. You'll learn more about Print Manager in Chapter 7.

Activating the Print Manager

Windows lets you install more than one printer. To add a printer, first select the Add Printer >> push button in the Printers dialog box. As you can see in Figure 3-28, the dialog box will expand to include a printer installation section, which contains a list of acceptable printers, and an Install... button.

Adding a printer

Figure 3-28

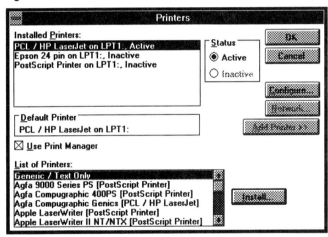

The Printers dialog box expands to include a printer installation section.

Notice that some of the printers have [PostScript Printer] or [PCL/HP LaserJet] after their name. These are printer groups. Installing any member of the group will put the group name, instead of the specific printer's name, on the Installed Printers list at the top of the Printers dialog box. You can select the specific printer later during the setup procedure, which we will explain in a moment.

After you have selected a printer from the List of Printers list box and pressed the Install... button, a Control Panel-Printers dialog box, like the one shown in Figure 3-29, will prompt you to insert into a disk drive a floppy disk with printer drivers. The printer driver will tell Windows how to use the printer and which fonts it can use. If you have already copied all the printer files onto the hard disk, just type the full path name into the text box so Windows can locate the necessary files. Select OK to continue, or press Cancel, which will return you to the Printers dialog box without making any changes. After the files are copied, the new printer will appear on the Installed Printers list. You will have to go through the configuration procedure to set the new printer's port and any customized parameters.

Figure 3-29

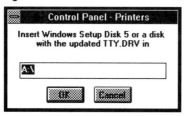

The Control Panel-Printers dialog box copies printer drivers to your hard disk.

If you try to install a printer that is already installed, Windows will display a warning message asking if you really want to reinstall the driver. If a driver is damaged, click on the New button to install a new driver. If you just made a mistake, you can click on Current or Cancel without making a change. Remember, printers come in groups, like PostScript printers. After you have installed one printer in a group, you don't need to install another. To change to another printer within a group, return to the setup procedures.

Removing installed printers

You may find you no longer need a printer you installed for Windows. For example, you may upgrade a printer or trade one in. You can remove a printer with the Installed Printers list box in the Printers dialog box. To do this, first click on the name of the printer in the Installed Printers list box. Next, click on the Configure... button to display the Printers-Configure dialog box. Finally, click on the Remove button to delete the printer name. When Windows presents a warning dialog box asking for verification, click Yes. After you click on OK in the Printers-Configure dialog box, Control Panel will return you to the Printers dialog box. Control Panel will delete only the printer name from the Installed Printers list; it won't delete the printer driver files from your hard disk. Later, if you want to reinstall the printer, Control Panel will add the printer's name to the list, but you won't have to copy any files onto your hard disk.

Setting up printers

Each printer has different setup options. Windows supports many printers, but we'll limit our discussion to three common printer types: the HP LaserJet Series II (PCL/HP), the Epson LQ2500, and the Apple Laserwriter II NT. When you click the Setup... button in the Printers-Configure dialog box, you can choose paper size and number of copies. Other options, such as orientation, memory, color, scaling (enlarging or reducing an image), or duplexing (printing both sides of a page), depend on the capabilities of the printer. If the printer doesn't have an option, you won't see one in the Printers-Configure dialog box. If the option is installed in your printer but dimmed (not available) in the dialog box, you don't have the correct printer chosen in the drop-down list box.

The Printer Setup... commands in your Windows applications bring up the same dialog box you see in Control Panel when you first set up your printer with the Setup... button, signifying how closely Control Panel works with your applications. You will see a detailed explanation of printer setup only in this chapter and not in the chapters about individual applications. If you install a printer that's part of a class or group of printers, like the PCL/HP LaserJet or PostScript printers, you must choose the specific printer to use during the setup procedure. Windows loads a generic driver, then refines it depending on the setup options.

Let's look at the HP LaserJet Series II setup process. In the Printers dialog box, choose PCL/HP LaserJet on LPT1: from the Installed Printers list box, then click on the Configure... button. Next, click on the Setup... button in the Printers-Configure dialog box. The PCL/HP LaserJet on LPT1: dialog box will appear, as shown in Figure 3-30. The title bar of this dialog box contains the name and port selection of the printer you are configuring.

Setting up the HP LaserJet Series II

Figure 3-30

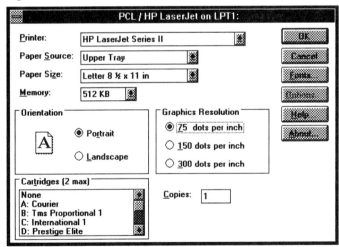

A printer-specific dialog box outlines detailed setup functions.

As you can see, the dialog box for your printer contains four drop-down list boxes that let you specify the printer, paper source, paper size, and installed memory size of your printer. For example, you could select HP LaserJet Series II from the Printer list box, Upper Tray from the Paper Source list box, Letter from the Paper Size list box, and 1.5 Mb from the Memory list box.

If you're printing large documents, your printer could run out of memory. If you get the error message *Out of memory*, you should install more memory in your printer. If more memory isn't available, you can reduce the dots per inch (dpi) setting in the Graphics Resolution section to free-up some memory. If your printout shows only half an image, your printer has a memory shortage—the printer's memory just couldn't hold more than half the picture.

Three sections of the dialog box give you control of orientation, graphics resolution, and font cartridges. The Orientation section allows you to tell the printer whether you want to print across the width or length of the page. Notice that when you select one of the two orientations, the sample page display changes to match your selection. Normally, you will use Portrait.

The Graphics Resolution section determines the quality of the output by setting the number of dots per inch. The higher the dpi, the crisper the image, but the greater the memory consumption.

The last section, Cartridges, provides a list of available font cartridges. A cartridge, an interface board inserted in the printer, contains fonts on a chip. Windows can look at the printer to determine which cartridges are in the printer's cartridge slots. Windows also knows how many cartridges the printer can use at one time and displays the maximum number at the top of the Cartridges section. The HP LaserJet Series II can use two.

You set the number of copies you want to print in the Copies text box. Simply double-click on the box to highlight the current number, then type in the new number of copies. The default setting is 1. If you don't provide a number of copies when you print, Windows will assume that you want one copy.

Installing printer fonts

To install a new printer font, click on the Fonts... button in the PCL/HP LaserJet on LPT1: dialog box to activate the Printer Font Installer dialog box shown in Figure 3-31. The left display box lists the currently installed fonts. The right display box lists fonts you can add. The option buttons under the display boxes designate selected fonts as permanent or temporary. Files marked as permanent have an asterisk next to their names. Windows loads a permanent font when you select the printer and a temporary font when you select the font. The buttons between these two display boxes exchange files between them. The left display box is the target, and the right is the source. The Move button moves a highlighted font from the source display box on the right and adds it to the target display box on the left. The Copy button will add the font to the target display box but won't remove it from the source. The Delete button removes any highlighted font. The Edit... button allows you to edit a font's title and options, such as the way the font is downloaded (permanent or temporary).

At the bottom of the dialog box, below the heavy line, is a status display area where Control Panel displays the file names as you add or delete them.

Figure 3-31

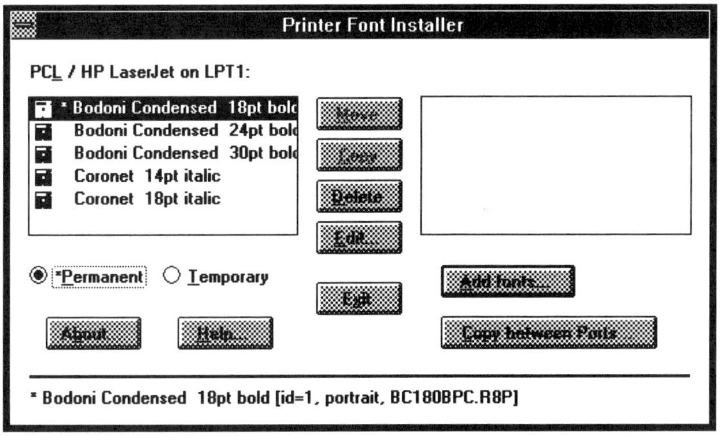

The Printer Font Installer dialog box adds printer font drivers to
your hard disk.

If your printer supports soft fonts (fonts that can be downloaded into your
printer's memory), then you can edit the soft font settings when you set up the
printer. For example, if you want to add Bitstream's Headline typeface soft fonts
to Windows, you need to select the PCL/HP LaserJet on LPT1: (or another port)
in the Printers dialog box, then click on Configure.... Next, click on Setup..., then
click on Fonts... to access the Printer Font Installer dialog box. Finally, click on
Edit... to display an Edit dialog box, as shown in Figure 3-32. You can change the
font name (in case different brands of soft fonts have the same name), change the
WIN.INI ID number, the method of downloading, and the font family. You can
even change several fonts at a time with the Edit Mode option.

Editing font settings

Figure 3-32

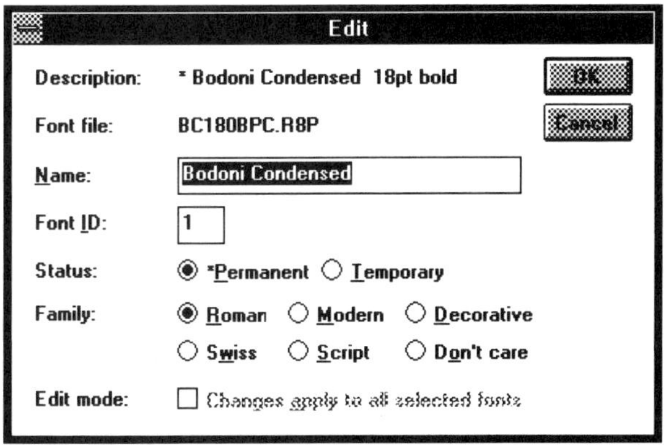

*The Edit dialog box
allows you to edit soft
font settings such as
the font name or
download capabilities.*

The top two lines of the dialog box displays the soft font official description (which appears in the Printer Font Installer dialog box) and file name. On the next line is a Name text box where you can alter the name that appears in font listings in applications (the unofficial description). On the next line is the Font ID text box, which allows you to change the number Windows assigns to the font in the WIN.INI file. Don't change this number unless you are familiar with editing the WIN.INI file. If you change the Font ID number incorrectly, you may lose access to the font from Windows applications.

Next, with the Status radio buttons, you can change whether the soft font is downloaded when you select the printer (Permanent Status) or when you select the font (Temporary Status). You can designate only one font on the list as permanent. When you designate a font as permanent, Windows will present a dialog box asking if you want the font downloaded immediately and/or automatically each time you turn on your PC. Check the Download at Startup box if you want Windows to modify your AUTOEXEC.BAT file to download the font when you turn on your PC or just reboot it (reboot means restarting the PC without turning it off by pressing [Ctrl][Alt][Delete]). A word of caution: It will take longer to start working on your PC when you boot your system because downloading takes a long time (how long depends on how much memory the font uses). However, your PC will prompt you with a message like *Download PCL fonts (y/n)?* so you don't have to download the fonts every time. However, if you need to download fonts, you'll see the Download options dialog box in Figure 3-33.

Figure 3-33

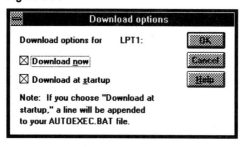

The Download options dialog box modifies your AUTOEXEC.BAT file to load fonts to the printer.

The next group of radio buttons defines the family or category of typeface. For example, the Roman radio button pertains to all serif fonts with variable character widths like Times Roman. Roman is the most common font family. Table 3-4 lists the font families and describes their distinguishing characteristics. If your soft font doesn't fit into any of the categories listed in the table, click on the Don't Care radio button to leave the family unspecified.

Table 3-4

Family	Description	Example
Roman	Serif font with variable character width	Times Roman
Swiss	Sans serif font with variable character width	Helvetica
Modern	Serif or sans serif font with non-proportional character width	Courier
Script	Cursive fonts	Script
Decorative	Unusual or novelty fonts	Old English

These font family categories group soft fonts by typeface features.

The last line in the Edit dialog box sets the edit mode with a check box. If you have more than one font selected when you click on the Edit... button in the Printer Font Installer dialog box, this option will be available. When you activate the check box by clicking on it, Windows will use all the options you set in the Edit dialog box for each highlighted font. (A word of warning: If you change the name of a font, then all highlighted fonts will have the same name.)

After you have set all the options, click on OK to return to the Printer Font Installer dialog box. The status area at the bottom of the dialog box will tell you how many fonts were edited, with a message like *3 fonts edited.*

The Add Fonts... button in the Printer Font Installer dialog box copies font files onto your hard disk. If you click on it, Windows displays the dialog box shown in Figure 3-34, which prompts you for a floppy disk. If you don't want to access a floppy disk in drive A, enter a new drive ID and path name in the text box.

Adding a font

Figure 3-34

The Add fonts dialog box copies font files onto your hard disk.

After the fonts appear in the right display box, the Add Fonts... button changes to a Close Drive button. If you click on Close Drive, the listed fonts will disappear, and Windows will reset the path to its default (C:\WINDOWS). If you don't click Close Drive and take the disk out, Windows will continue to prompt you for a disk for drive A whenever it wants to issue a command. Once you have established the correct drive from which to add fonts, highlight the fonts you want to add, and click on the Add Fonts.... button. In the Add fonts dialog box, either accept the default path for the files or enter a new one. After you click OK, Windows will copy the fonts onto your hard disk.

**Copying fonts
between ports**

The Copy between Ports... button in the Printer Font Installer dialog box lets you copy fonts between printers. Windows lets you select the destination port with the Copy between Ports dialog box shown in Figure 3-35. Click on the destination port, then click on OK. Windows adds a printer name with that port designation to the source display on the right side of the Printer Font Installer dialog box. Now you can copy fonts from one printer's memory into another printer's memory instead of only from a disk into a printer.

Figure 3-35

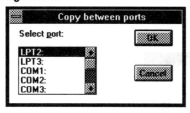

The Copy between Ports dialog box enables you to transfer fonts.

After you choose the fonts to install on the right display box and click on the Copy button of the Printer Font Installer dialog box, Windows will confirm any permanent font's download options and use the Print Manager to transfer the fonts to the other printers.

The Exit button will return you to the PCL/HP LaserJet on LPT1: dialog box. Closing the dialog box will also return you to the previous dialog box.

**When is the
Options... button
available?**

You may have noticed the dimmed Options... button in the PCL/HP LaserJet on LPT1: dialog box. You can click on the Options... button to see more settings for your printer, if there are any available. For example, if you want to use the HP LaserJet IID, you need to tell the printer that you want to use its Duplex Printing feature to print on both sides of a sheet of paper. Notice that the Options dialog box shown in Figure 3-36 has a Duplex Printing section. Duplex printing means printing on both sides of a piece of paper. If you select one of the radio buttons, the sample page on the left will change to illustrate that option. The None option is the default and will print single-sided normal pages. The Long Edge option duplexes portrait pages side by side for side binding. The Short Edge option duplexes portrait pages by the tops and bottoms for top binding.

Figure 3-36

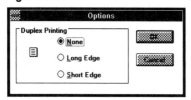

The Options dialog box for PCL/HP LaserJets will appear only if the selected printer supports any additional options.

If you use a dot matrix printer instead of a laser printer, you will see different options when you install the printer and set up its options. For example, when you install an Epson LQ2500, which is a near letter-quality printer with a color option, you will see a dialog box similar to the one in Figure 3-37. In the Epson 24 pin printer driver dialog box, you'll set printer model, graphics resolution, paper orientation, paper feed hardware, text quality, paper width, paper height, installed fonts, color option, and margins. The dialog box also provides information on dip switches—the small switches found on the printer's circuit board that control printer settings such as line feeds and carriage returns. To completely install the printer, you'll need to set all of these options.

Setting up the Epson LQ2500

Figure 3-37

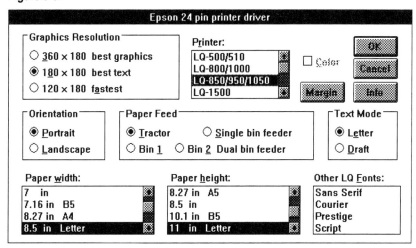

The Epson 24 pin printer driver dialog box sets up a high-end dot matrix printer.

You should begin setting up your printer by defining the hardware you're using. First, you have to choose which Epson model you're installing. When we choose the LQ2500 in the Printer list box, the color option becomes available. If you installed the color option kit on your Epson LQ2500, you can click on the Color check box to allow applications to print in color. (Note that the application, as well as Windows, needs to support the printer.) Next, choose which type of feed equipment you're using in the Paper Feed section. The Paper Feed section has radio buttons for Tractor, Single bin feeder, Bin 1, and Bin 2 Dual bin feeder options. By default, Windows uses the Tractor setting.

The last hardware setting you need to confirm is the suggested dip switch settings, which Control Panel displays when you click on the Info button. In Figure 3-38, you can see that the dialog box lists the settings by function below the

Required DIP switch settings heading. DIP switch settings can either be off or on. You'll need to refer to your printer manual to find their location and which switch number refers to which function so you'll be sure to flip the correct switch. After you've set the switches or made a note of the settings, click OK to return to the Epson 24 pin printer driver dialog box.

Figure 3-38

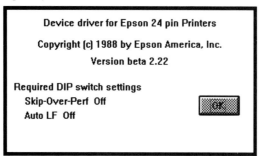

The Info button displays the printer driver version and the required DIP switch settings for an Epson 24 pin printer.

You can choose page setup options, such as minimum margins, paper width, paper height, and page orientation. If your printer has limits for margins, you can use the Margin button to open a dialog box, as shown in Figure 3-39, to set the minimum top and bottom margins. The Minimum Margins display box on the left lists the top and bottom margins for a tractor feed and sheet feed. The Select Margin Size list box lets you set the margin size. For example, if you want to print labels, you need to select 0 for the top and bottom margins. If you don't have a preference or need to reset the margins to the default, click on the Use Defaults button to reset the margins, in this case to .5". The left and right margins are set within the application you're using. Click OK to continue setting the other page setup options.

Figure 3-39

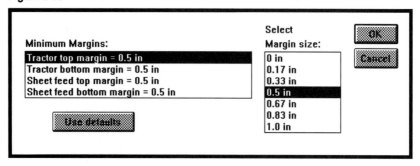

This dialog box lets you change the minimum top and bottom margins for a tractor feed or a sheet feed.

Because dot matrix printers use an adjustable tractor feed and aren't confined to a paper tray, they can use many sizes of paper. To set the paper width, click on one of the items in the Paper width list box in the Epson 24 pin printer driver dialog box. The default width is 8.5 in Letter. You also need to choose the paper height with the Paper height list box. The default for height is 11 in Letter.

If you want to print a spreadsheet that exceeds the width of the paper, you'll need to turn the printing sideways, or to Landscape orientation, in order to use the length of the page to gain more space. Not all printers have this capability, but Epson 24 pin printers do. To set the page orientation, simply click on one of the radio buttons in the Orientation group box. Windows uses Portrait orientation by default.

The rest of the options in the Epson 24 pin printer driver dialog box set the quality of the printout. You can change the resolution (density of dots) of the output. The highest quality of printing is the slowest, since a high resolution output uses more dots to form the characters or graphics and therefore takes more time to print. The Graphics Resolution group box has three radio buttons for three quality levels. By default, Windows uses the middle setting, which is best for printing text. If you want to print text in order to proofread a document, you can use the Draft option in the Text Mode group box. This way, the printer prints at the lowest quality and doesn't take as long to print or use as much of your printer ribbon.

If your printer came with several font cartridges, you'll probably want to click on one of the fonts in the Other LQ Fonts list box so you can access those fonts from your application.

Setting up PostScript printers

PostScript printers are similar to the HP LaserJet printers, but they have more options since they have more capabilities. When you select a PostScript printer in the first Printers dialog box and then configure it, you'll see a dialog box like the one in Figure 3-40 on the following page. You need to select the specific printer, paper tray, paper size, orientation, and copies, just as you did for the HP LaserJet. This dialog box also has an About... button for the driver version. You don't need to install fonts. PostScript printers come with their own outline fonts (similar to vector fonts) to create fonts of varying sizes. You can install screen fonts with Control Panel's Fonts feature, but you don't have to install printer fonts there. The PostScript printer options we haven't discussed previously include scaling, color, adding new PostScript printers, and printer communication options.

Scaling will enlarge or reduce the images sent to your printer. For example, a setting of 50 percent will cut the size by half, and a setting of 200 percent will double the size. You should set scaling to 100 percent for normal size images.

Color is available for specific PostScript printers like the QMS Color Script 100. If your printer can't print in color, the Use Color check box will be dimmed.

Figure 3-40

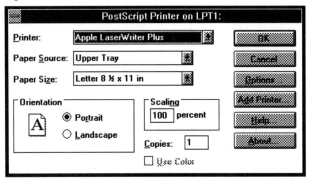

This dialog box sets PostScript printer options.

The Add Printer... button allows you to add a new PostScript printer to the list for this group. PostScript printers are relatively new so Windows will not always have a driver. With the Add Printer dialog box, you can add drivers later from the printer manufacturer or from Microsoft.

The Options... button in the PostScript Printer on LPT1: dialog box directs you to more setup details. In the Options dialog box, shown in Figure 3-41, you can send output to a file by changing the selection in the Print To section.

Figure 3-41

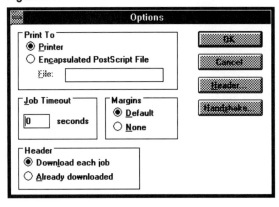

The Options dialog box will set printer-specific parameters.

Some of your applications, such as PageMaker, may be able to use an Encapsulated PostScript (EPS) File format. You can choose this file format by clicking on the Encapsulated PostScript File radio button. Normally, you'll use the Clipboard to transfer bit map graphics to another application, but bit map graphics take longer to print than EPS files. To speed printing, you can use the Encapsulated PostScript File to place the figure in PageMaker. In the Print To section, you can enter the name of the output target file. If you select the Encapsulated PostScript File radio button, the File text box will become available for text entry. You need to click in the File text box and enter the file name at the cursor. The Job Timeout text box lets you specify the number of seconds Windows will wait before giving you an error message about the file not printing if your printer doesn't respond. If, however, you are sending the information directly to the printer, the Margins section will let you disable the default margins set up by the printer. This is especially useful if you are trying to print labels that have no top or bottom margin.

Also in the Options dialog box, the Header... button will let you either send a header each time a file prints or let the software application take care of it. A header is unique to PostScript printers. A header is information sent to the printer to set up the printer with the correct page formatting and fonts. The Header dialog box, shown in Figure 3-42, provides the option of sending the header information to a file instead of to a printer. As you may know, PostScript files are more portable than application-specific files because you can use them across applications. If you send the header to a file or to the printer, Windows will present a warning dialog box asking you for verification.

Figure 3-42

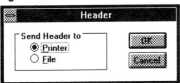

The Header... button will bring up the Header dialog box, which allows you to send header information to a printer or a file.

The Handshake... button in the Options dialog box will bring the option of hardware handshaking (in which the printer asks for more data from the application instead of the operating system) to an application instead of leaving it in the background. The Handshake dialog box, shown in Figure 3-43, also will give you a warning before making any changes.

Figure 3-43

Hardware or software can set up handshaking with a printer.

WINDOWS SETUP

The Windows Setup application makes it easy to recustomize Windows when you change your PC's hardware or add new applications. Any changes you make with Windows Setup are reflected in your WIN.INI and SYSTEM.INI files. The options you can change include settings for your PC's display, keyboard, mouse, and network (if applicable).

**Starting
Windows Setup**

To start Windows Setup, click on the Main group window to make it active, then double-click on the Windows Setup icon. A Windows Setup window, like the one in Figure 3-44, will appear. This dialog box displays all your current hardware settings and the size of the swap file used in memory operations. You'll need to use the commands on the Options menu to change hardware settings or install applications.

To exit Windows Setup, choose the Exit command from the Options menu.

Figure 3-44

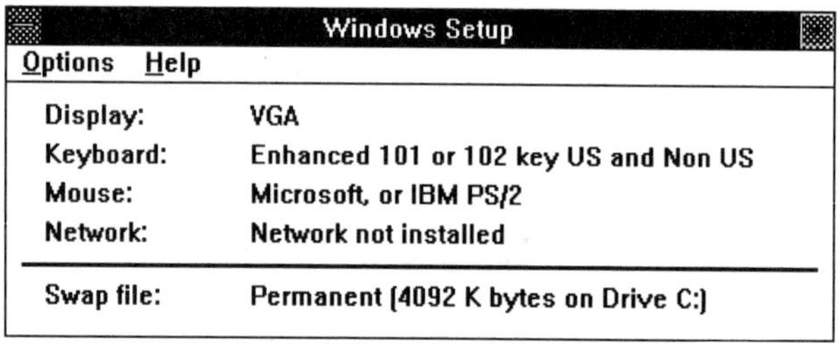

Windows Setup	
Options Help	
Display:	VGA
Keyboard:	Enhanced 101 or 102 key US and Non US
Mouse:	Microsoft, or IBM PS/2
Network:	Network not installed
Swap file:	Permanent (4092 K bytes on Drive C:)

The Windows Setup window displays the current hardware settings and size of the swap file.

If you change your hardware, for instance, if you upgrade to a VGA monitor, you'll need to change the hardware settings in Windows. To do this, choose the Change System Settings... command on the Options menu, and Windows Setup will display a Change System Settings dialog box, like the one in Figure 3-45. This dialog box provides drop-down list boxes to let you choose the Display (monitor), Keyboard, Mouse, and Network. These list boxes present the current settings for the various hardware categories. To change one of these settings, simply click on the list box's drop-down arrow, and click on a new setting. For example, if you currently have a Hercules Monochrome interface card and monochrome monitor and want to upgrade to a VGA interface card and VGA color monitor, click on VGA in the Display drop-down list box. Of course, you need to change your hardware by installing the new card and monitor so that when you start your next Windows session, you can use the new hardware. Note that if you change your hardware before you change the appropriate settings with Windows Setup, you may not be able to see the desktop, since Windows will still present it as if you had a monochrome monitor.

Figure 3-45

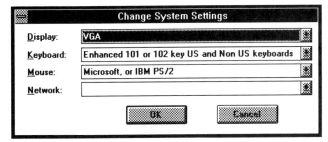

The Change System Settings dialog box lists the current hardware and network settings.

The keyboard and mouse system settings are similar to the display settings since they all depend on a type of hardware, but the network settings relate to a type of network software. As you can see in Figure 3-46, the Network list box provides a list of network software packages such as Microsoft's LAN Manager and Novell's Netware. If you have removed your PC from a network and don't want to see the *Connect to Network* prompt at the beginning of every Windows session, you can choose the No Network Installed selection to cancel that connect prompt.

Figure 3-46

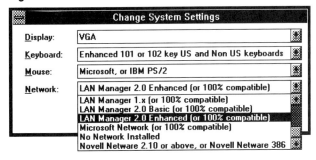

The Network list box displays network software packages.

After you've changed any hardware settings, click on OK to save your changes, then return to the Windows Setup window.

ADDING APPLICATIONS TO THE DESKTOP

When you buy a new software package to use with Windows, you'll need to add it to a Program Manager group window with Windows Setup. Before you can run Windows Setup, you must install the application onto your hard disk according to the instructions in the application's documentation. After the application is correctly installed on your hard disk, start Windows, then double-click on the Windows Setup icon. When the Windows Setup application window appears, choose the Set Up Applications... command from the Options menu.

By default, a Set Up Applications dialog box, like the one shown in Figure 3-47, will search your hard disk for all applications that Windows recognizes. This could take awhile if you've installed several applications on your hard disk. However, you can tell Windows to look at just one drive to speed up the process. For example, if the application you just installed was copied onto drive C, you would click on the drop-down arrow and click on drive C. After you clicked on OK, Windows would search for applications on drive C. If drive C is loaded with applications, a search through it would take a long time. As an alternative, you could instruct Windows to search the path you specified in the AUTOEXEC.BAT file, which lists the directories of all the major applications. To search the path, choose the Path Only selection in the list box.

Figure 3-47

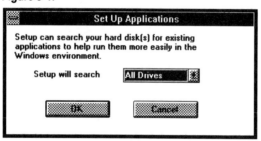

The Set Up Applications dialog box searches for applications on your hard disk.

After you click on OK, Windows will display a Windows Setup message dialog box that indicates the status of the search. The first line in the dialog box tells you which drive Windows is currently searching, with a message like *Searching Drive C:*. The next line changes often because it displays the path that Windows is looking at (*C:\WINDOWS\SYSTEM)*. Windows looks at each directory on your hard disk. The last line of text lists the name of the application that Windows finds. This line changes each time Windows finds a new application. The display bar at the bottom of the dialog box shows you how much of the search Windows has completed. When the bar is all blue, then the search is 100% complete.

As soon as the search is complete, another Set Up Applications dialog box will appear, like the one in Figure 3-48. Windows will list the applications it found in the left list box. To select an application, click on it. Windows will highlight the application name and frame it with a dashed line. If you want to remove the highlight and deselect an application, click on it again. After you select the applications you want to add to the Program Manager, click on the Add button. Now the highlighted application will appear in the right list box. If you added an application by mistake, you can use the Remove button to return it to the left list box. If you want to add all the items in the left list box and don't want to bother clicking on each one, you can simply click on the Add All button.

Figure 3-48

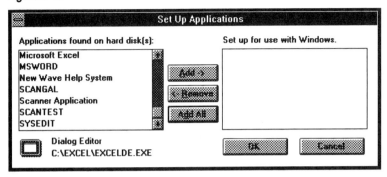

Another Set Up Applications dialog box lists the applications Windows found and allows you to choose which ones to add.

As you click on application names, you'll notice that the lower-left corner of the dialog box displays an icon, the application name, and its path. This display area is handy for verifying which application is being added, since you might have installed different versions of software under the same name. The path information in the display area will distinguish one software version from another.

When you've selected the applications to add, click on OK. Now Windows will add the applications to the Program Manager in the Windows Applications group window. It also will keep you informed of its progress in adding the application with a Windows Setup message dialog box like the one you saw when Windows searched the drives for applications. This time, the message dialog box will have three lines of text to tell you that Windows is *Building a Program Group...*, which group it is, and the name of the application. After you exit Windows Setup, you'll see the new icon in either the Windows or Non-Windows Applications group window. If the application wasn't originally designed for Windows but Windows recognizes it as compatible, Windows will write a PIF (Program Interface File) so that it can start the application correctly later. You can read more about PIFs in Chapter 17.

In this chapter

Getting Help 4

*S*ome programs offer so little assistance you may feel stranded when you encounter a problem. Windows Help is determined to change that feeling by offering a new and comprehensive approach to the standard Help feature.

In DOS applications, Help is part of the application you are running. In Windows, Help is a separate application devoted to providing information about Windows. Some applications written to work with Windows will use the Help application too, but with their own data files. The installed application will supply the information, and Windows will present it to you in the Help window. Applications that weren't designed to work with Windows have their own isolated Help systems, not the advanced and easily accessible Help system Windows provides.

As you work with the various Windows applications, you'll see a Help menu on every menu bar. Since Help works the same way for all applications, we'll explain how to use Help only in this chapter to avoid repetition as we explore the many Windows applications. However, you'll see Help buttons on dialog boxes throughout the book, and we will detail their uses and functions as necessary.

In this chapter, we will show you how to start Help and how to use all its features. For instance, you can get help on a specific topic with the Help Index. You can even print a particular topic and add notes to it. Finally, we'll show you how to exit from Help and return to the application you're working on.

Starting Help

Windows provides many avenues by which you can reach its internal Help application. You can use the Help menu on an application's menu bar, press a Help... button in some of the dialog boxes, or press [F1]. Some applications like PIF Editor and Windows Setup even provide context-sensitive help.

You can acesss Help from within an application by choosing commands on the Help menu. This menu features a list of commands that will generally include Index, Keyboard, Commands, Procedures, Using Help, and About.... The Program Manager and Paintbrush add to this list a few commands specific to those applications. For instance, the Program Manager also lists Basic Skills and Glossary, while the Paintbrush Help menu lists a Tools command.

When you choose one of these commands, Help will open a window on your desktop for the specified category. For example, if you want to see all the Help categories for the Program Manager, select the Index command from the Help menu on the Program Manager menu bar. Then, click on the Program Manager Help Index, listed in green under Help Indexes. The Program Manager Help Index lists the available topics grouped by category, as shown in Figure 4-1.

Figure 4-1

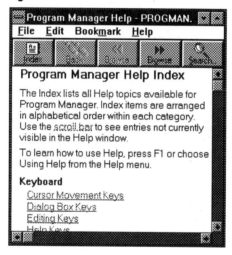

Help displays a list of available topics when you select the Index command.

If you press a Help... button in a dialog box, you'll see a topic related to the functions of that dialog box. (Note that you can still use the Help menu to view the same information.) For example, when you click on the Help... button in the Printer Font Installer dialog box, shown in Figure 4-2, Help will open a window like the one in Figure 4-3 to display an Index of topics related to installing fonts. After you exit the Help window, you'll return to the dialog box as you left it. We'll show you how to exit Help later.

When you press [F1], Help will display an Index for the active application (the window you're currently working with). This is the same Index you can reach with the Index command on the Help menu.

When you initially set up Windows and when you're working with the PIF Editor, you can get context-sensitive help without using the Index. If you press [F1], Help displays a topic about the highlighted portion of the window.

Figure 4-2

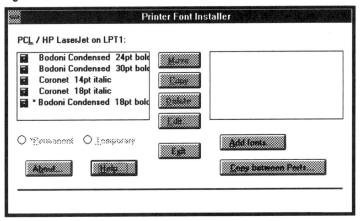

*The Printer Font Installer dialog box from Control Panel provides
a Help... button that leads to an Index of topics for installing fonts.*

Figure 4-3

*Help displays an Index of
topics germane to font
installing.*

Sizing Help

After you start Help, you can resize the window in order to work with multiple
windows, to use space more efficiently, or for easier viewing. You can adjust the
size of your windows by dragging the window frame or clicking on the Minimize
or Maximize box. As we showed you in Chapter 2, dragging the frame to a custom
size allows you to use the rest of the desktop so you can display several windows
simultaneously. If you click on the Minimize box, you gain the most desktop space
because Windows shrinks Help into an icon and places it at the bottom of the
desktop, as shown in Figure 4-4. Finally, clicking on the Maximize box expands
the Help window to fill the entire desktop, making the topics easier to read.

Figure 4-4

You can minimize Help into this icon to save desktop space.

HELP FUNCTIONS

The Help application supplies built-in tools to enable you to access information easily. Figure 4-5 shows Help's standard window controls, menu bar, and a row of function buttons. These five buttons—Index, Back, Browse backward, Browse forward, and Search…—will move you around the available Help topic.

Figure 4-5

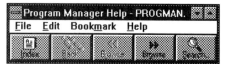

The Help window provides standard window controls plus five function buttons.

As you navigate through the Help information using the function buttons, you'll notice an occasional green keyword with a broken underline. If you click on a green keyword and hold down the mouse button, Help will display a glossary definition for that term. If you want to know the definition of *desktop* under the topic *Changing a Window's Size in the Program Manager,* move the pointer over the keyword *desktop,* then click and hold the mouse button. Help will then display a rectangular box containing the definition, as shown in Figure 4-6.

Figure 4-6

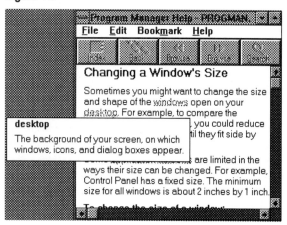

Help defines keywords when you click on them.

The Index button takes you to the top of the list of general categories, the subject headings, and specific topics, the titles of additional information. Keyboard, Commands, and Procedures are the categories you'll see most often. In the Index, the topics are green and underlined to point out that you can click on them to display related information. As you read the available information on a selected topic, you'll also see keywords in green, which you can click on to access related information. Help organizes the Index topics within each category. Since there are so many topics, you will need to use the scroll bars to see them all.

If you move the pointer over one of the topics, it will change from an arrow into a hand pointer. The change in the pointer is another clue that the topic has more information to offer. For example, in the Program Manager Help Index, if you want to know more about the Program Manager Keys topic, move the pointer over that topic, and select it. Notice all five function buttons are now available to you —since Help advanced a screen, you can use the Back or Browse backward buttons.

As you read through the available topics, you'll see a list entitled *Related Topics* at the end. This miniature Index provides a way for you to quickly click on another topic to continue reading about more information on a closely related subject.

Using the Index button

When you click on the Back button (or press [Alt]B), Help takes you to the previous screen and will backtrack through the topics in the reverse order you originally chose. Each time you select Back, you will return to the preceding screen. When you return to the category from which you started Help, the Back button will become inactive. For example, if you highlight the Procedures command on your Program Manager Help menu, the Back button will retrace any steps you've taken until you return to the Procedures category. Obviously, this can be a handy tool for quick referral to earlier information.

Using the Back button

You can browse forward or backward through a series of Help categories. To Browse through successive categories, click on Browse forward or press [Alt]O from the Index. For instance, to look at Write's Help categories, click on Browse forward from the Index. Help will then display each category as you repeatedly click on the Browse forward button. You'll see the categories Write Keys, Write Commands, and then Write Procedures. You can click on Browse backward to go back through the categories and return to the Index.

To browse through Help topics within a category, you must click on one of the category's topics before you click on the Browse forward button. That way, you'll start browsing within a category rather than between categories. For example, if you want to browse through Write's Procedures topics, click on a topic like Adding Headers, Footers, and Page Numbers. Now, when you click on Browse forward, Write will present another topic in the Procedures category. You'll need to use the Browse backward button (or press [Alt]R) to view all the

Using the Browse buttons

topics for Procedures since the series isn't a continuous loop (it doesn't restart displays from the beginning of the series) or in alphabetical order (you can't tell which topic is the first in the series.)

**Using the
Search... button**

When you select the Search... button (or press [Alt]S) in the Help Index window, Help will display the Search dialog box shown in Figure 4-7. Simply enter a topic in the Search For text box and press the Search... button. Help will quickly locate that topic. Incidentally, the Search feature is not case-sensitive. In other words, you can type either uppercase or lowercase letters in the Search For text box. As you type in the search text, the Search list box will automatically highlight the topic alphabetically closest to your entry.

Figure 4-7

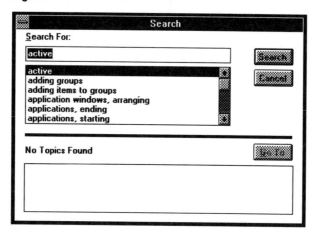

The Search dialog box finds words or phrases whether you enter the search text in uppercase or lowercase letters.

Rather than typing a topic in the Search For text box, you can select one of the keywords from the Search list box. For example, if you want to find out how to edit text in the Program Manager, you can either type *editing* in the Search For text box or select *editing* from the list box. After you specify the search text, select the Search button to begin. Windows will find the information or its closest alphabetic neighbor. Notice that three topics, Text Boxes, Editing Selected Text, and Editing Keys appear in the Topic Found list box as shown in Figure 4-8. At this point, you can select the Go To button to read about editing keys under the Keyboard category. It should be clear from this example that topics with similar names might not yield the results you desire, so you'll sometimes need a bit of persistence.

Figure 4-8

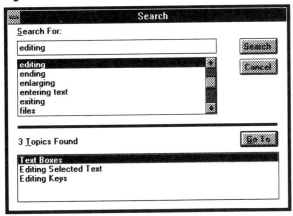

The Search dialog box will display in the Topic Found list box all topics related to the search text.

Windows provides Help for all applications, including Help itself. When you choose Using Help from the Help menu or press the accelerator key ([F1]), the Help Index shown in Figure 4-9 will appear. The Index contains such topics as Help Basics and Help Commands. To return to the original Help Index for the application you're working on, press the Index button.

GETTING HELP FOR HELP

Figure 4-9

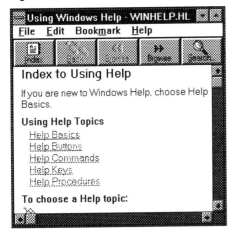

When getting help for Help, you can reference this Index.

In most applications, you probably won't use the About... command on the Help menu. The About dialog box that appears when you issue this command provides information you usually don't need—the application's name, version number, copyright date, and, sometimes, the name of the contributing programmer. However, the About dialog boxes for the Program Manager and the File

Using the About... command

Manager have an additional and potentially very useful piece of information. They display the amount of unused RAM, as shown in Figure 4-10. You'll find this information helpful when you're diagnosing problems and memory is a factor.

Figure 4-10

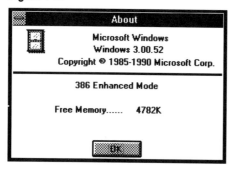

The About Program Manager... command displays the available RAM.

ADVANCED FEATURES

Among Help's advanced features are the ability to open Help topics for applications other than the one you're currently using and to transfer Help topics to a word processor, like Notepad. You can also define bookmarks and customize Help to add or find information within a Help topic.

Opening other Help files

From the File menu of your Help application, you can open Help files for other applications. For instance, suppose you're working in Write and need to know how to paste a Paintbrush file into your Write document. When you select Open... from Write's Help File menu, the File Open dialog box shown in Figure 4-11 will display all available files in the Files list box. All Help files have an .HLP extension. If the file you need isn't listed, you can look in other subdirectories of your hard disk by selecting one of the directories listed in the Directories list box.

Figure 4-11

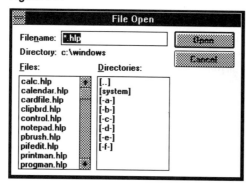

The File Open dialog box displays the available Help topic files.

To select the Paintbrush application's Help file, either double-click on the file (PBRUSH.HLP) from the Files list box or type the name in the Filename text box, and press OK. The Help title bar will change to *Paintbrush Help-PBRUSH.HLP*. When the new file appears on the screen, notice that the Back button is inactive. Remember, you can only retrace your steps through a file—not between files.

Using Help information in other applications

You can use the Copy command on the Edit menu to copy topic information from Help to another document. For instance, to copy a Help topic to a Notepad document, simply select a topic from the Program Manager's Help window, then select Copy from the Edit menu. Help will store the topic on the Clipboard. Exit Help by opening the Help File menu and choosing the Exit command. To complete the copy, simply activate the Accessories group window, and double-click on the Notepad icon. Then, select Paste from the Edit menu to place the topic in the new Notepad file.

If both a Notepad file and a Help window are already on the desktop, you can save yourself a few steps by resizing the Help window so Notepad's window is visible as well. After you have selected and copied the Help topic, just click on the Notepad window to make it active, then use the Paste command. Now, return to Help by clicking on the Help window, and you're ready to look at the next topic.

Defining bookmarks

A bookmark in Windows serves the same purpose as an actual bookmark—it lets you quickly return to a specific location. The Bookmark menu lets you define shortcuts to a Help topic. Instead of threading through two or three levels to find a related topic, you can just define a bookmark. For example, if you are working in Notepad and find yourself always looking up the Creating Time-Log Documents topic, you could set up a bookmark for it instead of scrolling through the Index and then choosing that topic.

Defining a bookmark is very simple. From within the Help Index, select a topic beside which you want to place a bookmark, then choose Define... from the Bookmark menu. When you do this, the Bookmark Define dialog box in Figure 4-12 on the next page will appear. Help will automatically accommodate as much of the topic name in the Bookmark Name text box as it can (up to 20 characters). Help will truncate the bookmark's name if necessary to fit it on the Bookmark menu below the Define... command. You can edit the name if it is cryptic or too long (you will want to be able to identify it easily, especially if your list of bookmarks contains more than a few names). When you're satisfied with the name, click on OK to add it to the list of bookmarks at the bottom of the Bookmark menu. Help adds a number nest to the bookmark for quick keyboard access. To return to a topic of interest, you need only open the Bookmark menu and click on the defined bookmark name (or type the number next to the bookmark). When you do, Help will display your topic.

If you no longer need a bookmark for a topic, you can delete it. To do this, open the Help Index and select the Define... command from the Bookmark menu to activate the Bookmark Define dialog box. Select the bookmark you no longer need from the list of bookmarks below the Bookmark Name text box and click on the Delete button. Then, click on OK to return to the Help topic.

Figure 4-12

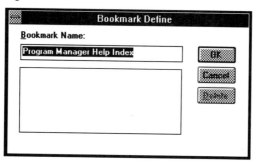

The Bookmark Define dialog box will let you type up to 20 characters for an entry in the Bookmark menu.

Customizing Help with Annotate...

You can make Help a little less generic by customizing it with the Annotate... command on the Edit menu. You can add a note to a selected topic to relate the command or function to specific tasks you do. For example, if you want a reminder that the Paste command is used to paste weather reports in a newsletter you've created, all you have to do is select Annotate... from the Edit menu. As you can see in Figure 4-13, the Help Annotation dialog box contains a large text box with a scroll bar. You can begin typing the desired text into this text box. As you type, Help will automatically wrap your text onto subsequent lines. If you want to force a line wrap before the end of a line, press [Ctrl][Enter]. (The [Enter] key by itself is used to activate the OK button and shouldn't be confused with a carriage return.) After you have finished typing, click on OK, and Help will add your note to the topic. You can have only one annotation for each Help topic.

Figure 4-13

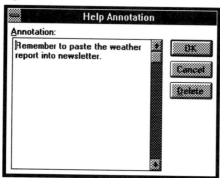

The Help Annotation dialog box includes a large text box in which you can type a note.

You can determine whether a topic contains an attached note by looking for the Paper Clip icon. In the Help window, the Paper Clip icon will appear at the top-left corner of the topic, as shown in Figure 4-14. The pointer will turn into a hand pointer when you move it over the icon, letting you click on the icon and open the note.

Figure 4-14

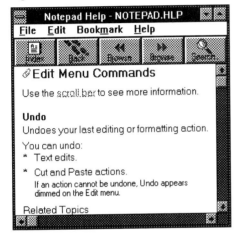

The Paper Clip icon reminds you that there is a note attached to a particular Help topic.

PRINTING

While you're learning a new technique in Help, you can print the accompanying Help topic so you don't have to keep Help open while you work. Printing a topic is a two-stage process. First, you need to set up your printer, and then you need to issue the Print Topic command.

Setting up the printer

To prepare to print a Help topic, you must make sure you have set up the printer correctly. The Printer Setup... command on the File menu allows you to make adjustments to all the printer's settings. The Printer Setup dialog box, shown in Figure 4-15, displays a list of printers. Just click on the printer you want to use, then click on OK. If you need to adjust the number of copies, paper orientation, and printer resolution, click on the Setup... button. (If you need more information about printer settings, see Chapter 3.) When you're satisfied with the settings, click on OK to return to the Printer Setup dialog box, then click on OK again to return to the Help window.

Figure 4-15

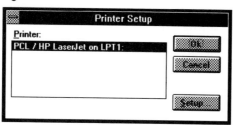

The Printer Setup dialog box provides a list of installed printers.

Printing a topic

A handy feature of your Help application is its ability to print specific topics from the Help Index. After the printer is set up, you can print a chosen topic by calling it, then selecting Print Topic from the File menu. A Help dialog box like the one in Figure 4-16 notifies you that the topic is printing. If the Help window is resized so you can see the lower part of the desktop, the Print Manager icon will appear. After the topic prints, the icon will disappear from the desktop. If you change your mind and want to cancel the Print Topic command, simply click on the Cancel button in the dialog box, or press the [Esc] key.

Figure 4-16

The Help dialog box notifies you that the topic is printing and that you can click Cancel to stop printing.

If your printed topic is misaligned or doesn't look like the topic on your screen, it's because your printer font isn't the same font that Help uses. When Help prints, it will use the fonts in your printer that are similar to the ones it was set up to use. Optimally, Help uses the Microsoft 1A font (cartridge for a LaserJet). If you see the font, then what you see on a maximized window will be exactly what you see when Help prints the topic.

EXITING HELP

To exit Help, choose the Exit command from the File menu. This command closes any open Help files and returns you to the point at which you started Help. For instance, suppose you started Help from the Notepad, where you were working on a document about weather reports. When you exit Help, you will return to the place where you were last working in your weather report document. In Chapter 9, we'll discuss exiting applications in more detail.

In this chapter

Program Manager 5

*T*he Program Manager lets you use Windows to find the right application for your job. Like a department store whose display windows line the sidewalk, each window of the Program Manager colorfully presents available applications. If one window doesn't have what you need, the next one probably will.

The Program Manager's series of internal windows (group windows) organize all the application icons. Each icon is a colorful graphic with a title to remind you of the application it represents. All you need to do is double-click on the icon whose application you want to use, and the Program Manager opens it for you.

As with store windows, you can customize the icons and their windows. In this chapter, we'll show you how to manipulate icons and their windows as we focus on how to move, create, delete, and edit them. In the Advanced Features section, you'll learn about representing documents as icons.

PROGRAM MANAGER

Unlike the other applications you'll use in Windows, you don't click on an icon to open the Program Manager; Windows starts it for you. When you begin a new Windows session, the Program Manager appears automatically. To start Windows, type *WIN* at the DOS prompt (C:>) and press [Enter]. (Chapter 1 explains more about starting Windows.) The first window you see is called the Program Manager.

The Program Manager is not a typical window. As you can see in Figure 5-1, the Program Manager consists of a window framing a series of smaller windows. The Program Manager window is a shell, which is a variation of an application window. The smaller windows, called group windows, are variations of document windows.

Starting the Program Manger

Figure 5-1

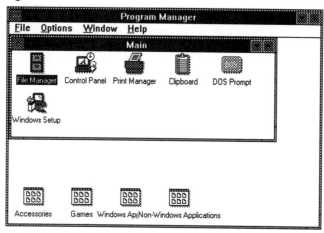

The Program Manager has a main window and a series of minimized group windows.

Group windows organize the application icons that the Program Manager launches. Just because Windows automatically puts the icons in certain groups doesn't mean they have to stay there. You can move the icons between the groups to sort them in any order you want. You can add applications to the groups by adding their icons. You can also delete those icons. We'll show you how to add and delete icons later in this chapter. You can edit group window titles and the titles that appear with the icons. In the Advanced Features section of this chapter, we'll show you how to convert a document into a launchable icon.

When you minimize a group window by clicking on the Minimize box in its upper-right corner, it will turn into an icon just like an application window. Program Manager will place the icon at the bottom of its window. To restore the group window to its previous size, simply double-click on its icon.

Minimizing group windows is a handy feature for keeping your desktop un-cluttered. For example, if you seldom use the Main group window, you can mini-mize it and keep other group windows open for easy access to their applications.

Minimizing the Program Manager

When you minimize the Program Manager, Windows will convert it into an icon and place it at the bottom of the desktop. There's even a way to set up Windows so the Program Manager is minimized into an icon for easy access every time you start an application. We'll talk about that later in this chapter.

NAVIGATION

As you work with the Program Manager, you'll need to move among its elements, such as menus, group windows, and icons, in order to use their functions. For example, if you want to start an application, you need to move to a group window. If you want to use the Program Manager's commands, you need to access the menus on the menu bar. You can access group windows and menus with both the mouse and the keyboard. Navigating in the Program Manager is easiest when you use a mouse.

If you want to use a group window, click on its title bar. When you do, the group window will become active or, in other words, move to the front of the stack so you can open the applications you need.

Mouse navigation

To use Program Manager's menus, you can click on a menu name to access the drop-down list of commands. You can also drag down the menu to quickly choose a command. (We explained menu bars in Chapter 2.) To open the Control menu (the box in the upper-left corner), simply click on it. Be careful not to double-click since this will close the window and end your Windows session. Group windows also have Control menus that you can open by clicking on them.

You can accomplish the same tasks (move between group windows, access the Program Manager menu bar, and open the Control menu) with the keyboard. Before you can move between group windows with the keyboard, you need to know how to use the Program Manager's menu bar. You access the menu bar with the keyboard the same way you do in any other application—by pressing [Alt] and the underlined letter of the menu name. For example, to open the File menu, you press [Alt]F since *F* is the underlined letter. Once the drop-down list of commands is open, you can use the arrow keys to move the highlight to the command you need.

Keyboard navigation

To move between group windows with the keyboard, you need to use the Window menu. When you press [Alt]W to drop down the Window menu, you will see a numbered list of the group windows represented by icons in the Program Manager window. Next, press the number of the group window you want to use. When you choose a number, the group window will become active and a check mark will appear next to the number on the menu. You can also use keyboard shortcuts to move between group windows. For example, you can press [Ctrl][Tab] or [Ctrl][F6] to move between group windows.

To open the Program Manager's Control menu with the keyboard, press [Alt][Spacebar] and close it by pressing [Alt]. To open the active group window's Control menu, you need to use a different key combination, [Alt]- (hyphen).

Icons are the most important part of the Program Manager because they allow you to start your applications. As its name implies, the Program Manager controls how applications or programs are started and how their icons are organized on the desktop. The Program Manager also allows you to add or delete application icons from the various groups and edit icon titles. You can even control the way an application starts.

MANIPULATING ICONS

Starting applications

You can use two methods to start an application: double-click on an icon or use the Open command from the File menu. With the mouse, you can click on an icon to select it and then choose the Open command or simply double-click on the icon. If you're using the keyboard, you need to highlight the correct icon (with the arrow keys) and press [Enter], or press [Alt]F to access the File menu, and press O to issue the Open command. As you can see, double-clicking is easier and quicker.

Minimizing the Program Manager automatically

If you often return to the Program Manager to start other applications during your Windows session, it would be a good idea to use the Minimize on Use option to keep the Program Manager icon handy. To turn this option on, choose the Minimize on Use command from the Options menu. A check mark will appear next to the command, indicating that the option is turned on. Now, every time you start an application, Windows will automatically minimize the Program Manager and place its icon at the bottom of the desktop. If you keep all the application windows sized so the bottom of the desktop is visible, then you'll be able to return to the Program Manager simply by double-clicking on its icon.

Moving application icons

You can reorganize the icons between the group windows by dragging them to another window. For example, if you add a new group window, you can put your favorite applications, like Word for Windows and Toolbook, in it. To do this, click on the Windows Applications group window, then drag the Microsoft Word icon to the new group. Release the mouse button to finish placing the icon. Next, drag the ToolBook icon to the new group. If you try to place an icon outside a group window, the pointer will change into a little circle with a slash through it (the prevent pointer). The slashed circle means the action you attempted is prohibited.

To reorganize icons with the keyboard, you need to use the Move... command on the File menu to move them from one group window to another. To move an icon, use the arrow keys to highlight it, then choose the Move... command. When you do this, a Move Program Item dialog box, like the one shown in Figure 5-2, will appear with a drop-down list box of the available destinations. Press [Alt]↓ to drop down the list box. Then, use the arrow keys to select the group to which you want to move the icon, and press [Enter]. The top of the dialog box displays the program item name and source group window.

Copying icons

Suppose you have an application, such as Paintbrush, that you customize for a specific job. If you have multiple copies of Paintbrush, each uniquely customized, you can place a separate PageMaker icon on the desktop for each customized version. To make a copy of an icon with the mouse, hold down the

[Ctrl] key as you drag the icon to another window or drag it to a new position in the same group window. The Program Manager will then create an identical Paintbrush icon. You can edit the new icon to change the path, start-up command, and title so it matches your customized version of Paintbrush. Later, we'll show you how to use the Properties... command to change an icon's start-up command, and title.

Figure 5-2

The Move Program Item dialog box moves icons between groups.

To copy an icon with the keyboard, you need to use the Copy... command on the File menu. Simply highlight the icon you want to copy, press [Alt]F to open the File menu, then press *C* to issue the Copy... command. The Copy Program Item dialog box, like the one shown in Figure 5-3, will appear. The Program Manager will display the name of the icon to be copied and its current group window location at the top of the dialog box. To choose the group window in which you want to place a copy of the icon, press [Alt]↓ to open the To Group drop-down list box. Now choose one of the listed group windows by highlighting it and then press [Enter] or [Spacebar] to close the dialog box and immediately issue the command. The destination group window will become active as Program Manager adds the copied icon.

Figure 5-3

The Copy Program Item dialog box copies icons from one group window to another.

You can add applications at any time by using the Windows Setup application or the Program Manager. In Chapter 6, we'll show you how the Windows Setup application works. For now, we'll use the Program Manager to add an application.

Adding applications

Before you can add an application, you need to decide which group you want to add it to, what you're going to name the icon, and which directory contains the application's program files so you can find its start-up command. When you have this information and are ready to begin, click on the group window in which you want to add the icon. Next, choose the New... command from the File menu. When the New Program Object dialog box appears, just click on OK. You don't have to select anything because the icon-adding option, Program Item, is the default and is already selected, as shown in Figure 5-4.

Figure 5-4

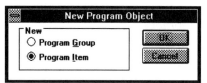

The New Program Object dialog box provides an option for adding items to a group window.

After you click OK in the New Program Object dialog box, the Program Item Properties dialog box appears, as shown in Figure 5-5. In this dialog box, enter the title for the icon in the Description text box. Next, enter the start-up command (the application's executable file name) in the Command Line text box.

Figure 5-5

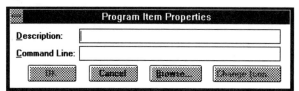

The Program Item Properties dialog box lets you name an icon and specify the application's start-up command.

If you need help locating the path and the start-up command for the application, Program Manager will help when you click the Browse... button. After you click on the Browse... button, you'll see a list of available program files in the Browse dialog box, shown in Figure 5-6. (By default, Windows will search for files with the .EXE extension. You'll need to change the file name specification in the Browse dialog box to search for executable files with .COM or .BAT extensions.) Table 5-1 lists the Windows program files and the applications to which they belong. You can either enter the file name in the Filename text box or click on a file in the Files list box. If you need to look in a different directory, use the Directories list box to change directories. After you find the file and select it, click on OK to continue.

Figure 5-6

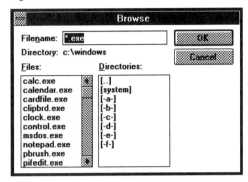

The Browse dialog box helps you find the right program file for the application.

Table 5-1

Program file	Application
CALC.EXE	Calculator
CALENDAR.EXE	Calendar
CARDFILE.EXE	Cardfile
CLIPBRD.EXE	Clipboard
CLOCK.EXE	Clock
CONTROL.EXE	Control Panel
MSDOS.EXE	DOS Prompt
NOTEPAD.EXE	Notepad
PBRUSH.EXE	Paintbrush
PIFEDIT.EXE	PIF Editor
PRINTMAN.EXE	Print Manager
PROGMAN.EXE	Program Manager
RECORDER.EXE	Recorder
REVERSI.EXE	Reversi
SETUP.EXE	Windows Setup
SOL.EXE	Solitaire
TASKMAN.EXE	Task Manager
TERMINAL.EXE	Terminal
WINFILE.EXE	File Manager
WINHELP.EXE	Help
WINVER.EXE	The About... commands
WRITE.EXE	Write

Each Windows application has a program file.

After you click OK in the Browse dialog box, the Program Manager will return you to the Program Item Properties dialog box so you can finish entering any parameters or options for your application's start-up command in the Command Line text box. A parameter is any character or combination of characters that modify how a program application runs. You can find these parameters in your application documentation. For example, with Windows, you type */3* after the word *WIN* to start the 386 enhanced version of Windows. Make sure you type a space between the file name and the parameters. Otherwise, Windows will think that the parameters are part of the file name. Finally, you're ready to click on OK and add the application to the group window.

If the application didn't have an icon designed for it by the software company, Windows will tuck it into a DOS icon resembling the one in Figure 5-7. For instance, applications that weren't designed for Windows won't have an icon.

Figure 5-7

Windows uses this DOS icon for a default icon when an application doesn't come with one.

Deleting application icons

You can delete an icon from the Program Manager if you no longer need an application or don't use it often. Deleting an icon doesn't mean that the Program Manager deletes the application; it's just a form of housekeeping to remove clutter from your desktop. You can still use the application without the icon. We'll show you how to start applications without icons later in this chapter.

To delete an icon, click on it and then choose the Delete command from the File menu. Windows will then present a message like the one shown in Figure 5-8, asking you to verify the deletion.

Figure 5-8

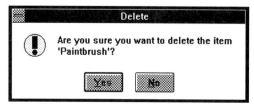

This message verifies that you want to delete an icon from a group window.

If an icon doesn't start an application the way you want it to or the title is wrong, don't worry. You can always modify an icon's start-up command or its title by using the Properties... command on the File menu. When you choose the Properties... command, the Program Item Properties dialog box will appear with the current information displayed. For example, when you highlight the Write icon, the Program Item Properties dialog box displays *Write* as the icon title and WRITE.EXE as the program file name, as you can see in Figure 5-9. When you upgrade application software, you'll often have to change the icon's properties. For instance, if you put the version number in the icon title, you'll need to edit it. You will edit or replace that information in the dialog box. When you're satisfied with your changes, click the OK button and the Program Manager will put those changes in place.

Editing icon properties

Figure 5-9

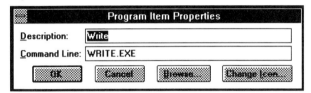

You can use the Program Item Proper-ties dialog box to edit icon properties.

If you add a DOS application to a group window and want to change the icon graphic to something other than the default DOS graphic, you can use the Properties... command to switch to another graphic. For example, if you're using a spreadsheet program that doesn't have a predefined Windows icon, you can choose the generic spreadsheet graphic to replace the DOS graphic. Table 5-2 on the following page lists the six generic graphics you can use. To change a graphic, first click on the icon you want to modify. Next, choose the Properties... command from the File menu to display the Program Item Properties dialog box. When you click on the Change Icon... button, Windows will display the Select Icon dialog box and place the current graphic in the center of it, as shown in Figure 5-10 on the next page. If you click on the View Next button, Windows will scroll through the different icons. You'll see a few other graphics besides the six generic ones, but Program Manager uses these graphics for its own elements, such as a minimized group window. When the new graphic appears in the dialog box, click on OK to use it and return to the Program Item Properties dialog box. When you click OK in the Program Item Properties dialog box, Windows will swap the icon graphics.

Changing icon graphics

Table 5-2

Icon	Definition
	DOS icon—This icon is the default for all DOS applications that don't have a predefined icon.
	Text icon—This icon represents a document-based application, such as a word processor or a desktop publishing application.
	Database icon—The small boxes on this icon look like fields in a database. You can use this icon with applications that manipulate data, such as databases or list utilities.
	Communications icon—The telephone in this icon is a clue that your application deals with communicating over the phone lines, as in PC-to-PC communications or terminal emulation.
	Generic icon—You can use this icon when none of the others is appropriate. Windows uses this icon when the start-up command is a program file with an .EXE extension. You'll also see this icon in File Manager.
	Windowed Application icon—If you create a PIF (Program Interface File) for an application so you can run it in an interactive window when it doesn't normally, you can use this icon to remind you that this version was set up to do so. You can refer to Chapter 17 for more about PIFs and windowed DOS applications.

You can customize applications with their own icon graphics.

Figure 5-10

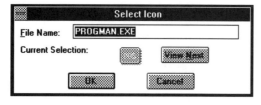

You can use the Select Icon dialog box to change icon graphics.

MANIPULATING GROUP WINDOWS

Group windows operate very much the same way that application windows do, except they allow you to customize Windows. In this section, we'll show you how to operate group windows, then we'll cover the more complex process of creating new groups, deleting old groups, and editing their properties. The basic operations include moving and resizing the windows, displaying group windows, and arranging their icons. You can move and resize group windows the same as you do application windows. However, the group windows are constrained by the boundaries of the Program Manager.

To move a group window, you can click on its title bar and drag it to a new location. Alternatively, you can press [Alt]- (hyphen) to access the active group window's Control menu and then press *M* to use the Move command. Refer to Chapter 2 for more information about moving windows.

Moving and resizing group windows

Resizing is just as easy. Simply click and drag the group window's frame to a new size. Keyboard users can take the Control menu route and use the Size command and the arrow keys to resize the group window.

Whenever you move or resize a group window, you must stay within the boundary of the Program Manager window. If you try to move the group window outside the boundary of the Program Manager window, scroll bars will appear to let you pull the group window back into view in the work area. If you want to avoid using the scroll bars, you can use the commands on the Window menu to resize the group windows so they'll fit into the workspace.

There are two ways to automatically arrange the group windows to fit in the Program Manager's workspace: by cascading or tiling. You can even realign the icons in a group window. The Program Manager provides Cascade, Tile, and Arrange Icons commands on the Window menu to let you rearrange the group windows and their icons.

Displaying group windows

To cascade the group windows as a stack with the titles showing, click on the Cascade command on the Window menu or press the accelerator keys [Shift][F5] to resize all the group windows and reposition them. By default, Program Manager automatically cascades the group windows when you first start Windows. The active group window appears in the front of the stack. If you click on one of the title bars in the stack, that window will appear in front of the other ones. To view all the title bars again, you'll need to reissue the Cascade command. Figure 5-11 on the following page shows how the Cascade command arranges the group windows in a stack.

Cascading group windows

If there are several group windows or if you've reduced the Program Manager window, rearranging the windows will create layers. For example, suppose you cascade five group windows into a small Program Manager window, like the one in Figure 5-12 on the next page. After four levels, the remaining group window will be stacked in the upper-left corner over other windows.

Figure 5-11

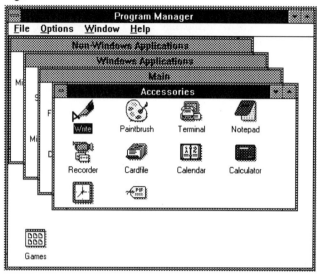

The Cascade command stacks the group windows so the title bars show.

Figure 5-12

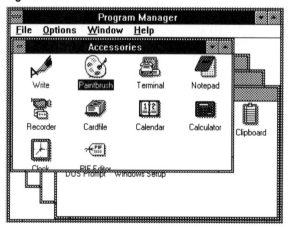

If the Program Manager window is too small, cascaded windows will begin layering.

Tiling group windows

When you want to see more than the group window title bar, you can tile the windows. The Tile command ([Shift][F4]) on the Window menu divides the workspace among the different group windows, as shown in Figure 5-13. The Tile command places the active group window in the upper-left corner when it rearranges the groups. When you click on another group window to make it active, its title bar will become highlighted and its position will not change.

Figure 5-13

The Tile command divides the work-space among the group windows.

Tiles can overlap but only in more cramped conditions than cascaded windows. After you open more than five group windows, it's better to tile them, since cascading will create covering layers and prevent you from viewing all the group windows.

After you tile the windows, you'll want to rearrange the icons for easier access. You can make the icons in the active window more accessible by using the Arrange Icons command on the Window menu. For example, in Figure 5-14 on the next page, we assembled the windows into tiles. In the Accessories window, we arranged the icons in two rows. After we issued the Arrange Icons command, the Program Manager organized the icons into two columns, which fit the shape of the window, as you can see in Figure 5-15 on the next page. Once you rearrange the icons, it will be easier to view and access them since Windows conserves space and work for you by removing one set of scroll bars. As you can see in Figure 5-15, after the Program Manager stacks the icons in the Accessories window, it needs only one scroll bar.

Arranging icons

You can avoid the hassle of selecting each group window and choosing the Arrange Icons command by turning on the Auto Arrange option. To turn on this option, choose the Auto Arrange command on the Options menu. A check mark will appear next to the command, indicating that it is active. Now, every time you use the Cascade or Tile commands, the Program Manager will rearrange the icons as it repaints the screen.

Arranging icons automatically

Figure 5-14

Although we rearranged the windows with the Tile command, the icons are still configured for a larger window.

Figure 5-15

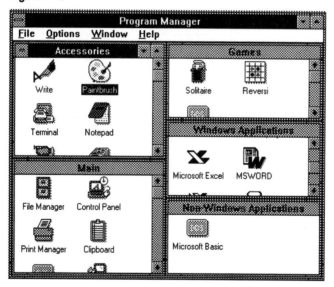

We used the Arrange Icons command to rearrange the icons in the tiled window.

Creating new group windows

Windows allows you to customize the Program Manager by adding group windows. For example, if you use Word for Windows and Toolbook exclusively, you'll want to add a group window for just those two application icons. Then, when you start Windows, you'll immediately be able to use both applications.

To add a group window, select the New... command from the File menu. When Windows displays the New Program Object dialog box, shown in Figure 5-16, choose the Program Group radio button and click OK. At this point, the Program Manager will bring up a Program Group Properties dialog box like the one shown in Figure 5-17. Enter the title for the new group window in the Description text box. You can enter a file name in the Group File text box or leave it blank and let Windows name the file for you. If you assign the file name, limit the name up to eight characters and use a .GRP extension. When you click OK to add the group window, Program Manager will place the new group window in the lower-right corner of its window.

Figure 5-16

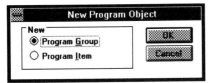

The New Program Object dialog box lets you customize the Program Manager with new group windows.

Figure 5-17

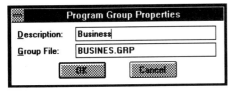

The Program Group Properties dialog box lets you name the new group window.

Let's go through the steps necessary to add a group window called *Business* to the Program Manager.

- Choose the New... command from the File menu.

- Choose the Program Group radio button from the New Program Object dialog box and click OK.

- Enter the title *Business* into the Description text box of the Program Group Properties dialog box.

- Leave the Group File text box blank so Windows will provide the file name, then click OK. Windows will name the file BUSINES.GRP.

- Program Manager will add the group window at the front of the stack, covering all the existing windows.

Deleting group windows

Deleting group windows is another aspect of customizing the Program Manager. When you reorganize the Program Manager by moving your application icons, you occasionally will empty a group window. If you're not going to use that window, you might as well remove it.

After all the icons are either moved to another group or the group window is minimized, you can delete the group window itself by first activating that window or icon and then choosing the Delete command from the File menu. When you do, Windows will present a warning message like *Are you sure you want to delete the group 'Business'?* to verify that you want to delete the group window.

Editing group properties

If you inherit someone else's PC with a lot of bizarre group window titles that you don't want to keep, you can retitle the windows. Before you can change the title, you must minimize the group window into an icon. Then, you can use the Properties... command on the File menu to change the title.

To edit a title, click on the group window so it becomes active. Next, minimize it and choose the Properties... command from the File menu. The Program Group Properties dialog box will then appear, displaying the information that belongs to the group. Now you can click on the Description text box and edit the title. You can also change the file name. After you've edited the information in the dialog box, click on OK to save and implement the changes.

ADVANCED FEATURES

So far, you've seen the Program Manager work with application icons. In this section, we'll show you how to use the Run... command to start applications that are not represented by an icon. The Program Manager can also start an application with a specified document already open. It can even turn a document into an icon and launch it like an application icon.

Using the Run... command

You can launch any application from the Program Manager, regardless of whether it has an icon. The Run... command on the File menu allows you to start an application by giving the Program Manager the details it needs. For example, if you want to use a program you don't work with very often, which you didn't bother adding to a group window, you can start it with the Run... command. To do this, select the Run... command to bring up the Run dialog box shown in Figure 5-18.

Figure 5-18

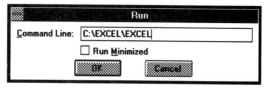

The Run dialog box lets you run applications that aren't represented by icons.

When you use the Run... command, you'll need to know where the application is stored on the hard disk (in other words, you'll need to know the application's path) and the command that starts the application. For example, if you've installed Microsoft Excel in the directory C:\EXCEL, and the command that starts Excel is simply EXCEL, you would type *C:\EXCEL\EXCEL* into the Command Line text box in the Run dialog box, as we've done in Figure 5-18, then click on OK. Note that you can type either the program file name in the Command Line text box or just the start-up command. Immediately, the Program Manager will start Excel. When you exit Excel, you'll return to the Program Manager.

If you want an application to have a temporary icon for a Windows session, you can use the Run Minimized check box in the Run dialog box. Windows will minimize the application into an icon as soon as it appears on the desktop. This is a good way to add an icon temporarily to the desktop instead of making it a permanent application icon in a group window. To open the application, double-click on the icon. If you exit the application, its icon will not appear on the desktop again. If you want to keep using the application during your Windows session, it's a good idea to minimize the application window before you exit so you won't lose the icon. If you exit the application and need to re-create the icon, you can reissue the Run... command and select Run Minimized.

Starting an application as a minimized icon

If you use a document frequently, such as a Write memo template or an Excel spreadsheet of your combined monthly sales, you can customize Windows to open a document as soon as you start the application. All you need to do is add a space and the document name after the start-up command that's already in the Command Line text box in the Run dialog box. That way, every time you start the application, Windows will open that document. If this doesn't work for you, your application may not have the capability to open a document on startup.

Starting an application with a document open

One of the Program Manager's most powerful features is its ability to transform a document into an icon so you can activate it from a group window. That way, you can double-click on the icon to start your application and immediately open a document. You can create a separate icon for each document. This will enable you to access that specific document without the hassle of opening the application.

Setting up a document as an icon

To create a document icon, you'll need to modify the properties of an application icon by adding the document name to the end of the entry in the Command Line text box in the Program Item Properties dialog box and changing the title in the Description text box. If you're starting a new icon instead of modifying an old one, you'll need to add the start-up command to the Command Line text box too. Application icons have default titles, but you can change the default and enter a unique title for the document icon. After you click OK, the Program Manager will add the modified icon to the desktop.

For example, if you want to add a Write report document to your Business group and use it as a template for other reports, you need to follow these steps:

- Activate the Business group window in which you want to add the document icon.

- Choose the New... command on the File menu, select Program Item in the New Program Object dialog box, then click OK.

- Enter the title of the report, such as *Monthly Report,* in the Description text box of the Program Item Properties dialog box, as shown in Figure 5-19.

- Click on the Command Line text box to make it active and then click on the Browse... button to display a list of commands.

- Double-click on a command, like WRITE.EXE in Figure 5-19, from the Files list to choose it and return to the Program Item Properties dialog box. Alternatively, you can use the Directories list box to look in other areas of the hard drive for the file you want.

- Click on the right half of the Command Line text box, and type the file name for the Write file you want to open automatically with this icon.

- Finally, click on OK to add the icon to the active group window. The icon will look like the Write application icon but will use *Monthly Report* for a title instead of *Write,* as shown in Figure 5-20.

Figure 5-19

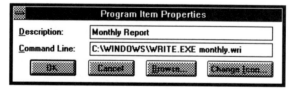

The Program Item Properties dialog box lets you enter a customized title, like Monthly Report, for an icon.

Figure 5-20

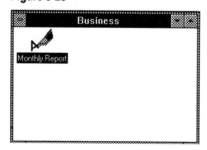

The Write graphic and a custom title form the Monthly Report icon.

When you exit the Program Manager, you exit from Windows and end your Windows session. When you're ready to leave Windows, choose the Exit Windows... command from the File menu. Windows will then display the Exit Windows dialog box shown in Figure 5-21. When you click on OK, Windows will return you to the DOS prompt.

Figure 5-21

The Exit Windows dialog box returns you to DOS.

You can save the position of the Program Manager and the group windows on the desktop by choosing the Save Changes check box in the Exit Windows dialog box. Then, the next time you start Windows, the Program Manager will appear as you left it, with your group windows open and ready for you to use.

In this chapter

File Manager 6

*F*or many personal computer users, the most fundamental piece of software they have ever used, DOS, has also been the most perplexing. In order to accomplish "basic" file management tasks under DOS, you must memorize cryptic commands with obscure parameters. Just moving a file takes two steps, and moving a directory requires even more. (In order to move a directory with DOS, you must actually copy all its files to a new directory, delete the original files, and finally delete the original directory.) To run an application under DOS, you need to know the directory in which it is located, and there's no easy way to browse through directories and their subdirectories. Now you can use Windows' File Manager to overcome the stodginess of DOS.

The File Manager performs all the file management tasks and uses Windows' graphical user interface to make it all seem easy. For example, in a single step, the File Manager lets you move a directory, with all its files and subdirectories, to a new directory. You can even use the File Manager to rename your hard drive or a floppy disk. Also, the File Manager can display more than one directory at a time, making it easy to see how directories branch under one another.

The File Manager, like the Program Manager, is a shell that creates a friendly interface that you can use to access DOS capabilities. You can use the File Manager to modify your files and their organization on your hard drive and to launch applications. For those of you familiar with earlier versions of Windows, the File Manager replaces the MS-DOS Executive that previously served as Windows' primary file management tool. The File Manager extends the graphical aspects of the old MS-DOS Executive and includes many new capabilities.

An important element of the File Manager is the Directory Tree, a visual representation of a directory system that you use to manipulate directories and files

FILE MANAGER

on a floppy, hard, or network drive. Applying the tree analogy, the root directory of a drive is like the trunk of a tree in that it provides a base from which subdirectories branch. Subdirectories are like limbs because they branch from the root directory and into other subdirectories. Files are like leaves on the tree since they are attached to the directories.

In this chapter, we'll show you how to start the File Manager, set up its work area, manage directories, and manipulate files. Then, we'll discuss advanced File Manager operations, including changing file attributes, launching documents and applications, and taking care of media maintenance (such as formatting a disk).

Launching the File Manager

You launch the File Manager from the Main group window in the Program Manager. To start the File Manager with a mouse, open the Main group window and double-click on the File Manager icon. To start File Manager with a keyboard, press [Alt]W to access the Window menu and then type the number for the Main window. Next, use the arrow keys to highlight the File Manager icon and press [Enter] to activate it.

You can customize Windows to make the File Manager replace the Program Manager as the first window you see when you load Windows. However, doing so requires manually editing your WIN.INI file, which is explained briefly in Appendix 1. If you make File Manager the initial window, the Program Manager will automatically be available as a minimized icon on the desktop.

When you are ready to exit File Manager, choose the Exit command from the File menu.

What you'll see

After you activate the File Manager icon, you will see the File Manager application window, shown in Figure 6-1. Initially, the File Manager displays in the workspace the Directory Tree document window, which lists the current drive's directories.

At the top of the Directory Tree, the File Manager displays disk drive icons representing the available disk drives or hard disk volumes. (You can also have icons for a RAM drive or a CD-ROM drive.) Note that floppy drive icons look like floppy drive faceplates with doors, and hard drive icons look like hard drive faceplates. To make the Directory Tree display the directory system for a particular drive, you simply click on that drive's icon. In order to access the disk drive icons with your keyboard, press the [Tab] key to place a selection frame around the currently highlighted disk drive icon, then use the arrow keys to position the frame around the drive you want to view. Next, press [Enter] to select the icon.

Directly below the disk drive icons, a status bar lists the current disk's name (if it has one) and the current path. The status bar at the bottom of the File Manager application window displays the letter of the current drive and the amount of storage space available on that drive.

Figure 6-1

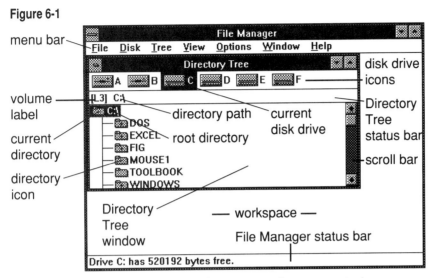

The File Manager application window can use document windows.

As we've already mentioned, the Directory Tree displays all the directories you can work with in the File Manager. The Directory Tree work area is an interactive display area that presents the directories as icons. Each miniature file folder icon in the Directory Tree window represents an individual directory or subdirectory. The name of each leveled directory appears adjacent to the icon's graphic instead of below the graphic as in application icons.

The Directory Tree arranges all the file folder icons at the same level in alphabetical order for easy access. If you double-click on a directory icon, the File Manager will open a new document window to display the files in that directory.

Using the Directory Tree

You'll notice small plus (+) and minus (-) signs on some of the directory icons in the Directory Tree. A plus sign indicates that there are more directory levels under the directory represented by the icon. You can click on any icon with the plus sign to make the Directory Tree display the directories at the level immediately below that directory. At the next level, you might see more directory icons, including some with plus signs. You can keep clicking on the icons to expand further into the different branches. Note that you need to click exactly on the icon and not in the general area of the selection frame in order to expand the directory. To expand a directory with the keyboard, use the arrow keys to move to the directory icon, then type * (asterisk).

The File Manager also provides a shortcut you can use to expand all the directories in the Directory Tree in a single step. To expand every directory marked with a plus sign on the Directory Tree, including those that are more than

Displaying directories

one level below the currently displayed directories, issue the Expand All command on the Tree menu. You can also press [Ctrl]* (asterisk) to universally expand the Directory Tree.

Where do the minus signs enter the picture? After you expand a directory, the directory icon's plus sign turns into a minus sign. If you click on a directory icon marked with a minus sign, all the branches extending from that icon will collapse, and the minus sign will change back to a plus sign. To collapse an expanded directory with the keyboard, use the arrow keys to highlight the directory, then press - (hyphen).

As we just pointed out, the File Manager offers a shortcut for completely expanding the Directory Tree. While the File Manager does not include a command to collapse the directory branches you have expanded, you can perform this task in just two steps. First collapse the branch at the root directory (the first directory icon at the top of the Directory Tree, such as C:\) by clicking on the directory icon, then re-expand that branch by clicking on the icon again. After you do this, only the subdirectories immediately below the root directory will appear on the Directory Tree, and the icons representing subdirectories with subordinate directories will include plus signs. You can adapt this technique to "prune" all the branches stemming from a particular directory, showing only the branches immediately below the directory. All you have to do is collapse the branch at the directory, then expand it again to show the immediately subordinate directories.

Viewing directory windows

The Directory Tree displays all the directories and subdirectories on a drive, but you cannot see any of the files on a drive until you open a directory. You can open a directory by double-clicking on the directory's icon or name or by highlighting the directory name and pressing [Enter]. As an alternate keyboard technique, you can also highlight the directory's name and issue the Open command on the File menu.

When you open a directory, the File Manager will display a directory window listing all the files and subdirectories in that directory. For example, Figure 6-2 shows the directory window for the C:\WINDOWS directory. Notice that the title bar shows the path to the displayed directory along with the file name pattern *.*. This title bar displays the file name pattern along with the directory path because you can describe a file name pattern to limit the types of files that appear in a directory menu. Later in this chapter we'll show you how to use the Include... command to accomplish this.

When you open a directory window, the File Manager's status bar changes to display the number of files currently selected, the number of bytes in those files, and the total number of files that appear in the window. This information can be very valuable as you are working with files. For example, you can use the status bar to determine if the selected files will fit into the available space on a disk.

Figure 6-2

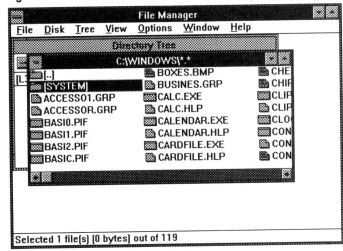

*A directory
window lists
the directory's
path and types
of files.*

If a directory window contains too many files to fit in the window, the File Manager will add a horizontal scroll bar to the window so that you will be able to view all the files. You can resize a directory window to display more of the directory's files. However, some directories will have so many files that you'll never be able to see all of them at once; even if you maximize the window, you'll still have to use the scroll bar to view the remaining files.

Like the Program Manager, the File Manager provides a shortcut for maximizing document windows. If you double-click on the title bar of a Directory Tree window or a directory window, that document window will expand to fill the File Manager window.

Although the Directory Tree can display the directory structure of only one drive at a time, the File Manager will allow you to have directory windows from several drives open at the same time. For example, after you launch the File Manager, you can open a directory window for the C:\WINDOWS directory in drive C, then select the A drive icon to display the Directory Tree for the floppy disk in drive A. When you do this, the C:\WINDOWS directory window will remain open even though the Directory Tree window will now display the structure of the directory system for drive A. As we'll show you later in this chapter, being able to open directory windows from multiple drives is a valuable feature when you are moving and copying files and directories between drives.

If you minimize a directory window, or the Directory Tree, the window will become an icon at the bottom of the File Manager application window. You can move the icon anywhere on the File Manager workspace and use the icon in several of the File Manager operations we will explain in this chapter.

Opening another directory from a directory window

The same techniques you use to open directories on the Directory Tree will also let you open a directory listed in a directory window. To see the contents of a directory that appears in a directory window, double-click on the directory's icon or name. You can also use the keyboard to highlight the directory, then press [Enter] or issue the Open command on the File menu.

Reusing the same directory window

As you open additional directories, the File Manager will open a new directory window to hold the contents of each new directory. Often you will want to keep all the directory windows open so you can copy and move material among the windows. However, if you are merely scanning through directories looking for a file, the multiplying directory windows can be quite a bother. To prevent a crowd of directory windows from taking over your computer screen, you can make the File Manager reuse the active directory window to display directories as you open them. To activate this feature, choose the Replace on Open command on the View menu. After you choose this command, a check mark will appear next to it on the View menu to indicate that the feature is active. From that point on, whenever you open another directory, its contents will replace the current contents of the active directory window. You can reset the File Manager to open a new window for each directory by selecting the Replace on Open command again. Later in this chapter, we'll show you how to use this feature to simplify the process of copying and moving files.

Navigating around the File Manager

If you open several directory windows under the File Manager, you'll probably want to move among them. Fortunately, moving between document windows in the File Manager is as easy as clicking on the window to which you want to move. To use the keyboard to move to a window, press [Alt]W to display the Window menu, then type the number corresponding to the directory window to which you want to move. (Number 1 will always correspond to the Directory Tree window.)

You also can use the keyboard to move through directory windows in the order in which you placed them on the work area. To move to the next window in this order, simply press [Alt]- (hyphen) to access the active document window's Control menu and select the Next command from it.

You can use standard navigational techniques to move through a document window. For example, you can click on an element to highlight it or use the arrow keys to move the highlight bar from one icon to another.

Table 6-1 lists the accelerator key shortcuts you can use to navigate in the File Manager. You can read Chapter 2 to learn about standard accelerator key techniques that apply to all applications, including the File Manager.

Table 6-1

Keyboard	Function
In the Directory Tree	
[Home]	Move to the root directory
[End]	Move to the last listed directory
→	Move to the first subdirectory of selected directory
←	Move to the directory in the previous directory level
[Page Up]	Move up one directory window
[Page Down]	Move down one directory window
[Ctrl]↑	Move to the previous directory in the same level
[Ctrl]↓	Move to the next directory in the same level
n	Move to the directory whose name starts with n
[Ctrl]n	Select and activate the disk drive called n
- (hyphen)	Collapse highlighted directory
+ (plus)	Expand highlighted directory
* (asterisk)	Expand entire branch of highlighted directory
[Ctrl]* (asterisk)	Expand all directory branches
In directory windows	
↑	Move to file or directory above current one
↓	Move to file or directory below current one
[End]	Move to the last file or directory in the list
[Home]	Move to first file or directory in the list
[Page Up]	Move to first file or directory in previous window
[Page Down]	Move to last file or directory in next window
n	Move to the file or directory whose name starts with n
[Ctrl]/ (slash)	Select all files in list
[Ctrl]\ (backslash)	Deselect all files in list
In the File Manager	
[Enter]	Open the directory or file
[F7]	Issue the Move... command
[F8]	Issue the Copy... command
[Delete]	Issue the Delete... command
[Shift][F5]	Cascade all document windows
[Shift][F4]	Tile all document windows
[F5]	Issue the Refresh command
[Ctrl][Tab] or [Ctrl][F6]	Move between document windows

You can use these shortcuts to navigate through the File Manager.

Rearranging the workspace

You can rearrange the File Manager workspace to make it easier to access the Directory Tree and the directory windows. The Window menu's Cascade and Tile commands rearrange all these document windows. By default, the File Manager cascades the Directory Tree and directory windows as you open new directories. Stacking the windows in a cascade pattern enables you to see the titles of all the windows below the active window in the workspace. However, as you jump from window to window, the active window will probably cover the title bars of other windows. If you choose the Cascade command, the File Manager will rearrange the windows so you can see all their title bars, as shown in Figure 6-3.

Figure 6-3

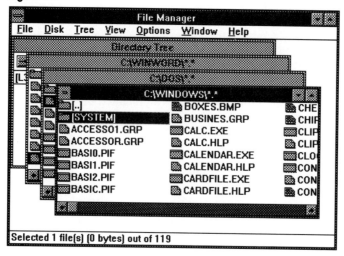

By default, the File Manager tiles the Directory Tree and directory windows.

If you choose the Tile command, the File Manager will resize the document windows and place them next to each other, as shown in Figure 6-4. As you use the File Manager, you'll find that tiled windows are generally easier to work with when you need to use more than one directory window at a time. The only problem with tiling the directory windows is the next directory window opens by default as a cascaded window and covers the tiled windows already in the work area. To bring the new window in line, simply choose the Tile command again. The File Manager will tile the window along with the others.

While you are working with the directory windows, the displayed data will often change as a result of your or others' activities. If you are working on a network, the data on network drives sometimes may not update automatically. You can make the File Manager update the active directory window by issuing the Refresh command on the Window menu or by pressing [F5].

Figure 6-4

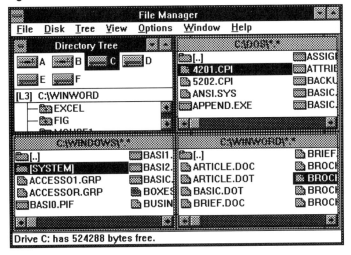

You can tile all the File Manager's document windows with the Window menu's Tile command.

If you want to close all the directory windows on your workspace at once, instead of double-clicking on each window's Control menu, you can issue the Close All Directories command on the Window menu. You can close all the windows in the File Manager's workspace except the Directory Tree window.

If you want to temporarily make extra room on the workspace, you can minimize any directory window or the Directory Tree window into an icon. The File Manager places the icons at the bottom of the workspace. Figure 6-5 shows the File Manager with the Directory Tree and three directory windows minimized.

Figure 6-5

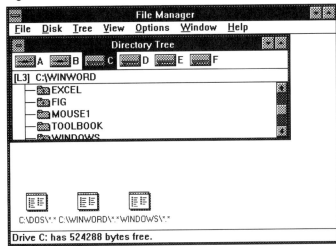

The File Manager places minimized directory windows at the bottom of the workspace.

**Removing
the status bar**

You can remove the status bar at the bottom of the File Manager application window by issuing the Status Bar command on the Options menu. The File Manager will place a check mark next to the command to show that it is on. Issuing it again will toggle the command off and redisplay the status bar. Removing the status bar gives you more room to display files and directories in the work area, but the information that appears on the status bar is often very useful.

**Changing text
to lowercase**

Some people prefer to see text on a computer screen displayed in uppercase, while others prefer lowercase. By default, the File Manager capitalizes all letters in directory and file names. If you want to change all the text that appears in the Directory Tree and the directory windows from uppercase to lowercase, you can issue the Lower Case command on the Options menu. Reselecting this command toggles the text back to uppercase.

**DIRECTORY
FUNDAMENTALS**

Now that you are familiar with the Directory Tree and the rest of the things you are likely to see in the File Manager application window, we'll turn our attention to the tasks the File Manager is designed to handle. Most of these tasks involve file management, and one of the most important concepts of file management is that of directories.

Directories let you create a structure for organizing your files. A well-planned directory structure can make finding files quick and easy, regardless of the size of the drive on which they are located. It's a good idea to have a directory for each application and separate directories for your data files. The data files should also be organized according to the project or subject to which they pertain instead of according to the application you use to work with them. You'll be able to remember the subject of the project more easily than the application in which you wrote the report or generated the data.

If the files on your hard drive are not currently organized in a directory system, don't worry. The File Manager contains all the tools you need to reorganize them. In the rest of this chapter, we'll show you how to use the File Manager to work with directories and files.

Creating directories

You can use the Create Directory... command on the File menu to add directories to hard drives or floppy disks. You can add a directory in the Directory Tree window or in a directory window. To add a subdirectory to the Directory Tree, click on the directory to which you want to add it. Next, issue the Create Directory... command to summon a Create Directory dialog box like the one shown in Figure 6-6. This dialog box displays the name of the directory under which the File Manager will place your new one. You enter a name for the new subdirectory in the Name text box. After you select the OK button, the File Manager will add it. Then, the File Manager will immediately add a plus sign to the current directory (if it didn't have one already), indicating that now there is a subdirectory one level below it.

Figure 6-6

The Create Directory dialog box allows you to enter eight characters and a three-character extension for a directory name.

To add a directory from a directory window, you also issue the Create Directory... command. It doesn't matter which file or directory is highlighted when you issue the command. The File Manager uses the current path—that is, the directory whose name appears in the current directory window's title bar—as the location for the new subdirectory.

As you work with files and directories in the Directory Tree and directory windows, you need to follow certain DOS rules for naming new files and directories. Many of the same rules apply to directory and file names, but there are a few differences.

Naming directories and files

DOS requires that file and directory names include no more than eight characters, and does not allow you to use a . (period), , (comma), / (slash), \ (backslash), | (vertical bar), [ ] (brackets), ; (semicolon), : (colon), or " (quotation marks) as one of the up to eight characters in a name. In addition to these character restrictions, Windows reserves some names and characters to represent devices and parameters in commands. You can't use CON, AUX, COM1, COM2, COM3, COM4, LPT1, LPT2, LPT3, PRN, or NUL as a directory or file name.

In addition to its one-to-eight-character base, a file name can also include an extension of up to three letters (which will be separated by a period from the base name). Many applications use file name extensions to recognize files they create. For example, many spreadsheet packages assign extensions that begin with the letters *WK* to all worksheet files. Other applications allow you the flexibility of using any extension you want, enabling you to identify groups of files. For example, if you use Word for Windows to write memos for five managers, you can use their initials as extensions for the memos' file names. (This system might produce the file name 5-1-90.RJO for a memo you wrote for Robert J. Ober on May 1, 1990.) This way, you can easily identify the memos for a particular manager. If you don't want to use a file extension to group memos by manager, you can keep all the memos for a manager in a directory named with that manager's last name or initials.

You can use the same basic techniques to copy, move, rename, and search for files and directories with the File Manager. You can expand an operation that you perform on one file, such as copying it, to involve several files by selecting

WORKING WITH DIRECTORIES AND FILES

them before you begin the operation. You can also increase the scope of an operation by performing the action on a directory that contains several files. Another method of identifying files for an operation is by selectively displaying files in a directory window.

In order to perform any of these varied operations, you must first display and/ or select the files with which you want to work. We'll begin our discussion of working with directories and files by showing you how to display and select them.

Controlling the display of directories and files

By default, in a directory window, the File Manager lists directories first and then files, sorting the names in each group in alphabetical order. The File Manager's View menu provides commands that allow you to sort the files listed in a directory window, show different types of information about a file, and determine which types of files are included in the listing. Changing the display is useful when you are looking for a particular file or when you want to issue a command that affects a certain group of files.

Figure 6-7 shows a directory window that displays icons for several subdirectories and files. The File Manager uses icons to represent three types of files: data files, application-specific data files, and launchable files. The icon that looks like a blank piece of paper with one corner turned down represents a data file. If the File Manager knows which application created a file (by its extension), then the file will have an icon that looks like a ruled page with one corner turned down. Launchable files include program files (identified by the extension .COM or .EXE), batch files (.BAT), and Windows' own program information files (.PIF). Launchable files have icons that look like a rectangle with a blue stripe across its top, which gives the icon the appearance of a window with a title bar.

Figure 6-7

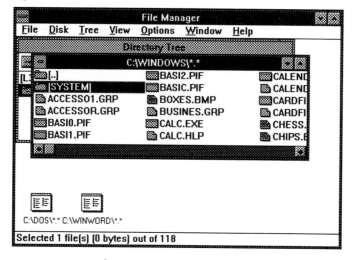

The File Manager uses icons to identify the three types of files.

The File Manager keeps track of more information about a file than you usually see listed in a directory window. By default, the File Manager displays only the file name, but you can also display a file's size, modification date (date you saved the file), modification time (time you saved the file), and attributes (hidden, read-only, archive, or system). We'll talk more about file attributes later in this chapter. If you want to display all the available file information, issue the File Details command on the View menu. After you issue this command, the File Manager will convert the directory window's work area to list only one file per line with additional information after each file name, as shown in Figure 6-8. After you issue the File Details command, the check mark next to the Name command on the View menu will move to the File Details command.

Expanding file information

Figure 6-8

File Manager				
File Disk Tree View Options Window Help				
C:\WINDOWS*.*				
[..]		01/24/90	03:30:50 AM	——
[SYSTEM]		01/24/90	03:30:54 AM	——
ACCESSO1.GRP	7159	01/23/90	05:42:48 AM	——A
ACCESSOR.GRP	7159	03/07/90	12:56:44 AM	——A
BASI0.PIF	545	01/24/90	09:08:42 PM	——A
BASI1.PIF	545	02/10/90	03:50:34 AM	——A
BASI2.PIF	545	02/14/90	09:00:02 PM	——A
BASIC.PIF	545	01/11/90	02:10:44 AM	——A
BOXES.BMP	630	11/07/89	12:28:24 PM	——A
BUSINES.GRP	5280	01/18/90	11:42:54 PM	——A
CALC.EXE	38992	12/05/89	08:50:26 PM	——A
CALC.HLP	23155	12/05/89	09:08:38 PM	——A
CALENDAR.EXE	64240	12/05/89	08:50:30 PM	——A
CALENDAR.HLP	43115	12/05/89	09:08:40 PM	——A

Directory Tree

Selected 1 file(s) (0 bytes) out of 118

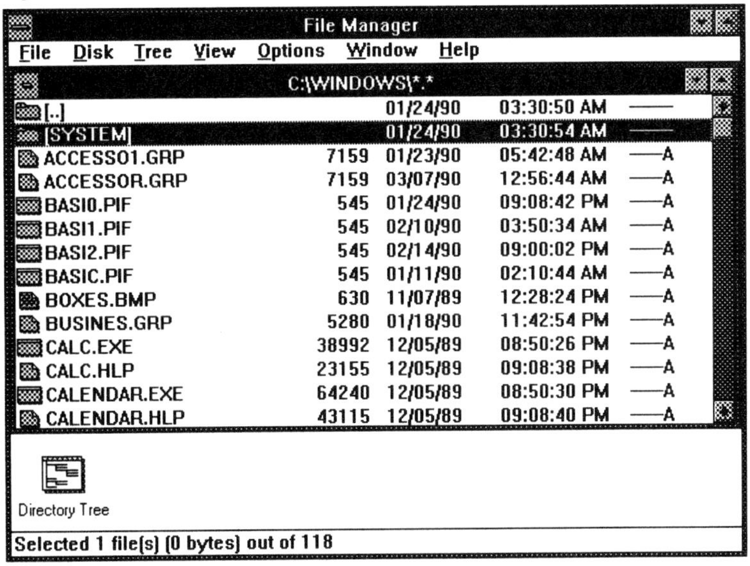

This directory window displays all the information for files.

If you don't want to see all the information about your files, you can use the Other... command on the View menu to choose certain parts of the information. When you issue the Other... command, the View Other dialog box, shown in Figure 6-9, will appear. You can use the standard mouse or keyboard techniques to choose any combination of settings. After you select your desired settings and choose OK, the File Manager will immediately restructure the directory window to display the selected information. The File Manager will still list the files one line at a time, even if you select only one of the information options. After you use the Other... command, it will remain check marked on the View menu until you issue the Name or File Details command to change the file display again.

Figure 6-9

You can choose from these options to display all or some of the extra file information.

The Set System Default check box in the View Other dialog box allows you to apply your choices to any new directory windows you open. We'll discuss the Set System Default check box in detail later in this chapter.

Sorting files

Although the File Manager by default lists file names in alphabetical order, you can also sort files by their type (extension), size, or modification date (date you saved the file). You can group the files according to their extensions by issuing the By Type command on the View menu. The File Manager will immediately group the files alphabetically by extension and then by name within the extension group.

You need to issue the Sort by... command on the View menu in order to specify a display sorted by file size or modification date. After you issue the Sort by... command, the File Manager will present the Sort By dialog box, shown in Figure 6-10. This dialog box has four radio buttons that you can use to choose a sorting criterion. The Name and Type buttons produce the same effect as the By Name and By Type commands. The File Manager provides these duplicate commands on the View menu because they are the two sort orders you are most likely to use.

Figure 6-10

The Sort By dialog box sets the sorting criterion for the files in a directory window.

If you want to see the files in a directory with the largest files at the top of the list, select the Size radio button and choose OK. To view the files in chronological order, with the most recently modified files first, select the Last Modification Date radio button and select OK. Even if you sort by size or date, you won't be able to see file sizes or modification dates in a directory window unless you use the File Details or Other... command to display this information.

Like the View Other dialog box, the Sort By dialog box includes a Set System Default check box that you can use to determine the sort order of new directory windows. We'll discuss this setting in detail later.

If you have so many files in a directory that it's hard to find the one you want, you can tell the File Manager to filter out the files you don't need to see. To do this, issue the Include... command on the View menu. In the Include dialog box, shown in Figure 6-11, you can use a combination of wildcards and file type options to select the files you want the File Manager to list.

Excluding files

Figure 6-11

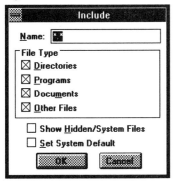

You can tell the File Manager which files to list with a combination of wildcards for a file name and a selection of file type categories.

You can use wildcards in the Name text box to specify which file names to include in the list. The File Manager uses ? (a question mark) to represent individual characters and * (an asterisk) to represent any series of characters. For example, if you want to see only the files with a .WKS extension, you would type *.WKS in the Name text box. If you want to see files with the extension .WKS, .WK1, and .WK2, you could use the wildcard pattern *.WK?.

To look for a group of files that don't have a common extension or similar file name, but share other traits, you can use the options in the File Type group box to limit the scope of the listed files. You can use the other options in the File Type group box to display directories, programs, documents, or files that don't fit into any of these groups. For example, to look for a Word for Windows document file that was misplaced in another directory, select only the Documents check box to view all the files with document icons. If you select more than one File Type check box, Windows will display all the types of files you select.

You can force the File Manager to display hidden or system files (files that don't normally appear in a directory window) by selecting the Show Hidden/ System Files check box. Applications hide files to prevent misuse or deletion.

The Include dialog box also contains a Set System Default check box you can use to change the display format of new directory windows. We'll talk about changing the default display next.

Changing the default view

Usually, the display changes you make by altering settings in the View Other, Sort By, and Include dialog boxes affect only the active directory window. However, you can make the options you choose in these dialog boxes become the new defaults for all new directory windows. As we've mentioned, each of these dialog boxes contains a Set System Default check box. If you select this check box, the settings you choose will control the display of every directory window you open from that point on. For example, if you open the Include dialog box, select the Programs check box, and choose the Set System Default check box before you choose OK, the current directory window and all subsequently opened directory windows will display only program files.

You can also change the display options for all new windows by making the Directory Tree active before you issue a command on the View menu. Although the command you issue will not affect the Directory Tree window, it will control the appearance of any directory windows you open. Using this technique lets you change the default view of new directory windows without changing the display of an existing window.

Neither technique for changing the default display will affect the appearance of directory windows (other than the active window) that are already open on the workspace. To change the appearance of an existing window, you need to make it the active window, then issue the appropriate commands on the View menu to change the active window in the manner you want.

Changes that you make to the default appearance of directory windows remain in effect until you specify new defaults or end the File Manager session. When you exit the File Manager, the Exit File Manager dialog box shown in Figure 6-12 will appear. If you leave the Save Settings check box in this dialog box selected and choose OK, the File Manager will save the changes you made to the default view and activate those defaults the next time you launch the File Manager. If you toggle off the Save Settings check box, the File Manager will restore the original defaults when you reload the File Manager.

Selecting directories and files

Before you can issue a command, you need to select the file or directory upon which you want the command to act. You can select directories one at a time from either the Directory Tree or a directory window. Because files appear only in directory windows, you can select a file only in a directory window. In directory windows, it is possible to select more than one file or directory at the same time.

Figure 6-12

If you leave the Save Settings option selected in the Exit File Manager dialog box, the File Manager will save your directory display defaults.

To select a file or directory with the mouse, you simply click on it. With the keyboard, you can use the direction keys ([Home], [End], [Page Up], [Page Down], ↑, ↓, ←, →) to highlight a file or directory.

In a directory window, you can select a series of neighboring files and directories, or you can select them out of sequence. To select consecutive items, click on the first in the series, move the pointer to the last one, press [Shift], then click. All the files between the two on which you clicked will become highlighted. To make the same kind of selection with the keyboard, use the arrow keys to highlight the first item, then hold down the [Shift] key while you move to the last item you want to select.

To select items that aren't adjacent, click on the first item and then press [Ctrl] and click on each additional item. To select non-neighboring items with the keyboard, first press [Shift][F8] to tell the File Manager you're going to select items out of sequence. When you do this, a blinking selection frame will appear around the selected item. Now use the direction keys to move the selection frame around the directory window, and press [Spacebar] to select files and directories. You can continue to use the [Spacebar] to select items until you press [Shift][F8] again to let the File Manager know that you are finished selecting.

If you want to select several blocks of neighboring files within a window, use the [Shift] click technique to select your first block of items. Then, select the first item in the next group by using the [Ctrl] click technique. Next, [Ctrl][Shift] click on the last item in that group to select it and all the files and directories between it and the first item in the second group. You can then repeat the [Ctrl] click and [Ctrl][Shift] click techniques to select additional groups of neighboring items.

If you are a keyboard user, you can select the first group in the normal manner (by holding down [Shift] while you move around with the arrow keys). To select the next group, press [Shift][F8], then move the blinking selection frame to the first item in the next group and press [Spacebar] to select it. Next, press [Shift] while using the direction keys to highlight the remaining items in the second group. After you have finished selecting the second group, use the arrow keys by themselves to move to the first item in the third group, press [Spacebar] to select it, and use the [Shift] and arrow keys to select the rest of the items in the third group. When you're completely finished highlighting, press [Shift][F8] again to turn off the blinking selection frame.

If you decide to select all the files in a directory window, simply issue the Select All command on the File menu (or press [Ctrl] /). You can also tell the File Manager to deselect any of the selected items in the directory window by issuing the Deselect All command on the File menu (or by pressing [Ctrl] \). However, if you want to deselect only one item from a group of selected files and directories, you can [Ctrl] click on it or press an arrow key. Keyboard users need to press [Shift][F8], move the blinking selection frame to an item, then press [Spacebar] to deselect it. After you've finished deselecting with the keyboard, remember to press [Shift][F8] again to return to normal operations.

You can reduce the effort and frustration of selecting files scattered throughout the directory window simply by displaying only the files you want to select. For example, if you want to perform an operation on all the Paintbrush (.PCX) files in the current directory, you can use the Include... command to show only .PCX files in the directory window, then use the Select All command to highlight them before you issue the command that produces the desired operation.

Deleting directories and files

Now that we've talked about displaying directories and files and selecting them for File Manager operations, we are ready to begin discussing the operations available in the File Manager. We'll start by showing you how to delete directories and files.

If you don't need to use a directory or file anymore, you can delete it with the Delete... command on the File menu or the [Delete] key on your keyboard. To delete a file or group of files in a directory window, first select the file or files, then issue the Delete... command on the File menu or press [Delete]. After you do this, a Delete dialog box, like the one shown in Figure 6-13, will appear. The Delete text box in this dialog box displays the names of the files you selected for deletion. Each name will include a period, even if it lacks an extension, and a space will separate the listed file names. If you want, you can remove file names from the Delete text box at this point to prevent their deletion by highlighting them and pressing [Delete] or [Backspace] or by using standard editing techniques. To delete the listed files, select the Delete button. Or, select Cancel to leave the Delete dialog box without deleting any files.

Figure 6-13

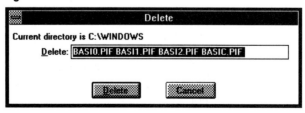

The Delete dialog box displays the current directory and the list of files you want to delete.

If you choose the Delete button, the File Manager will present a series of dialog boxes like the one shown in Figure 6-14, letting you verify the deletion of each individual file. If you select Yes when you see one of these dialog boxes, the File Manager will delete the file named in the dialog box and continue through the list of selected files, deleting each in turn. If you choose No, the File Manager will not delete the listed file but will continue with the deletion process. If you select the Cancel button at any time, the File Manager will not delete the current file and will abort the process of deleting the remaining selected files.

Figure 6-14

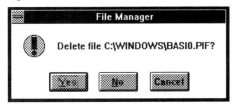

After you approve the deletion once, the File Manager will present this message dialog box for each file you are deleting.

To delete the contents of an entire directory, begin by selecting that directory in either the directory window of its parent directory or the Directory Tree window. By the way, the File Manager will not allow you to delete a root directory since you would make your disk unreadable. When you issue the Delete… command, a Delete dialog box like the one shown in Figure 6-13 will appear, but only the directory's name will appear in the Delete text box. (If you select a directory for deletion in the Directory Tree window, the Delete dialog box will list that directory as the current directory. If you select a subdirectory for deletion in a directory window, the directory whose name appears in the directory window's title bar will be the current directory.

For example, if you select in drive C the C:\DATA subdirectory on the Directory Tree, then press [Delete], the Delete dialog box will show C:\DATA as the current directory and list the entry *C:\DATA* in the Delete text box. If you click on the Delete button, the File Manager will present a series of dialog boxes, like the one shown in Figure 6-14, asking you to verify the deletion of each file. The last File Manager dialog box will verify your intention to delete the subdirectory and the selected directory itself.

The File Manager works its way from the lowest level of files and subdirectories under the selected directory to the selected directory itself. This progression forces you to empty the contents of every directory you are deleting before giving you the chance to delete the directory itself. If you use the No option in a delete message dialog box to prevent the deletion of a file or subdirectory under the selected directory, the File Manager will not allow you to delete the selected directory. If you select Yes to delete the selected directory, the File Manager will show you a message dialog box like the one in Figure 6-15. To avoid this type of impasse, you need to move the files or subdirectories you want to keep out of harm's way before you select the parent directory for deletion. We'll show you how to move files and directories in the next section of this chapter.

Figure 6-15

If you try to delete a directory that is not completely empty, the File Manager will display this message dialog box.

A word of caution: The File Manager provides several opportunities to back out of deleting the files and subdirectories under a selected directory, but doesn't supply an "undo" feature that you can use to reverse the process. Once you delete a directory, it and all its files and subdirectories are gone.

Just as you can use multiple selection techniques to select several files for deletion, you can select several directories for deletion. You can also select files and directories for deletion at the same time. The names of all the files and directories you select will appear in the Delete text box of the Delete dialog box, and the File Manager will prompt you to verify every file and subdirectory explicitly and implicitly included in the deletion.

All of the confirmation prompts can become annoying if you are well aware of the consequences of your deletion. At the end of this chapter, we will show you how to control the number of verification prompts the File Manager displays.

Moving directories and files

At the beginning of this chapter, we mentioned how complicated it is to move directories and files and with DOS commands. The File Manager makes it easy to move directories and files within a drive volume or between drives.

Moving items around on a drive

Moving files around on a drive is especially easy. Before you move a file or directory, you must first decide where (that is, to which directory) you want to move it. Next, you need to make sure that the destination directory is represented somewhere on the File Manager workspace. The destination directory can appear as an icon on the Directory Tree, as an icon in a directory window, as an open directory window, or as an icon representing a minimized directory window. The next step is to select the item or items you want to move.

You can select a single directory on the Directory Tree or make a single or multiple selection of files and/or subdirectories in a directory window. After you select the item(s), click and hold down the mouse button anywhere in the highlighted selection area to grab the selected item or items. When you grab the selection, the mouse pointer will change appearance to indicate that you are moving a selection. If the selection contains a single directory or file, the mouse pointer will change into the icon that represents the selected item (a folder for a directory or the appropriate file icon). If the selection includes multiple files or directories, the mouse pointer will change into an icon that looks like three stacked cards. If you drag the selection icon into an area where the File Manager can't move the selection, the pointer will change to a prevent pointer (a slashed circle). The mouse pointer changes similarly when you select items for copying.

After you grab the selection, drag it to the destination directory and release the mouse button. When placing the selected material, you release it in the directory window of the destination directory or on top of any icon representing the destination. After you release the mouse button, a message dialog box, like the one shown in Figure 6-16, will appear to verify your intention to move the selection. If you select Yes, the File Manager will move your selection. If you select No, the File Manager will not move the files.

Figure 6-16

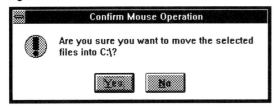

The File Manager will display this message dialog box before moving a file or directory.

If you place selected items in the directory window of the destination directory, be careful not to release the selection on top of a directory icon inside the window. If you place the icon on top of a directory icon, the File Manager will move the selected items to the directory represented by the icon, instead of the directory displayed in the directory window, after asking you to confirm the move. To place the selected items in the directory window, you must position the mouse pointer in an empty portion of the directory window when you release the mouse button.

Keep in mind that when you move a directory to another directory, the File Manager actually places the directory you are moving within the destination directory. It does not merely move the files from your directory into the destination directory. If you want to move all the files in one directory to another directory, you need to open the directory containing the files, select all the files, then move them to the destination directory.

At the same time, you should remember that when you move a directory, you move all its files and subdirectories. If you want to relocate any specific files or subdirectories separately from the directory, you need to select and move them separately.

Moving between drives

Moving files and directories from one drive to another requires one extra step not required when you move a selection from one location to another on the same drive. Again, you need to make sure that the item(s) you want to move are available in the Directory Tree window or an open directory window and that the destination directory is accessible somewhere on the workspace. After you select the material you are going to move, press [Alt] before you drag the selection. When the pointer is over the destination directory window or icon, release the mouse button before you release the [Alt] key. The File Manager will present a message dialog box. Click Yes and the File Manager will complete the move.

If you want to move a selection to the last active directory of a drive, you can do so by dragging the selection to one of the drive icons at the top of the Directory Tree window. For example, let's assume that you had been working in the \MEMO directory on the C drive but had closed that directory window and are now working with files on drive B. If you select a file and press [Alt] while you drag its icon to the C drive icon, Windows will move the file from the current directory on drive B to the \MEMO directory on drive C since that was the last active directory on the C drive. You can also make a directory the last active directory on a drive by simply highlighting that directory before switching to another drive in the Directory Tree window.

Moving with the keyboard

If you want to move a selection on a drive or between drives with the keyboard, you need to use the Move... command on the File menu. After selecting the item(s) you want to move, press [Alt]F to access the File menu, then press *M* or [F7] to issue the Move... command. Next, the File Manager will display a dialog box like the one shown in Figure 6-17. The Move dialog box lists the names of every selected item (directories and files) in the From text box and prompts you for a destination path in the To text box. You should type the name of the directory to which you want to move the selected item(s) in the To text box. For example, to move selected items to the C:\DATA directory, you would type *C:\DATA*. After you enter the destination, press *M* to select the Move button, and the File Manager will complete the move.

Figure 6-17

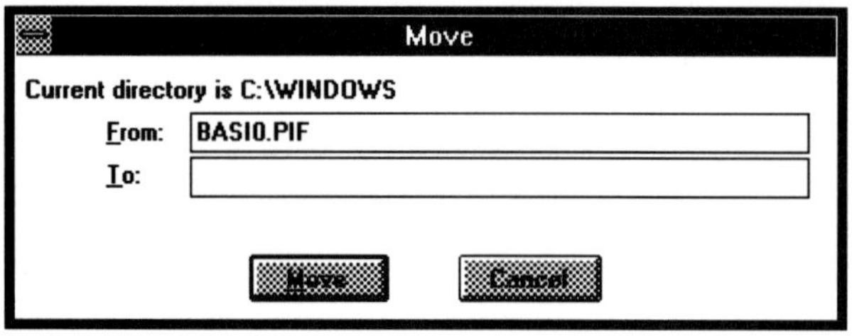

The Move dialog box prompts you for a destination path.

Copying directories and files

While you are more likely to move items within a drive, you are more likely to copy between drives. In this section, we'll show you how to copy items between drives and how to copy items on the same drive.

Copying between drives

To copy files or directories between drives, simply select the items you want to copy in either the Directory Tree window or a directory window, click in the selection area to grab the items, and drag the selection to the icon or directory window of the directory to which you want to copy the items. The File Manager will present the dialog box shown in Figure 6-18, asking for confirmation that you want to proceed with the copy.

Figure 6-18

Before copying your selection, the File Manager will ask you to verify your intention to copy.

As you can see, this process requires the same steps as moving selected items between different locations on the same drive. When you simply click and drag a selection to a new directory, the File Manager automatically moves the selected items if the source and destination directories are on the same drive, but copies the items if the source and destination directories are on different drives. As we mentioned above, this automatic decision by the File Manager makes it easier to use the moving and copying features in the situations in which you are most likely to want them.

Copying on the same drive

If you want to copy files or directories from one location to another on the same drive, press and hold down the [Ctrl] key while you grab and drag the selection to the destination directory. Release the mouse button and then the [Ctrl] key to complete the copy. Before completing the copy, the File Manager will display a message dialog box similar to the one shown in Figure 6-18.

Copying with a keyboard

Keyboard users can use the Copy... command on the File menu to copy directories or files. To copy an item or group of items, first select the items in the Directory Tree or in a directory window. Next, press [Alt]F to access the File menu and press *C* to issue the Copy... command. At this point, a Copy dialog box, like the one in Figure 6-19, will appear. (You can also press [F8] to display the Copy dialog box.) The File Manager inserts the names of all selected directories and files in the From text box. You have to enter the path of the destination directory in the To text box. When you're ready to finalize the copy, press *C* to activate the Copy button.

Figure 6-19

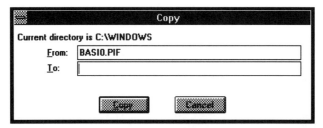

The Copy dialog box inserts the source, while you enter the destination for the copied directory.

Changing the name of a copied file

Whether you use a mouse or the keyboard exclusively, the Copy... command has one characteristic that you will probably take advantage of from time to time. You can use the Copy... command to make a copy of a file and change its name in the copying process. To make a copy with a new name, select the file you want to copy, then issue the Copy... command. When the File Manager presents the Copy dialog box, only the name of the selected file will appear in the From text box. You type the file name you want to assign to the copy in the To text box. In order for the File Manager to place the copy in the current directory, you should not specify a directory path in the To text box.

For example, suppose you want to make a copy of a file named REPORT.DOC and name the copy REPORT.BAK. First, select the REPORT.DOC file and issue the Copy... command. When you see the Copy dialog box, type REPORT.BAK in the To text box, and select the Copy button.

You can type a new file name in the To text box only if you have selected a single file for copying. If you select multiple files or a directory before you issue the Copy... command, the File Manager will accept only an existing directory's name in the To text box. Since every file in a directory requires a unique name, you can't specify one name for multiple files. On the other hand, if you copy the files one at a time, you can change their names and they can stay in the same directory. If you attempt to enter new names for multiple files, the File Manager will display a fatal warning dialog box (a red stop sign) and abort the copy.

Copying an application to a Program Manager icon

One special copying feature the File Manager provides is a quick and easy method of creating DOS application icons you can use in the Program Manager. If you copy a launchable file to the Program Manager, the icon for the file will become a DOS application icon. Normally, the addition of a DOS application icon in a Program Manager document window requires the use of a few dialog boxes and the setting of several options.

To use the File Manager to add an application icon to the Program Manager, first resize the File Manager application window so that part of the Program Manager is visible on the desktop. (See Chapter 2 for more about resizing windows.) Next, select the application file and drag it to one of the Program Manager group windows. As soon as you release the mouse button, Windows will add a DOS icon to the Program Manager, using the file name (without the extension) as the icon's title.

If you reorganize your hard disk and want to change a directory name or the names of files to reflect the new structure, you can use the Rename... command on the File menu. To rename a directory, simply select it in a directory window or the Directory Tree window and choose the Rename... command from the File menu. At this point, the File Manager will display a Rename dialog box, like the one in Figure 6-20, listing the old directory name in the From text box. All you have to do is enter the new name in the To text box and select the Rename button.

Renaming directories and files

Figure 6-20

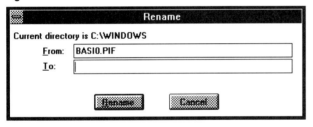

When you issue the Rename... command, the File Manager will display the Rename dialog box.

When you are entering the new directory name, you shouldn't include any of the directory path that precedes the name of the selected directory. For example, to change the name of the directory C:\DATA\DOCS to C:\DATA\DOCUMENT, you would type only the name *DOCUMENT* in the To text box. After you enter the new name and select the Rename button, the File Manager will immediately change the name of the directory you selected wherever it appears on the Directory Tree and in any directory windows.

To rename a file, select it and issue the Rename... command. Again, the File Manager will present a Rename dialog box, this time listing the name of the file you selected in the From text box. It's up to you to enter the new file name in the To text box. As with directories, you shouldn't include the directory path before the file name you enter in the To text box.

A word of warning: Don't rename any of the Windows program files. If you do, Windows may not work properly, if at all. Also, if you rename a file and the new name is the same as an existing file, the File Manager will replace the existing file, but only after you get a chance to confirm it with one of the File Manager's message dialog boxes.

Assigning extensions to several files

You can use the Rename… command to assign file extensions to several files by selecting the files before you issue the Rename… command. When the Rename dialog box appears, it will list the names of all the selected files in the From text box. In the To text box, you should type an * (asterisk) followed by a period and the extension you want to assign to the files. For example, if you want to change a group of batch files (with the extension .BAT) to backup files with the extension .BAK, select all the batch files and issue the Rename… command. In the Rename dialog box, type *.BAK in the To text box and select the Rename button.

Changing the extension of a file can affect much more than just the file's name. Because DOS and Windows recognize launchable files by their extensions, changing a program or batch file's extension alters the very nature of the file. When you change a file's extension from .BAT to .BAK, you change the file from an executable DOS program to a simple text file. As a result, the File Manager will change the file's icon from that of a launchable file icon to that of a data file.

Searching for directories and files

After you've added several directories and files to your hard disk, you may at times have trouble finding the one you need. If you know the name of that elusive directory or file, you can use the Search... command on the File menu to find it. To locate a file or directory, issue the Search... command to summon the Search dialog box shown in Figure 6-21. All you have to do is type the name of the item you want to find into the Search For text box. By default, the File Manager will search through the entire drive. To search only the current directory, toggle off the Search Entire Disk check box. Begin the search by choosing OK.

Figure 6-21

The Search dialog box provides a text box for search text.

The File Manager displays all the matches to your search text as icons in a Search Results document window. Each icon has the full path listed next to it, and you can use the icons in a Search Results window as you would those in a directory window. You can open, delete, and rename any of the items listed in the Search Results window. You can also copy or move the files out of the Search Results window, but you can't copy or move directories into it. You can minimize or maximize the Search Results window just as you would any other directory window. The File Manager lists the Search Results window on the Window menu so keyboard users can access it. When you've finished with the window, double-click on its Control menu to close it.

If you're unsure what you named the directory or file you are trying to locate, you can use wildcards to replace the forgotten areas of the item's name. For instance, if you know the directory started with an *S*, you could enter *S** in the Search For text box. The * (asterisk) is a wildcard for any number (and any type) of characters. You can also use question marks to represent individual characters in your search text. If you want to look for all directories and files with a five-letter name beginning with *N*, you should enter the search text *N????* in the Search For text box.

If you are looking for files with extensions, you need to include the extensions in your search text, using either characters or wildcards in the extension. For example, to locate every batch file on your hard drive, you could enter the search text **.BAT*. If you want to find every file with the name WINDOWS, regardless of the files' extensions, you should use the search text *WINDOWS.**.

Controlling messages sent by the File Manager

The File Manager can nag you to death if you let it. The File Manager's usual routine is to ask for verification for a command by presenting a dialog box in which you select or verify options that affect the command. Windows adds another layer of verification by having the File Manager present message dialog boxes. Windows considers this necessary since you're manipulating the underlying foundation of your computer, its directories, and files. You must not only say what you want the File Manager to do, but must mean what you say. Thus, if you didn't mean to issue an instruction, Windows will give you yet another chance to avoid a possibly dangerous error. If you think you can manage by yourself not to commit a serious offense, you can turn off this extra warning message.

To change the confirmation message system, issue the Confirmation... command on the Options menu to display a Confirmation dialog box like the one in Figure 6-22. By default, all the check boxes are selected. Simply click on a check box to toggle it off. If you're using a keyboard, you'll use the arrow keys to move the selection frame and then press [Spacebar] to toggle a check box. Table 6-2 on the next page lists the check boxes and the functions they confirm.

Figure 6-22

The Confirmation dialog box allows you to choose which functions will have an added layer of message dialog boxes.

Table 6-2

Option	Function
Confirm on Delete	Deleting files
Confirm on Subtree Delete	Deleting directories
Confirm on Replace	Copying or moving files that replace another file with the same name
Confirm on Mouse Operation	Dragging files or directories to copy or move them

Each confirmation option sends messages when you perform a certain function.

Once you're familiar with the File Manager and its commands, you can speed up operations by disabling the confirmation messages before you undertake a large project like deleting a directory with many files. If you don't turn off Confirm on Delete and Confirm on Subtree Delete, File Manager will force you to click on OK for each directory and file deleted. Assuming you intentionally deleted those directories and files, you may want to skip this confirmation step and get on with your work. After you've deleted a directory and its files, it's a good idea to turn the confirmation back on to help prevent unintentional deletions.

Printing files

The File Manager allows you to print an ASCII text file with the Print... command on the File menu. You can actually print any file, but only ASCII files will print recognizable and properly formatted text. You should print the other files with the application you used to create them.

One good time to use the Print... command is when you want a hard copy of README.TXT files that often come with commercial software packages. Typically, README.TXT files include recent additions and corrections to software documentation. You can also use the Print... command to send a Notepad .TXT file to a printer to test whether the printer is set up and connected properly.

To print a file, select it, then issue the Print... command. The File Manager will display a Print dialog box like the one in Figure 6-23, with the file name highlighted in the Print text box. When you click on OK,the Print Manager icon will appear on the desktop as the File Manager sends the file to the printer.

Figure 6-23

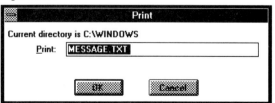

File Manager will present a Print dialog box like this one when you issue the Print... command.

The File Manager's repertoire of functions exceeds basic DOS functions like copying and renaming files. The File Manager also provides tools for changing file attributes, launching a document, and launching an application. You can also use the File Manager to perform media maintenance chores on disks and hard drives, like formatting (disks only), copying, and labeling.

Changing file attributes

File attributes are notes DOS makes about a file to remind it that there are limitations to what a user can do with that file. The four attributes are Read Only, Archive, Hidden, and System. The File Manager enables you to change a file's flag, or the attribute assigned to the file, with the Change Attributes... command on the File menu. In addition, the File Manager allows you to determine a file's attributes with the File Details command on the View menu. When you issue that command, you can see all the file attributes for each file in the directory window.

A Read Only flag means no one can make any changes to the file. You can't write any more information to it; you can only look at it.

An Archive flag means you have made changes to a file. DOS's BACKUP and XCOPY commands toggle this flag off after they run. That way, you will back up only the files that have changed instead of all the files on your hard drive.

A file flagged Hidden will not appear on a normal directory listing. Files can be hidden by DOS, applications, and users as a form of copy protection for files they don't want changed or copied. Since you can't see the file in a directory, you can't manipulate it. However, you can instruct the File Manager to reveal hidden files by selecting the Show Hidden/System Files option with the Include... command on the View menu.

A System attribute marks DOS system files such as the IBMBIO.COM and the IBMDOS.COM files in the root directory of your hard drive. These files are also hidden from view (so you can't delete or modify them unintentionally) until you tell the File Manager to display them with the Include... command menu.

If you have a file you want to share with other users, but you don't want any changes made to it, you can flag the file as Read Only with the Change Attributes... command on the File menu. The Change Attributes dialog box, shown in Figure 6-24, provides a check box for each type of file attribute. To flag a file as Read Only, simply click on that check box and then click on OK. Notice that you can have any combination or all four flags selected for a file. You can click on the check box again to remove an attribute.

Figure 6-24

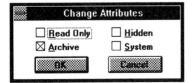

The Change Attributes dialog box lets you choose a combination of file attributes.

Launching a document

In Chapter 5, we explained how to create a launchable application icon for a document in the Program Manager. You can also launch an application's document from the File Manager. You can think of an icon that launches an application and immediately opens a specific file as a launchable document icon. The document's parent application determines the icon's graphic; the document's name is the icon's title. All you have to do is supply the File Manager with the name of the document's parent application by issuing the Associate... command. After the file is associated with an application, you can simply double-click on the file's icon, and the File Manager will open the application with the specified document displayed in its work area.

To associate an application with a file, first click on the file, then issue the Associate... command on the File menu. In the Associate dialog box, enter the application's file name in the text box and click on OK. Now the file's icon will change into a document icon (a ruled page).

When you use the Associate... command, the File Manager associates each file name extension with a specific application. Therefore, when you associate a selected file with a specific application, you associate any other files bearing the same extension with that application too. For example, if you associate a Write memo named MEMO.WRI with Word for Windows, all your files with a .WRI extension will be associated with Word for Windows instead of with Write.

If you later want to unassociate a file, select that file and reissue the Associate... command. Then, delete the application name in the text box and click OK. The File Manager will convert the file's icon back into a generic file icon (a blank page).

Another way to launch a document along with its parent application is to drag the document file on top of an application file. For example, if you want to work with a monthly report created in Excel, you can simply drag the MONTHLY.XLS file on top of the EXCEL.EXE program file. Then, the File Manager will verify that you want to start Excel with your monthly report as the initial file by displaying a message dialog box like the one in Figure 6-25. After you click on Yes, the File Manager will open Excel's application window and immediately open your monthly report. When you exit Excel, Windows will return to the File Manager.

Figure 6-25

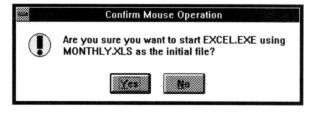

This message dialog box verifies that you want to launch an application and immediately open a specific file.

You can launch any file with a launchable icon (a rectangle with a blue stripe) next to the file name. To launch a file, simply double-click on the file's name or icon. The File Manager will immediately open either a DOS full-screen process or a window, depending on the application. If you launch a Windows application such as Calculator (CALC.EXE) from the File Manager, then the Calculator application window will appear on the desktop just as it does when you launch its icon from the Program Manager. To launch a highlighted file with the keyboard, you can issue the Open command on the File menu or simply press [Enter].

If you're going to launch applications from the File Manager, it's handy to automatically minimize the File Manager into an icon to save desktop space. To do this, issue the Minimize on Use command from the Options menu. This setting is toggled on until you issue it again or exit the File Manager. However, you can keep it toggled on between File Manager sessions by selecting the Save Settings check box in the Exit dialog box when you exit the File Manager.

It's much more elegant to use the File Manager than it is to try to launch DOS commands. If you're familiar with DOS and would rather double-click on a DOS command than use the File Manager's commands, you should be aware that it will take longer to issue the same command in DOS. When you issue a DOS command, the File Manager has to start a DOS full-screen process before the command can work. Also, after the command is completed, Windows returns you immediately to the File Manager. If the command simply displays information, as does CHKDSK (check disk), you may not have time to read all the information.

You can double-click on COMMAND.COM so File Manager will provide a DOS prompt. If you absolutely need to launch a DOS command, you should go to the Program Manager and start a DOS session with the DOS Prompt application. A word of warning: You should never run another DOS utility from the File Manager because the DOS utility could severely undermine Windows. For example, if you tried to launch PC Tools to compress your computer's hard drive from the File Manager, the DOS utility could alter the memory on your hard drive. As a result, Windows would no longer run on your machine.

You can also use the Run... command to start an application from the File Manager. First, highlight the directory in the Directory Tree where the application is located, or open that directory as a directory window. Next, issue the Run... command on the File menu. Now you can enter the application's file name and any parameters (such as a document file to open) in the Command Line text box. If you prefer, you can select the Run Minimized check box to run the application in the background on your desktop. After you click on OK, the File Manager will launch the application.

The File Manager provides simple, accurate methods to format, copy, and label floppy disks and hard drives. You can even use the File Manager to modify a disk so you can boot your PC with it (by making it a system disk).

Formatting

Before you can store data on any type of magnetic media, you need to prepare it by formatting it. A disk can't hold any information until the media is mapped out so the data has a defined place to be stored. Formatting a disk is also a good way to erase all the information on a disk so you can reuse it. You can format a disk if parts of the media become damaged. Reformatting a disk remaps the bad spots so the PC knows not to use them.

To format a disk, place the disk in a floppy drive and issue the Format Diskette... command on the Disk menu. The File Manager will present the Format Diskette dialog box, shown in Figure 6-26, so you can indicate which floppy drive the disk is in. For example, if you want to format the disk in drive A, select *A:* in the Disk drop-down list box. Next, the File Manager will warn you that formatting will erase all the information on the disk and prompt you for confirmation with the message dialog box shown in Figure 6-27. When you click on Format... to continue, the Format Diskette dialog box will change to prompt you to insert the disk and tell the File Manager whether you want to format the disk for high capacity (1.44Mb or 1.2Mb disks). You can also instruct the File Manager to copy the boot information immediately after formatting the disk by selecting the Make System Disk option and clicking on OK.

Figure 6-26

If you have more than one drive, the Format Diskette dialog box asks you to specify which drive to use.

Figure 6-27

This message dialog box asks you to verify with the Format... button if you want to erase all the data on the floppy disk.

The File Manager tells you its progress in formatting the disk by displaying the percent of formatting completed in the Format Diskette dialog box. You can click on Cancel in the Format Diskette dialog box to stop formatting the disk. When the File Manager finishes formatting the disk, it will ask if you want to format another disk with a Format Complete dialog box like the one in Figure 6-28. If you click on Yes, the File Manager will return to the Format Diskette dialog box. If you click on No, the File Manager will return you to the regular workspace.

Figure 6-28

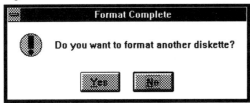

The Format Complete dialog box lets you immediately format another disk in the same drive.

You can create a system disk with the Make System Diskette... command on the Disk menu. You may need a disk to boot your PC (or load DOS into memory so you get a DOS prompt). A system disk is useful in emergencies, such as when the hard drive fails to boot by itself. You can use the Make System Diskette... command to copy the hidden files and COMMAND.COM to boot up your PC.

To make a system disk, click on the drive icon in the Directory Tree that has the system files (such as drive C) and issue the Make System Diskette... command on the Disk menu. If you have two floppy drives, the File Manager will ask you to specify which one you want to use. The File Manager presents a Make System Diskette dialog box for this information. Next, the File Manager will confirm that you want to copy the system files by displaying a message dialog box. If you answer by selecting the Yes button, the File Manager will provide a dialog box with a Cancel button so you can stop it from copying the files at any point during the process. When the copy is complete, the File Manager will return you to the Directory Tree.

You can use any empty formatted disk for a system disk. The disk must be empty because the File Manager needs to put the system files at the very beginning of the disk. If there is any data on the disk, the data will cover the area targeted for the system files. If you try to copy the files anyway, the File Manager will display a message dialog box telling you it's *Unable to add system files to this disk.*

When you want to make working copies of application disks or copy a data disk, you can use the Copy Diskette... command on the Disk menu. The destination disk doesn't even need to be formatted as it would if you used a regular Copy... command. However, the Copy Diskette... command works only if the two disks are the same capacity, such as both 1.44Mb (3.5"). The File Manager will format the target disk as it copies the information on it. Watch out: If there's data on the destination disk, it will all be erased. This command will also give the destination disk the same name or label as the source disk. By the way, the Copy Diskette... command works the same way as DOS's DISKCOPY command.

To copy a disk, first click on the drive icon that will be the source and then issue the Copy Diskette... command on the Disk menu. If you don't select a drive first, the File Manager will admonish you with a message dialog box, telling you to specify a drive first. Once you indicate a source drive and issue the Copy

Making a system disk

Copying disks

Diskette... command, the File Manager will ask you to specify the destination disk in a Copy Diskette dialog box. Simply click on the drop-down arrow to display a list of available destination disk drives. Select the one you want (in this case, the same drive as the source, drive A) and then click on OK.

Next, the File Manager will warn you with a message dialog box that it will erase all the files on the destination disk before copying any files. It actually reformats the destination disk. When you click Copy... to continue, the File Manager will ask you to insert the source disk with a Copy Diskette dialog box. After you insert the disk and click on OK, the File Manager will begin copying the data into your PC's memory. The File Manager keeps you informed of its progress by presenting another dialog box. Once the File Manager copies a chunk of data and prepares to write it to your destination disk, it will present a dialog box prompting you for the disk. After you insert the next disk, click on OK to begin the transfer. After the File Manager is finished writing, it will ask for the source disk again (with a dialog box). It will repeat the sequence of copying the information from the source disk into memory and then transferring it to the destination disk until it copies all of the source disk.

Even if you have only one floppy drive, you can still copy disks. The File Manager will prompt you when it's time to add the next disk. If you have two drives, you can still use only one to complete the copy by specifying the same drive as both the source and the destination drive. You may need to use this technique if your PC has two drives of different capacities installed, such as 1.2Mb (5.25") and 1.44Mb (3.5").

If you specified a drive for the destination disk that is different from the source disk, the File Manager will not repeatedly prompt you for disks. It will ask you for the source disk once, then ask you for the destination disk once. The copying process will also be quicker since you don't have to keep inserting disks.

If you really need to copy two kinds of disks, you can force the File Manger to copy them anyway. First, format the destination disk to erase any data. You'll need to add a label to it manually (with the Label Disk... command), if you want one. Next, click on the drive icon that the source disk is in, which is A. This action will display a directory icon in the Directory Tree for your source disk. Now drag the directory icon over the destination disk icon, which is B. The File Manager will display a message dialog box asking if you really want to copy all the files. When you click Yes, the File Manager will essentially copy the disk in drive A to the disk in drive B. This way, it doesn't matter if the disk in A is 1.44Mb (3.5") and the one in B is 1.2Mb (5.25") or vice versa.

In this chapter

Print Manager 7

*H*ow often have you had to wait for your applications to finish printing so you could get on with your work? When you're battling a deadline as you insert last-minute revisions and reprint portions of a report or presentation, waiting for one file to print before you can open the next file for editing can give new meaning to the saying "hurry up and wait."

Print Manager—Windows' built-in print spooler—lets you get back to work fast after you send a file to the printer. No longer must you wait for your document or file to finish printing before you can begin editing the next file. Instead of your application sending information directly to the printer, Print Manager steps in to divert the information to your hard disk. (Sending the print job to disk is normally much faster than sending the same job to the printer, especially if you are printing a long text document.) Then, operating in the background while you go on with other work, Print Manager directs the print files from your disk to the printer. Although this adds a step that actually slows printing an individual file, it lets you get more work done by minimizing the time your application is tied up sending information to the printer.

PRINT MANAGER

Because Print Manager can hold multiple print jobs on disk and send them to the printer in sequence, you can send Print Manager another print job, even before the first file is finished printing. Print Manager maintains a "print queue"— a list of files awaiting printing—for each of the printers installed on your system and lets you delete and rearrange items in the queue to control your printing.

Using Print Manager is optional. You can deactivate it when you install Windows, or later, using Control Panel. To activate or deactivate Print Manager, choose Control Panel from the Main group window in Program Manager. Double-click on the Printers icon to open the Printers dialog box shown in Figure 7-1.

Select the Use Print Manager check box in the lower-left corner of the dialog box to activate Print Manager. Deselect it to disable Print Manager. Once you tell Windows to use Print Manager, it will send each print job from a Windows-based application to Print Manager automatically.

Figure 7-1

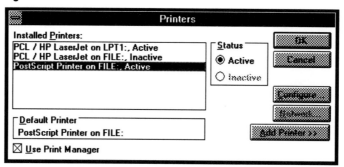

Select the Use Print Manager check box to activate Print Manager as an automatic feature of Windows.

Printing from Windows applications

Since Print Manager is a built-in feature of Windows, you don't have to do anything special to use it to manage your printing. You simply use the normal printing procedure in your Windows-based application (usually, you choose the Print... command from the application's File menu). The application will create a print file and send it to Print Manager instead of to the printer. Then, Print Manager will forward the file from its print queue on your hard drive to your printer and free you to work in other applications.

Print Manager doesn't modify the print file it receives from your application, so the availability of features such as fonts and formatting depend on the originating application, not Print Manager. Some applications use the full range of fonts and printer effects, while others use only a default typeface. Some preview the printed output with surprising accuracy; others do not. To avoid unpleasant surprises, you'll need to be familiar with the printing characteristics of your applications.

Starting Print Manager

Normally, Print Manager operates entirely in the background. Windows automatically invokes Print Manager when your application sends something to the printer and automatically closes Print Manager when the last print job in its print queue goes to the printer. Print Manager runs minimized as an icon on your desktop when it is queuing print jobs. If you need to view or manipulate the print queue, you can open the Print Manager application window simply by double-clicking on its icon or using the Task Manager to switch to Print Manager from your current application. If you need to open Print Manager when it isn't already on your desktop, you can double-click on the Print Manager icon you'll find in the Main group window in the Program Manager.

If Print Manager is operating normally as an icon on your desktop, it will close automatically when the last print job in its queue goes to the printer. It will start again automatically when you start the next print job. If the Print Manager window is open, it won't automatically close—even if the window is inactive. To exit from Print Manager when it's running in an open window, choose the Exit command from the Options menu.

Exiting from Print Manager

Your non-Windows applications cannot use Print Manager. Whether they operate in a window or as full-screen applications, each of your DOS applications will use its own procedures to send data directly to the printer. Each DOS application will need its own printer drivers and configuration for your printer and will demand exclusive access to the printer when it prints. Since DOS applications were conceived as stand-alone operations rather than part of a multitasking environment, they typically have no provision for sharing resources such as printers. Consequently, there is a potential for conflict if a non-Windows application tries to print while Print Manager is printing. If you use Windows' standard mode, there is no problem since all background operations—including Print Manager—are suspended when you run a DOS session. In 386 enhanced mode, Windows can exercise some control over contention for shared resources. Chapter 3 explains using the controls for the 386 enhanced mode.

Printing from non-Windows applications

Print Manager adds to Windows' "network awareness" by intelligently sensing print jobs destined for a network printer and handling them differently from files you send to a local printer. Since most networks have their own print spoolers, sending a print job through Print Manager would be redundant. Instead, your network print jobs normally go directly to the network; they aren't added to Print Manager's queue, and the Print Manager icon doesn't appear while the file is queued or printing on the network. Print Manager includes several features to help you manage your network printing. We'll discuss network printing, along with other network operations, in the next chapter.

Printing with a network

When you open the Print Manager window, by double-clicking on the icon on your desktop or by selecting Print Manager from the Main group window in Program Manager, you will see a window like the one in Figure 7-2. Below the usual menu bar, you'll see the Pause, Resume, and Delete buttons and the message box, which gives a slightly more complete summary of the highlighted item's status. The rest of the work area in the Print Manager window is devoted to print queues for each of the printers installed on your system (at least, each of those you have set up as active printers in Windows). If you are connected to a network, you may also see a queue for the files you've sent to the network. The detail that Print Manager can display about your network print jobs depends on the network software, as we'll explain in the next chapter.

EXAMINING THE PRINT QUEUE

Figure 7-2

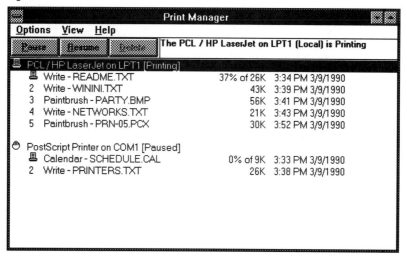

The Print Manager window includes information on each printer and each file in the print queues waiting to be printed.

Printer information line

The first line (highlighted in Figure 7-2) is the printer information line for the first printer. Here you'll find the name of the printer, the port the printer is connected to, and its current status. Notice the icon at the beginning of the line that indicates the printer is printing. The message box below the menu bar gives more information on the highlighted line; in this case, the LaserJet printer. Near the middle of the window, you can see another printer information line for a PostScript printer. The icon and the *[Paused]* notation indicate that printing is temporarily suspended.

File information line

Below the printer information lines are file information lines for each file in the print queue. The file information lines start with either the "printing" icon or a number showing each file's position in the queue. Beside the number (or icon) is the title of the print job—typically, the name of the originating application and the file name. On the right side of the window, Print Manager lists the size of each file and shows the portion of the file that it has sent to the printer. The last entry on each file information line is the time and date Print Manager received the file from your application. If you highlight a file information line by clicking anywhere on the line, a slightly more detailed version of this same information will appear in the message box.

Time/Date and Print File Size displays

The file information line normally includes the date and time the file was sent to Print Manager and the file's size. You can suppress either or both portions of the information lines. When you select the View menu, you'll notice check marks beside the Time/Date Sent and Print File Size commands, indicating that the options are active. To turn off the time and date or file size portion of the file information lines, choose the corresponding command. The check mark beside the command and the information in the Print Manager window will both disappear. To reinstate the display, choose the command again.

Print Manager messages

Although Print Manager normally operates in the background and typically needs very little interaction with you, it occasionally needs to display a message, such as a notice that the printer is out of paper or jammed. You can choose the way you want Print Manager to handle messages—how persistent it should be in interrupting you when it needs your attention.

You can choose one of three alert commands on the Options menu—Alert Always, Flash if Inactive, or Ignore if Inactive—to control how Print Manager will display messages. These commands control how Print Manager will alert you when it is an inactive window or icon. Of course, messages always appear immediately when Print Manager is the active window. A check mark indicates which message alert mode is active. To change the way Print Manager displays messages, choose one of the three commands.

If you choose Alert Always, Print Manager will immediately display a message box over the foreground application when it encounters any situation that needs your attention.

The default message display mode is Flash if Inactive. In this mode, you will hear a beep, and the Print Manager icon (or the title bar of the inactive Print Manager window) will flash to let you know Print Manager is waiting with a message. When you restore Print Manager from an icon (or make it the active window), you'll see the message and be able to respond.

If you don't want to be bothered, and are willing to have your printing stalled without notice, choose Ignore if Inactive. This mode ignores messages unless Print Manager is the active window.

The command you select will remain in effect until you change it. Regardless of the command you choose, you will still see system messages, such as a notice the printer is off-line.

CONTROLLING PRINTING

Print Manager normally sends print files to the printer in the same sequence it received them from your applications. But, if you want to rearrange the printing sequence, Print Manager allows you to manipulate the print queue and manage your printing tasks. You can change the order of the items in the print queue and cancel the printing of individual print files. You can also suspend printing temporarily and change the printing speed.

Rearranging the queue

Changing the order of the items in the print queue is easy. You simply highlight the file you want to move by clicking anywhere on its file information line, then drag it into the new position. To perform the same operation with the keyboard, first use the arrow keys to move the highlight to the correct file information line, then press and hold the [Ctrl] key while you reposition the file with the arrow keys. Release the [Ctrl] key when the file reaches its new position.

You can rearrange files in the queues only for local printers; and, for obvious reasons, you can't move the file that is currently printing. Although Print Manager can show the status of some network print queues, you can't manipulate those queues with Print Manager. You'll need to use the network printer control facilities for that.

Pause/Resume printing

One of Print Manager's handier features is its ability to temporarily suspend printing. Whether you need to interrupt printing to change a ribbon or cartridge, add paper, or just quiet a noisy printer while you take a phone call, you'll appreciate this capability. To suspend printing, select the printer you want to interrupt by clicking on its information line, then click on the Pause button. With the keyboard, use the arrow keys to move the highlight to the printer information line, then press [Alt]P. Print Manager changes the printer information line to show that printing is paused.

To restart a paused printer, select the correct printer information line and then click on the Resume button. The keyboard equivalent for the Resume button is [Alt]R. Sometimes when the printer develops a problem, such as running out of paper, you'll see the *[STALLED]* notation at the end of a printer information line. After you correct the cause of the problem, you'll need to use the Resume button to restart printing.

Another way the Pause command can be very useful is to allow you to do your printing in "batches." Perhaps you share a printer with someone, or perhaps you just don't like the distraction of the printer chattering or whirring while you work. You can use the Pause command to hold your print jobs in Print Manager's queue and defer printing to a later time. The trick is to pause the printer before sending any print jobs to Print Manager. If you haven't started printing, Print Manager won't be available as an icon on your desktop. Open Print Manager by choosing it from the Main group window in Program Manager. Select the printer you will be using and click on Pause, then minimize Print Manager. Now you can issue the Print... command or its equivalent as usual, but instead of going to the printer, your file will remain in Print Manager's queue. When you decide to print the batch of files, just open Print Manager and select Resume.

Deleting a file from the queue

You don't have to waste paper or time printing a file that you decide you don't need after all. You can simply delete the file from the print queue if it hasn't started printing. To delete a file from the queue, select the file by clicking anywhere on its information line, then click on the Delete button or press [Alt]D. Print Manager will open a dialog box like the one in Figure 7-3 asking you to confirm the action. Click on OK to remove the file from the queue or Cancel to change your mind.

Figure 7-3

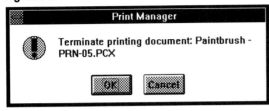

Print Manager will ask for confirmation when you delete a print file from the print queue.

You can delete all the files in the queue by choosing Exit from the Options menu and confirming the action by clicking on OK in the dialog box. This action will remove all the print files from the print queue and close Print Manager.

Print Manager allows you to delete the file that is currently printing, thus aborting what could be a long print job in midstream. However, if you do, you may need to reset the printer. You may only need to click on the Resume button if the printer information line shows *[STALLED]*; but, depending on your printer, you may also need to manually reset the printer (turn it off, and then turn it back on) or re-initialize it before printing another file.

Adjusting the printing speed

You can control how fast Print Manager sends data to your computer's printer port with three commands—Low Priority, Medium Priority, and High Priority—on the Options menu. By changing the priority Windows will give printing activity relative to your foreground application's activities, you can exercise control over how fast both operations will run. A check mark appears beside the command that is active (Medium Priority is the default). To change the priority printing will receive, choose one of the three commands from the Options menu.

Low Priority assigns more of the computer's resources to your foreground applications, causing them to run faster and causing printing to be slower. Medium Priority gives approximately equal time to Print Manager and to the foreground applications. High Priority gives Print Manager more computer resources, which maximizes printing speed at the expense of performance in the foreground applications. Choose the priority setting that meets your needs. The printing priority will remain in effect until you change it.

PRINTING TO A FILE

Occasionally, you may want to send your application's printer output to a file instead of to the printer. You may need to merge a file into another document, to delay printing a document for several hours, or even days, or to print it at another location. Whatever the reason, the procedure is the same.

- Open Control Panel by double-clicking on its icon in the Main group window in the Program Manager.

- Open the Printers dialog box by double-clicking on the Printers icon.

- Choose the printer you eventually expect to use to print the file from the Installed Printers list box.

- Click on the Configure... button to open the Printers-Configure dialog box.

- Select File from the Ports list box, then choose Setup to verify the settings.

- Click on OK in each dialog box to install the settings and close the Control Panel.

- Open your application, select the printer you just configured with File as the port, and print normally.

Print Manager opens a Print To File dialog box like the one shown in Figure 7-4 to prompt you for a file name each time you print with this option. Print Manager will save each print job destined for this printer in a separate file until you reconfigure the printer back to its normal port with Control Panel.

Figure 7-4

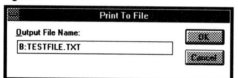

When you print to a file instead of a printer, Print Manager will prompt you for a file name with this dialog box.

In this chapter

Networking 8

*H*ow will a network affect your work with Windows? On a network, you'll be able to use network resources such as printers and modems and multiple hard drives. While the network provides more resources for you, it actually saves your company's resources by eliminating the costly duplication of equipment and software. In fact, the computer industry provides application licensing and devices designed expressly for networks.

Fortunately, Windows facilitates using these added resources with features in Control Panel, the File Manager, Print Manager, and Windows Setup. In this chapter, we'll introduce you to the concepts of networking, then take you on a tour of Windows' networking functions via two scenarios: using a Windows application with a network and using a network-installed application with Windows. Finally, we'll show you how to communicate with other users on your network. If you are already familiar with the basic concepts of a network, you can skip the first section and go directly to the next section where we discuss how Windows works with the network.

NETWORK NUTS AND BOLTS

Your PC provides a wide range of capabilities that you can implement by attaching devices. For example, your PC is capable of addressing (or routing information to) drive IDs from A to Z. It can also use printer ports LPT1, LPT2, and LPT3 plus serial ports COM1, COM2, COM3, and COM4.

Even though your PC is capable of attaching to many devices, realistically, it has only a few physically installed. A typical PC uses drive IDs A and B for floppy disks and C for a hard drive and commonly has a printer attached to the LPT1 printer port. After connecting all the basics (two floppy drives, a hard drive, and a printer), your PC still has the capacity to address drives D through Z, two more printers, and four serial devices.

Instead of outfitting each PC with all the peripheral devices it can use and might need, you—and other users—can share resources and information through a network. When you access a network, you usually access another PC like your own, called a server. The server has a hard drive, that is divided into volumes with unique path names and printers and modems attached to its printer and serial ports. These resources of the server are shared by the users of the network..

But how do you gain access to the network resources? How do you connect your PC to a printer, hard drive, and modem connected to another PC that may be in a different part of the building—all through a single network cable? You do it by establishing links—or associations—between some of the unused device addresses (drive IDs, printer ports, or serial ports) of your PC and the resources of the network. The network software and hardware will then be able to intercept information and requests destined for one of your phantom devices and redirect them to the network devices linked to that address. For example, you could link your PC's drive ID F to the path called \\SERVER\EXCEL on the server's hard drive to access Excel from the network. You could also link drive ID G to the server's path called \\SERVER\WORD to access Word for Windows and link drive ID H to the path \\SERVER\XWS to access Crosstalk for Windows. Once you made these links, you could use drive F to run Excel, drive G to run Word for Windows, and drive H to run Crosstalk for Windows from the network.

In addition to linking your PC to the server's applications, you can link your printer ports to the server's printers. For example, if you wanted to use the server's printer, you could link it to your PC's LPT2 printer port. You could also link LPT3 to the server's color printer and link the server's modem to your PC's COM2 port.

Your resources would grow from a PC with two floppy drives, a hard drive, a dot matrix printer, and your own applications, to a system with all of these things plus the resources of the network. These network resources include the addition of the Excel, Word for Windows, and Crosstalk applications, as well as two added printers and a modem.

To use all these resources, you must abide by the network's rules. These rules include permission from the server to use network applications and devices. We'll explain later how you gain permission. As you would expect, the software on a network must be specifically licensed for multiple users, just as you must license your personal software.

Before you can expand your PC's (called a work station on the network) capabilities with network resources, you must first learn how to use the network with Windows. We'll introduce you to the resources of networks and also point out the rules governing user access.

Introducing the server

Many of the capabilities of a network depend on the capabilities of its server. As we've explained, the server provides resources that everyone on the network can use. All network users granted permission will have access to the server's volumes and devices. (We'll use Microsoft's LAN Manager for our examples.) Windows will list in the network dialog boxes resources from which you may choose. We'll show you how to browse through these various lists.

You also should be aware that there can be more than one server on your network. In fact, LAN Manager sets up special names for groups of servers called domains (think of a domain as a server neighborhood).

Servers not only share their resources, they protect them too. Since all the server's resources are potentially available to every user, the server must impose order on the chaos of many work stations PCs scrambling for resources. The server acts as a traffic cop to ensure that connecting to resources is orderly and nondestructive to applications and devices.

Sharing resources

The server can provide access to its resources in two ways: through user level or share level access. User level access assigns rights and restrictions to individual users. Users who can access the server have rights to all its applications and devices. Share level access is more restrictive since it requires specific rights to each volume and device individually. Users with rights to network resources, from either user level or share level access, have a password that enables them to connect to a server or to individual volumes and devices.

Restricting access to files

After you gain access to a server volume, the server imposes another level of protection on the paths in that volume. The server provides this protection by issuing privileges that define the extent to which a user can manipulate a file in a specific path on the server volume. (Files include data, program, command, and batch files.)

These privileges allow users access to each path in varying degrees. Privileges are similar to file attributes (read-only, hidden, system, and archive, which we discussed in Chapter 6), but they are much more extensive. Privileges limit access to all the files in a network path on the server. Some types of networks can even assign unique privileges to specific files in the path. Networks commonly use privileges such as read-only, create, delete, write, and open.

For example, when a server shares a network version of Excel, it can protect Excel's program files by assigning a read-only privilege to its path. Read-only means a user can launch Excel but can't save any changes to the application's setup in the restricted path. You would need to save your work in another location.

Restricting access to printers

The server also restricts access to printers. Each time a user asks for access to a printer, the server verifies that the user has access privileges. For example, a printer dedicated to printing invoices on six-part invoice stock could be accessed only by the accounting department that issues the invoices. This restriction would help prevent other users from printing memos on accounting's invoice printer.

Connecting to applications

In order to access the applications installed on the server, you need to create a bridge between your PC and the server. A network drive forms this bridge by associating a drive ID on your PC to a path name on the server (such as \\SERVER\EXCEL). As we mentioned, you can assign any letter from A to Z to a drive ID as long as your PC isn't currently using it for its own drives.

It's important to consistently connect network resources to the same drives. For example, if you set up an application icon for a network version of Excel and you defined the command line as G:\EXCEL\EXCEL, you'll need to make sure drive G is consistently assigned to Excel in order for the icon to launch properly. After all, the Program Manager won't know to look anywhere else. We'll show you how to connect to network drives and create network application icons later in this chapter.

Connecting to devices

In general, more than one user can access a network device, such as a printer, modem, or CD-ROM (a drive that stores large amounts of read-only data), at one time because the server can juggle everyone's requests to use it. If the server is juggling the requests of other users as well as your requests, it will assess the various user needs and privileges, and assign you a turn for a percentage of the time. Don't worry—this juggling happens in milliseconds so there will be only a minor decrease in response time.

Connecting to a printer

To print on a network printer, you must tell Windows which printer on the server you want to use and which printer port on your PC will link to it. Windows provides a list of network printers via Control Panel. Once you choose a network printer, you specify which port on your PC will represent the port on the server. In this way, you equate your PC's port, like LPT1, to the server's LPT1 port and form a logical connection. Thereafter, anything you print from an application to a printer with an LPT1 port listed in a Printer Setup dialog box is actually sent to a network printer. We'll show you later how to connect to printers.

After you connect to a network printer and print a file, the file will stand in line at the server along with other files until its turn to print. This waiting line, called a network print queue, is the server's way of sharing the printer. While your file is in the network print queue your PC is free for other work. You don't have to wait for the file to print before you can continue working in your application.

Connecting to a modem

Connecting to a modem works differently than connecting to a printer. In general, only one user can connect to a modem at a time. (You can't queue modem communication.) The next user that requests a connection to a modem will either connect to an available modem on the server or receive a message similar to *Device not available.* When you connect to a modem, you use a serial port like COM2 instead of a network drive ID to form the bridge between your PC and the modem.

CD-ROMs are another type of device you can access on the network. When you connect to a CD-ROM, you use the same technique you use with any other network volume. You link a drive ID to the name of the CD-ROM. However, when you use a CD-ROM that exchanges large chunks of information at once, you will notice the response time will decrease quickly as more users try to access its data simultaneously.

Connecting to a CD-ROM

In our explanations so far, the server seemed to magically assign user access rights and path privileges. It's not magic, but hard work by the network administrator, who must define these rights and privileges. The network administrator installs and sets up the network for you and others to use. When the network administrator sets up the server, he or she divides the hard drive into sections called volumes, giving each volume a unique name (such as SERVER or ACCOUNTING1). Next, the network administrator installs several applications, sets up all the printers, and defines who is allowed to use which server volumes and applications. Finally, the network administrator assigns passwords to each user of the server or to the server's volumes and devices.

The network administrator

The network administrator also serves as the network problem solver. If you see a message dialog box regarding a network error, you need to inform the network administrator so he or she can fix the problem. For example, with several printers serving the needs of many users, you may accidentally send your letter to a printer set up for envelopes. A message dialog box will alert you to the problem, so you can notify the network administrator if you need help.

If your needs for network resources change, and you want to gain access to another application or printer, you should contact your network administrator to broaden your access.

Windows acts as a liaison between your PC and the network. Because Windows equips its applications with certain functions to deal with networking issues, you never have to leave Windows' friendly graphical user interface to use networking functions. Windows Setup sets the stage for networking by allowing you to install network drivers on your PC. The File Manager connects to network paths with its Connect Net Drive... command. Control Panel devotes a specialized feature just to networking functions such as logging on to the network and sending messages. Print Manager lets you observe the network print queues. We'll talk about all of these functions later in this chapter.

Windows as a network liaison

Since you have access to so many additional resources, working on a network can be confusing. We'll start by guiding you through some basic network functions, then we'll show you how to manage more complex network functions. The first operations we'll explain include accessing the network, using an application on your PC while working with data on the server, printing to a network

TESTING THE WATER WITH NETWORK

printer, and leaving the network. Our discussion of more complex network functions will include installing Windows from the server, changing your password, and launching applications from the File Manager and the Program Manager.

In the following examples, we'll use Microsoft's LAN Manager 2.0 network software installed on a 386 PC server. An HP LaserJet IIP printer will provide network printing services. The figures in the examples show LAN Manager dialog boxes and windows. Although other brands of networks have unique dialog boxes pertinent to their software, the basic functions are similar.

Now that we've introduced you to the basics of networking, let's go through an example using a network. Suppose you have a draft quality dot matrix printer connected to your PC and you need to print an important report for the officers of your company. You'll want to print your report on a more sophisticated printer so your work will look professional. Instead of taking a disk containing your report to another office that has a laser printer connected to a PC, you can use the laser printer connected to the network—from your own PC. You can even share the report file with other users on the network.

Installing network capabilities from your PC

Before using Windows on a network, you must specify the type of network to which you're connecting. After you start your Windows session, you can install network capabilities for Windows with Windows Setup. However, before you run Windows Setup, the network administrator must install the software and hardware connecting your PC to the network.

To start Windows Setup, double-click on its icon in the Main group window. Next, issue the Change System Settings... command on the Options menu in the Windows Setup window shown in Figure 8-1. To select the network type in the Change System Settings dialog box shown in Figure 8-2, click on the Network list box's drop-down arrow to display the list of networks. To choose a network, click on the appropriate network name. Next, Windows will prompt you for a disk that contains the Windows network files for your type of network. Insert the appropriate disk in the drive, and press [Enter] to copy the files onto your hard drive.

Figure 8-1

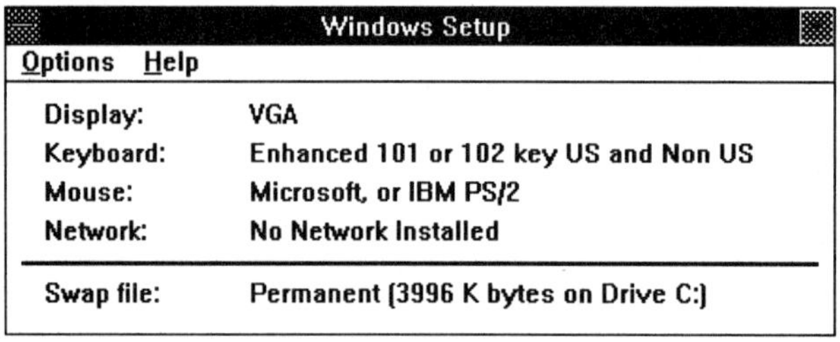

Windows Setup	
Options Help	
Display:	VGA
Keyboard:	Enhanced 101 or 102 key US and Non US
Mouse:	Microsoft, or IBM PS/2
Network:	No Network Installed
Swap file:	Permanent (3996 K bytes on Drive C:)

The Windows Setup window displays your currently installed hardware.

Figure 8-2

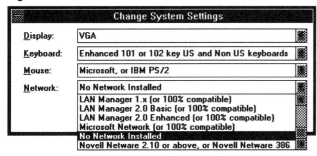

The Change System Settings dialog box lets you change your installation options, including network type.

After Windows copies the files and modifies the SYSTEM.INI file, it will present a message dialog box asking if you want to reboot your PC or return to DOS. You'll need to restart Windows in order to use the new network options.

Logging on the network

Before you can use the server's resources, you must log on the network. Logging on is a network user's way of getting the server's attention by establishing a software rapport between his or her PC and the server. Logging on involves telling the server who you are with a user name and supplying a password. You'll need to ask your network administrator for a user name and password.

To log on the network, activate the Control Panel application in the Main group window of the Program Manager. Next, activate the Network icon on Control Panel to display the Networks-LAN Manager window shown in Figure 8-3. Before you log on, Control Panel will enter a *Not currently logged on* message where your user name usually appears. Now issue the Logon... command on the Account menu to access a dialog box like the one in Figure 8-4 on the next page, and enter your user name in the Username text box. (This text box isn't case-sensitive; you can use either uppercase or lowercase.) By default, Control Panel enters the network's generic user name in the text box. For LAN Manager, the default user name is USER. Finally, click on the Logon button to log on the network. When you are logged on the network, Control Panel automatically will enter your user name into the Username text box.

Figure 8-3

Networks - LAN Manager			
Account	Message	Options	Help

Your Username:	(not currently logged on)
Your Computername:	COMPAQ386
Your Domain:	DOMAIN

The Networks-LAN Manager window displays your user name, PC network name, and network neighborhood or domain.

Figure 8-4

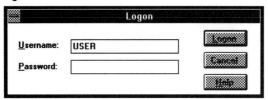

*The Logon dialog box
displays your user name
and requests a password.*

If your network requires passwords, you must enter your password in the
Password text box before the network will let you in. After you enter the
password, click on the Logon button to connect to the server. If your network
software includes a Help feature, as LAN Manager does, you can click on the Help
button to find out about logging on to the network. If you decide not to log on
to the network, simply click on the Cancel button to return to the Networks-LAN
Manager window.

**Connecting to
a network path**

One of the main benefits of a network is its ability to share data. With the File
Manager, you can specify a network path and establish a network drive ID. For
example, if your department uses the \\ACCOUNTING\PAYROLL path on the
server to share common data, you could connect it to drive G.

Through the File Manager, you can connect to this path and assign it a network
drive ID (in our example, G) so you can access it from your applications. Begin
by starting the File Manager and choosing the Connect Net Drive… command from
the Disk menu. In the Connect Network Drive dialog box, shown in Figure 8-5,
select a drive ID (such as G) in the Drive Letter drop-down list box and type the
server path (\\ACCOUNTING\PAYROLL) into the Network Path text box. If you
don't know the path, you can click on the Browse… button to display a list of
available paths in the Network Disk Resources dialog box shown in Figure 8-6.
To choose a path, simply click on a path listed in the Resources list box, then click
on OK. Now the Connect Network Drive dialog box will list that path in the
Network Path text box.

Figure 8-5

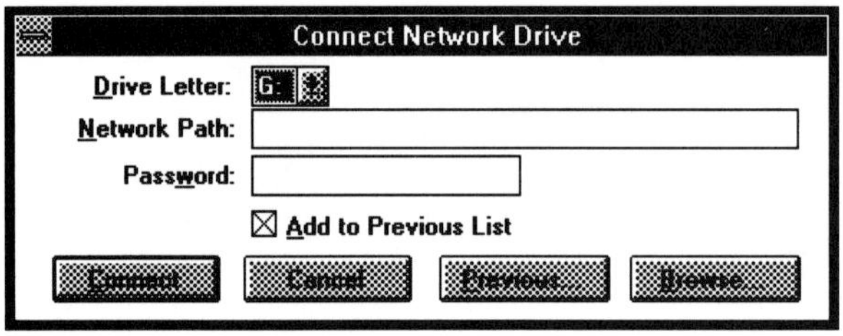

*The Connect Network
Drive dialog box
prompts you for a
drive ID to associate
to a server path.*

Figure 8-7

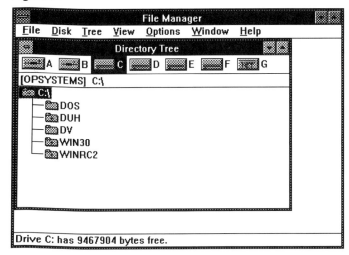

The File Manager adds a special network drive icon when you connect to a network path.

file
ork drive

If you want to save a report you created with Write on a network drive, such as drive G, you would follow a process similar to saving a file on your PC. Simply issue the Save As... command, then choose the network drive ID from the Directories list box in the File Save As dialog box, like the one shown in Figure 8-8. Now enter the file name in the Filename text box and click on OK. Windows will save the file on the server. When you save the file, it typically receives privilege attributes similar to the other files in the same server path. In other words, if you save your file to your department path for which only your department has privileges, no other departments will be able to use it.

The process for assigning privilege attributes to files depends on which network you're using. You should check with your network administrator about how your network assigns privileges to new files.

Figure 8-8

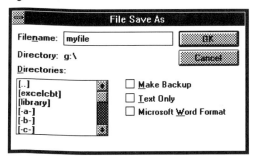

The File Save As dialog box's Directories list box will list any network drive IDs to which you're connected.

Figure 8-6

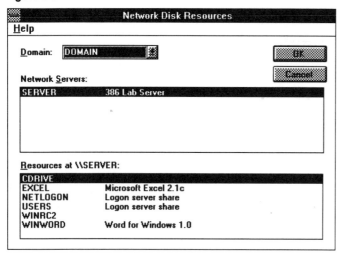

The Network Disk Resources dialog box lists the available paths on the server hard drive.

File Manager maintains a list of the connection you've previously established between drive IDs and network paths. By default, the File Manager toggles on the Add to Previous List option in the Connect Network Drive dialog box. That way, the next time you want to use the same connection, you can simply click on the Previous button to cycle through the connections the File Manager lists instead of typing in the path or browsing through all the available paths.

When you're ready to make the connection to the network path, click on the Connect button. The File Manager will immediately add another drive icon to the Directory Tree and label it with the drive ID you chose. In Figure 8-7 on the next page, notice that the drive icon is slightly different from the other hard drive icon because the word *Net* appears on the icon to indicate it's a network icon.

If you connect to a path on the server for which you don't have privileges, you won't be able to open files. When you try to open a directory window for the path in the File Manager, you'll get a message stating that the directory contains no files. Actually, the files are there, but you aren't allowed to see them. You need to connect to a different path for which you have privileges, or ask your network administrator to change your resource privileges.

If you connect to a read-only network path to run an application stored there, you should connect a drive ID to another path (that isn't read-only) so you store your files. You can share a document, such as a newsletter, with anyone on the network by specifying the drive ID for a shared network path when save the file.

When you use the File Manager to establish the network connections, those connections will remain effective even if you exit Windows. This is good news and bad news. The good news is that you can use Windows to quickly and easily set up the network connections for a non-Windows application you normally run from DOS. Simply set up the connections with the File Manager, exit Windows, then run your application. The bad news is that you need to take another step to disconnect a network drive ID in the File Manager. Of course, if you do something drastic like log off the network, then all your network drive connections and links to other network resources, like printers, will be terminated. A safer way to disconnect from a network drive is to issue the Net Disconnect... command from the Disk menu in the File Manager. When the File Manager displays the Disconnect Drive dialog box, shown in Figure 8-9, you'll need to choose the network drive ID you want to disconnect in the drop-down list box. Then, click on OK to complete the disconnection. Now you can reassign that drive ID.

Disconnecting from a network drive

Figure 8-9

The Disconnect Drive dialog box lets you disconnect a drive ID from a network path.

Before you can print with one of the network printers, you must inform Windows of the available network printers. Activate the Printers icon on Control Panel. Assuming you are connected to the network (logged on), the Network... button in the Printers dialog box will be available, as you can see in Figure 8-10. Click on the Network... button to start the process of installing the list of your network's printers.

Connecting to network printers

Figure 8-10

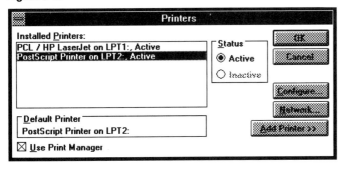

The Printers dialog box provides a Network... button to set up network printers.

In the Printers-Network Connections dialog box, shown in Figure 8-11, you need to click on the Browse... button to display a list of network printers to which you can connect. In the Network Printers dialog box, shown in Figure 8-12, Control Panel lists the printers by server. Just click on the server you want to use in the Network Servers list box, assuming there is more than one server on your network. If you have only one server, it will be automatically selected. In fact, Control Panel lists the servers, grouped by domain. If your network has more than one domain, be sure to select the one with the server you need. (Since multiple domains and servers can be confusing, you should get a list or map from your network administrator to use for reference.)

Figure 8-11

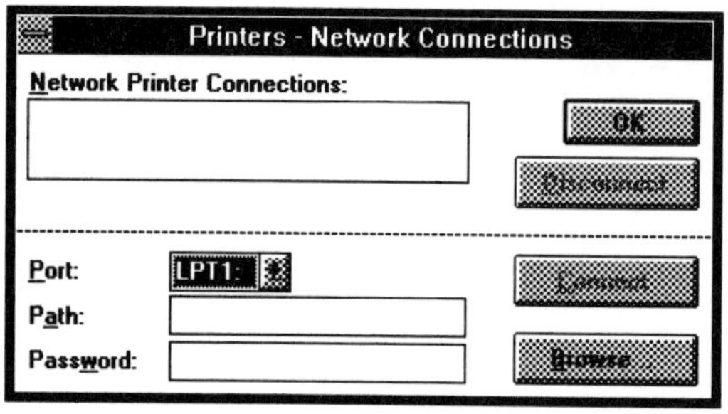

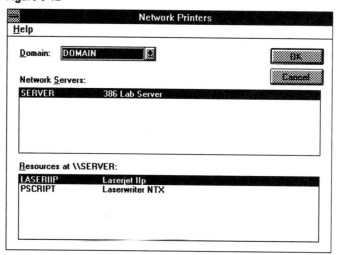

The Browse... button in the Printers-Network Connections dialog box offers the first step toward setting up network printers.

Figure 8-12

The Network Printers dialog box lists the available domains and their servers, with the active server's printers displayed below.

After you select a server, its network printers will appear in the Resources list box at the bottom of the Network Printers dialog box. Now you can click on one of the printers and click on OK. Control Panel will insert the selected printer's name in the Path text box in the Printers-Network Connections dialog box. Next, you need to inform Control Panel which port (for example, LPT1) you want associated with the network printer by selecting one from the Port drop-down list box.

Before you can connect to the printer, you need to enter its password in the Password text box in the Printers-Network Connections dialog box. If the printer doesn't have a password, click on the Connect button to finish connecting to the network printer. After the printer is connected, Control Panel will list the printer in the Network Printer Connections list box. These connections are active and displayed until you log off the network.

When you've connected to the network printer, click on OK to return to the Printers dialog box. You still have one more step to ensure that your file will print properly. You must match the specifications of the network printer to the printer listed in the Installed Printers list box in the Printers dialog box for the port you specified in the Printers-Network Connections dialog box. For example, if you usually print on an Epson printer from your PC's LPT1 port but now redirect LPT1 to the network laser printer, Windows will send all your files to the printer in Epson printer language, which the laser printer won't understand. To avoid this miscommunication, you must set up an HP LaserJet on LPT1 in the Printers dialog box so you can use it to send files to the network laser printer.

To verify that Control Panel has selected the correct printer, click on the Configure... button in the Printers dialog box and then click on the Setup... button in the Printers-Configure dialog box. Now Control Panel will display the PCL/HP LaserJet on LPT1: dialog box. If the Printer drop-down list box doesn't list the HP LaserJet IIP, click on the drop-down arrow and select it from the list. Now click on OK in the PCL/HP LaserJet on LPT1: dialog box and in the Printers-Configure dialog box to return to the Printers dialog box. Finally, click on OK in the Printers dialog box to use all your new settings.

If you want to disconnect from a network printer, click on its name in the Network Printer Connections list box, then click on the Disconnect button.

Normally Windows bypasses Print Manager to speed up printing on the network. However, you can still use Print Manager to view the status of your file in a network queue. You'll need to manually activate Print Manager by double-clicking on its icon in the Program Manager's Main group window.

Printing from an application

Once you set up your printer, you can access your application normally and print your report. To demonstrate how you would print on a network, we'll use a report we created in Write for an example. Begin by activating the Write application icon in the Program Manager. To send your document to the network printer, you complete the same process you use without a network. First, set up your page layout, then set up the printer with the Printer Setup... command on the File menu. In the Printer Setup dialog box, choose the active printer that matches the type of network printer and the port to which you assigned it from Control Panel (in our example, PCL/HP LaserJet on LPT1: with Lan Manager). Now issue the Print... command on the File menu. Instead of printing on the printer connected to your PC, Windows will send the file to the server for printing. After the server prints the document, it will display a message dialog box telling you that the network has sent a message. After you click on Yes to read the message, Windows will display the message (like the one in Figure 8-13) via the WinPopup icon to tell you that your file has been printed. You can read more about the WinPopup icon in the section on sending messages.

Figure 8-13

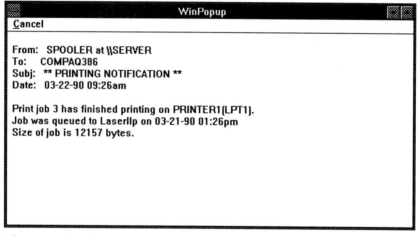

The server displays a message when it prints your document.

Viewing the network queue with Print Manager

As we explained, Windows bypasses Print Manager by default. Since Print Manager enables you to pause a file or stop a file from printing, you won't have these capabilities on the network. However, you'll be able to use Print Manager if, prior to sending the file to the printer, you issue the Network... command on the Options menu in Print Manager and toggle off the Print Net Jobs Direct option in the Network Options dialog box shown in Figure 8-14. When you deselect the Print Net Jobs Direct check box, instead of printing directly to the network, you use Print Manager's functions to print.

Figure 8-14

The Network Options dialog box bypasses Print Manager by default.

Now when you print a file, it will go to Print Manager first and then to the network's print queue. After the file reaches the network, you can look at the print queue to check on the printing progress of your file by choosing the Selected Net Queue... command from the View menu. Print Manager will display a dialog box, like the one shown in Figure 8-15, which displays the selected printer in the title bar and lists all the print jobs currently waiting in line.

Figure 8-15

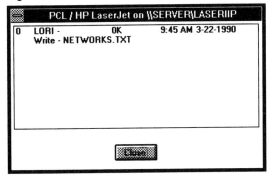

The Selected Net Queue... command displays all the files waiting to print on the network printer to which you're connected.

If you want to look at a print queue for another printer or even for another server's printer to which you're not currently connected (for example, if you have an old job waiting to print), issue the Other Net Queue... command on the View menu to display the Other Net Queue dialog box shown in Figure 8-16. After you enter the printer name in the Network Queue text box, Print Manager will display the queued jobs for that printer. You can find the full printer name via Control Panel's Printers icon. If you click on the Network... button in the Printers dialog box, and then click on Browse..., Control Panel will list the names of the printers connected to the server.

Figure 8-16

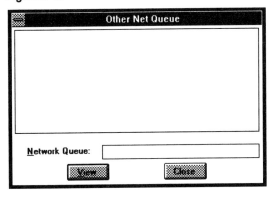

The Other Net Queue dialog box lists print jobs from another network printer.

If you try to look at a network queue with either the Selected Net Queue... or Other Net Queue... commands, but Windows doesn't find the printer (even when you know the name is correct), then the printer either is not responding or isn't connected to the port. The queue of files will appear only if a printer is connected to the port and is functional (turned on and on-line).

Logging off the network

After you've finished using the network for the day and want to disconnect from it entirely, you can either turn off your PC or leave your PC running and log off the network. Turning off your PC is a quick way to tell the network server and its connections to close down—but may cause problems with some networks. A better course of action is to log off the network from the Network window in Control Panel. Simply choose the Logoff command from the Account menu, and Control Panel will disconnect you from the network. Logging off will disconnect any network drive IDs. If you still have network drives connected and you log off, Control Panel will prompt you for verification with a message dialog box like the one in Figure 8-17. After you click on Yes, Control Panel will finish logging you off the network.

Figure 8-17

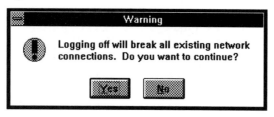

Logging off will break all existing network connections. Do you want to continue?

Control Panel warns you that you'll disconnect any existing network drive connections with this message dialog box.

Remember, when you log off, all the network printer and file commands in Windows will be dimmed and unavailable until you log on to the network again.

SENDING MESSAGES

Control Panel's Network icon comes with a function that allows you to send a message to anyone on the network who is also running Windows and network software. To send a message, select the Send... command on the Message menu from Control Panel's Network application window. In the Send dialog box from the LAN Manager, first enter in the To text box the user name of the person to whom you're sending the message. You don't have to supply your user name to indicate who is sending the message. The network will identify you and supply that information in the Send dialog box. Next, type your message in the Message text box. When you've finished typing, click on Send to transmit the message across the network to the recipient's PC.

You can receive a message at any time with LAN Manager because it installs a message application icon called WinPopup. By default, LAN Manager keeps a WinPopup icon on the desktop to handle the background message functions. When a message arrives, the icon will blink and your PC will beep to indicate you have a message. You'll also see a WinPopup dialog box like the one in Figure 8-18, telling you that you have a message. When you click on OK, the message will appear in a WinPopup application window similar to the one in Figure 8-19. After you've read the message, minimize the window to delete the message, and make room for the next one.

Figure 8-18

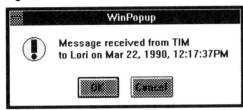

When a message from the network arrives, Windows notifies you with this message dialog box.

Figure 8-19

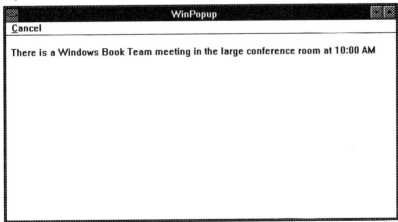

The actual message appears in a WinPopup application window.

Now that you've tested the water, you're ready to dive into the full network capabilities of Windows. Some of these added capabilities include: installing Windows so all your files are automatically stored on your private network drive and all Windows program files are on the server, changing your log-on password, starting applications on the server from the File Manager, and starting applications on the server from the Program Manager.

**DIVING INTO
NETWORKING**

Installing Windows from the server

Instead of using the stand-alone copy of Windows on your PC, you can use the server's copy and keep only the personal files that customize Windows. You can install Windows without disks by using the server as the source for any requests for a disk. (However, the network administrator must copy all the files to the server before you can install Windows on your PC.)

To install Windows from the server, first log on to the network from the DOS prompt, then type *SETUP /N* to install only the files necessary to run the network version of Windows with your PC. Windows will verify the hardware you're using and the applications you want to add to the Windows Applications and Non-Windows Applications group windows. With this type of installation, any defaults you change with Control Panel, such as screen colors or printers, will be kept separate from other network users' preferences in separate files on either your PC or the server.

Changing your password

If your network administrator requires you to change your password periodically (to maintain security), you can use Control Panel's Network icon to enter a new password. After you open Control Panel and activate the Network icon, issue the Change Password... command on the Account menu to display the Change Password dialog box. LAN Manager displays your user name by default. To change a password, first enter the domain in the Change Password at text box (other networks will ask for different information, such as a server name). Next, enter your current password in the Old Password text box, then enter the replacement password in the New Password text box. As you type, Control Panel will display asterisks (*) instead of characters to maintain password security. At this point, the dialog box will look like the one in Figure 8-20. After all the data is correct (and you've noted your new password), click on OK to make the change. LAN Manager will ask you to confirm the new password by entering it into a dialog box one more time.

Figure 8-20

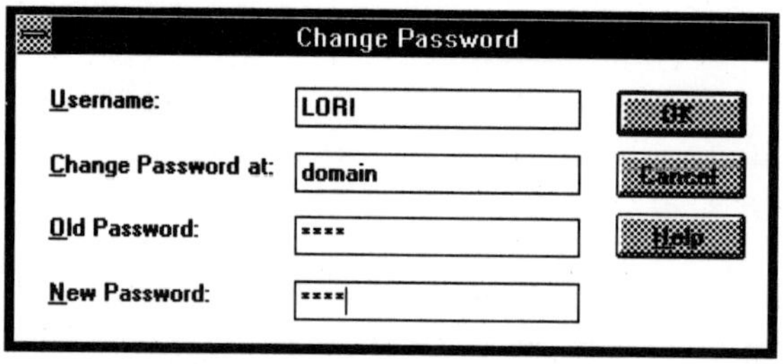

The Change Password dialog box displays your current user name and password, and allows you to enter a new password.

If you forget your password, you'll need to contact your network administrator so he or she can reset it.

The easiest way to dive into network applications is from the File Manager. Connect to the network resource via the Connect Net Drive... command on the Disk menu, then open a directory window for that path. Now all you have to do is double-click on the program file for your application, and Windows will open a full-screen window or an application window in which to run your application. When you exit the application, Windows will return you to the File Manager.

The File Manager as a diving board

For example, if you want to run a network version of Excel from your PC, you can issue the Connect Net Drive... command to display the Connect Network Drive dialog box. You can either leave the drive ID as the default (the next available drive ID) or specify an unused drive ID by clicking on the drop-down arrow and then clicking on a letter. Next, either enter the network path for Excel in the Network Path text box or click on Browse... to select a path from the Network Disk Resources dialog box so the File Manager will enter it for you. If there's a password (if you don't specify one when you should, you won't be able to connect to the network path at all), enter it in the Password text box. Finally, click on OK to establish the network connection.

After the network drive icon appears on the File Manager's Directory Tree, click on it to place a directory icon on the Directory Tree work area. Now double-click on the directory icon to open a directory window for the network path. To launch Excel, scroll through the list of files until you find EXCEL.EXE and then double-click on that file. Since Excel can run in a window, Windows will add an application window to the desktop (on top of the File Manager) for Excel.

If you're running in 386 enhanced mode, all the settings in the 386 Enhanced dialog box on Control Panel will apply to the network applications as well as your PC applications. When you run a network application, the server will load the application's program files into your PC's memory. Therefore, your PC's CPU will do all the work even when you run a network application.

One incentive to develop a thorough understanding of your network commands from the DOS prompt is that with them, you can create shortcuts for launching network applications. The process involves creating a batch file (a file containing a series of commands that you can launch to execute the commands) and an application icon on the Program Manager from which you can launch your network applications.

The Program Manager as a launching pad

The only way to connect and assign a drive ID to a network path consistently is with a batch file. The batch file needs to list the network commands you enter at a DOS prompt to accomplish the connection you made earlier with the File Manager. You can use Notepad to create a batch file—like the one shown in Figure 8-21—to launch Excel. The batch file first connects the \\SERVER\EXCEL path to drive G, then issues a command to change the DOS prompt to that drive ID. Next, it issues the command to start Excel with the program name EXCEL. The next lines clean up by changing the DOS prompt back to C and then disconnecting your PC from the network drive.

Figure 8-21

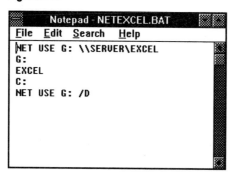

*This batch file, created in Note-
pad, connects to a network drive,
launches Excel and, after you
exit Excel, disconnects from the
network drive.*

To add an application icon for a network application with the Program
Manager's New... command, you must be able to connect to a specific network
resource (server path) with a specific drive ID (these are arbitrarily assigned)
consistently in order to accurately specify the command line. A word of warning:
Each network application you launch must have a unique drive ID. Otherwise,
the next application connecting to the same drive ID will disconnect the previous
path. For instance, you might obliterate your Excel application window if you
launch another application that uses the same drive ID while Excel is still running.
If the application's path isn't marked as read-only, you could damage program and
data files.

**When Windows
can't find your
network**

If your PC can't access the network (for example, because the server is down,
your cable is unattached, or the network software on your PC is damaged),
Windows will display a message dialog box warning you that you can't access the
network. Once you know about the problem, you'll want to disable the warning
so it won't continue reappearing restart Windows to correct the problem. To do
this, select the Don't Display this Warning in the Future check box and click on
OK. After you disable the warning and correct the problem, you'll notice a change
on the Options menu in Control Panel's Networks-LAN Manager window. By
default, the Enable Initial Warning Message command is selected, but when you
disable the message dialog box, you automatically toggle on the Disable Initial
Warning Message command. You'll need to select the Enable Initial Warning
Message command to reset the Options menu so Windows will warn you the next
time it finds a problem when it's establishing network communications.

Section 2

Using Program Manager Applications

In this chapter

Introducing Applications 9

Without applications, your computer would be a useless piece of hardware. For most people, applications are the lifeblood of their computers. Just as compact disks enable you to use your CD player, applications unleash the power of your computer. In essence, an application is simply a program that enables you to accomplish a task with your computer.

You've probably already worked with at least one application. If you use a word processor, you may work with an application like WordPerfect. If you use a spreadsheet, you most likely use an application like Lotus 1-2-3. Windows comes with a number of applications. In fact, all the icons you see shown in Figure 9-1 start applications. In this section of the book, we'll discuss some of Windows' applications, including Write, Paintbrush, Terminal, Recorder, Notepad, Calendar, Cardfile, Calculator, Clock, Reversi, and Solitaire. In this chapter, however, we'll acquaint you with applications in general. We'll present the features of PIF Editor in Chapter 17.

Figure 9-1

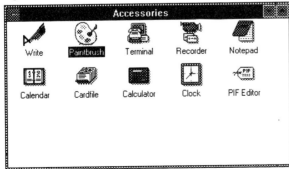

Each icon in the Accessories group window opens an application.

All Windows applications have a few things in common. Windows applications start the same way; and after you open them, you'll see they share similar commands on the menu bar. Furthermore, most of these applications use a data exchange utility called Clipboard to share information between them. (Even non-Windows applications have a few of these common characteristics when you start them from Windows.) In this chapter, we'll identify common characteristics of Windows applications and explain how those elements operate. After you master some basic techniques, you'll be able to apply them to virtually all the applications that you work with in Windows.

First, we'll show you how to launch an application and issue commands. The commands we'll examine open files, edit text, save files, define page layout, and print files. We'll also show you several ways to exit an application. Then, we'll work on such advanced features, as copying data within a document or between applications. In addition, we'll explore the options that change the work area in a window. Finally, we'll discuss running non-Windows applications and explain how you can still share data between Windows and non-Windows applications with Windows' data exchange capabilities.

LAUNCHING APPLICATIONS

The first step in using any application is to start or launch it. The most common place to start an application is from the Program Manager. Simply double-click on the application icon in the Program Manager window to tell Windows to open the application window.

Launching applications without icons

If the application you want to start isn't represented by an icon, you can launch it with the Run... command on Program Manager's File menu. As we showed you in Chapter 5, you need to provide the application's path and program name so Windows knows which application to start. One advantage in starting an application with the Run... command is that you can instruct Windows to open a specific document or graphic file immediately after starting the application. For example, if you use a Write document template for all your memos, you can instruct Windows to start Write and immediately open the memo file. But you'll probably want to use the Run... command to start only applications you use infrequently because you add an extra step or two dealing with a dialog box instead of simply double-clicking an icon.

Launching applications from the File Manager

You can use the File Manager to locate a program file and launch the application. As we showed you in Chapter 6, you can use the Run... command on File Manager's File menu to launch the highlighted file. As a shortcut, simply double-click on the file. If the file is an executable file (that is, one with an *.EXE, *.COM, or *.BAT extension), Windows will run the application and either open a window for it or start it in a DOS session.

You also can use the Open... command on the File menu to launch a DOS application. The Open... command launches the highlighted file, places a DOS icon at the bottom of the desktop, and then converts the screen from a graphical interface into a DOS-like interface with a black screen and a DOS prompt, such as *C:>*. This DOS-like interface is called a full-screen window since Windows is still running while you see the DOS prompt. As an alternative to the full-screen window, some non-Windows applications can operate in a regular application window. In standard mode, an active non-Windows application prohibits your interaction with all other applications. (This barrier is overcome when you run Windows 386 enhanced mode.)

Launching non-Windows applications

If you want to launch a non-Windows application, you can run the application from the DOS Prompt application. DOS Prompt lets you run an application in DOS without exiting Windows. Windows starts a full-screen window for the DOS prompt. At that point, you can use DOS commands to run your application. When you want to return to Windows, simply type *EXIT* at the DOS prompt and press [Enter]. Windows will then terminate the DOS session and return you to Windows.

Creating document icons

If you find yourself using the Run... command often to start an application and open a document simultaneously, you'll want to create an icon for the Program Manager that accomplishes this task for you. As we showed you in Chapter 5, you can use the New... command on the Program Manager's File menu to add a new icon to a group window. In the Program Item Properties dialog box, shown in Figure 9-2, enter the path and start up command into the Command Line text box to start the application, and append the appropriate file name to that command. You also need to enter a title for the icon in the Description text box; we titled ours *Memos*. For example, if you use a memo template document frequently, you can create an icon that, when clicked on, both launches the application and opens the template file.

Figure 9-2

You can add a new icon that starts an application and opens the document you specify.

Issuing commands in a Windows application is as easy as pulling down a menu and selecting a command name. In addition, the consistency in command names that perform the same function throughout the various Windows applica-

ISSUING COMMANDS

tions facilitates your work without testing your recall skills. Windows has even unified the keyboard equivalents that issue commands in the various applications. In Chapter 2, we explained how to issue commands, use keyboard shortcuts, and enter text in dialog boxes.

Opening files

When Windows opens an application window, the application's work area will contain an empty new file by default. If you want to work on an existing file, you will need to use the Open... command on the File menu. The File Open dialog box displays a list of existing files. For example, after you start Write and issue the Open... command, you'll see a list of files like the one in Figure 9-3. All Write's file names have a .WRI extension. (Each application uses a unique file name extension so it can identify its own files.) To open a file, you can either click on an item in the Files list box or type the complete file name with its extension in the Filename text box. When you click OK, Write will open the file.

Figure 9-3

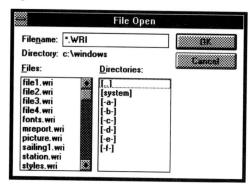

This File Open dialog box lists files you can use in Write.

Listing all the files

If you saved your file without an extension and you don't remember what you named it, all is not lost. Although you can't type the name in the Filename text box, you can direct Windows to display in the Files list box all the files in the current directory. To list all the files, type *.* in the Filename text box and press [Enter]. (The asterisks are wildcards that represent all files with any name and any extension.) Now Windows will display all the files in the current directory, which is noted below the Filename text box, so you can find the file you want.

Using the Directories list box

If you don't find the file you want to open in the current directory, you can use the Directories list box to move to another directory or to a floppy disk to find the file. After you change the directory by clicking on a directory name (or a letter for a drive), Windows will display the files it finds in the active directory. The directories are listed by name. For example, in Write's File Open dialog box shown in Figure 9-3, the subdirectory SYSTEM appears in the Directories list box. The double periods represent the directory one level higher in the directory hierarchy.

The letters below the directories represent the two disk drives (A and B) and the various hard drive volumes or drives (C through F). You'll see a range of letters for drives because a PC can have more than one hard drive, and a hard drive can have more than one 33Mb volume.

To open a new file, you'll use the New command on the File menu. When you issue the New command, Windows will close the current file and place an empty new file in the work area.

Opening a new file

In all Windows applications, you must select text before you can edit it. In this section of the chapter, we'll review the procedures for undoing changes, selecting text, and deleting text through Windows applications. You can refer to Chapter 2 for more details on these procedures.

Editing

The most often-used editing command is the Undo command. Undo is context-sensitive, meaning its name changes depending on the context of your last action. For example, if you accidentally change all the characters in your document to italic and want to undo the change, the Undo command becomes Undo Formatting. The name change lets you know what action Undo can reverse, in this case, the formatting. If an application can't undo your last action, the Undo command appears in inverse video. Note that Undo's versatility has two major limitations—you may undo only your last action, and some actions are irreversible.

Using Undo

Selecting text works much the same way throughout the applications, including selecting text in text boxes. To select text, click on the character or place you want to start, then drag to the last character or ending position of your selection and release the mouse button. The selected characters will appear in inverse video. In other words, they're highlighted.

Selecting text

You can use either the [Delete] or [Backspace] key to delete characters in a document or in a text box. The [Delete] key deletes the character to the right of the cursor. The [Backspace] key deletes the character to the left of the cursor. If you want to replace the text in a text box, you can either delete the characters one at a time, or you can highlight all the text and then press [Delete] to delete all the characters at once. If you highlight the text and then begin typing, your new text will immediately replace the old.

Deleting text

Windows provides several ways to save a file. As you may know, to save a file, select the Save or Save As... command from the File menu. The first time you save an untitled file—whether you select Save or Save As...—you'll see the Save As dialog box shown in Figure 9-4. Once you have assigned a name to a file, however, you can bypass this dialog box by issuing the Save command to save the file, along with any changes you've made, under its original name.

Saving files

Figure 9-4

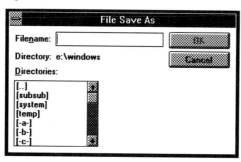

The File Save As dialog box prompts you for a file name for the document.

The first thing you need to tell Windows is where you want to store the file, using the Directories list box. Once you decide where you want to store your file, you must provide Windows with a name for the file. If you don't give the file name an extension, the application will add one for you. The application adds an extension that associates the file with the application. For example, Notepad adds a .TXT extension while Write adds a .WRI extension. Remember, you can have up to eight characters in a file name. After you have entered the file name, click on OK to save the file.

Later, if you want to save the file under a different name, you can use the Save As... command to enter another file name. You'll want to use this technique if you work with templates. For example, if you use a memo in Write as a template, you won't want to overwrite the file every time you create a new memo. You can save the altered memo with a new file name and leave your original template intact.

If you want to delete a file, you must use the File Manager, which we discussed in Chapter 6.

Printing

You'll probably want to print the documents you create in Windows applications. In most applications, this multistep process includes setting up your page layout, setting up your printer, and issuing the Print command.

Setting page layout

If an application doesn't have its own unique commands for letting you adjust the page margins (as Write does), the File menu offers a Page Setup... command that lets you specify margin settings as well as create headers and footers. When you choose the Page Setup... command, a Page Setup dialog box like the one in Figure 9-5 appears. This dialog box has a text box for the header and one for the footer. The Margins section has four text boxes to set the left, right, top, and bottom margins.

Figure 9-5

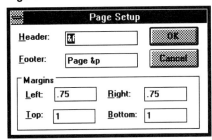

The Page Setup dialog box sets headers, footers, and margins.

Setting margins

Windows formats the text in a document to conform to the margins specified in the Page Setup dialog box. By default, the top and bottom margins are 1" and the left and right margins are .75". To change a margin setting, simply highlight the old margin setting and type the new setting. Windows will accept any whole number for a margin. If you enter a fraction, like $^3/_4$, Windows will warn you with a message dialog box that it can't use that number. Windows will, however, accept a decimal value, like .75".

As you set your margins, keep the limitations of your printer in mind. If you set the document's left and right margins to .25", but your printer's default minimum margin is .5", your text will be truncated on the left and right margins.

Creating headers and footers

You tell Windows what text you want to use for a header and footer in the Header and Footer text boxes of the Page Setup dialog box. The header and footer will always appear .75" from the edge of the page, so be careful not to set your top or bottom margin less than .75". Otherwise, your document text will overlap your header.

To enter text for a header or footer, click in the Header or Footer text box. A cursor will appear and you can begin typing. If there is text in the text box already, highlight it and then begin typing. That way, the new text will replace the old text.

Windows will help you create and format your header and footer text. If you're using Windows' built-in applications, you can use special codes made up of an & (ampersand) and a letter to insert header or footer text or change its alignment. Table 9-1 lists the codes for header and footer entries. To enter a code for a header or footer, click in the Header or Footer text box and type a code. For example, if you want to print a page number on the bottom of each page, and you want the word *Page* to appear next to the number, you would enter *Page &p* in the Footer text box.

Table 9-1

Code	Function
&c	Centers the header or footer
&d	Prints the system date
&f	Prints the active file name
&l	Left-aligns the header or footer
&p	Prints the page numbers
&r	Right-aligns the header or footer
&t	Prints the system time

You can use these codes to tell Windows to supply header and footer information and to format headers and footers.

Setting up your printer

Since Windows allows you to install more than one printer, you need to choose the printer you're going to use. When you issue the Printer Setup... command, you'll see a Printer Setup dialog box like the one shown in Figure 9-6. From the list of installed printers in the Printer list box, simply select the one you want to use and then choose OK.

Figure 9-6

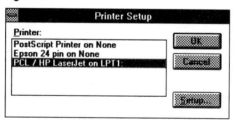

The Printer Setup dialog box lists the installed printers.

If the printer you want to use is not assigned a device name (LPT1, COM1, etc.), you must use the Control Panel to assign one. Chapter 3 shows you how to do this.

If you want to change any of the default printer settings, such as page orientation (Portrait or Landscape) or the number of copies, you'll need to click on the Setup... button to display the printer options in a dialog box. If, for example, you want to print three copies of a Landscape-oriented spreadsheet on an HP LaserJet printer, you need to choose the PCL/HP LaserJet on LPT1: selection in the Printer list box and click on the Setup... button. When Windows displays the PCL/HP LaserJet on LPT1: dialog box, you can click on the Landscape radio button and enter the number of copies in the Copies text box. After you've made the changes, click on OK to return to the Printer Setup dialog box. Now click on OK again to return to your document.

To send a document to the printer, simply select the Print command on the File menu. The application will display a dialog box showing that the file is being sent to the printer. Next, the Print Manager icon will appear on the desktop. At this point, you can resume working with your application while the Print Manager handles the printing of your file in the background. After the Print Manager sends the entire file to the printer, its icon will disappear from the desktop. If something goes wrong while you're printing (for example, the paper runs out), then the Print Manager will alert you to the problem with a warning dialog box. After you resolve the problem, you'll need to access the Print Manager to resume printing. Chapter 7 explains how to resume printing with the Print Manager.

Issuing the Print command

As we explained in Chapter 2, it's always better to exit with the Exit command on the File menu instead of using the Close command on the Control menu. The Close command will remove the application from the desktop, but it won't clear the application from your PC's memory or, in some cases, save the file.

Exiting applications

Windows makes it easy for you to share data between applications. With Clipboard, you can cut or copy data from one application and paste it into another. If you want to establish a dynamic link between two applications, you can do so by using Windows' dynamic data exchange (DDE) facility. DDE enables Windows to update data in one application with data that has changed in another application.

SHARING DATA

Clipboard is a storage area for information copied or cut from any Windows application. The information in Clipboard can be retrieved by most Windows applications. The information can be text, a Paintbrush graphic, or even a screen capture. For text and graphics, you'll need to use the Cut, Copy, and Paste commands on the Edit menu. For screen captures, you'll use the [Print Screen] and [Alt][Print Screen] keys. All the information passing between applications occurs invisibly. Unlike the Print Manager, Clipboard's icon doesn't appear on the desktop when it is in use. However, you can double-click on Clipboard's icon to open Clipboard and view the data in its memory.

Using Clipboard

Clipboard can hold only one item at a time. Therefore, if you copy text to Clipboard without pasting it somewhere and then cut or copy a graphic, Clipboard will replace the text with the graphic. You'll have to copy the text again before you can paste it. Windows imposes no specific limits on the length of text you may cut or copy to Clipboard in one operation.

Moving text and graphics within an application is the most common use of Clipboard. To move text, highlight it, then issue the Cut command on the Edit menu. Now position the cursor in the place you want to move the text and choose the Paste command. Windows will insert the text at the cursor position. For more information about editing text, see Chapter 10.

Moving text and graphics

Moving graphics is similar to moving text. First, select the graphic and then choose Cut. Next, position the cursor in the new location and choose Paste. Windows will insert the graphic at the cursor position. Moving graphics can be more involved in Paintbrush than in other applications because you have more options. Chapter 11 provides details about moving graphics in Paintbrush.

Copying text and graphics

You'll probably want to copy text nearly as often as you want to move it. Unlike cutting text, copying text provides a safety net in case you change your mind and want to leave the selected text in its original location. Copying also provides an easy way to repeat a phrase, such as a product or company name, throughout a document. To copy text, just highlight it and then choose the Copy command on the Edit menu. Whenever you want to insert the copied text, just issue the Paste command. You can continue to paste that text as many times and in as many locations as you like until you replace it on Clipboard with something else by using the Copy or Cut command again.

Sharing text and graphics between applications

Windows lets you share data between applications or documents by activating the appropriate application and opening the destination document (the document to which you'll add text) before you issue the Paste command. For example, you might want to copy a company name and address from your Cardfile phone number file and use it in a business letter in Write. To begin the transfer, you need to first open Cardfile, highlight the data on the card, then issue the Copy command. Next, return to the Program Manager (remember, you can minimize or resize Cardfile's application window so you can use the Program Manager window) and start Write. When Write's application window appears, open the business letter and issue the Paste command to insert the address at the cursor position.

Capturing screens

Windows can copy the current screen or active window to Clipboard. This capability is handy for creating presentations about software or about data the software displays. To capture the entire desktop, press the [Print Screen] key. To capture only the active window, press [Alt][Print Screen]. Now you can paste the screen as a graphic into another application, like Paintbrush, so you can print it. (You may want to edit the screen in Paintbrush before you print it.)

If, for example, you need to teach your co-workers how to calculate the budget using Excel, you could illustrate each step with a figure. The figure would include the active Excel window and a caption. To create the figure, you need to arrange the spreadsheet the way you want it, then press [Alt][Print Screen] to capture the active window into Clipboard. Later, you can use Paintbrush to paste the screens from Clipboard into a file and then print or modify the screens.

You can open the Clipboard application icon on the Main group window to view the data on Clipboard or change some of the default settings. Figure 9-7 shows the Clipboard application window after we copied some data. By default, the application's work area always displays scroll bars.

Figure 9-7

The Clipboard application window has a large work area to display the data in memory.

The Display menu lets you choose a format for displayed data. By default, the Display menu uses the Auto command, which automatically selects a data format for you that best fits the data. The Auto command chooses an ASCII text format (characters with no formatting codes) for any text and the bitmap format for any graphics. OEM (Original Equipment Manufacturer) and Owner Display (original application's screen font) are the two data formats that use characters with formatting which you need to specifically select. You would choose the OEM text command from the Display menu if you wanted to retain font information and other formatting when you are pasting information between compatible applications. However, if two applications aren't compatible because they don't use the same kind of data files, such as Word for Windows and Micropro's WordStar, then you'll need to specify Auto loading to use the ASCII text format to establish a common meeting ground.

Choosing a data format

If you want to delete the data in Clipboard's memory so you can make that memory available for your applications, you need to open Clipboard and use the Delete command on the Edit menu. Choosing the Delete command or pressing the [Delete] key will clear the work area and Clipboard's memory.

Clearing the work area

If you want to save the data in Clipboard before you clear the work area, you can issue the Save As... command on the File menu. The File Save As dialog box, shown in Figure 9-8, will appear with the file name DEFAULT.CLP displayed in the Filename text box. Clipboard will save any file with a default .CLP extension

Saving the data in a Clipboard file

if you don't specify a file name extension. Note that you can save Clipboard data to another application by pasting the data into the application's work area and then issuing the application's Save command.

Figure 9-8

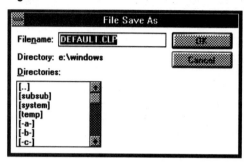

Clipboard's File Save As dialog box displays the default file name.

Opening Clipboard files

If you have a favorite graphic or a commonly used address, you can copy it to Clipboard from its originating application and save it as a Clipboard file. That way, you can use the Open... command to reopen the file and place the data back onto Clipboard, and then you'll be ready to paste it into an application's document. To open a Clipboard file, choose the Open... command from the File menu to display the File Open dialog box. You can use this dialog box as you do any of the Open dialog boxes for other applications. Simply click on a file in the Files list box and then click on OK to open the file and place the data in Clipboard's work area and memory.

Exiting Clipboard's application window

To exit from Clipboard's application window, choose the Exit command from the File menu. Clipboard will not prompt you to save your changes with a warning dialog box; it simply will close the application window. Therefore, if you want to save the displayed data in a file, make sure you issue the Save As... command before exiting Clipboard.

Using DDE

One of Windows' most exciting features is its ability to perform dynamic data exchange (DDE), because with DOS you cannot dynamically exchange data. In DOS, you must work in one application, close it, then start the next one. With Windows, however, you can load multiple applications and allow them to dynamically exchange data. That is, data that changes in one application will change in the other.

To illustrate how DDE works, let's suppose you create a summary report in Word for Windows that garners information from an Excel spreadsheet. You need to copy all the pertinent information from the spreadsheet into your Word document. Without DDE, you would either have to print the spreadsheet and type in the information, or copy and paste the data into your Word document with Edit commands. If some of the data in your report changes, you would have to recalculate and print the spreadsheet again and copy and paste the correct information into your summary document in Word. Wouldn't it be nice to eliminate some of these steps and still ensure the accuracy of your reports?

Let's repeat our scenario using DDE. Suppose you completed all your statistics in Excel and are creating a summary report in Word for Windows. You can link data in the Excel spreadsheet to the Word report. That way, any time the data in the Excel spreadsheet changes, Windows will update the numbers that appear in the Word report with the new values. In other words, the DDE acts as a conduit for the updating process.

In order to facilitate DDE, Windows reserves a special area of your computer's memory to store the data that is dynamically exchanged between applications. Windows monitors that area of memory and, as soon as the data in that region of memory changes, automatically updates the data file of the application receiving the data. When the transfer is complete, Windows deletes the data from memory.

How does DDE really work ?

Global memory is allocated in chunks of 64Kb or 128Kb. This means that DDE can be used in real mode with the 640Kb of DOS memory, as long as there's enough left over from the applications. DDE is more feasible if you use it with extended memory (which is beyond 1Mb), if your computer has at least 2Mb of memory, and if you are running Windows in either standard or 386 enhanced mode. If you are running Windows in 386 enhanced mode, Windows even provides virtual memory (swap disk) to accommodate DDE requests.

To use DDE, you tell an application to retrieve data from another application with commands unique to each application. You need to supply the name of the source application (the application that will supply the information) and the name of that application's data file. Windows supplies the format of the data involved. Like the Clipboard, DDE transfers data as ASCII text, bitmap graphics, and OEM text. As you might expect, individual applications provide their own techniques for making DDE requests.

After the receiving application requests the data, the source application places the data in the special area of memory and marks that memory location with a DDE handle. Windows immediately locks that memory location so other data can't be written there. The receiving application looks for that handle and retrieves the data. Afterward, Windows unlocks the memory and deletes the data.

A hot link tells the source application to automatically update the data in the receiving application as soon as linked data changes. On the other hand, a warm link updates data only when the receiving application (or user) approves the transfer. (By the way, a cold link is simply unchanging data, the kind of data that is pasted with Clipboard.)

Why use DDE?

The best feature of DDE is that the source application does all the hard work in the background while you write your report. For example, if you are downloading stock reports from a bulletin board service with Crosstalk (the source application) to an Excel spreadsheet (the receiving application) that calculates trends and charts the data, then Excel can continuously update the chart (with a hot link) as it receives new information. In turn, the chart is part of a Word for Windows summary report linked to Excel. Therefore, as the stock information changes in Crosstalk, Crosstalk updates Excel and Excel updates Word for Windows. Not only is the report going to be accurate, it will be timely.

ALTERING THE WORK AREA

As you use the various Windows applications, you'll notice that several menu bars have a View menu. The View menu doesn't work with files or the data in the work area as the other menus do; instead, it works with the work area itself. In Calculator, the View menu lets you switch between two calculators, standard and scientific. As you can see, the View menu has different commands for different applications but performs a common function—changing the work area. Of course, some applications, like Notepad, will not have a View menu since their work areas cannot be changed.

USING NON-WINDOWS APPLICATIONS

If you're very fortunate, all the applications that you'll use with Windows will be designed to work in Windows. Realistically, you'll probably need to use at least one non-Windows application to get your job done. Windows enables you to run non-Windows applications and, in some cases, even lets you share data between non-Windows and Windows applications via Clipboard.

You can launch a non-Windows application with the DOS Prompt icon in the Main group window as we showed you earlier in this chapter. Additionally, you can use the Run... command from either the Program Manager or the File Manager. The File Manager provides two additional ways to open a non-Windows application. You can issue the Open... command or simply double-click on the application's name to launch the application.

The best way to use a non-Windows application with Windows is to manually set the memory and other program options in a PIF (Program Information File). Windows automatically checks for a PIF when it starts an application. If Windows doesn't find one, it uses its default PIF. You can read more about PIFs and their settings in Chapter 17.

If you run Windows in real or standard mode, non-Windows applications will run full-screen and suspend the running of all other applications. However, you can switch to any other application by using the Task Manager, which we introduced in Chapter 2. To access the Task Manager while running a full-screen, non-Windows application, simply press [Ctrl][Esc] and Windows will display the Task List dialog box. After you click on the name of the window you'd like to switch to, Windows will display a *Switching...* message on the screen. When Windows displays the desktop, the non-Windows application will appear as a minimized application icon. While an icon, the non-Windows application is on hold or paused. You can return to the non-Windows application by double-clicking on the icon.

In Windows 386 enhanced mode, non-Windows applications may run in a window with a Control menu and run concurrently with other applications. In fact, the non-Windows application continues running while minimized into an icon.

If you want to transfer information from a non-Windows application to another application (either Windows or non-Windows), you can use the 386 Edit commands. You'll find these commands on the Control menu of a non-Windows application window only if you're running 386 enhanced mode. When you click on the Control menu, you'll see a menu like the one in Figure 9-9. To copy data to Clipboard, choose the Edit cascading menu to display the 386 Edit commands also shown in Figure 9-9. Note that you can't copy graphics to non-Windows applications—just text. The Mark command allows you to select information to copy onto Clipboard. The Copy command, of course, copies the selected information. The Paste command inserts the contents of Clipboard in the application at the cursor position. The Scroll command moves the application work area so you can copy the next screenful of information.

Using the 386 Edit commands

Figure 9-9

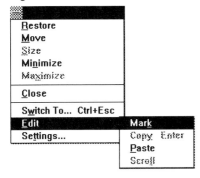

You can copy text from non-Windows applications to the Clipboard using commands on the 386 Edit menu.

If you're running Windows in standard mode, check to see if the Windows application supports the Control menu by pressing [Alt][Spacebar] to open it. If the Control menu doesn't appear, then the editing commands are not available. You can access the Task Manager even if you can't open a Control menu.

When you're working with a full-screen application, you can copy only the entire screen onto Clipboard. You can't select information; it's all or nothing. You can press [Print Screen] to copy the current screen onto Clipboard.

Even though you can place information onto Clipboard, you may not always be able to paste it into another application. The destination application must be able to accept the data in the original format (such as ASCII text or OEM).

In this chapter

Using Write **10**

*W*hat would you do without a word processor? Fortunately, Windows has one built in, called Write. In this chapter, we'll describe the anatomy and basics of Write, discuss formatting and editing, and show you how to add graphics to your documents. At the end of the chapter, we'll demonstrate how Write handles files, printing, and page layout.

Write is an application that will let you create, edit, print, and save documents. Write can also import text and graphics from other applications, and you can save Write documents in a form that other applications understand.

WRITE

Starting Write

To start Write, just double-click on the Write icon in the Accessories group window within the Program Manager. Windows will bring up an application window for Write, complete with a menu bar and the other controls associated with an application. As you can see, this application window has a work area for a document instead of separate document windows because Write is incapable of using document windows. You'll see separate document windows in other, more powerful Windows-based applications, such as Word for Windows or Excel.

However, you can create the effect of having multiple documents open on your desktop. When you want to work with another document as well as the one already on the desktop, you need to return to the Program Manager and start Write again. In the additional Write window, you can start the new document. At that point, you'll have two copies of Write on the desktop—each with different documents. We'll show you how to copy information between these two documents later in this chapter.

**The Write
application
window**

The Write application window in Figure 10-1 appears when you start Write. It has all the basic elements of an application window: a title bar, Control menu, Minimize and Maximize boxes, menu bar, scroll bars, and a size-adjustable frame. In addition to the basic elements, Write features a page status bar at the bottom of the window to the left of the horizontal scroll bar. This area will indicate the current location of the cursor. The work area is the major part of the window and contains the end-of-file marker, the cursor, and the page-break marker. The icon next to the cursor is the end-of-file marker, which automatically appears at the end of your text. The page-break marker, which looks like a right-pointing chevron, will appear in the work area when you issue the Repaginate... command. Later, when we talk about pagination, we will show you how to insert page breaks in your document.

Figure 10-1

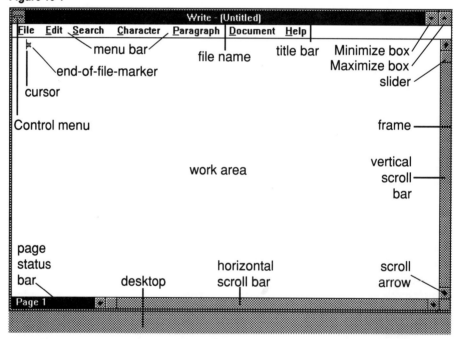

The Write application window has all the standard window elements plus a page status bar.

The ruler

The ruler is one of the features Write provides to make your work easier. To display the ruler, choose the Ruler On command from the Document menu. Figure 10-2 shows how the ruler will appear on the screen. Since the Ruler On command works like a toggle switch, after you display the ruler, the Ruler On command name will change to Ruler Off.

Figure 10-2

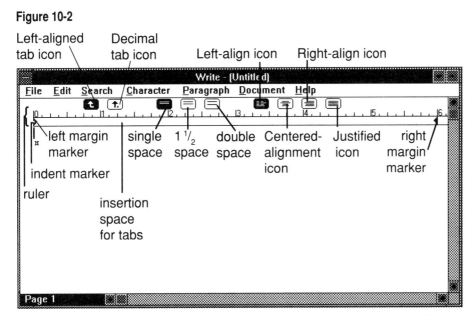

You can add a ruler to the window by choosing the Ruler On command from the document menu.

As you can see in Figure 10-2, the ruler contains nine icons that are organized into three functional groups: tab icons, spacing icons, and alignment icons. We'll show you how to use these icons to format paragraphs later in this chapter.

The ruler's scale displays inches or centimeters, depending on the settings you choose with the Page Layout... command on the Document menu. By default, the ruler display is set for inches. Figure 10-3 on the next page shows a metric version of the ruler. Below the scale on both versions of the ruler is an open line where you can place the tab, indent, and margin markers. The tab markers look just like the graphics on the tab icons. The indent marker is a dot embedded in the left margin marker and controls the indention of the first line of a paragraph. The opposing triangles under the ruler are the left and right margin markers.

It's a good idea to turn on the ruler whenever you use Write. The only time you might not want to use the ruler is if you need more space to display your document. For instance, if you are working on a table or are trying to place a large graphic, you may need more of the work area.

WRITE BASICS

In order to create a document with Write, you need to master a few basic skills. Specifically, you need to know how to enter text, navigate through your document, select text, and edit your work. After you learn these basics, you'll be ready for the section on formatting.

Figure 10-3

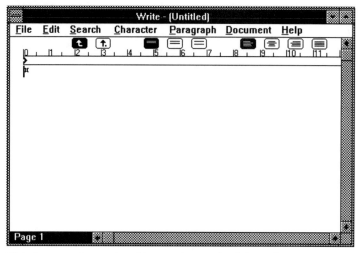

This is a metric version (in centimeters) of the ruler.

Entering text

As you type, Write will enter the text into your untitled document. Write displays the text as it will appear on a printed page. This is commonly referred to as WYSIWYG (What You See Is What You Get).

Entering text in Write is actually easier than typing text on a typewriter. A special facility called Word Wrap lets you type a constant stream of characters without having to use carriage returns at the end of each line. If you are new to word processing, you may be tempted to press the [Enter] key as you approach the end of a line of text in order to move to the next line. Not to worry—if there is not enough room for the word you are typing on the current line, Write will move that word to the beginning of the next line automatically.

In fact, the only time you will need to press the [Enter] key as you enter text in Write is when you want to start a new paragraph. You can hinder significantly your editing and formatting capabilities by placing carriage returns at the end of each line. If you decide later to insert or delete text or change your margins, you'll have to edit each line manually in order to reset your line breaks. If you let Word Wrap handle this task for you, you can change the content, format, and layout of your document, and Write will automatically reflow the text for you.

The text you enter into a document will appear at the cursor (blinking vertical line). If you want to enter text in another part of your document, you need to move the cursor. To do this, move the pointer (which looks like an I-beam) to the new location and click. The cursor will then move to that spot. At that point, you can begin entering more text.

Navigation

As you polish the documents you create in Write, you'll need to move the cursor to edit the text. In Table 10-1, you'll find a description of keyboard shortcuts you can use to move the cursor quickly through the text of your document. For example, to move the cursor to the top of the document, press [Ctrl][Home]. Holding down any of the key combinations (continuous selection) listed in Table 10-1 will repeat the function until you release the key(s). For example, if you want to advance the cursor a word at a time continuously until you reach the correct one, simply hold down the [Ctrl]➡ keys. In the table, the [Goto] key is the number 5 key on your keyboard's numeric keypad.

Table 10-1

Keystroke	Movement	Keystroke	Movement
↑	Up one line	[Goto]➡	Next sentence
↓	Down one line	[Goto]⬅	Previous sentence
➡	Right one character	[Goto]↓	Next paragraph
⬅	Left one character	[Goto]↑	Previous paragraph
[Ctrl]➡	Right one word	[Goto][Page Up]	Previous page
[Ctrl]⬅	Left one word	[Goto][Page Down]	Next page
[Home]	Go to beginning of line	[Page Down]	Down one window
[End]	Go to end of line	[Ctrl][Home]	Go to beginning of document
[Page Up]	Up one window	[Ctrl][End]	Go to end of document

These key combinations provide shortcuts for navigating in your document.

Not only can you use key combinations to move through your document, you can also use the Go To Page... command on the Search menu or the accelerator key ([F4]) to move to a different page. But before selecting the Go To Page... command, you must use the Repaginate... command on the File menu to repaginate your document. After you add text to your document, you must issue the Repaginate... command to update the page numbering. After all the pages have numbers, the Go To Page... command will then be able to access the page you specify. Remember, you only need to re-issue the Repaginate... command when you add new text that will change the page numbers. (We'll show you how to use the Repaginate... command later in this chapter.) When you select the Go To Page... command from the Search menu, the Go To dialog box in Figure 10-4 will appear. To designate the page you want to move to, just type the page number, and click on OK. Write will then move the cursor to the top of that page. However, if you haven't repaginated the document, then any page number you enter in the Go To dialog box will return you to the beginning of the document.

Figure 10-4

To move to another page, enter the page number in the Go To dialog box, and click OK.

Selecting text

You can manipulate or edit large parts of your document while leaving the rest alone. To do this, select only the text you want to edit, format, or move. To select text, just drag the I-beam pointer over the text you want. As you select the text, Write will highlight it (that is, Write will display it in inverse video). You can highlight only one block of text at a time. As soon as you click somewhere else, Write will remove the highlight from the selected text.

If you want to highlight an entire line, move the pointer to the selection bar (on the far left side of the work area) until it changes to a standard arrow pointer. If you click once, you will highlight the line next to the pointer. If you click and drag down, you will highlight multiple lines of text. If you double-click in the selection bar, you will highlight the entire paragraph. If you hold down the [Ctrl] key and click once in the selection bar, you will select the entire document.

Of course, if you need to select a large block of text and not the entire document, you might find it tiresome to drag through line after line of text. Another technique for selecting text is with the [Shift] key. For example, suppose you want to highlight all the text in Figure 10-5 beginning with the words *Wind brushed* in line 4 of the first paragraph and ending with *seat compartments* in line 7 of the second paragraph. Begin by clicking just to the left of the word *Wind*, then hold down the [Shift] key and click just to the right of the period that follows the word *compartments*. Figure 10-6 shows the results.

If you prefer using just the keyboard, you can refer to Table 10-2 on page 212 for the appropriate keystrokes to select text in your document. These keystrokes are also good shortcuts for large-block selections. For example, [Ctrl][Shift][Home] selects all the text from the cursor to the beginning of the document.

Figure 10-5

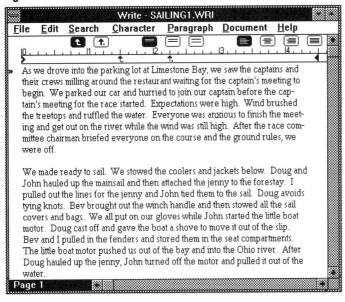

You can use your mouse and the [Shift] key to select a block of text.

Figure 10-6

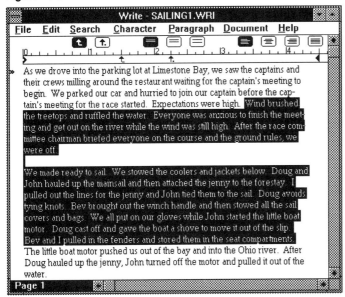

This is the same document with the text selected.

Table 10-2

The Keystroke...	Selects...
[Shift]←, [Shift]→	one character to the left or right. If the character is already selected, and you move back over it, the selection will be cancelled.
[Shift]↑, [Shift]↓	one line of text up or down. [Shift]↓ selects the current line, and then subsequent lines when you repeat the keystroke. If the line is already selected, moving over it again will cancel the selection.
[Shift][Page Up]	text up one window. Repeating the keystroke over the same area cancels the selection.
[Shift][Page Down]	text down one window. Repeating the keystroke over the same area cancels the selection.
[Shift][Home]	text to the beginning of the line.
[Shift][End]	text to the end of the line.
[Ctrl][Shift]←	previous word.
[Ctrl][Shift]→	next word.
[Ctrl][Shift][Home]	text to the beginning of the document.
[Ctrl][Shift][End]	text to the end of the document.

You can use these key combinations to select text.

Basic editing techniques

You can replace or remove one character or a selected block of text at a time. To replace text, first highlight the old text and then begin typing to replace it with new text. The [Backspace] and [Delete] keys remove text. The [Backspace] key removes text to the left of the cursor. The [Delete] key removes text to the right of the cursor. If you press [Backspace] or [Delete] while text is highlighted, Write will delete all the highlighted text.

If you delete something accidentally, you can use the Undo command on the Edit menu to recover deleted text. The Undo command is context-sensitive. For example, when you press the [Backspace] key to delete a word, the command becomes Undo Editing. When you press [Enter] for a paragraph, the Undo command changes to Undo Typing. If the command is simply Undo, then the last command or action will be reversed. The accelerator keys to undo an action are [Alt][Backspace].

Table 10-3 summarizes the basic editing keys. They include the [Backspace] and [Delete] keys and the accelerator keys for the Edit menu commands.

Table 10-3

Keystroke	Function
[Backspace]	Deletes a character to the left of the cursor. It will also delete selected text.
[Delete]	Deletes a character to the right of the cursor. It will also delete selected text.
[Alt][Backspace]	Undoes the previous editing command or function.
[Shift][Delete]	Deletes the selected text and places it on the Clipboard.
[Ctrl][Insert]	Copies selected text onto the Clipboard.
[Shift][Insert]	Inserts, or pastes, text from the Clipboard into your document at the cursor.

You can use these key combinations to edit your document.

FORMATTING

You can enliven and clarify your text with Write's formatting capabilities. For instance, you can enhance your document by centering and boldfacing a title at the beginning of an article or italicizing a book title in a report. You can format characters, paragraphs, or pages. In this section, we'll show you how to change character styles, fonts, and point sizes. Then, we'll teach you how to use optional hyphens, add and delete paragraph breaks, set alignment, choose spacing, set up indention, and set up tabs. Finally, we'll go over page formatting, which includes pagination and creating headers and footers.

Character formatting

You can choose a character format before you begin typing or for highlighted text. Characters can be formatted for style, font, and point size. For example, the default for Write is a *Normal* style, Courier 10-point font (not italic, bold, etc.).

Using styles

Character styles can add emphasis to your text. For example, you can use the italic style for a book title. You can make a character bold, italic, underlined, superscripted, subscripted, or any combination of the above. Figure 10-7 shows a sample of each style. A style is linked to a paragraph or a character. Write's Character menu will display check marks beside the active styles of selected text. To turn off a style, open the Character menu, then select the style again to toggle off the check mark.

Figure 10-7

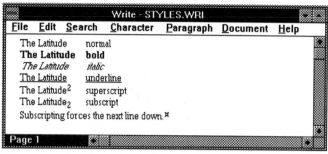

Write provides these character styles.

If you want to start typing text in a new style of type, make your choices on the Character menu, and resume typing. The new text you enter will be in the new style and will continue in that style until you change it with the Character menu again.

You can change the style of a selected block of text by highlighting the text and choosing the style from the Character menu. Only the text in the highlighted area will change.

You can turn off all the styles in the selected text by choosing Normal on the Character menu. This option is especially helpful if you have more than one style active. You can simply select Normal and cancel all special formatting instructions.

You can use accelerator keys for the Normal, Bold, Italic, and Underline commands on the Character menu. To select Normal, press [F5]. To select Bold, Italic, or Underline, press [Crtl]B, [Crtl]I, or [Ctrl]U, respectively.

When you use the Superscript and Subscript commands, Write has to make room between lines for the superscripted or subscripted characters. Write compensates by changing the space (or leading) between the line above and below the superscripted character. Lines 5 and 6 in Figure 10-7 show how Write adjusts the line spacing to accommodate these characters.

Using fonts

In addition to style, the Character menu lets you choose the font you want to use. Below the list of styles is a numbered list of fonts. For example, if you install an HP LaserJet printer during installation and make it the active printer, you might be able to choose from these HP LaserJet fonts: Courier, Helvetica, LinePrinter, Modern, Roman, Script, and Times Roman. Figure 10-8 provides a sample of each font. However, by default, Write will display Courier, LinePrinter, and Roman on the Character menu. It is important to note that Write will display only three fonts on the Character menu at a time.

Figure 10-8

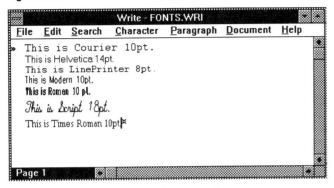

The HP LaserJet setup provides seven fonts.

You will use the same technique to apply a font that you use for a style. You can select a font for new text or change a block of text to a selected font. You can even have multiple fonts on a page. You can switch fonts any time by selecting a new font from the Character menu and resuming typing. The text you type from that point on will reflect your new font choice. If you want to change existing text to a new font, highlight the text, and choose a new font from the Character menu.

Sometimes your printer will have a larger font repertoire than Write. If you choose a font for your printer that Write doesn't have, then Write will substitute a screen font that will approximate the printer font you chose. Write will use the same spacing for the screen text as the printer will use for its output. That way, you'll have a better idea of how the page will look, and how to set your tabs and spacing to achieve the desired formatting.

Adding fonts to the Character menu

The Character menu displays only three fonts. If you want to use a font that isn't on the menu, you can use the Fonts... command to select one of the others. Write will place the font on the Character menu.

Changing the font point size

You can change the point size of a font in one of three ways. First, you can change the font point size with the Reduce Font and Enlarge Font commands on the Character menu. After you select the text you want to size, you can use the Reduce Font or Enlarge Font command to adjust the point size by 2 points. If the screen font doesn't change, that means the printer doesn't support that point size. If you use the Reduce Font and Enlarge Font commands repeatedly and don't remember the final point size, you can check the highlighted text by using the Fonts... command to bring up the Fonts dialog box and check the current size in the Point Size text box.

The second way to change the point size of your text is to use the Sizes list box in the Fonts dialog box, as shown in Figure 10-9. To do this, highlight the text, and choose the Fonts... command from the Character menu. Click on the font you want to use, and then click on the desired point size in the Sizes list box. The Point Size text box will change to match your selection.

Figure 10-9

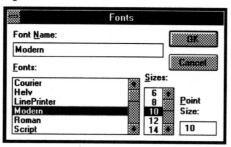

The Fonts dialog box allows you to choose a font and its point size.

Finally, you can change the text point size by entering the size in the Point Size box in the Fonts dialog box. Again, highlight your text, and choose the Fonts... command from the Character menu. Click on the font you want to use, then click on the Point Size text box, and type in the new size. Remember, if this size doesn't match one that is listed in the Sizes box, the printer can't print it.

Using optional hyphens

As you type, Write will wrap the text to fit the margins so you don't have to keep pressing [Enter]. Sometimes Write will have to wrap a long word that doesn't quite fit in the rest of the space on a line. When the word moves to the next line, it can leave a large empty space on the line above. If you want to reduce the white space or smooth a jagged right margin, you can insert an optional hyphen in a word. Optional hyphens will show up only if the word needs to be wrapped to the next line. To insert an optional hyphen in a word, position the pointer in the word where the hyphen should appear, and click to move the cursor there. Then, to add the hyphen, press [Ctrl][Shift]-.

Of course, you can also use a regular hyphen. If your line ends abruptly, you can fill it with part of a word from the following line. Just insert a hyphen between syllables as you do when typing. Write will move the letters before the hyphen to the previous line, if they fit. If they don't fit, then they won't move until you reposition the hyphen so fewer letters move to the previous line. Figure 10-10 shows a paragraph with regular hyphens. Be careful when you use regular hyphens. The hyphen may show up in the middle of a line if you edit the document and change the spacing.

Figure 10-10

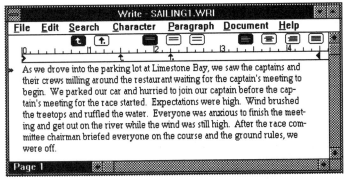

Some of the lines in this document end with hyphenated words.

Paragraph formatting creates the overall look or design of your document. You can set the alignment of the text, the line spacing, and the paragraph indentions. Alignment and spacing are linked to paragraph markers, which Write inserts when you press [Enter]. Paragraph markers don't have a visible character, but they do take up a space. You can highlight and edit them like any other character. You can find them at the end of a paragraph or the beginning of a blank line. In Figure 10-11, we highlighted two paragraph markers.

Paragraph formatting

Figure 10-11

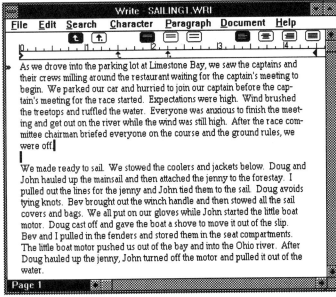

We highlighted two paragraph markers.

If you place your cursor anywhere in a paragraph and change the alignment or spacing, the entire paragraph will change. You can change more than one paragraph at a time if you highlight all the necessary paragraphs. If you hold down [Ctrl] and click once in the selection bar to select the entire document, you can even change the paragraph formatting for the whole document.

You can use a paragraph marker to format paragraphs repeatedly. Since all the alignment and spacing settings are linked to the paragraph marker, copying the marker will copy the settings too. First, highlight the paragraph marker, and copy it with the Copy command on the Edit menu to place it on the Clipboard. Next, highlight the paragraph marker you want to replace, and choose the Paste command to replace it with the copied marker. Write will then reformat the paragraph with the new settings. You can use this method to repeat formats in a document.

The Paragraph menu controls alignment, spacing, and indention. You can reset any of these formats to their defaults with the Normal command on the Character menu. When you highlight a paragraph and select the Normal command, the paragraph will be left-aligned, single spaced, and not indented.

Setting alignment

Now that you know how paragraph markers work, let's look at how you set paragraph alignment. You can instruct Write to left-align, right-align, justify, or center your text.

There are two ways to set alignment. You can use the alignment icons on the ruler or use the Paragraph menu commands. If you use the icons, just click anywhere in the paragraph, then click on the appropriate icon to change the paragraph's alignment. For example, in Figure 10-12, we clicked on a paragraph and then clicked on the Centered-alignment icon to center all the lines. Write centered only the paragraph that contained the cursor.

Figure 10-12

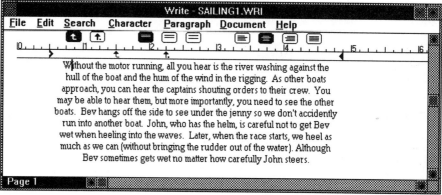

We used the Centered-alignment icon to center this paragraph.

Instead of using the alignment icons, you can use the Paragraph menu to change the alignment. To do this, select a paragraph as you did before, but this time select one of the alignment commands on the Paragraph menu. A check mark will appear next to the command you choose. You can check only one alignment command at a time. (A check mark also will appear next to the command on the Paragraph menu when you use the icons on the ruler.)

Defining the space (or leading) between lines is similar to setting the alignment since you can set the spacing with a ruler icon or from a menu. You can choose single-, $1^1/_2$-, or double-spaced lines. Again, the only paragraphs affected by your choices are the ones selected. To use an icon to change spacing, select the necessary paragraphs and click on a spacing icon. Write's default is single spacing. You can format a new paragraph with different spacing by pressing [Enter] and then clicking on one of the spacing icons. You also can use the Paragraph menu to redefine the space between lines. Just click on one of the menu commands to change a paragraph's spacing. As we mentioned earlier, after each formatting choice, a check mark will appear next to the active command.

Spacing options

In addition to changing the space between the lines of a paragraph, you can change indention and margin settings from the menu or the ruler. Commonly, paragraphs have the first line indented five spaces. Instead of typing five spaces at the beginning of each paragraph, you can tell Write automatically to indent the line that follows a paragraph marker. To set the indention, use the Indents... command on the Paragraph menu. The Indents dialog box, shown in Figure 10-13, provides three text boxes in which you can enter a left, first-line, or right indention. The Left Indent text box controls the left margin for all the lines of the paragraph. The First Line text box sets the left margin for just the first line. The Right Indent text box controls the right margin for all the lines. To indent the first line $^1/_2$ " enter *.5* in the First Line text box, and click OK to continue. Figure 10-14 on the next page shows a paragraph with a First Line setting of .5".

Setting indentions and margins

Figure 10-13

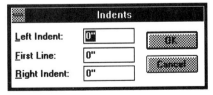

You can enter indention or margin values in the Indents dialog box.

Figure 10-14

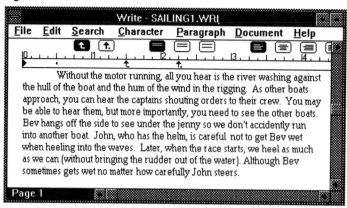

This paragraph has a First Line setting of .5".

If you want to create new margins for an entire paragraph, you can use the Left Indent or Right Indent text box. Figure 10-15 shows a paragraph with the Left Indent and the Right Indent text boxes, set at .5". These settings will establish margins on both sides of the paragraph, a useful format if you need to accent a paragraph or distinguish between speech and narrative.

Figure 10-15

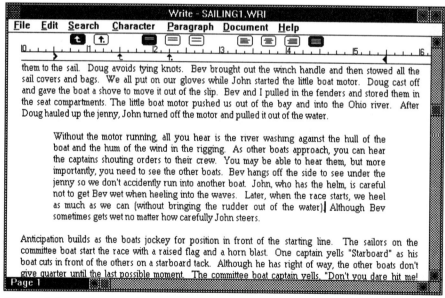

We used the Indents dialog box to set this paragraph apart.

You can use a combination of indention settings to create hanging indents. In a paragraph with a hanging indent, the first line extends farther into the left margin than the following body of text. To create a hanging indention, click on the paragraph you want to indent, then choose the Indents... command from the Paragraph menu. Next, you can choose to set the Left Indent text box to .5" and the First Line text box to -.5". This will indent the body of the paragraph .5" and leave the first line at the original left margin. Figure 10-16 shows a paragraph with a hanging indention.

Creating hanging indentions

Figure 10-16

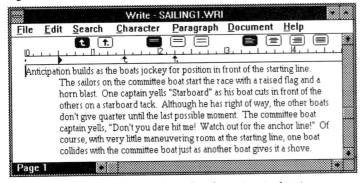

We formatted this paragraph with a hanging indention.

Using the ruler to set indents is faster than using the Indents dialog box. The text will change as you move the indent marker, so you will see the results sooner too. To change the indents, just drag the indent marker on the ruler, as shown in Figure 10-17 on the following page. The first-line indent marker is a dot that is embedded in the left margin marker. You can drag the dot off the marker to create a first-line indent or a hanging indent, depending on the direction you drag the marker. As with other paragraph settings, the changes you make with the ruler will be reflected in the Indents dialog box.

Creating indentions with the ruler

Tabs are invisible markers that you can set at any point along the ruler. You can use tabs to line up text to form columns and create tables. When you press the [Tab] key, the cursor will advance to the next tab marker on the current line of the document. By default, Write sets left-aligned tabs every half inch. When you set a new tab, Write deletes any default tabs to the left of the new tab. A word of caution: Tab settings apply to the whole document. If you create tables in a document, and change the tab settings for one of the tables, Write will change the tab settings for the other tables as well. To modify the default tab settings, you can either use the ruler or the Tabs... command on the Document menu to set the new tabs.

Working with tabs

Figure 10-17

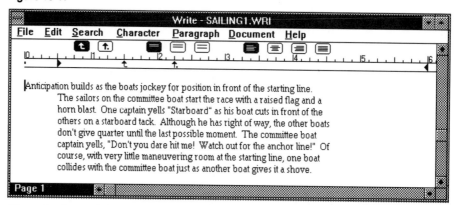

The ruler has a left margin marker, right margin marker, and a first-line indent marker.

Write offers two kinds of tabs: left-aligned and decimal. The Left-aligned tab formats text to the right of the cursor. The Decimal tab will let you add text to the left of the cursor until you type a period, and then it will add text to the right of the period. To use a Decimal tab, press [Tab], enter the first part of your number, type a period, and then enter the rest of the number. The Decimal tab is handy for lining up columns of numbers in a table, as shown in Figure 10-18.

Figure 10-18

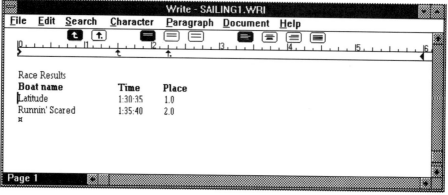

This table has both Left-aligned and Decimal tabs.

To set tabs with the ruler, simply select the Left-aligned tab icon or the Decimal tab icon, and click on the ruler at the position you want to place the tab. As we mentioned earlier, the new tabs you set will replace the half-inch default tabs. You can move the tab markers on the ruler by dragging them. To delete a tab, just drag the tab marker below the ruler. If you move or delete a tab, the text attached to that specific tab marker will change to match the new settings.

To set tabs with a command, select the Tabs... command from the Document menu. As you can see in Figure 10-19, the Tabs dialog box provides 12 text boxes to enter tab positions (in inches). By default, all of the text boxes are empty. The Decimal check boxes below the Positions text boxes indicate with an X that a position will use a Decimal tab. Before you start entering position numbers, you need to determine where you're going to place the tabs. The Tabs dialog box will help you by displaying the location of any tabs you have set previously with the ruler, thereby providing you with a frame of reference. You can change the tab settings or add more, and you can enter the tab positions in any order. Write automatically sorts them in numeric order. After you have added the new tab positions, click OK to return to the document and apply the new tab settings. Although you can be more precise by using the Tabs dialog box, it's easier to set tabs with the ruler because you can see the text change to match the tab settings.

Setting tabs with the ruler

Setting tabs with a command

Figure 10-19

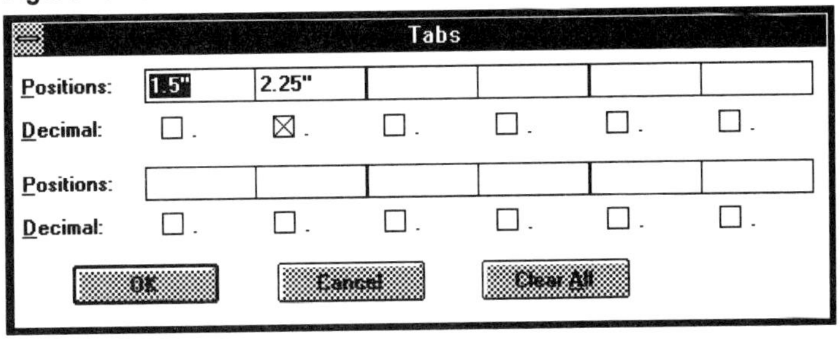

You can enter tab positions in any of the 12 boxes in the Tabs dialog box.

To delete a tab using the Document menu, first open the Tabs dialog box with the Tabs... command. Next, highlight the tab position you want to remove, and then press [Delete]. Write will delete the value and remove the tab position. If you want to delete all the tab positions, click on the Clear All button. After you have cleared all the tabs, Write will restore the default half-inch tabs. If you press Cancel, Write will change nothing and return you to the document.

Page formatting

The last formatting topic you need to consider is page formatting. Page formatting includes margins, page numbers, headers and footers, and page breaks. You'll use the Page Layout..., Header..., and Footer... commands on Write's Document menu and the Repaginate... command from the File menu to format your pages.

Setting margins and page numbers

The Page Layout... command on the Document menu provides a dialog box to set the margins and the page numbers. The Page Layout dialog box, shown in Figure 10-20, contains text boxes for left, right, top, and bottom margins. By default, Write sets the top and bottom margins to 1" and the left and right margins to 1.25". Write will print page numbers in your document, beginning with the page number displayed in the Start Page Numbers At text box.

Figure 10-20

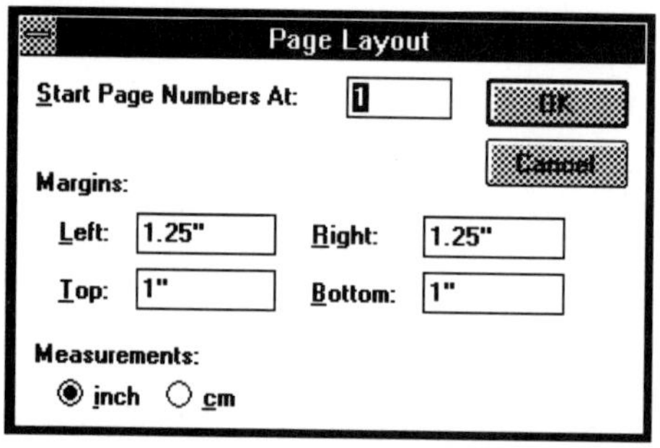

The Page Layout dialog box sets the margins and the beginning page number.

Setting page breaks

Write doesn't automatically set page breaks. You need to tell Write to set the page breaks with the Repaginate... command on the File menu before you print your document. Write's Repaginating Document dialog box lets you either automatically set all the page breaks or lets you confirm them individually. When you choose the Repaginate... command, a Repaginate Document dialog box appears as shown in Figure 10-21. To begin automatically repaginating, click OK. When Write is repaginating the document, a dialog box with a *Repaginating document* message will appear. If you want to stop the repaginating, click on Cancel.

When you use the Confirm Page Breaks option, Write will verify each page break. After Write finds a line on which to insert a page break, it will highlight the line and then prompt you for verification with the Repaginating Document dialog box, as shown in Figure 10-22. You can change the page break by clicking on the Up and Down buttons, which move the highlight to another line. Click on Confirm once the page break is where you want it, and Write will continue to the next page. Write marks the new page break with a dotted line to remind you that it is now a manual rather than an automatic page break (which is designated by double chevrons). The page-break marker in the selection bar will move to the line below the manual page break. Figure 10-23 shows an example of a manual page break. If you don't want to complete the process of repaginating, click on Cancel in the Repaginating Document dialog box.

The accelorator key for manual page breaks is [Ctrl][Enter]. First position the cursor at the desired spot and press [Ctrl][Enter]. Write will insert a dotted line above the cursor for the manual page break.

Figure 10-21

The Repaginate Document dialog box has a Confirm Page Breaks check box.

Figure 10-22

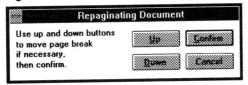

The Repaginating Document dialog box allows you to move the page break or confirm its placement.

Figure 10-23

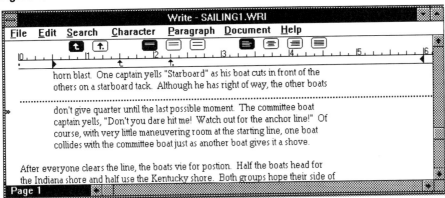

When you move a page break, Write will place a dotted line in your document to show the new placement.

After working with a document, you may be dissatisfied with some of your manually set page breaks. When this happens, you can delete the manual page break by highlighting the dotted line and then pressing [Delete] or [Backspace].

If you repaginate with confirmation after you manually placed a few page breaks, Write will display the dialog box shown in Figure 10-24, asking if you want to keep them. You can keep the page break, remove it, or cancel the operation with this version of the Repaginating Document dialog box.

Figure 10-24

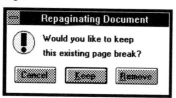

You'll see this version of the Repaginating Document dialog box when you need to repaginate and confirm existing manually set page breaks.

Creating headers and footers

You can annotate the top and bottom of every page of your document respectively, with headers and footers. A header is a line of text or numbers Write will print at the top of every page. Footers will be printed at the bottom of every page. Both headers and footers will appear in the margin space you specified with the Page Layout... command. By default, they will be left-aligned and .75" from the top and bottom of the page, but you can specify a custom setting for your header or footer.

To create a header, choose the Header... command from the Document menu. A blank document window, like the one in Figure 10-25, will appear along with the Page Header dialog box. The blank document, labeled *HEADER* in the title bar, will contain an end-of-file marker and a blinking cursor. At this point, the document is active and the dialog box is inactive. First, type the text you want for the header. Note that you can use the commands on the menu bar to format the text any way you like (usually, you can't access the menu bar when a dialog box is open). You can even have more than one line in your header; you can have as many lines as will fit in the margins. After you enter the text, you can insert a dynamic page number (a code that Write automatically changes to match the page you're printing) by using the Insert Page # button in the Page Header dialog box. If you do, Write will print only the page number. If you want the word *Page* to precede the number, you need to type it into the header and then choose the Insert Page # button. The resulting code will look like this: *Page (page)*. Figure 10-26 shows a sample header.

The Page Header dialog box allows you to customize your header. Normally, the page number and other header information begin on the second page. However, if you want to print the header on the first page, you can select the Print on First Page check box.

By default, Write starts inserting the header .75" from the top of the document and continues until it reaches the top margin setting specified with the Page Layout... command on the Document menu. You can make more room for the header by starting it closer to the top of the page. For instance, to add .25" to the header, change the Distance from Top value to .5" in the Header dialog box.

After you enter text in the header, Windows will print it on every page. If you don't want to print the header anymore, you must delete all the text and codes from the header window. Instead of doing this manually, you can click on the Clear button in the Page Header dialog box to accomplish the same thing. When you are satisfied with the header text, just click the Return to Document button to resume working on your document.

Figure 10-25

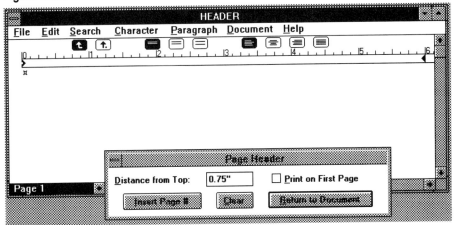

The Header... command brings up a blank document window and a Page Header dialog box.

Figure 10-26

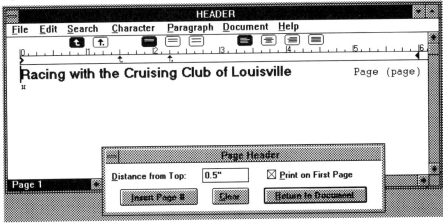

This is a sample header.

Footers work the same way as headers. When you choose the Footer... command from the Document menu, Write will bring up a blank document window labeled *FOOTER,* along with a Page Footer dialog box, as shown in Figure 10-27. In the Footer document window and its attendant dialog box, you can enter text, insert a dynamic page number, decide if the footer goes on the first page, then enter a quantity in the Distance from Bottom text box. If you don't want a footer after all, you can use the Clear button. To return to the document work area, just click on the Return to Document button.

Figure 10-27

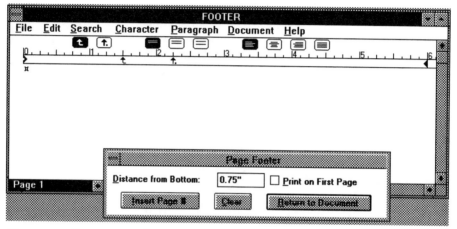

To create a footer, issue the Footer... command on the Document menu.

EDITING

After you have written a document, you're ready to polish it. We've already explained some basic editing techniques, such as deleting text, selecting text, and moving around the document. Now we're going to show you how to copy text, how to move it, and how to find and change words in your document.

Copying and moving text

The commands on the Edit menu let you copy and move text. With these commands, you can remove text from one area and add it to another. You can also duplicate the text and move a copy to another area. Before you use any of these commands, you need to select the text you intend to change.

If you want to place selected text in another part of your document, use the Cut command. The Cut command will delete the selected text and place it on Clipboard. Then, move the cursor to the place you want the text to appear. Choose the Paste command and Write will add your text to the left of the cursor.

If you want to reuse some text in another part of your document, you can use the Copy command to duplicate it. The Copy command will store a copy of the selected text on Clipboard. When you choose the Paste command, Write will add the text to your document at the position of the cursor.

With a combination of two commands, Find... and Change..., you can systematically go through your document and change every occurrence of specified text. For instance, you can use this technique to correct spelling, add an address, or make a name change. If you're trying to find a specific topic so you can edit that topic, you can search for a key word in your document to move quickly to that part of the document.

Finding and replacing text

To locate a specific string of text, you use the Find... command. When you choose the Find... command from the Search menu, the dialog box in Figure 10-28 will appear. The Find dialog box displays a text box for the search text and two check boxes to qualify the search. When you enter search text, Write will look for every occurrence of that series of characters, starting from the current location of the cursor. For example, if you enter *cat*, Write will stop at *Cat, catch, catacomb,* etc. If you want to look just for the word *cat*, you need to check the Whole Word check box. If the word you're looking for is capitalized, you need to enter the search text with a capital letter and check the Match Upper/Lowercase box. After you have specified the search text, click on the Find Next button to start the search. If Write can't find a match, it will give you a *Search text not found* message.

Using the Find... command

Figure 10-28

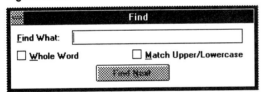

The Find dialog box lets you enter search text in a text box and specify details in two check boxes.

When Write finds a match, it will stop on the first characters that match your search text and highlight those letters. You can click in the document and make any changes without closing the Find dialog box. It just becomes inactive. To continue searching, click on the Find Next button in the dialog box. The Find dialog box will become active, and Write will move to the next match. After Write finds the last match, it will present a *Search complete* message. If you don't want to search for other words, just close the Find dialog box to return to the document.

You can tell Write to search only a selected portion of a document. If you want to find a word and you know it's on one of three pages, you can highlight or select those pages and then use the Find... command. After Write reaches the end of the section, the search stops and you'll get a *Search complete* message.

One very helpful feature of Write's Find... command is its ability to use the question mark character (?) as a wildcard. You can use a ? in place of any single character in your search text. For example, if you enter *ba?e* as your search text,

Using wildcards in searches

Write will highlight occurrences of *bale, base, bane, bake* and any other words that begin with *ba* followed by a single character and an *e.*

Wildcards come in handy for a variety of situations. For example, suppose you are working on a document in which you have not been consistent in spelling the name *Petersen.* In some cases, you have entered *Peterson* with an *o,* and in other cases, you've entered *Petersen* with an *e.* You can find all occurrences of the name by using the Find... command and entering *Peters?n* as your search text. Of course, you will probably want to change some of the occurrences so that the spelling will be consistent throughout the document. We'll show you how to do that when we discuss the Change... command.

Since Write considers a question mark in your search text to be a wildcard, you may be wondering how you can search for a literal question mark in a document. Fortunately, there is a way to do this. Just enter ^? (a caret followed by a question mark) as your search text. This tells Write that, instead of using the ? as a wildcard, you want to find all occurrences of a literal question mark. Of course, you can combine ^? with other characters as you enter the search text. For example, suppose you want to find all occurrences of the question *Is this correct?* in your document. You can do this by entering *Is this correct ^?* or perhaps just *correct^?* as your search text.

When you use the question mark as a character wildcard, you need to select the Whole Word check box in the Find dialog box because Write treats spaces and punctuation as characters. This means Write will find character patterns that cover part of two adjacent words. For example, suppose you entered *s?on?*as the search text without selecting the Whole Word check box. Write would find *stone, others on,* and *sailors on.*

Finding special characters

Another useful feature of Write's Find... command is its ability to search for special characters in a document, such as spaces, tabs, paragraph markers, or manual page breaks. To find a special character, you must insert a caret (^) followed by a specific character to complete your search string, as shown in Table 10-4.

Table 10-4

Search text	Finds all occurrences of...
^w	spaces
^t	tabs
^p	paragraph markers
^d	manual page breaks

These codes search for special characters with the Find... command.

When you're searching for a word that needs to be changed, you can use the Change... command to find and change automatically all occurences of that word in your document. When you choose the Change... command on the Search menu, you'll see a Change dialog box like the one in Figure 10-29. The Change... command can help you correct spelling errors. For example, instead of just finding all the occurrences of *Peterson* and then changing each one to read *Petersen*, you could use the Change... command to correct all of them for you. To do this, first enter the misspelled version in the Find What text box. Then, enter the correct spelling in the Change To text box. For example, you would type *Peterson* in the Find What text box and *Petersen* in the Change To text box. You need to check the Whole Word and Match Upper/Lowercase check boxes.

Using the Change... command

Figure 10-29

Change
Find What: `a particular phrase`
Change To: ` `
☐ **Whole Word**   ☐ **Match Upper/Lowercase**
[Find Next] [Change, then Find] [Change] [Change All]

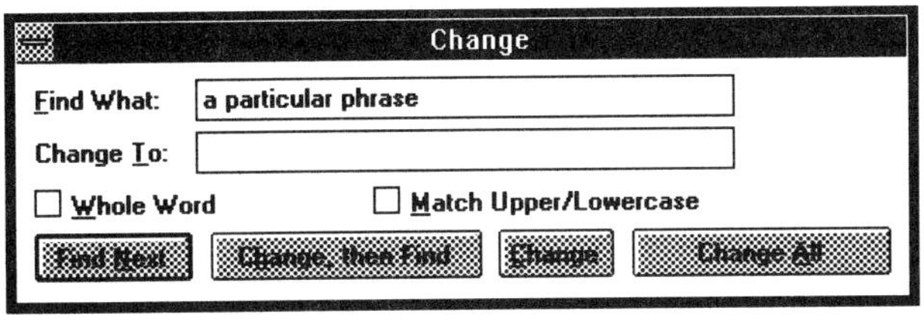

The Change dialog box lets you find and change text.

Now you need to determine how Write will search and replace your text with the four buttons at the bottom of the Change dialog box. The Find Next button will find and highlight the characters matching the search text. The Change, then Find button will find the first match, change it, and then find the next match. The Change button will change only the highlighted text from a search. The Change All button will change all of the matching search text throughout the document. If you select part of your document and then choose the Change... command or return to the Change dialog box, the Change All button will convert to Change Selection. The Change Selection button will change all the matches in the selected part of the document.

When you've finished changing text, you need to remove the Change dialog box from the desktop. The quickest way to close it is to double-click the Change dialog box's Control menu.

In both the Find What and Change To text boxes, you can use the wildcards you used with the Find... command.

You won't always need to make global changes. You might need to vary your modifications for each match. If you simply want Write to find text but not change anything or bring up any dialog boxes, you can use the Repeat Last Find command on the Search menu. (The accelerator key is [F3].) After you set up the search with the Find... or Change... command, you can close the dialog box and press [F3] to start the search through your document. Write will highlight one match every time you press [F3].

Repeating the last search

ADDING GRAPHICS

In addition to working with text, Write can also work with graphics. Write lets you place graphics from other applications, like Paintbrush, into your document. If you can copy the graphic onto Clipboard, you can import it into Write. You can learn how to copy graphics in Paintbrush in Chapter 11. Once the graphic is in your document, Write can format, move, and size it. Keep in mind that your graphic may look distorted when you bring it into Write because the graphic's resolution is based on your printer's capabilities. If your printer has a higher resolution than your screen, then the graphic won't look as sharp on your screen as it will when it's printed. For example, a typical VGA screen's 72 dpi (dots per inch) resolution is less sharp than a 300 dpi printout from a laser printer.

Importing a graphic

After you select and copy a graphic with Paintbrush or another graphics program, exit that application, and start Write to place the graphic. Remember, you can have both applications on the desktop; just click on the Write application window instead of exiting the first application. When your document is on the screen, move your cursor to the place in the work area you want to insert the graphic. Now, use the Paste command on the Edit menu to place the graphic. Figure 10-30 shows a graphic we've added to our sailing document. Write will treat the graphic as a paragraph, which means you can't wrap text around your graphic. As a result, text can appear only above and below the graphic.

Formatting a graphic

Once you've placed a graphic in your document, you can format its alignment just as you format text, using the menu commands or the ruler icons. First, you need to select the graphic by clicking on it. The graphic will change to inverse video to show it has been selected. Next, choose one of the alignment commands on the paragraph menu or click on an alignment icon. Write will format your graphic according to your selection. For example, we centered the sailboat in our sailing document in Figure 10-31.

Moving a graphic

Besides aligning a graphic, you can move it to a unique alignment or to another part of the document. To align the graphic, select the graphic, then choose the Move Picture command from the Edit menu. Write changes the pointer into a set of nested boxes (a box within a box). When you move the pointer away from the graphic, you'll see a gray frame that represents the size of the graphic. Click to place the graphic at the new location. Then, click again on a different line in the document to deselect the graphic. Your pointer will re-assume its normal shape and function.

The Move Picture command only moves the graphic to a different position on the same line. However, you can use the Cut and Paste commands to move the graphic to a new location in your document. To do this, first select the graphic and choose the Cut command on the Edit menu to store it on Clipboard. Then, move the cursor to the graphic's destination and select the Paste command to retrieve and place the graphic back into the document at the position of the cursor.

Figure 10-30

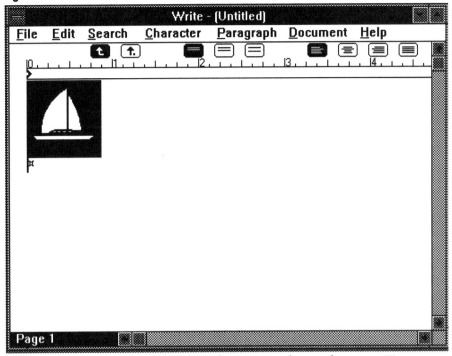

You can copy graphics from other applications and paste them into Write.

Figure 10-31

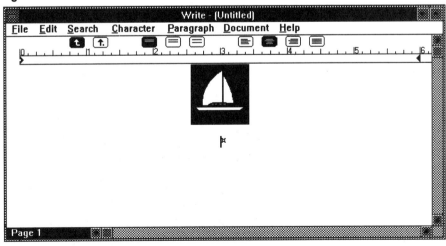

We centered the sailboat by selecting the graphic and then choosing the Centered command from the Paragraph menu.

Duplicating a graphic

Not only can you move a graphic with Cut and Paste; you can duplicate it with the Copy and Paste commands. To copy a graphic, double-click on it to highlight it in your document. Next, choose the Copy command from the Edit menu. Position your cursor on the line where you want the graphic inserted. Choose Paste from the Edit menu to place the graphic on that line. You can continue to paste the graphic until you issue another Cut or Copy command.

Although you can duplicate the graphic, you only can add one graphic to a line in your document. If you want a line filled with graphics, then you need to create the original graphic large enough to fill the line. For example, you could create multiple graphics in Paintbrush, then copy them as a group onto Clipboard before pasting them into Write.

Sizing a graphic

If you want to produce a smaller or larger version of the original graphic, you can use the Size Picture command on the Edit menu. First, click on the graphic to select it, then choose the Size Picture command. When you do, the pointer will change into the nested boxes. As you drag the nested box pointer, a gray frame appears as a guideline for changing both the horizontal and vertical dimensions of the graphic. To see how these dimensions change as you move the frame, look at the status bar at the bottom of the work area. The status bar changes to display the X and Y coordinates of the pointer. The X represents the horizontal position, and the Y represents the vertical position. To keep the graphic proportional, drag in a diagonal direction from the lower-right corner, keeping the coordinates equal as you drag the pointer. You can prevent distortion if you drag the frame so that the coordinates are equal, whole numbers.

Creating letterhead

Now that you know how to format text and graphics, you can combine them to create letterheads. Once you save a file, you can use it as a template for memos and letters. Let's examine the procedure by creating a letterhead file for the Cruising Club of Louisville. We'll use the sailboat graphic you saw earlier.

- First, create the sailboat graphic in Paintbrush, and copy it to Clipboard.

- Next, start Write, and use the default new document to begin the stationery.

- Since the graphic is supposed to be at the top of the document, place the cursor on the first line of the document and issue the Paste command.

- Now add the name and address in 10-point Times Roman type. To make the name and address bold, highlight it, and then issue the Bold command on the Character menu.

- Finally, highlight the graphic and the text, then click on the left alignment icon to create the final version of the letterhead shown in Figure 10-32.

Figure 10-32

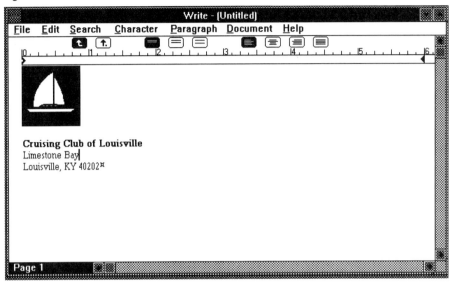

The logo for our letterhead combines text and graphics formatting techniques.

Once you've placed your text and graphic, it's relatively easy to reformat them as a unit. You'll need to experiment to achieve the effect you want. For example, we didn't like the way our letterhead looked, so we selected the text and the graphic and aligned them with the Right command on the Paragraph menu. You can see the effect of this change in Figure 10-33 on the next page.

When your letterhead looks the way you want it, save it under a name that will identify it as your template. To use the letterhead file as a template, just open it, add your text, then save it under a different name. It's crucial that you save your letterhead file under a new name each time you use it so you don't replace the original letterhead file. This way you can use the letterhead file as a template for all your correspondence.

After you've finished working with a document, you need to save your work. **FILE HANDLING** Write provides options that let you save the document as a Write document or save it so you can use it with another word processing application. After you save your work, you're ready to create a new document or work on an existing one. The File menu commands let you do all these things.

To save your work, use the Save or Save As... commands on the File menu. **Saving your work** The first time you save a file with the Save command, Write will ask you for a file name. The next time you save the file with the same command, Write will automatically save the file by replacing the old one. If you don't want to replace the old file, you can use the Save As... command to create a separate copy of the old file with a new file name.

Figure 10-33

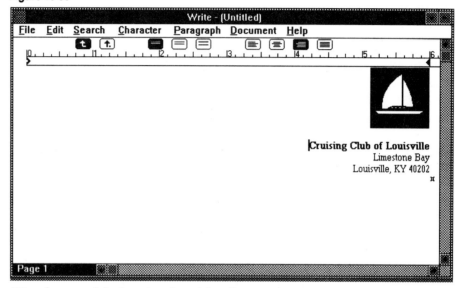

We reformatted the letterhead to right-align our logo.

Exporting files

The Save As... command enables you to save a file in other formats. As you can see in Figure 10-34, two of the check boxes in the File Save As dialog box specify file formats. The Text Only check box will save your file as an ASCII text file. You can use text files to export Write documents into other applications, such as WordPerfect or WordStar, which will convert the text file into their own file format. The Microsoft Word Format check box will let you save the Write file so Word can open the file without converting it itself. A word of warning: Do not use the Microsoft Word Format if you have graphics in your document because Windows will remove them during the conversion.

Backing up your work

The other check box in the File Save As dialog box can create backup copies automatically. When you save the file with the Save As... command and the Make Backup option, Write will back up your file whenever you save it again. You can save the file with either Save command and still keep making a backup. When Write makes a backup copy, it saves the file with a .WRI extension and saves a copy with a .BKP extension in your current directory. The first part of the file name is the same, so you can match originals with backups.

Figure 10-34

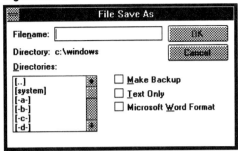

Write's File Save As dialog box lets you specify other file formats.

If you want to stop making a backup copy, use the Save As... command, toggle off Make Backup, and then save the file again. That way, Write won't make a backup every time you save the file. However, this will cause a large gap between the date in the backups and in the current file. Since this discrepancy could be misleading, you should use the File Manager to delete the backup copies or rename them to avoid confusion. For more on deleting files, see Chapter 6.

Starting a new file

When you want to create a new document, you can either start one when you first bring up Write, or you can use the New command on the File menu. Write calls the new document *Untitled* until you save it and assign it a name. If you start a new document before saving the current one, Write will present a dialog box like the one shown in Figure 10-35, asking if you want to save the changes. After you close the warning dialog box, Write will replace the current document with an untitled one on your desktop.

Figure 10-35

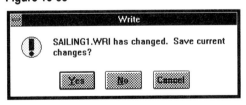

Write will ask if you want to save your changes before starting a new document.

Opening a file

If you want to open an existing file, you can use the Open... command on the File menu. When you issue the Open... command, Write will display the File Open dialog box shown in Figure 10-36. All the available Write files are listed in the Files list box. Notice that all the files Write creates use a .WRI extension in their file name. You can either click on one of these file names in the list or type the name in the Filename text box. You can use the Directories list box to choose a different path or drive if your file is at a location other than the one in which it was created. Click OK, and Write will find your file and display it in the work area.

Figure 10-36

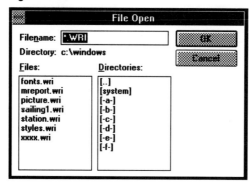

The File Open dialog box allows you access to the available Write files.

PRINTING YOUR DOCUMENT

After you've written the document, formatted, edited, and perhaps added a few graphics to it, you're almost ready to print it. Before you print the document, however, it's always a good idea to save the file so you won't lose any work. To get ready to print, you need to select a printer, set the page orientation, and set the printer resolution. For a more detailed examination of printing basics, see Chapters 3 and 9.

Preparing to print

Before you can print a document, you need to choose the printer you're going to use from the list of installed printers. To choose a printer, select the Printer Setup... command on the File menu. The Printer Setup dialog box, shown in Figure 10-37, will appear. Write displays only the active printers. You can change any printer option such as page orientation or printer resolution, with the Setup... button. These printer options are explored in greater detail in Chapters 3 and 9.

Using the Print... command

After you select a printer and specify the appropriate settings, you're ready to print the document. First, choose the Print... command from the File menu. Write will then present a Print dialog box like the one in Figure 10-38. The name of the printer you select will appear at the top of the dialog box. First, enter the number of copies in the Copies text box, then specify which pages to print. You can select the All button or select the From and To buttons to specify the starting and ending page numbers. If you prefer to get a rough draft quickly instead of printing at the highest resolution, click on the Draft Quality check box. However, when you print with draft quality, graphics will appear as empty boxes. When you click OK, Write will display a dialog box with a message telling you that your document is printing.

Figure 10-37

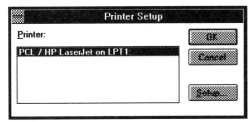

The Printer Setup dialog box displays a list of available printers.

Figure 10-38

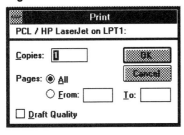

The Print dialog box lets you select the number of copies and the range of pages to print, and lets you choose draft quality for quicker printing.

At this point, Write will send the file to the Print Manager. You can cancel sending the file by clicking on the Cancel button in the Write message box. If the icon area of your display is uncovered, you'll see the Print Manager icon on the desktop. After the file is sent to the Print Manager, the Write message box will disappear. Print Manager, in turn, sends the file to the printer.

If your printer isn't connected, the Print Manager will send a message informing you that it can't send anything to the port. Click OK in the message dialog box, and the Print Manager will pause printing until you resolve the problem. After the printer is connected, you need to tell the Print Manager to resume printing by double-clicking on the Print Manager icon and clicking on the Resume button on the Print Manager window. When you minimize the Print Manager, Windows will return you to your document. You can read more about the Print Manager in Chapter 7.

EXITING WRITE

After you've finished working with Write, you can exit the application and return to the Program Manager by choosing the Exit command from the File menu. If you didn't save your document before you selected the Exit command, Write will present a message asking if you want to save it. If you click Yes, Write will save your file. Click No, and Write will not save your changes, or click Cancel, and Write will return you to the current document. For more about exiting applications, read the detailed discussion in Chapter 9.

In this chapter

Using Paintbrush **11**

*P*roducing a memo, report, or newsletter with correctly spelled words and printing it with attractive fonts isn't enough in today's communications-saturated world. The printed page needs a dash of flash in order to capture anyone's attention. Windows has the answer. Its graphics application—Paintbrush—lets you spice up mundane documents.

Paintbrush helps you create graphics for many types of documents, such as greeting cards, newsletters, and memos with letterheads. In this chapter, we'll show you how to use Paintbrush's tools to create simple and complex drawings and how to make customized wallpaper for your desktop. We'll also show you how to use a scanner with Paintbrush.

PAINTBRUSH

We created the poster in Figure 11-1 on the next page to demonstrate the capabilities of the Paintbrush tools. (A color version of Figure 11-1 appears in Appendix 2.) We'll show you how we made the poster at the end of this chapter. You'll see each of the elements in the poster as you learn about Paintbrush.

As you read this chapter, keep in mind that Paintbrush uses both the left and right mouse buttons. The left button is the primary button and the right one is for special functions. If you are using a keyboard, you can press the [Delete] key instead of clicking the right mouse button and press [Delete][F9] for a right button double-click.

To start Paintbrush, click on the Accessories window of the Program Manager, then double-click on the Paintbrush icon. The Paintbrush application window will then appear, as shown in Figure 11-2.

Starting Paintbrush

Figure 11-1

This poster presents a variety of images you can create with Paintbrush.

Figure 11-2

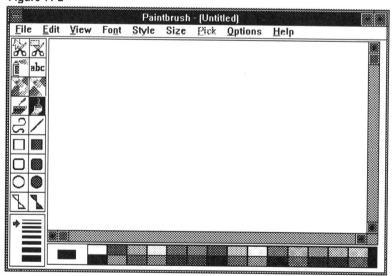

The Paintbrush window includes a Toolbox, Linesize box, and Palette.

Paintbrush provides a wide assortment of tools and functions. On the left of the application window, you'll see all the "tools" in a vertical stack known as the Toolbox. Below the Toolbox is the Linesize box, which contains a series of increasingly thick lines. To the right of the Linesize box, you'll find the Selected Colors box that sets foreground and background colors. Next to the Selected Colors box is a set of colors, called the Palette. The middle of the window is your work area. By default, Paintbrush adds horizontal and vertical scroll bars to the window so you can move to all parts ofthe work area.

GETTING YOUR SUPPLIES

Before you begin drawing a graphic, you'll want to determine the size of your image and the color scheme for it. The Image Attributes… command on the Options menu lets you do this. In the Images Attributes dialog box, shown in Figure 11-3, you choose a unit of measurement and specify a width and height for your work area. In the Colors section, you can choose either the Black and White or Colors radio button to define your Palette. By default, Paintbrush sets up a Color Palette and a 6.67" by 5" work area when you start Paintbrush. You can also create a custom Palette, which we'll discuss later in this chapter.

After you make all your selections, you need to start a new work area (or file) in order to implement the new Image Attribute settings. To do this, issue the New command on the File menu or simply double-click on the Eraser tool.

Figure 11-3

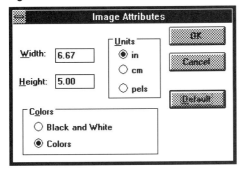

The Image Attributes dialog box lets you choose the size of your work area, the colors, and the unit of measurement.

MOVING AROUND YOUR DRAWING

When you specify large dimensions for a drawing, you'll need to scroll through the work area as you create and modify the drawing. Paintbrush provides some shortcuts for moving around your drawing. Although you can use the scroll bars, the accelerator keys listed in Table 11-1 offer a faster means of navigation; when you use accelerator keys, Paintbrush doesn't need to repaint the screen each time as it does when you click on a scroll arrow. For example, if you finished drawing shoelaces on the tennis shoes of a tall basketball player, and you wanted to start drawing his eyes, instead of scrolling through the whole drawing, you could just press [Home] to move to the top of your drawing.

Table 11-1

Key Combination	Function
[Home]	Move to top
[End]	Move to bottom
[Page Up]	Move up one screen
[Page Down]	Move down one screen
[Shift]↑	Move up one line
[Shift]↓	Move down one line
[Shift][Home]	Move to left edge
[Shift][End]	Move to right edge
[Shift][Page Up]	Move left one screen
[Shift][Page Down]	Move right one screen
[Shift]←	Move left one space
[Shift]→	Move right one space

You can use these shortcuts to move around your work area.

DRAWING BASICS

To create your masterpiece with Paintbrush, you'll need to know what tools are available, how to use them, and how to use the Color Palette. The following section will explain how to use the graphics tools, Text tool, and editing tools. We'll also show you how to manipulate the elements you create with the tools.

Tool overview

Table 11-2 lists all the tools in the Toolbox and shows their icons and the tool-specific pointer you'll see when you select each one. To use a tool, click on it and move the pointer into the work area, where it will assume its tool-specific shape. Clicking will activate the tool for the duration of the click; holding down the mouse button will continuously activate the tool. Dragging the tool moves the pointer while keeping the tool active. Some tools perform advanced functions when you select them by linking another key (like [Ctrl] or [Shift]) with the mouse button. We'll show you these special functions when we talk about the applicable tools.

Dealing with color

You'll probably use the Palette as much as you'll use the Toolbox. The Palette, located at the bottom of the screen, provides a choice of 28 colors. With the Palette, you tell Paintbrush which colors you want to use for foreground and background colors. The center box in the Selected Colors box contains the foreground color, and the surrounding box contains the background color. When you click with the left mouse button on a color in the Palette, you choose the foreground color. When you click with the right mouse button on a color, the background area in the Selected Colors box assumes that color. As you draw with Paintbrush's tools, Paintbrush will use the foreground color for the lines you draw and for filled shapes. However, Paintbrush borders shapes with the background color. For instance, if you draw boxes with the Filled Box tool, the boxes would be the foreground color, framed in the background color. If your background color is white, like the work area background, the border shows up only when one box crosses another, as shown in Figure 11-4.

Table 11-2

Tool Name	Tool Icon	Tool Pointer	Tool Name	Tool Icon	Tool Pointer
Scissors		┼	Pick		┼
Airbrush		┼	Text	abc	I
Color Eraser		⊞	Eraser		□
Paint Roller			Brush		▪
Curve		┼	Line	/	┼
Box	□	┼	Filled Box	■	┼
Rounded Box		┼	Filled Rounded Box		┼
Circle/Ellipse	○	┼	Filled Circle/Ellipse	●	┼
Polygon		┼	Filled Polygon		┼

You can use all these tools to create drawings.

Figure 11-4

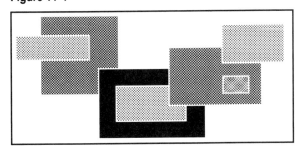

Because our background color is white, these overlapping boxes have white borders.

On the other hand, if you don't want lines to show up around the boxes, you can eliminate the distinction between the background and the foreground. To make the background color match the foreground, click with the right mouse button on the same color. The Selected Colors box will change to match your choice. Figure 11-5 shows overlapping boxes without a border.

Figure 11-5

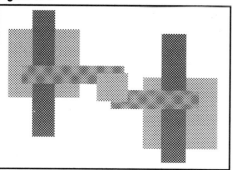

These overlapping boxes don't have borders because the background color matches the foreground color.

You also can change the foreground color in the Selected Colors box. Click on the color you want using the left mouse button, and the foreground section of the Selected Colors box will change to that color.

If you are going to print your graphic and don't have a color printer, you will need to use the Black and White Palette. If you are going to plot your graphic or send the image to color printer, you'll want to use color. In any case, the techniques described in this chapter apply to both the Color and the Black and White Palettes.

Some of the colors on the Palette work in a unique way with the Paint Roller tool. These colors (marked with an X in Figure 11-6) are actually patterns or composites of two colors. When you color an area with a pattern, you can't repaint it again with the Paint Roller tool. Later, we'll show you how you can use the Color Eraser tool to replace the patterned color.

Selecting a line size

You can vary the thickness of the lines you draw with the Linesize box. The Linesize box doesn't simply affect line width; it affects other graphic tools too. The thicker the line you choose, the larger the area the tool affects. For example, if you use the Brush tool, the width of the Brush pointer will widen as you increase the size of the line. Figure 11-7 shows the changes in the Brush pointer as the line in the Linesize box gets thicker. Linesize affects all the tools except the Text tool, the Paint Roller tool, and the Scissors and Pick tools.

Figure 11-6

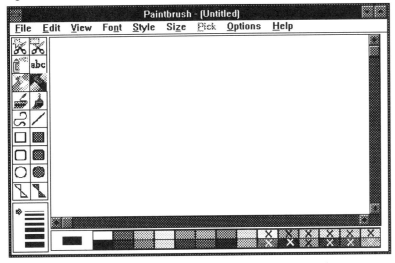

We marked the 12 mixed colors in the default Palette with Xs.

Figure 11-7

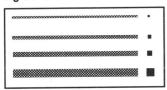

The Brush shape on the right gets thicker as you choose wider lines.

If you're using the Line tool to click the mouse once and draw a dot, you'll notice the dot changes as the line size changes. (The finest line doesn't form a dot with a single click.) Paintbrush uses a unique shape to create each of the available line thicknesses in the Linesize box. Figure 11-8 illustrates the different widths and shapes. The wider the line, the more nearly round the ends. In fact, when you draw the widest line, the ends of the line will be round. Later, when we show you how to use the Eraser tool, you can square off the ends of the line.

Figure 11-8

The single-click shape changes as you choose various line sizes.

A TOUR OF TOOLS

Paintbrush's Toolbox has a wide assortment of tools: graphic tools, a Text tool, and editing tools. The graphic tools include the Line, Box, Filled Box, Rounded Box, Filled Rounded Box, Circle/Ellipse, Filled Circle Ellipse, Polygon, Filled Polygon, Curve, Brush, Airbrush, and Paint Roller tools. The editing tools include the Eraser, Color Eraser, Scissors, and Pick tools.

A look at graphic tools

The graphic tools can create a variety of shapes and patterns, such as lines, squares, circles, polygons, and curves. You also can create freehand shapes with the Brush or Airbrush tool. If you want to change a large area to a new color, you can use the Paint Roller tool.

Using the Line tool

You can draw horizontal, vertical, and diagonal lines, and small shapes (such as tiny square dots) with the Line tool. To draw a line, first choose the Line tool, position the pointer in the work area where you want to start the line, and click there to anchor the line. Then, drag the pointer to stretch the line to its destination point. When you stretch the line, a guideline will appear to simulate where the line will go. When you release the mouse button to finish the line, the guideline will change into a line with the color and thickness you selected.

Paintbrush is very careful to do exactly what you tell it. However, the result might not always be what you want. If you want a horizontal or vertical line but release the mouse button one bit off a perfectly straight line, you will end up with a jagged line. To avoid mishaps, hold down the [Shift] key while you drag the guideline. Using the [Shift] key will tell Paintbrush to allow only perfectly horizontal, vertical, or diagonal lines. Paintbrush assumes a 45-degree angle for its diagonal lines.

You also can use a combination of lines to create free-form polygons. After you draw one line, leave the Line tool in the same place and then start drawing again in a different direction. All you have to do to start another line is click and then drag the guideline to the next spot.

Besides the common horizontal, vertical, or diagonal line, you can use the Line tool to create small shapes such as a square dot. If you click once without dragging the mouse, you will create the shortest possible line—a dot.

For example, you can create a flower using only the Line tool. Figure 11-9 illustrates the steps necessary to draw a dandelion.

- To draw the flower, open the Image Attributes dialog box, select a Black and White Palette with a page size of 2.5" by 1.5", then double-click the Eraser tool to start a new work area.

- After choosing a dark gray from the Palette, select the Line tool, hold down the [Shift] key, and draw a vertical line for the stem, as shown in step one.

- Add a series of light gray, thin diagonal lines for dandelion fluff, as shown in step two. Don't use the [Shift] key here because you need a variety of diagonal lines instead of just 45-degree lines.

- Put leaves on the stem of the flower by creating a dark gray, jagged-edge polygon, and use a fine, dark gray line to add seeds to the dandelion by clicking to create small shapes, as shown in step three.

Figure 11-9

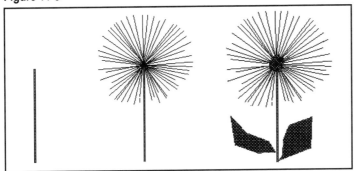

You can use the Line tool to create this dandelion.

The Box tool lets you create rectangles, perfectly proportioned boxes, and lines. The Box tool uses the foreground color for its frame and leaves the interior empty/unfilled. The Filled Box tool is the reverse; its frame is the background color and the interior is the foreground color. (Note that the background color in the Selected Colors box is, by default, the color of your work area.)

To draw a box, choose your foreground color and line width, then select the tool (Box or Filled Box). Position the pointer where you want to start your box (the pointer becomes a crosshair), then click. When you do, you'll see the guidelines anchored at the corner you clicked. Click and drag the box guidelines until they are the size and shape you want, then release the mouse button. The guidelines will turn into a final graphic with the line width and color you selected.

In addition to rectangles and boxes, you can draw lines with the Box tools. If you create a rectangle with no height or one with no width and then release the mouse, the final shape will be a line. This technique is useful when you want to draw a quick line without changing tools.

When you draw nested boxes with the Filled Box tool, you might end up with white frames like the ones you saw in Figure 11-4. To avoid odd-colored frames, choose the same colors for foreground and background when you are drawing layers of boxes. If you want the frame around a filled box to be a different color for contrast, you can choose a different background color with the right mouse button and then draw the box.

Using the Box tools

You can use the Box and Line tools to draw a cube. As you can see in Figure 11-10, it takes just a couple of steps to complete the graphic.

- Draw a small box and then draw a larger box on top of the first one but offset to the lower right, as shown in step one.

- With the Line tool, draw connecting lines to the corners of the boxes, as shown in step two.

Figure 11-10

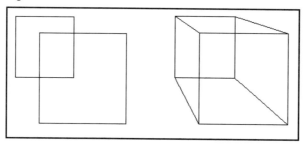

With only the Box and Line tools, you can draw a cube.

Using the Rounded Box tools

The Rounded Box and the Filled Rounded Box tools form boxes with rounded corners, like the keys on an electronic piano. When you click and drag these tools, the guidelines form a box with rounded corners. When you release the mouse button, the final box will reflect your choice of line size and color. Figure 11-11 shows the steps to draw an electronic piano keyboard.

- First, choose white for the foreground and then draw the full-length white key with the Filled Rounded Box tool, as shown in step one.

- For step two, draw another white key with the Filled Rounded Box tool and add a black key on top of the two white keys (remember to change the foreground color to black before drawing the black keys). Keep adding more keys (black and white) to form an electronic piano keyboard.

- Finally, add shading (a gray line) and a frame (a black unfilled rounded box). (We used the Text tool, which we will discuss later, to add a logo.)

Figure 11-11

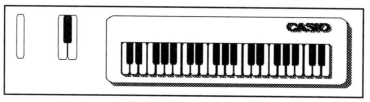

We created a keyboard with the Rounded Box and Line tools.

With the Circle/Ellipse and the Filled Circle/Ellipse tools, you can create filled and unfilled ellipses, circles, and ovals of various sizes. As you did with the other tools, first select the line width and color. Next, select one of the Circle/Ellipse tools and move the crosshair pointer to the work area. To start drawing your circle, click to anchor the guidelines and then drag them to form the circle. If you want to draw a perfect circle instead of an ellipse, hold down the [Shift] key while you drag the guidelines to the size you want. Figure 11-12 shows the shapes you can create with the Circle/Ellipse tool. As with the Box tools, if you use the Circle tools to draw a circle with no height or width, the result will be a line.

Using the Circle/ Ellipse tools

Figure 11-12

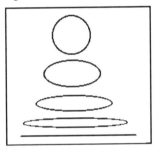

The Circle/Ellipse tool can create an evolving series of circular shapes.

For example, you can use a combination of the tools we talked about so far to draw a full cookie jar. You will use circles and lines to draw the cookie jar. Figure 11-13 on the next page shows the series of steps.

- Use ellipses (unfilled circles) for the base and top of the glass jar, as shown in step one.

- Add lines to connect the circles. Step two shows the cookie jar at this point.

- To create a cookie, first draw a brown filled ellipse. Next, add chocolate chips by adding smaller darker filled ellipses. If you like Oreos better, draw black filled ellipses on either side of a white rounded box. As you can see in step three, we put both chocolate chip cookies and Oreos in our cookie jar.

- To put a cover on the jar, use the Circle/Ellipse tool to create the different diameters of the lid. Finally, connect the lid's circles with lines to finish the shape. You'll learn how to erase the overlapping lines with the Eraser tool later in this chapter so your lid will look like the one in step four.

Figure 11-13

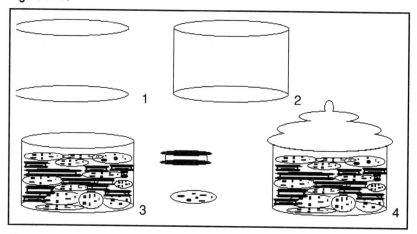

You can create a cookie jar using the Circle/Ellipse and Line tools.

Using the
Polygon tools

The Polygon and Filled Polygon tools are different from the tools we've used so far because they don't have predetermined shapes. Instead, the Polygon tools let you continue putting sides on a graphic until you close it with the last line. You can draw lines, triangles, trapezoids, parallelograms, and so forth, with the Polygon tools.

To draw a polygon, select the Polygon tool (or the Filled Polygon tool) and move the crosshair pointer into the work area. Click and drag to form the starting line and then release the button. When you click in another part of the work area, Paintbrush will add a line connecting the two points. You could also click to start a new line and then drag the line to its new location. The graphic won't be complete until you connect to your starting point to close up the shape. To close the shape, you can either click on the first point again or double-click to have Paintbrush automatically add the final line and complete the shape. Double-clicking is easier than trying to hit the first point exactly. After the shape is closed, the lines become the width and color you selected. If you were using the Filled Polygon tool, Paintbrush will fill any enclosed areas with the selected foreground color.

You can use the Polygon tool and a double-clicking technique as a quick way to draw a triangle. After you draw the base line, move the pointer into position for the third point of the triangle and double-click to connect to both ends of the starting line, forming a triangle.

To create a perfectly straight horizontal, vertical, or diagonal line, use the [Shift] key while you drag the guidelines. While you drag the guideline, it shifts to horizontal, vertical, or 45-degree diagonal lines.

You can use the Polygon tool with the Box tool to draw a wood plank. Follow the steps shown in Figure 11-14 to create a wood plank.

- Set up the drawing for a 4" by 6" area with color, then double-click the Eraser tool to start a new work area.

- Select a thin line size and choose the Box tool. Now draw a rectangle for the basic shape for a wood plank, as shown in step one.

- Form the wood grain inside the rectangle with the Filled Polygon tool by creating narrow long multi-edged shapes, as shown in step two. Now you have a wood plank that you can use to "build" complex shapes. We'll use the wood plank again later in this chapter.

Figure 11-14

By simply drawing a rectangle and filling it with a series of long narrow varied polygons, you can produce a wood plank.

Using the Curve tool

The Curve tool is like the Line tool, with a twist. After you draw the line, you can pull on either side of it to form a curve. The final curve will reflect the foreground color and line size width you choose. The Curve tool can draw curved lines, double-curved lines, and other complex shapes.

To draw a curved line, select the Curve tool and move the crosshair pointer to the work area. Click and drag the guideline to the length you want, then release the mouse button. Next, click on the guideline and drag to either side of the line. Notice that the guideline bulges and curves in the direction you drag the pointer. You are creating a mid-point that pulls the line into a curve, anchored at the two end points. Each line you create with the curve tool can have two mid-points. Release the mouse button to place the first mid-point, then click on the guideline again and drag the pointer in a different direction to create a compound curve. After you release the button the second time, the curve will be finalized. If you don't want a double curve, you can click on the ending point of the line to finish the curve.

The Curve tool can create other complex graphic shapes besides the double curve. You can flex the curved line into a loop by double-clicking and dragging the guideline, instead of just clicking and dragging it. A double-click will put the starting and ending points of the guideline in the same place. Now you can drag to form a narrow loop. Next, click on the guideline and drag it to one side to pull open the loop. After you release the mouse button, the shape of the graphic will be final.

Figure 11-15 shows a variety of curves you can create with the Curve tool. The first curve is a line pulled up with the pointer. The second is a line pulled down. The third and fourth are pulled right and left, respectively. The fifth is pulled up on one end and down on the other. The sixth is a loop created by a closed curve.

Figure 11-15

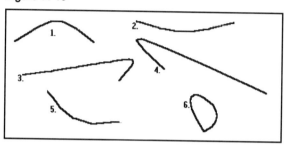

You can use the Curve tool to create a variety of curved lines.

You can use all these curved lines with the tools we've talked about so far to create a balloon like the one in Figure 11-16. The following steps explain how to create a balloon.

- Draw a filled circle for a guideline, as shown in step one.

- Use the Curve tool to draw sloping sides on the balloon, as shown in step two.

- With the Box and Line tools, add the basket for the balloon, as shown in step three.

Figure 11-16

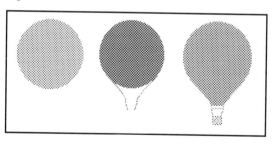

You can use the Paintbrush tools we've discussed to draw a balloon.

Using the Brush tool

The Brush tool lets you draw freehand with six kinds of brushes. Not only can you choose how large the brush is with the Linesize box, you can also choose the brush shape from the Options menu. The Brush tool paints with the foreground color.

To draw freehand, select the Brush tool and move the pointer into the work area. Notice that the pointer changes into a small square—the default brush shape. If you click and drag the Brush tool, a line will trail behind the pointer. This is a final line and not a guideline. The Brush tool lets you draw lines, curves, and shapes. By clicking once, you can draw a dot that is the same shape as the brush.

You can change the brush shape with the Brush Shapes… command on the Options menu. You can also double-click on the Brush tool for a shortcut to the Brush Shapes dialog box. The Brush Shapes dialog box in Figure 11-17 shows a box around the shape we are currently using. You can change the brush into a circle, horizontal line, vertical line, diagonal right line, or diagonal left line by clicking on one of the brush shapes and then clicking OK. The pointer changes to match your choice. The brush shapes apply only to the Brush tool.

Figure 11-17

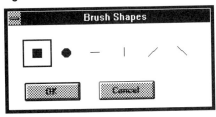

The Brush Shapes dialog box lets you choose from six brush shapes.

When you draw one line on top of another, the line on top determines the color of that area. The colors won't mix; they just cover each other up.

You can create calligraphy letters like the ones we used to spell *Kentucky* in Figure 11-18. If you want to create more than one letter, it's a good idea to draw some guidelines before you start writing. We used the [Shift] key as we drew our guidelines so they would be perfectly straight. If you draw a guideline with a color that isn't used in the rest of the drawing, you'll be able to erase just that color with the Color Eraser tool, which we'll discuss later. You can see a color version of Figure 11-18 in Appendix 2.

Figure 11-18

You can use the diagonal brush shape to pen calligraphy letters.

Here's a trick you'll want to try with the [Shift] key: As you draw a line, hold down the [Shift] key, and you will be able to move the pointer to the other end of the line and continue drawing in that direction without starting a new line. You must be moving in one direction (horizontal or vertical) before you press the [Shift] key or your line may shift directions.

**Using the
Airbrush tool**

The Airbrush tool is similar to the Brush tool because it creates free-form shapes. The Airbrush tool simulates a burst of spray paint, creating a circular pattern of dots. The color on the drawing increases in density as your dragging speed decreases (just like spray paint). You also can use the Airbrush tool to add shading to your drawing for a three-dimensional effect.

Select the Airbrush tool and move the crosshair pointer into the work area. Click and drag the crosshair to begin coloring. If you keep going over an area with the Airbrush tool, the color will become more intense (more like a solid color). When you move the pointer slowly, the area also looks more like a solid color. If you select the Airbrush tool, hold down the [Shift] key, and drag the pointer, you'll produce a perfectly horizontal or vertical line. Using the [Shift] key also will let you go back over your line to extend it in either direction. If you click the button once, the Airbrush tool will create a shape that is the lightest density; you won't be able to make it any darker by clicking on it again. To make the line darker, you need to drag the pointer.

Since you can see through the shape you're drawing (because the background isn't completely covered), you can draw on top of another color and simulate mixing the two colors. The Airbrush tool uses the foreground color. If you move the pointer quickly, to get a lighter density of dots, you'll get a better mix of colors.

You can use the Airbrush tool to create clouds by airbrushing the darker background color with white. In Figure 11-19, we created clouds to form a backdrop for our balloon drawing. We made the centers of the clouds opaque by moving the airbrush slowly and going over the area several times. The edges get their transparent look from moving the airbrush quickly, leaving a thinner pattern of white dots over the blue of the background.

**Using the
Paint Roller tool**

The Paint Roller tool, like a real paint roller, covers a wide area with color. In fact, the Paint Roller tool will keep filling in color until it reaches the boundaries of a graphic or framed area. If the frame isn't perfect (for example, if you leave a small opening), the color could spread into another area or even the entire drawing. Never fear: An Undo command on the Edit menu will remove all the color the Paint Roller tool dumped into your drawing.

Figure 11-19

You can use the Airbrush tool to create clouds.

To use the Paint Roller tool, select it from the Toolbox and move the pointer into the work area. When you do, the pointer looks like a paint roller. Select the foreground color you want to use, then move the pointer to the area that needs the new color, and click. The area will change to your selected color.

You can also change line colors with the Paint Roller tool, but you must be very careful. Remember, the active area of the Paint Roller pointer is the point formed by the paint dripping from the roller. In order to change the color of a line, you must position the pointer's active area precisely on top of the line. When you do, the pointer (at the tip) will change to another color (the pointer changes to contrasting colors as you move it over different colors) to let you know that the pointer is in the correct place. Then, you can click to change the line's color.

A word of warning: If you use the Undo command to remove a color, Undo will remove everything you have done with the Paint Roller tool since you last selected it. Therefore, it's a good idea to reselect the Paint Roller tool for each color or area you're painting. Also, if you change a line to the same color as the fill of the shape by mistake, when you try to change the line back to its original color, the fill will change too. Unfortunately, Paintbrush assumes that everything of one color (the frame and the filled area) is one shape and replaces it all.

In the case of complex graphics with overlapping lines, a fill may not work in detailed areas when the Paint Roller's active area is not fine enough to fit. You'll need to use the Zoom In command on the View menu to color in the small areas. We'll talk about the Zoom In and Zoom Out commands later in this chapter.

For example, if you want to fill in the background of the *Kentucky* calligraphy, first choose the Paint Roller tool and then a color for a new background. Click on the work area outside the letters so the Paint Roller tool will fill it in. We'll fill these in later when we talk about the zoom commands. Next, click on the inside of the letters to fill in the white spaces. In Figure 11-20, notice the isolated white pixels in the letters that didn't fill in.

Figure 11-20

The Paint Roller tool filled in the background but missed the areas blocked off.

A look at the Text tool

Paintbrush provides the Text tool to give you the power to add text to your graphics. However, the text you add will actually be a graphic itself. In other words, it isn't a specifically coded character (ASCII code) that you'd find in a word processor like Write. Each letter Paintbrush adds to your drawing is a bit map that looks like a letter. Since each letter is a miniature drawing, you can't edit Paintbrush text as you would regular text. In this section, we'll show you how to choose colors, fonts, sizes, and styles for letters of Paintbrush text.

Using the Text tool

abc

The Text tool is very easy to use. To add text to your drawing, select the tool and move the I-beam pointer into the work area. Click to position the cursor where you want Paintbrush to add the text. The cursor will assume the height of the text and move to the right as you type. (A word of caution: The text will overwrite any graphics already in your drawing.) Because Paintbrush won't wrap the letters when you reach the right side of the drawing's work area, you will have to press [Enter] to move the cursor to the next line. The cursor will return to the same horizontal position where you first started your text.

You can continue to change your text (active text) until you make it final by doing one of the following: choosing another tool, clicking somewhere else on the drawing, or scrolling the drawing. You can use the [Backspace] key to delete any mistakes. To save time and avoid frustration, create your text in small sections. You'll need to make any changes for a section before going on to the next one. That way, if one section contains a mistake, you can undo it without undoing all your text.

The Text tool uses the foreground color, which can be any color you choose, including colors that are patterns. The background color in the Selected Colors box is not used by the Text tool.

Setting the font

Paintbrush comes with nine fonts. The Font menu lists these fonts and places a check mark next to the one that the Text tool is currently using. Paintbrush will add or subtract fonts on the list to match the capabilities of your printer. If you don't have a printer installed, Paintbrush will use the fonts your monitor supports.

Paintbrush allows you to use multiple fonts in your drawing. In order to use a new font, you need to select it before you click to start your text. You can change fonts while you are entering text. Just select a font, and any text you've already typed will change to that font. However, after you finalize the text (for example, by choosing another tool), you can't change the font.

Choosing point size

Besides changing the font, you can vary the size of your text. The Size menu lists all the point sizes of the current font. Notice the asterisk, check mark, and black and gray numbers in the menu in Figure 11-21. The asterisk next to the black number is the point size that your printer already has (available precision sizes). The check mark indicates the size the Text tool is currently using. The gray numbers are point sizes your printer can't use (unavailable sizes), while the black numbers are point sizes that Paintbrush has rescaled from the ones with asterisks.

Figure 11-21

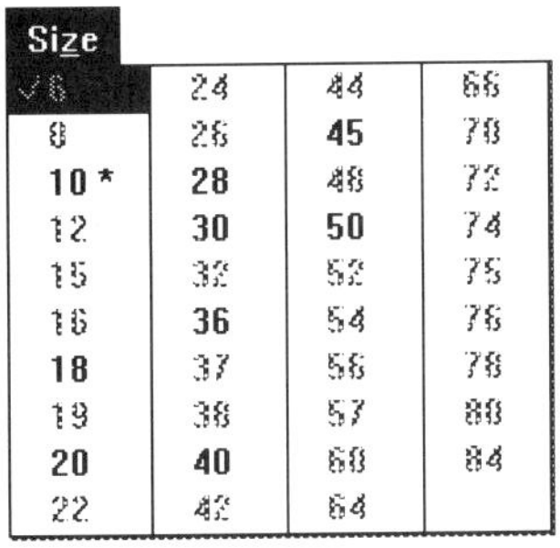

Size			
✓6	24	44	66
8	26	45	70
10 *	28	48	72
12	30	50	74
15	32	52	75
16	36	54	76
18	37	56	78
19	38	57	80
20	40	60	84
22	42	64	

The Size menu lists the range of point sizes for the currently selected font.

You can change the point size in the same way you can change the font. It's a good idea to decide on all the fonts and point sizes you will use before you begin typing since you can't change them after you've finalized your text. To choose a point size, open the Size menu and click on the size you want. When the menu closes, Paintbrush will automatically resize your active text. You can continue to change the point size for your text until you finalize it by clicking on another tool or clicking somewhere else on the drawing with the Text tool.

Enhancing your text

Besides changing the size and font, you can change the style of your text by using the six commands on the Style menu. As you can see in Figure 11-22, the Style menu is divided into three sections. The first section contains the Normal command, which cancels any styles you've assigned to your text. The next section's commands are Bold, Italic, and Underline. When you select one of these style commands, a check mark will appear next to it to show it's active. (You can have more than one style command chosen at a time.) If you select the command again, it will toggle off. The last section contains the Outline and Shadow commands. Unlike the previous section, which lets you choose more than one style command at a time, only one of these choices can be active at once. When you use the Outline or Shadow command, the outline or shadow color will be the background color. Figure 11-23 shows a sample of each of these styles.

Figure 11-22

The Style menu enables you to apply styles to text.

Figure 11-23

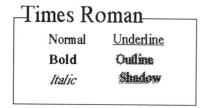

Here are samples of the six styles you can use for text.

Paintbrush also provides some shortcuts for changing the style of your text. You can press [Ctrl]B for Bold, [Ctrl]I for Italic, or [Ctrl]U for Underline.

A look at editing tools

Now that you know how to add text and graphics to your drawing, let's see how you can use the editing tools to edit the various elements of your drawing. Paintbrush dedicates four tools specifically for doing this: the Eraser, Color Eraser, Pick, and Scissors tools. The [Delete] and [Backspace] keys also can remove elements from your drawing.

With the Eraser and the Color Eraser tools, you can remove or even change colors in your drawing. As we'll explain in a minute, the Eraser tool changes a color, while the Color Eraser tool erases colors selectively. The pointer for the Eraser tool is a box; the Color Eraser pointer is a crosshair inside a box. The box determines the arca that is erased. You can change the size of the box with the Linesize box. Keep in mind that the finer the line, the smaller the box.

When you move the Eraser tool over an area, anything the pointer covers will change to the background color. If you change the background color, the Eraser tool will change the color of anything it encounters to match the new background color. For example, you can use the Eraser tool to clean up any stray lines in your drawing. Remember the wood plank we drew with the Polygon and Box tools? As you can see in Figure 11-24, we used the Eraser tool to remove any part of the wood grain that overflowed the boundaries of the wood plank.

Using the Eraser and
Color Eraser tools

Figure 11-24

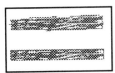

*We used the Eraser tool to clean up any
stray lines on our wood plank drawing.*

If you want to be a bit more selective, use the Color Eraser tool. It will erase only colors that match the selected foreground color. The Color Eraser tool changes any pixels of the foreground color it encounters into the selected background color, offering a good way to change only part of your drawing.

You can click and drag the Eraser tools to remove colors, or just click the button once to remove one box of color. Since the Eraser tool moves in a free-form pattern like the Brush tool, you can use the [Shift] key to move the Eraser tools in a perfectly straight horizontal or vertical line. Just as you can extend either end of a line with the Brush tool using the [Shift] key, you can extend color changes in the same manner with the Eraser tools.

For example, you can erase the calligraphy guidelines from Figure 11-18 with the Color Eraser tool since they are a different color than the calligraphy. To do this, choose the guideline color for the foreground and white for the background. Now you can erase the guidelines without removing the calligraphy.

You can also color parts of a complex drawing with the Color Eraser tool. If you want to change one color on a part of the drawing, like the red on a rose petal, just change the foreground color to red and the background to a new color (pink). Now move the Color Eraser tool over the area to be changed. The Color Eraser tool changes only the red and leaves the white background and green stem alone, as you can see in Figure 11-25. Appendix 2 has a color version of Figure 11-25.

Figure 11-25

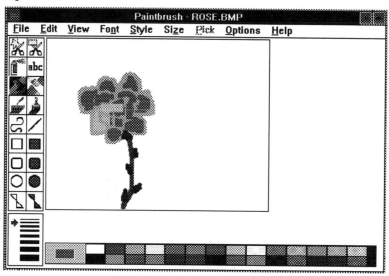

The Color Eraser tool changes only one color and leaves the other colors alone.

You can use the Color Eraser tool to make global changes to your drawing. Suppose you want to change everything that is blue on your drawing to purple, but the background, and many small items, are blue. Using the Paint Roller tool or erasing with the Color Eraser tool to make a change would involve a great deal of work. However, you can take a shortcut with the Color Eraser tool to change the colors. First make the foreground of the Selected Colors box blue and the background purple, then double-click the Color Eraser tool. All the blue in your drawing will change to purple.

Using the Scissors and Pick tools

The Scissors and Pick tools, are also called the pick tools because you can use the Pick menu commands only after you select something with them. These tools use a dotted line as a guideline to show you what area is selected. After you select a part of your drawing, you can move it, use the Pick or Edit menu commands, or even "sweep" the image to form a series of duplicates (we'll talk about sweeping later in this chapter).

To select a graphic from your drawing, you'll want to use the Pick tool. To use this tool, select it from the Toolbox and then move the crosshair pointer into the work area. Click to anchor the guidelines in one corner and then drag to form a box that encloses the graphic you want to select. If you make a mistake, you can click the right mouse button to start over. You also can click in another spot to remove the guidelines. When you use the Pick tool, the background around the shape will also be captured in the selection.

If you don't want to include the background in your selection, you should use the Scissors tool. To use the Scissors tool, select it from the Toolbox and move the crosshair pointer into the work area. Then, click near the shape or text you want to select, and drag the guideline around the shape. To finish selecting, connect the line to the starting point. If you release the mouse button before you arrive at the starting point, Paintbrush will connect the line.

You can use the editing features of Paintbrush to improve on the basic design of your drawing. You can rearrange the graphics in your drawing or even duplicate them. Paintbrush's editing functions give you artistic license to manipulate your drawing without starting over. In this section, we'll show you how to make changes via Clipboard and Edit menu commands, with advanced functions of the pick tools and the Pick menu. When you're finished, you'll be able to move graphics, change their size, flip them horizontally or vertically, invert their colors, and even tilt them.

Improving on the basic design

In Chapter 9, we showed you the basics of moving data around in a file with the Cut, Copy, and Paste commands. You use the same commands to move graphics around in your drawing. To use the Edit menu commands, first select a graphic with the Pick or Scissors tools. Next, issue the command you need to move or copy the graphics. Cutting the selected shape will remove it from the drawing and keep it on Clipboard. Copying will not remove the shape from the drawing but will store a copy of the shape on Clipboard. Pasting will add the contents of Clipboard to your drawing in the upper-left corner of the work area. The pasted copy will appear already selected so you can easily move it to a new location. You can paste an object more than once, quickly reproducing a common element in your drawing. We used the Copy and Paste commands to facilitate drawing the electronic keyboard in Figure 11-11.

Editing via Clipboard

You don't have to use special commands on a menu to move and copy your selected graphics. You can use the Pick or Scissors tool to move, copy, or sweep a selected graphic.

Selection tool functions

If you want to move a graphic that you selected with the Pick or Scissors tool, just move your pointer into the interior of the guideline box. The pointer will change from a crosshair to a regular arrow pointer. At this point, you can click and drag the graphic anywhere in your drawing.

Moving cutouts

If you select only a part of a graphic, only that part will move. If you make a mistake and don't get all of the graphic in your selection, you can use the Undo command to return the graphic to its original condition, providing you haven't performed any intervening actions. However, Undo works only for your last action; when you choose another tool, you can't undo your previous action.

After you select an entire graphic or part of one, you're ready to move it. You can place a graphic two ways; transparant placement and opaque placement. If you move an unfilled box using the left mouse button, when you place the graphic on top of another graphic, you will see the lines of both graphics (transparent placement). If you move the graphic with the right mouse button, it will be opaque (and will include any background you selected) and cover up the other graphic (opaque placement). Figure 11-26 shows a series of transparently moved and opaquely moved boxes.

Figure 11-26

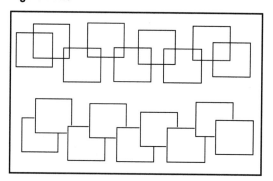

The top series of squares uses the transparent placement of a graphic; the bottom series uses opaque placement.

Using the Pick tools to copy a shape

If you find yourself repeatedly creating the same element, you can use a shortcut to simply duplicate the element and place it in your drawing. To copy an element, first select it with the Pick tool and then press [Shift] and drag the graphic with either the left mouse button (for a transparent copy) or the right mouse button (for an opaque copy). The pointer will pick up a copy of the element. For example, to reuse the wood plank you created earlier to draw the horse stable shown in Figure 11-27, you need to observe the following steps.

- Open the file in which you saved the wood plank. Select the wood plank with the Pick tool, and copy it to Clipboard using the Copy command on the Edit menu.

- Open a new file by choosing the New command on the File menu.

- Paste the wood plank into your new file by choosing the Paste command on the Edit menu.

- Click on the wood plank and then [Shift] drag to duplicate the plank. We used a combination of vertical and horizontal planks to build the walls and stable door shown in Figure 11-27.

- You can add such details as hinges and a handle to the door by using the Box, Circle, and Polygon tools. We also added straw with the Line tool and then copied it to spread it on the floor. We drew the horseshoe above the stall with the Curve tool and placed the transparent copy over the door.

Figure 11-27

By duplicating the wood plank, you can create a building like this stable.

Instead of cutting and pasting a graphic repeatedly to create a series, you can sweep the graphic to form a cascade of opaque or transparent images. A transparent sweep looks like Figure 11-28, while an opaque sweep looks like Figure 11-29 on the next page. As you can see, the lines from the underlying shapes show through in a transparent sweep, but not in an opaque sweep.

Sweeping a graphic

Figure 11-28

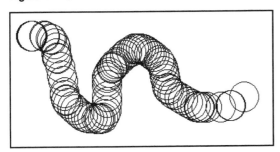

This is a transparent sweep of circles.

Figure 11-29

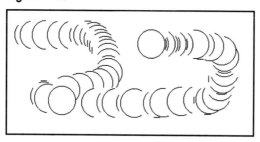

This is an opaque sweep of circles.

All you have to do to sweep a graphic is select it with the Pick tool, then hold down the [Ctrl] key and click and drag the graphic where you want to place it. To complete the sweep, release the mouse button and the [Ctrl] key. Use the left mouse button if you want a transparent graphic, and use the right button if you want an opaque one. You can change the graphic effect by altering the speed of your mouse movements.

Improvising with the Pick menu

Once you select a graphic with one of the pick tools, you can improvise on that graphic theme with the commands on the Pick menu. You can resize the graphic, flip it horizontally or vertically, tilt it, and invert its colors. You also can tell Paintbrush to remove the original graphic and replace it with the new version by using the Clear command.

Sizing selected graphics

As you know, it's much easier to draw a large graphic than a small one, but with Paintbrush, you can draw a large graphic and then make a reduced copy of it with the Shrink + Grow command on the Pick menu. When you're ready to shrink the graphic, frame it with the Pick tool and select the Shrink + Grow command. After you select the command, click and drag the pointer to form a guideline box representing the new size you want. You can change the proportions of the graphic by making the guideline box longer or wider. If you want the new size to have the same proportions as the original graphic, hold down the [Shift] key as you drag the guideline box. Figure 11-30 shows a series of balloons we created with the Shrink + Grow command.

When you select the Shrink + Grow command, Paintbrush adds a check mark next to the command. The command will remain selected until you toggle it off or reselect a graphic with one of the pick tools. Note that you must turn off the Shrink + Grow command before you can use the Flip Horizontal, Flip Vertical, or Inverse commands.

Figure 11-30

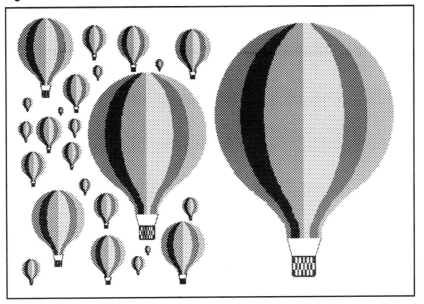

The Shrink + Grow command lets you create proportional copies of balloon graphics.

Flipping a graphic

Not only can you change the size of a selected graphic, you can flip it horizontally or vertically. To flip a graphic, first select it with the Pick tool, then choose one of the flip commands from the Pick menu. You can follow the steps below to flip a graphic, as illustrated in Figure 11-31 on the next page.

- Follow the arrows in step one as a reference so you can see the new orientation as the square flips.

- To flip the square horizontally, first select the square with the Pick tool and then choose the Flip Horizontal command from the Pick menu. When you flip the square, it will look like step two.

- If you flip the original square vertically with the Flip Vertical command instead, it will look like step three.

If you try to flip a graphic but nothing happens, check to see whether a toggle command on the Pick menu—either Shrink + Grow or Tilt—is turned on. These commands must be inactive before you can continue flipping the graphic. Another way you can tell if one of these toggle commands is on is that the guidelines won't remain when you try to select the graphic.

Figure 11-31

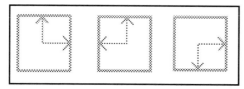

These are the steps for flipping graphics.

Tilting a graphic

In addition to flipping or resizing a graphic, you also can tilt it. All you have to do to tilt a graphic is select it and then choose the Tilt command from the Pick menu. Because Tilt is a toggle command, once it's active, you can keep producing tilted shapes. After you activate the Tilt command, move your pointer into the work area and click to draw the guideline box and anchor one corner. Now drag the pointer to change the orientation of the box. The farther you move the pointer from the anchor point, the greater the tilt. When you release the mouse button, the graphic will orient itself to the tilt of the guideline box. Figure 11-32 shows the "Leaning Tower of Louisville" straight and then tilted with the Tilt command.

Figure 11-32

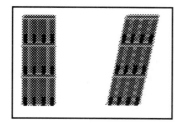

We created a leaning tower with the Tilt command.

Inverting a graphic

We've talked about changing the shape of a graphic: now let's talk about changing the colors with the Pick menu. The Inverse command on the Pick menu will change all the colors of a selected area to their complementary colors. (A complementary color is one that is opposite a selected color on a color wheel. For example, the complement of red is green.) You must carefully select the area you want to invert because both the foreground and background colors will be affected. If you use the Pick tool to select a graphic, the frame and the interior will change color, as well as any exterior selected area. If you invert a pattern, all the dots that make up that pattern will change to their complementary colors.

Using the Clear command

The Clear command on the Pick menu works with the Tilt and Shrink + Grow commands. The Clear command helps reduce the number of duplicate graphics in your work area by clearing the original selected graphic from the work area after you create a variation with the Tilt or Shrink + Grow commands. You need to reissue the Clear command to toggle it back off so you can leave the original graphic untouched while creating variations.

Instead of attempting to produce a perfect drawing on the first try, you can use the zoom commands to clean up your drawing and add fine detail. We used the zoom commands on all the graphics in this chapter to clean them up. In this section, we'll also show you how to use the Cursor Position box as a ruler for your drawing. The Cursor Position box is a special dialog box that dynamically displays the coordinates (X,Y) of your mouse pointer in the work area.

ADDING DETAIL

To view and adjust the minute details of your drawing, you can use the Zoom In command on the View menu to look at the bits that form images. When you choose the Zoom In command, the pointer will turn into a box. Move the box pointer over the area you want to start viewing, then click the left mouse button. As you can see in Figure 11-33, Paintbrush will display a grid of bits that is an enlarged view of the section of the graphic you selected with the box pointer. To provide a reference point, a box in the upper-left corner of the work area displays the actual size of the part of the graphic you're viewing. By using the scroll arrows, you can look at minute aspects of your graphic. Both the bit map and the display box will present a new part of your drawing when you use the scroll arrows.

Zooming in for a closer look

Figure 11-33

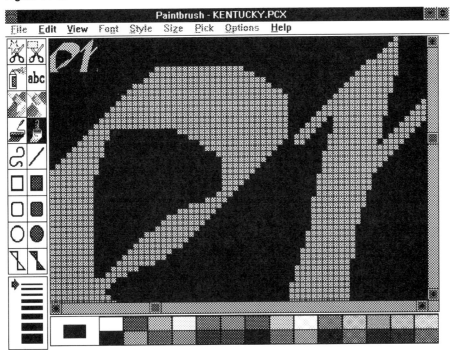

After you use the Zoom In command on the View menu, the work area turns into a bit map with an actual size view in the upper-left corner.

If you want to change any of the bits on the bit map, you must use either the Brush or the Paint Roller tool. You'll find that you can't select any of the other tools in the Toolbox or their related commands. The Brush tool will let you change one bit at a time. If you select the Brush tool and then move the pointer into the work area, you will notice that the pointer doesn't change a brush shape but remains an arrow pointer. The Paint Roller tool's pointer, on the other hand, keeps its unique shape and functions.

With the Brush tool, you can click on a single bit to change it to the selected foreground color or click and drag to change bits as you move the pointer. As you change the bits in the bit map, the actual-size view changes to match your bit changes, giving you a better idea whether the drawing looks the way you want.

For example, if you wanted to clean up the edges on a graphic because it had gaps and you couldn't fill it with the Paint Roller tool without filling the rest of the drawing, you could zoom in to fix it. To do this, select the Zoom In command, place the box pointer over the offending area of the graphic, and click. Once the bit map appears, choose the Brush tool and make sure the selected foreground color is the one you want. Next, move the pointer into the work area and click on the bits that will fill in the gap.

If you have an enclosed space to fill in the repaired graphic, go ahead and choose the Paint Roller tool. As you move the Paint Roller tool onto the zoomed-in graphic, the Paint Roller pointer will appear. The Paint Roller tool can only fill in the area displayed on the screen. Therefore, if part of a graphic isn't displayed, you can't fill it in. You'll need to scroll through the rest of the shape as you fill in all the bits with the new color.

You can see why the Zoom In command is used only for detail and not for large areas. For example, small areas like the ones in the *Kentucky* calligraphy need to be filled in with the Paint Roller tool and the Zoom In command. In Figure 11-34, we zoomed in on one part of the *Kentucky* calligraphy that needed the background filled in, then filled it in with the Paint Roller tool.

When you have finished working with the zoomed-in graphic, choose Zoom Out on the View menu to return to your original work area. If you want to go a step further, you can choose the View Picture command on the View menu to view the entire drawing instead of just what is displayed in Paintbrush's window. When you click on this command, Paintbrush will display the entire drawing without the Toolbox, Linesize box, Palette, menus, or other screen elements. To return to the regular Paintbrush window, click anywhere on the screen. Figures 11-35 and 11-36 on page 272 show a regular view and a View Picture view of the same drawing. (See Appendix 2 for a color version of Figure 11-36.)

Figure 11-34

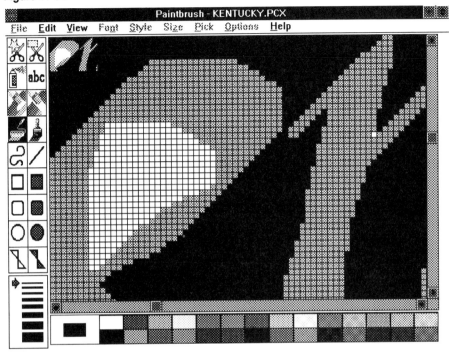

We zoomed in on part of the calligraphy that needed the background filled in.

If you want Paintbrush to display more of your drawing so you can manipulate it without relying heavily on the scroll bars, you can temporarily remove the Toolbox, Linesize box, or the Palette. When you select the Tools and Linesize commands on the View menu, the Toolbox and the Linesize box will disappear. If you look at the View menu again, you'll notice that the check mark next to Tools and Linesize is gone. If you select it again, the check mark, and the Toolbox and Linesize box, will reappear.

The Palette command on the View menu is also a toggle command. If you toggle the check mark off the Palette command, Paintbrush will remove the Palette from the work area.

If you want to see the entire drawing and still be able to work on it, you can use the Zoom Out command with a normally sized drawing. After you issue Zoom Out, Paintbrush will redisplay the entire drawing in the boundaries of your work area, regardless of the window size. However, not all the tools are active. You can use only the Pick tool and some Edit menu commands (Cut, Copy, Paste, Copy To..., and Paste From...), which we'll discuss at the end of the chapter.

Figure 11-35

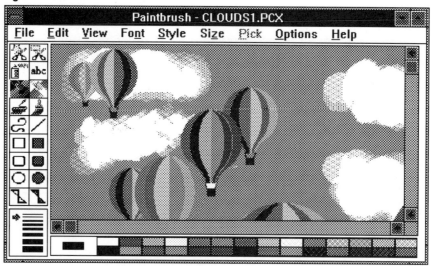

The work area displays only part of the balloons.

Figure 11-36

The View Picture command shows all the balloons.

Although you can't display a ruler in the Paintbrush window, you can use the Cursor Position command on the View menu to give yourself a reference and add consistency and accuracy to your drawing. When you select the Cursor Position command, a dialog box like the one in Figure 11-37 will appear on the menu bar.

Using cursor position as a ruler

Figure 11-37

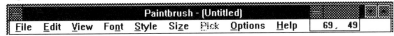

The Cursor Position dialog box tracks the horizontal and vertical coordinates of the pointer in your drawing.

The dialog box displays two numbers: the horizontal and vertical coordinates. The upper-left corner of a drawing has the coordinates 0,0. The coordinates of the lower-right corner depend on the size of your drawing. If the window is maximized, the lower-right coordinates can be as large as 543,369 in a default-sized drawing. However, you can use any dimensions you want for your drawing, meaning the coordinates for the lower-right corner can exceed the default coordinates. If the pointer leaves the work area, the values in the dialog box will freeze at the exit point's coordinates.

Let's suppose you want to draw a stack of boxes. Instead of guessing how wide the first one is when you're trying to match the second one, you can use the Cursor Position dialog box as a reference. Just remember the starting and stopping horizontal points when you draw the first box. You can move the Box tool to the exact horizontal starting point before you draw the next box so the boxes will be the same width. If you want identical heights for the boxes, you can increment the vertical coordinates the same amount for each box. Of course, if you want identical boxes, it would be easier to select the first with the Pick tool, then use the Copy and Paste commands.

You can close the Cursor Position dialog box either by toggling off the Cursor Position command or by double-clicking on the dialog box's Control menu. If you minimize the Paintbrush window while the Cursor Position box is displayed, Paintbrush will remove it once the window becomes an icon. When you restore the window, you'll need to issue the Cursor Position command to redisplay the box.

As soon as you complete a drawing or even a major portion of it, you should save your work. You can save the file on your hard drive or on a floppy disk. To save the file, choose the Save command on the File menu. A File Save As dialog box, like the one in Figure 11-38, will appear.

SAVING YOUR WORK

Figure 11-38

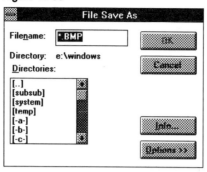

The File Save As dialog box has a text box for the file name.

When you save the file, Paintbrush saves it with a .BMP or .PCX file name extension depending on the file type. To see the available file types shown in Figure 11-39, click on the Options >> button. After you type in the file name and specify the correct directory (Paintbrush puts it in the Windows directory automatically) or drive in the Directories list box, click on OK. After the file is saved, you'll notice that the Paintbrush title bar displays the new file name. From that point, when you use the Save command, Paintbrush won't ask for a file name; it will update the file it already has.

Figure 11-39

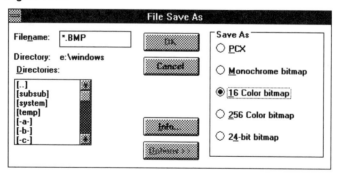

If you click the Options >> button, Paintbrush will list all the possible file extensions.

If you want to save a copy of your drawing in a different file, you must use the Save As... command on the File menu. Then, you can enter the new file name in the File Save As dialog box. Even if you don't want to see another copy under a different name, you can still use the Save As... command to save the file in a different place on your hard drive or on a floppy. It's a good idea to keep a backup copy on a floppy disk in case of accidents or equipment failure. In addition, it's always a good idea to save your drawing before you print. That way, if the printer causes your PC to lock up and you have to reboot, you won't lose any of your drawing in RAM.

At some point, you'll want to print your drawing. Before you can send your drawing to the printer, you need to make sure that the page and printer are set up correctly. Setting up a page involves setting the margins for a printout of your drawing. To set up a printer, you specify any variations in the options of an active printer (such as page orientation or number of copies). After the page and printer settings suit you, issue the Print... command to tell Paintbrush to print the drawing. You also can specify how much of the drawing to print. In this section, we explain the commands and settings you'll use to print your drawings. We'll also explain your options for printing partial drawings or multiple copies.

PRINTING YOUR DRAWING

Before you issue the Print... command, you need to tell your printer how you want the drawing positioned on the page. The Page Setup... command controls the header, footer, and margins. When you choose the Page Setup... command from the File menu, the Page Setup dialog box will appear. By default, the Header and Footer text boxes are empty in Paintbrush . For details on headers and footers, you can read the section on page setup in Chapter 9 and refer to Table 9-1.

The margins are also set up in the Page Setup dialog box. The header and footer will always be .5" from the top and bottom of the page. Paintbrush won't let you change those margins.

Page setup

After you have set up the page as you want it, you need to verify that the printer is also set up the way you want it. To do this, choose Printer Setup... from the File menu. When the Printer Setup dialog box appears, the default printer will be highlighted and all the active printers listed. Make sure the printer that is hooked up and installed on your PC is highlighted and is using the right port. If it doesn't have a port or the correct port, you need to use Control Panel to assign one. In Figure 11-40, the highlighted printer name shows that we're connected to an HP LaserJet on LPT1:. If you want to change the resolution, orientation, cartridge, or the number of copies, you'll have to use the Setup... button.

Printer setup

Figure 11-40

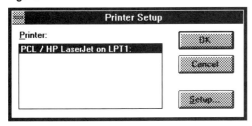

The Printer Setup dialog box highlights the active printer.

**Using the Print...
command**

Now that you have set up the page and printer, you're ready to actually print a drawing. When you choose the Print... command from the File menu, the Print dialog box in Figure 11-41 will appear. In this dialog box, you can choose the quality for the printout, the part of the drawing to print, the number of copies, and the printer resolution setting.

Figure 11-41

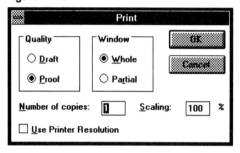

The Print dialog box appears when you use the Print... command.

Setting the quality

You can control the quality of your printout by selecting the Proof or Draft setting in the Quality section (if your printer has one). A high-quality printout, or a proof, uses all the features of your printer but prints more slowly than a printer that provides lower-quality printouts. A lower quality printout, or a draft, prints faster but ignores the advanced features of your printer. If you have a dot matrix printer, the draft printout will be lighter than a proof and the image will have rough edges. In a proof, the printout will be dark and the edges of the images and text will be smooth. Drafts are good for checking your work before you print the final copy. Remember that you can use the View Picture command on the View menu to see the entire drawing on the screen and catch mistakes before you print.

**Choosing the
number of copies**

The Number of Copies text box in the Print dialog box lets you specify the number of copies you want to print. Simply type a number (by default, the text box is selected when you open the dialog box) to change the number of copies.

As we explained in Chapter 9, you can also set the number of copies while setting up the printer. Since you can establish the copy setting in two places— the Print dialog box and the printer-specific setup dialog box—the number of copies your printer returns may be greater than you expect. For example, if you specify two copies from Paintbrush's Print dialog box and two copies in the printer-specific dialog box, you will actually receive four copies. To avoid printing extra copies, keep your printer set up for the default (one copy) and let the application specify the number of additional copies.

Another setting you may need to adjust is the printer resolution. The Use Printer Resolution check box in the Print dialog box tells the printer to use its idea of how large a pixel is instead of how large the screen thinks it is. Your screen uses larger pixels than your printer does. If you leave this option deselected, Paintbrush will size your image according to your specifications in the Image Attributes dialog box—it should approximate the image size on your screen. If you select Use Printer Resolution, the printer will translate each screen pixel to one of the printer's native size pixels. For example, a 300 dpi laser printer will reduce an image that fills your VGA screen to only $1^1/_2$" high.

Using the printer resolution

You may need to adjust your printer resolution again if you run into memory problems. The larger the number of pixels, the more memory it takes to print a drawing. If your drawing is only partially printed even though you selected Whole from the Print dialog box, you may have exceeded the limits of your printer's memory. Try reducing the resolution of the printer in the Print dialog box with the Scaling text box, either reducing the area being printed, or reducing the pixel dimensions, so you can work within your printer's memory limits.

If you want to print your drawing on a color printer, you need to be aware that if you use a Palette with more colors, or if your drawing includes scanned images, printing the drawing will consume more memory. A 256 gray level scanned image actually is 256 colors. Refer to your color printer's manual for details about memory management.

Although you'll usually want to print your entire drawing, at times you may prefer to print only part of it. Windows allows you to print part of a drawing by offering the Whole or Partial options in the Window section of the Print dialog box. A whole printout, of course, prints everything. A partial printout will send only a selected area to the printer.

Selecting all or part of a drawing

To select an area, choose the Partial radio button and click on OK. The entire drawing will appear in the work area with a crosshair pointer. You can click and drag the pointer to form a selection box around part of the drawing. After you have outlined the part you want, release the button to send the selection to the printer.

When you send a whole or partial printout to the printer, Paintbrush lets you know it's printing by displaying a Printing message dialog box. If you want to cancel, just click on the Cancel button. After the dialog box appears, you'll also see the Print Manager icon on the desktop (only if the icon area of the desktop isn't being used).

After the drawing is sent to the Print Manager, the Printing dialog box will close, but the Print Manager icon will stay on the desktop until your drawing comes out of the printer. If you are having trouble or want to stop printing, double-click the Print Manager icon. See Chapter 7 for more about using Print Manager.

OPENING FILES

You can either start a new untitled file with the New command on the File menu or you can open an existing file. If you want to work on a drawing you already started, choose the Open... command from the File menu. The File Open dialog box, shown in Figure 11-42, has a text box to enter the file name of the drawing you want to work on. If the file is in another directory or on a disk, you can use the Directories box to move to that path. The available files are displayed in the Files list box, where you can click on the file name instead of typing it into the text box. Paintbrush normally looks for .BMP extensions when listing files. If you want to look for files that have .MSP or .PCX extensions, you must choose one of the appropriate radio buttons in the Open From group box. An .MSP file is used with the old version of Microsoft Paint. A .BMP extension is used by Paintbrush wallpaper files and .PCX extension is used by Paintbrush.

Figure 11-42

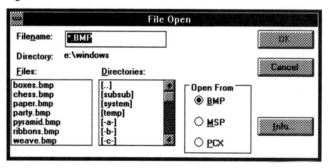

The File Open dialog box lets you choose from a list of files and file types.

If you try to open a file or start a new one without saving the existing one, Paintbrush will present a message dialog box asking if you want to save the drawing. If you click Yes, Paintbrush will update the file or ask you for a file name. If you click No, Paintbrush will not save the file and replace it in memory with the next file. If you click Cancel, Paintbrush will not save the file or open another file but will return you to the drawing.

ADVANCED PAINTBRUSH FEATURES

Now that you know everything you need to create basic drawings with Paintbrush, you're ready to explore advanced Paintbrush features. In this section, we'll explain the complex features of Paintbrush, such as converting old Microsoft Paint files, exporting files to other applications, creating custom colors, converting color Palettes, using a scanner, and making wallpaper files for the desktop.

So far, you've only been able to open other Paintbrush files. If you have Microsoft Paint files that you created with an older version of Windows, you can convert them into Paintbrush files. If the file has an .MSP extension, Paintbrush will know what kind of file it is and automatically convert it into a Paintbrush file with a .PCX extension. All you have to do is use the Open... command on the File menu and, when you enter the file name, include the .MSP extension. Paintbrush will do the rest.

Once a file has been converted into Paintbrush format, you won't be able to convert it back. If you want to use a file with both Microsoft Paint and Paintbrush, you must copy the file and then convert the copy to Paintbrush.

Converting old Microsoft Paint files

As we mentioned in the introduction, you can use the graphics you create in Paintbrush with other applications to make letterheads, greeting cards, newsletters, and so forth. If you want to use a logo you created in Paintbrush as part of your letterhead, you can do so just by adding your address and phone number. Then, you can add letterhead to a letter in Write by copying it to Clipboard with the Copy... command on the Edit menu and pasting it into your document with the Paste command on Write's Edit menu. It's best if you use black-and-white colors for your image attributes if you have a black-and-white printer. If you have a color printer that Windows supports (for example, the IBM Color Graphics printer), your letterhead can be in color. Remember that you can have both a Paintbrush window and a Write window open on the desktop to facilitate this process. We explained how to open multiple windows in Chapter 2.

Using drawings in other Windows applications

In addition to saving entire documents, you can save parts of your drawings in separate files so you can reuse them for future projects. For example, if you use your company logo or slogan with most of your presentations or graphs, it would be handy to paste it instead of having to open a file, select the graphic, copy it, open the file where you want to use it, and paste it in. With the Copy To... and Paste From... commands on the Edit menu, you can avoid time-consuming steps.

To save a graphic to a special paste file, first use the pick tools (the Scissors or Pick tools) to select the graphic you want. Then, select the Copy To... command to save the selected graphic to a file. Paintbrush will present a Copy To dialog box, as shown in Figure 11-43 on the following page, asking you for a file name. Just name the file, then, when you want to use that drawing again, select the Paste From... command and choose the file you want from the Paste From dialog box, as shown in Figure 11-44 on the next page. Paintbrush will paste the drawing in the upper-left corner of the work area, as it does with other graphics you paste into your work area.

Saving graphics to a file

Figure 11-43

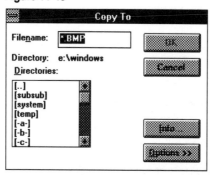

Paintbrush presents a Copy To dialog box when you use the Copy To... command to save a graphic.

Figure 11-44

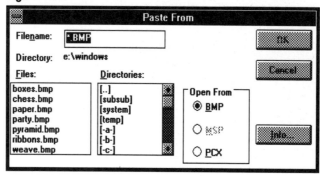

This Paste From dialog box appears when you use the Paste From... command to retrieve a graphic you saved with the Copy To... command.

You also can paste an entire drawing into the work area with the Paste From... command. Simply issue the Paste From... command, then select the file name of the drawing and click on OK. Paintbrush will insert the drawing into the work area the same way the Paste command inserts a graphic from Clipboard—by selecting it with a guideline and placing it in the upper-left corner of the work area.

For example, we decided to save our Best seal in a file so we could use it in various drawings. You can follow the steps listed below to create a reusable graphic, as shown in Figure 11-45.

- Open the original drawing file and select the graphic.

- Choose the Copy To... command and save the graphic file (we called ours BEST.PCX).

- Close the first file and open the target drawing file.

- Choose the Paste From... command and select the graphic file (for instance, BEST.PCX).

- Relocate the graphic (our Best seal) within the drawing.

Figure 11-45

We saved the Best seal as a reusable graphic.

Now whenever we want to use the Best seal, we can simply use the Paste From... command. Although the process of storing the graphic into a file takes as long as using the regular Cut and Paste commands, you save time later when you need to reuse the graphic.

In Chapter 9, you learned how to capture the screen or active window to Clipboard. Now we'll show you how to paste the image into Paintbrush. Once the image is on Clipboard, you can use the Paste command from the Edit menu to place it in the work area, where you can edit it. If you need to export the image, you can save it in a different file format. We used the screen capture feature to help create the figures for this book.

Using screen capture files

Another advanced feature of Paintbrush is its ability to customize the colors on the Palette. All you have to do is choose the Edit Colors... command on the Options menu to see an Edit Colors dialog box like the one in Figure 11-46.

Creating custom Palettes

Paintbrush displays the current foreground color in the display box on the right of the dialog box. The three scroll bars represent the three primary colors —red, green, and blue. All colors can be defined by mixing the three primary colors in different proportions. You may remember the Custom Color Selector in Control Panel's Color dialog box had red, gree, and blue values as well as hue, saturation, and luminosity.

Figure 11-46

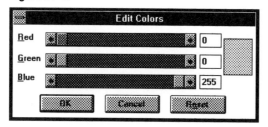

The Edit Colors dialog box lets you customize any of the Palette colors.

If you want to change the color, just drag the sliders on any of the three bars until the box on the right displays the color you want. Changing a color on the Color Palette doesn't change that color in your drawing, it simply gives you more colors to work with. If all three sliders are on the left of the scroll bars, the color will be black. If they are all on the right, the color will be white. The numbers corresponding to the position of the slider range from 0 to 255. The colors mix like light instead of like paint. That's why the primary colors are red, green, and blue (light primaries) instead of red, yellow, and blue (paint primaries). When you've finished changing the color, click on OK to add it to the Palette. After you finish using your new color, you may want to reset the sliders to restore the original color settings. Simply click Reset to return to the original color settings. The new color will be effective until you quit Paintbrush. When you start Paintbrush again, the original Color Palette will return.

You can use a shortcut to see the Edit Colors dialog box. All you have to do is double-click in the Color Palette on the color that you want to work on. The Edit Colors dialog box will appear with that color in the display box.

After you have changed the necessary colors, you can save those changes to use again later. To save the changes, choose the Save Colors… command on the Options menu. The Save Colors As dialog box, shown in Figure 11-47, will appear. All the palettes are named with a .PAL extension. The Directories list box will let you save the file anywhere on the hard drive or on a floppy. After you type in the new file name, click on OK to save the file.

When you want to use the colors you just saved, all you need to do is select the Get Colors… command from the Options menu. The Get Colors dialog box, shown in Figure 11-48, displays all the available .PAL files. Click on the one you want and choose OK to replace the current palette with the new one.

Figure 11-47

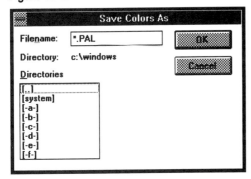

The Save Colors As dialog box saves your color changes in a .PAL file.

Figure 11-48

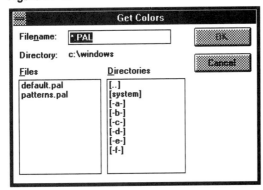

The Get Colors dialog box re-places the current palette with the selected.PAL file's palette.

It's a good idea to save the original palette with a file name like DEFAULT.PAL so you can return to the original default Color Palette without having to exit and restart Paintbrush.

Converting a drawing to black and white

Paintbrush can convert a graphic file from color to black and white (the color graphic needs to be in a file created with the Copy To... command or saved in a regular file). First, you must set up a drawing using the Black and White option in the Image Attributes dialog box or simply open a black-and-white drawing (it must use a Black and White Palette and not just the black and white colors from a Color Palette). Next, issue the Paste To... command to paste the graphic file into the work area. Paintbrush will convert the graphic into black and white. All solid colors will translate to black, while patterns translate into a black-and-white composite of colors that looks like gray. You can also paste a graphic from Clipboard into a black-and-white drawing to achieve the same effect.

**Importing
scanned images**

Apart from the Paintbrush tools you can use to create images, you can use a number of popular scanners. You can scan a picture (photo, artwork, and so forth) and then add the resulting graphic to your drawing. (We used an HP ScanJet Plus with HP's Scanning Gallery software to import photographs into Paintbrush.) If your scanning software won't produce a .PCX file for Paintbrush to read, you may need to use a conversion utility, like Hijaak to convert the file to a .PCX format. Now you can open the file like any other Paintbrush file.

Scanners convert you photo or artwork into a graphic, replacing the colors with shades of gray (gray scales). You can also set up a scanner to produce a graphic using only black and white with no gray shades.

Resolution plays an important role in the scanning process. You need to consider three resolution variables: scanner resolution for creating the graphic, printer resolution for printing it, and screen resolution for viewing it. The scanner can vary the resolution of the graphic when it scans (digitizes) your photo. The scanner determines the graphic's inherent resolution. When you print the graphic, you can vary the graphic's resolution again with the Printer Setup dialog box settings. For example, we scanned images at 75 dpi with the HP ScanJet Plus and HP Scanning Gallery software, then imported the images into Paintbrush for editing. The images were nearly actual size on our screen since the VGA resolution of 640 x 480 pixels approximates 72 dpi on a standard size monitor. We printed on an HP LaserJet, letting Paintbrush, not the printer, control the final image size.

When you save the scanned image with the scanning software, such as HP's Scanning Gallery, select a Paintbrush format (.PCX) or a TIFF (Tag Image File Format) format option. If you use a TIFF format, you will have to convert the file to a Paintbrush-compatible file format with a purchased file utility, such as Hijaak, to convert the files. Once you have a .PCX file, you can open it with Paintbrush.

You can put your company logo in your documents by scanning it and pasting it to Clipboard. You can use the Copy To... command to place the logo in a reusable format. You can paste your logo into any application that accepts graphics, like Write or Word for Windows. We scanned our logo, shown in Figure 11-49, converted the TIFF image to a .PCX file, then opened it.

Figure 11-49

*You can scan your logo, convert it,
then modify it with Paintbrush.*

Making wallpaper

Paintbrush lets you make your own wallpaper to customize the background for your desktop. You can make it full-screen or you can make a smaller image that can be tiled. Simply save your drawing in a file with a .BMP extension.

When you create a drawing for wallpaper, you need to choose the correct size for your work area. If you want the wallpaper to cover the whole screen on a VGA monitor, use a pixel setting of 640 (height) by 480 (width). If you want it smaller so you can tile it, use a setting of 320 by 240. If you don't want to tile the image, you can make it any size smaller than 640 by 480. If it's larger, it won't show up on the desktop when you select it for wallpaper. You can create a small image (32 by 32) and tile it for a pattern like the Pyramids that come with Windows. Figure 11-50 shows the Pyramid and a resulting section of a tiled desktop.

Figure 11-50

The Pyramid building block is a small graphic that you can tile to fill the Desktop.

For example, in the following steps, we created a full-screen wallpaper file using a scanned picture of horses and roses. Figure 11-51 illustrates the steps.

- Activate the Paintbrush icon twice and set up both work areas with default image attributes of 640 by 480 pixels, then select Colors for a Color Palette. (One window will serve as a sketch pad and the other as the destination window for your drawing.)

- Retrieve one of the image files, such as a scanned rose in the sketch pad window.

- Select the rose with the Pick tool and manipulate it with the Shrink + Grow command. Flip the images horizontally or vertically to vary the orientation of some of the images. Choose the variations you want to use, select them with the Pick tool, and then use the Copy command to copy them to your Clipboard.

- Click on the destination window in which you're creating the wallpaper, and choose the Paste command on the Edit menu to paste the image into the work area. Drag the image to the place you want it. Repeat the copy and paste routine as many times as it takes to include all the images in the wallpaper file.

- Add color to your wallpaper with the Color Eraser or Paint Roller tool. If you want to change only selected areas of the dark gray to red, use the Color Eraser tool to change only those areas. You can change all the dark gray to red for the roses and the horses by double-clicking the Color Eraser tool. You can also use the Zoom In command to clean up any stray marks or paint that overflows a graphic from the Paint Roller tool.

Figure 11-51

You can create wallpaper like this with scanned images.

Wallpaper can be more than just decorative. You can create some stock messages in Paintbrush and then put them on the desktop when you need them. You can create messages like *GONE TO STAFF MEETING*, *OUT TO LUNCH*, or *DON'T TOUCH—PROCESSING*. Figure 11-52 shows an example of an *OUT TO LUNCH!* message. Appendix 2 has a color version of the OUT TO LUNCH! wallpaper drawing shown in Figure 11-52.

Figure 11-52

You can leave messages on your desktop with wallpaper.

HOW WE MADE THE POSTER

At the beginning of this chapter, you saw a poster we created using a variety of Paintbrush's tools. Now that you've been introduced to all of Paintbrush's capabilities, we'll show you how we made the poster. As we present the steps, we'll briefly list the tools we used and any special settings. We won't show each brush stroke because we've explained many of them throughout this chapter.

- We used the wallpaper from Figure 11-52 as a starting point for our poster by opening its file and using the Save As... command to save a duplicate for the poster called POSTER.PCX.

- We used the Paste From... command on the Edit menu to add other drawings to the poster. We added the *Kentucky* calligraphy and the balloons to the drawing, then changed the background to create a blue sky.

- We added the text *The Bluegrass State* with the Text tool.

In this chapter

Using Terminal **12**

*E*lectronic mail, file transfers, mainframe communications, bulletin boards, information services—these are hallmarks of the information age! Personal computers are rapidly evolving from isolated number-crunching tools into the vital links of a worldwide information network. Many must share information with other computers in the next office, the next city, or on the other side of the world.

TERMINAL

Terminal—the communications application supplied with Windows—allows your computer to converse with remote computers and transfer files. You can check on your stock portfolio with an information service, correspond with a colleague via electronic mail, get sales data from the corporate mainframe, or send a spreadsheet file to an associate in another city.

Like the other Windows accessory applications, Terminal is limited but functional. It offers a scant selection of file transfer protocols and terminal emulations, and there is no scripting capability. Although Terminal lacks some of the features of sophisticated applications such as Crosstalk for Windows, it may be all you'll need for basic communications.

Of course, you'll need some extra hardware for your computer to talk to the outside world. You'll need a Hayes-compatible modem, an available COM port or address, and access to a phone line for the computer. (You may need to bypass your office switchboard since some electronic phone systems are not compatible with data communications.) You can substitute a null modem cable for the modems and phone line if you want to connect two computers in the same room.

In writing this chapter, we've assumed that you are familiar with some basic communications concepts. However, you need not have a detailed understanding of all the settings, such as baud rate, parity, and flow control. For successful communications, Terminal's settings must be appropriately adjusted for each host computer; but you can just get the correct settings from the host computer's operators and match those settings in Terminal.

Starting Terminal

You'll find Terminal in the Accessories group window of the Program Manager. Simply double-click on the icon to launch Terminal. Terminal is designed to communicate; all its features won't come alive until you begin a dialog with another computer. However, you can explore most of the menus and settings without dialing another computer. When you get ready to leave Terminal, select Exit from the File menu.

The Terminal window

As you can see in Figure 12-1, the Terminal window has the usual menu bar across the top, above a large workspace where Terminal will display your dialog with the remote computer. This workspace will be empty until you establish a connection and begin to exchange information. Terminal's work area will be linked to your modem. It will "echo," or display on-screen, the prompts your modem receives from the remote computer and the responses you type at your keyboard. You can only type in the work area during a communications session; you cannot type directly into the work area as if it were a document in Write. Along the bottom edge of the work area is a status bar where Terminal will keep you informed of its progress during file transfers. Of course, the status bar will be empty except when you are transferring files.

Figure 12-1

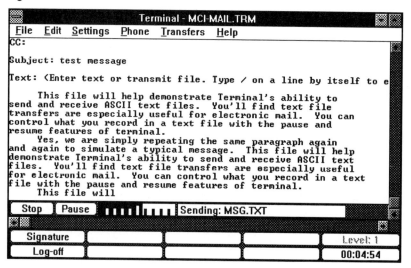

This figure shows the Terminal window during a file transfer. The optional Function Key display is visible at the bottom of the window.

At the bottom of the Terminal window, you'll find the optional Function Key display. As we'll explain later, Terminal allows you to define custom functions for these on-screen buttons. Along with the function keys, Terminal will display a timer in the box in the lower-right corner that tracks the duration of your communications session.

As you read this chapter, it will be helpful to remember the fundamental steps you'll go through each time you communicate with a remote, or host, computer. The details will vary greatly depending on the nature of the remote computer and your on-line activities, but the overall framework of your communications session will remain consistent.

Profile of a communications session

- Establish (or verify) the hardware connections—make sure your modem, COM port, and phone line are all connected and operating properly.

- Launch Terminal.

- Adjust Terminal's settings to match the remote computer's requirements, either individually or by opening the appropriate Terminal settings file.

- Dial the remote computer using Terminal's Dial command.

- Identify yourself to the remote computer by completing the log-on procedure.

- Read and send messages, transfer files, and conduct your other on-line business.

- Sign off from the remote computer using the suggested log-off procedure; don't just hang up.

- Hang up the phone line with the Hangup command.

- Save the Terminal settings for this remote system in a file for future use.

- Exit from Terminal.

TERMINAL SETTINGS

The world of data communications is a complex one with numerous "standards" for dealing with the many complicated issues that arise when two computers try to exchange information over telephone lines. Despite all the complications, diverse computers can talk to each other successfully if they both agree to use a common set of rules. So, obviously, you must adjust Terminal's settings to match the settings of the remote computer with which you wish to communicate.

Setting communications standards and protocols for two computers is not unlike arranging negotiations between two opposing factions. Before either party will begin discussions, you must first obtain agreement on the number and rank of the representatives from each side, the shape of the table and seating arrangements, how meal breaks will be scheduled, even the language that will be used for the negotiations.

Fortunately, you have an advantage over the diplomats and negotiators; you won't have to guess what settings will be acceptable to both computers or find out by trial-and-error. The operators of most remote systems make the protocols and settings for their systems available to their potential users. The large information services such as CompuServe and MCI Mail supply sign-up kits. If you need to connect to your company's mainframe or network, you can probably get the correct settings with a quick phone call to the corporate computer center. You don't need to understand what all the settings do to use them—just match Terminal's settings to those of the remote system, and the computers should be able to communicate.

Once you've configured Terminal to communicate with a specific remote computer, you can save the settings in a file. The next time you communicate with that remote system, you can open the file to repeat the settings. In fact, you can use TRM (Terminal) files from previous versions of Windows' Terminal.

Using the Settings menu

So, what are these settings? Some, such as the phone number of the remote computer, are obvious and self-explanatory. Others, such as Parity, may be harder to understand if you don't happen to have a background in data communications. Most of Terminal's settings are "host specific." By that we mean you must set them according to the requirements of the remote computer. The sheer number of possible options may seem intimidating, but using them is actually easy. You don't need to worry about why you should use one option instead of another. You simply match your settings with those the host computer expects of its users. Generally, if the host system does not specify a selection for one of Terminal's options, you can assume that the default will work.

To adjust Terminal's settings to communicate with a new host, select commands on the Settings menu, one by one, and review or adjust the options in the dialog boxes Terminal opens. Initially, it is probably a good idea to make sure you select every command on the Settings menu each time you set up for a new host—so you won't forget to adjust any settings. After adjusting Terminal's settings to work with your modem and a remote computer, you can save the settings in a file. Later, when you become familiar with Terminal's options, you can quickly create a Terminal settings file for a new host by using an existing file as a template. You can open a file for a host that uses similar settings, change only the settings that are unique to the new host (such as the phone number), and use the Save As... command to save the new settings in a file with an appropriate name. Let's examine the commands on Terminal's Settings menu.

The Modem Commands dialog box displays the commands that Terminal will use to instruct your modem to dial a phone number, hang up the phone line, and so on. Although the Modem Commands… command is near the bottom of the Settings menu, it's probably the first group of settings you should check before you begin to use Terminal. Once you establish the correct modem commands for your modem, they will normally remain the same for all your communications with various hosts.

Terminal comes configured to work with most Hayes-compatible modems, and the odds are good that the defaults will work without alteration. However, if you need to fine-tune the way Terminal works with your modem, you can change the commands in the Modem Commands dialog box. Be sure to consult your modem's documentation before you change any of these commands.

Select Modem Commands... from the Settings menu to open the dialog box shown in Figure 12-2. The radio buttons in the Modem Defaults group box allow you to change the defaults that appear in the Commands group box. Initially, when you enter Terminal, the defaults you'll see are for Hayes and Hayes-compatible modems. You can switch to the default commands for the other listed modems if you have one of those modems. Selecting the None radio button erases the default commands so you can enter a custom set of commands required by your modem.

Figure 12-2

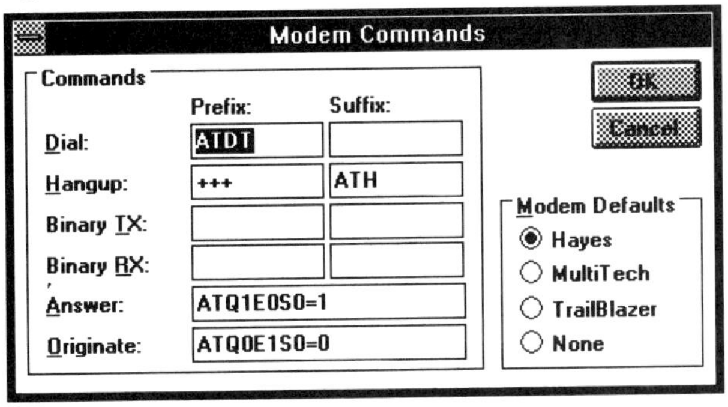

In this dialog box, you specify the commands Terminal will use to control your modem.

In the Commands group box, the first line is the Dial command for your modem, with text boxes for a Prefix and Suffix. Terminal uses the Dial command to tell the modem to dial the remote computer's phone number. ATDT tells the modem to dial using touch tones. If you are connected to older, rotary pulse phone lines, you should change this setting to ATDP to tell the modem to dial with pulses rather than tones. Following the dial prefix, Terminal will send the remote computer's telephone number (which you'll enter later in the Phone Number dialog box) to the modem and then add the suffix to the end of the number to complete the dialing instruction for the modem.

This prefix/data/suffix format affords considerable flexibility as you build the Dial command. For example, if you must dial 9 for an outside line on your office phone system, you could add the 9 and a comma to the prefix (the comma instructs Hayes-compatible modems to pause for two seconds). Terminal would dial 9 for the outside line and then pause before dialing the phone number. Similarly, you could add your long distance ID code in the Dial Suffix text box to follow the telephone number. You can also incorporate the 9 for an outside line, or the long distance code in the Phone Number dialog box; either of these techniques will work equally well.

Another useful trick is to automatically disable Call Waiting by changing the Prefix to *ATDT*70,,*. Although Call Waiting is a handy feature of modern phone service, the click or beep that alerts you to another caller on the line can disrupt a data communications session, especially during a file transfer. Dialing *70 and waiting for a second dial tone before you dial a phone number will usually disable Call Waiting for the duration of that call. (The procedure or code that disables Call Waiting may vary in some areas; check with your local phone company.)

Immediately below the Dial command is the Hangup command. Terminal will send the command it finds here to the modem when you select Hangup from the Phone menu. Your modem documentation may call this action "disconnect," "drop carrier," or going "on-hook." Whatever the name, most modems will sever a connection when they receive *+++ATH* from the computer.

When you send a binary file, Terminal uses the settings you enter in the Binary TX Prefix and Suffix text boxes to signal the modem at the beginning and end of the transmission. The Binary RX commands' Prefix and Suffix settings serve the same function when you receive a binary file. Normally, the Prefix and Suffix text boxes for these commands are empty. Check your hardware documentation to see if your modem requires the Binary TX and Binary RX commands.

The last two commands switch the modem into Answer or Originate modes, respectively. The defaults should handle most situations. Check your modem documentation if you need to make any changes.

Communications settings

The dialog box accessed by the Communications... command is where you get into the real minutiae of data communications. These settings are crucial. But, as we've said before, you can simply match them with the specifications your host supplies. If terms such as "data packet" and "parity" seem intimidating, just think of these as the computer's grammar and punctuation rules.

When you select Communications... from the Settings menu, Terminal will open a Communications dialog box like the one shown in Figure 12-3. All the settings in this dialog box must be correct before you call the remote computer.

Figure 12-3

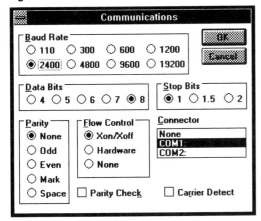

The Communications dialog box allows you to match Terminal's communications settings to the remote system.

"Match the specifications from the host." Sounds simple, and sometimes it is when the specifications use the same terminology you see in Terminal's dialog box. Often, however, the remote system's operator will use a sort of shorthand to describe the correct settings. Our heading, N81 at 2400 baud, is typical. It means the remote computer operates at No parity, 8 data bits, 1 stop bit, and at speeds up to 2400 baud. Let's use this description as an example and adjust the settings in the Communications dialog box accordingly.

N81 at 2400 baud

Baud rate is the speed at which the modems send data back and forth. Normally, to transfer information as quickly as possible, you'll want to set Terminal to operate at the highest speed supported by both your modem and the remote computer's modem. If you have a 2400-baud modem, you would click on the 2400 radio button in the Baud Rate group box to tell Terminal to operate at that speed. If your modem operates at a maximum of 1200 baud, you would select 1200. Typically, you can expect the remote computer's modem to adjust automatically to the slower speed. (Nearly all modems can function at their rated speed, or at any of the slower, standard speeds.) Occasionally, you may want to use a slower baud rate to compensate for noisy phone lines or to take advantage of lower connect time charges on the commercial information services.

Data bits are the number of digits in the binary numbers that computers use as "words." Click on the radio button beside 8 in the Data Bits group box to tell terminal to use 8-digit "data packets." Most remote computers will use either 7 or 8 data bits, with 8 being the most common. If the remote computer uses less than 8 data bits, you will not be able to use the XModem protocol for binary file transfers.

Stop Bits are like the spaces between words in a sentence. They keep the words from running together into an unintelligible string of letters. To match our example settings, click on the 1 radio button in the Stop Bits group box.

Parity is a rudimentary form of error checking the computer can use to verify the data it receives. Since parity checking "borrows" the eighth data bit, parity checking isn't possible when all 8 data bits are used for data. Terminal recognizes this and automatically sets Parity to None when you select 8 Data Bits. It will also change your Data Bits setting to 7 if you select any of the radio buttons in the Parity group box except None.

More nitty-gritty

The Xon/Xoff selection is the default in the Flow Control group box, and you should rarely need to change it. The Flow Control setting dictates the method Terminal will use to tell the remote computer "Whoa, you're going too fast for me." Normally, Terminal will use "software handshaking" (Xon/Xoff) to tell the remote system to stop sending data when Terminal has all the data it can handle, and to resume transmitting data when Terminal catches up. Some systems use hardware rather than software to control the flow of data, and a few remote systems use no flow control at all. Xon/Xoff flow control is not compatible with hardware flow control, so to configure Terminal to communicate with a host using hardware flow control, you would click on the Hardware radio button. You would also need to make sure your hardware is compatible with the remote system.

Select the communications port your modem uses from the list in the Connector group box to tell Terminal where to find the modem. You should note that while Terminal is running, the settings in this dialog box will supersede those you established with Control Panel for this COM port.

The Carrier Detect check box allows you to switch between two methods of detecting a successful connection to another computer (as opposed to a human voice or FAX machine). One method is built into your modem; the other is within Terminal. If all the other settings are correct and you still have trouble connecting to a remote computer, change this setting and try calling the host again.

The Parity Check check box enables a diagnostic tool you'll probably never need. If you select this option, Terminal will display the byte in which a parity error occurs instead of a question mark when it receives a corrupted character.

Phone number

The Phone Number dialog box appears when you select the Phone Number... command from the Settings menu. As you can see in Figure 12-4, the Dial text box, where you enter the remote computer's telephone number, is the main feature of this dialog box. Since your modem will ignore parentheses, hyphens, and spaces, you can use those characters to make the phone number easier to read. You can also enter commas (for a 2-second pause) and other characters that will have a special meaning to your modem. For instance, *9, 1 (800) 555-0000* would instruct the modem to dial 9 for an outside line, pause, and then direct-dial the long distance phone number.

Figure 12-4

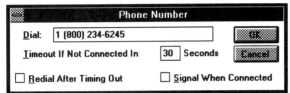

In the Phone Number dialog box, you specify the number you want Terminal to dial and how long to wait for a connection.

The Timeout If Not Connected In option controls how long Terminal will wait for the remote computer's modem to respond. Terminal starts counting as soon as it begins dialing, so you may want to change the Timeout value to 45 or 60 seconds, especially for long-distance numbers.

Two check boxes complete this dialog box. If you check Redial After Timing Out, Terminal will hang up and dial the number again if it does not successfully establish a connection within the time limit you specified in the preceding option. It will keep trying until it connects with the remote computer or until you click on the Cancel button in the dialog box Terminal displays while it is dialing. If you activate the Signal When Connected option, Terminal will beep to alert you when it establishes a connection. These two options can be especially helpful when you are attempting to call a computer system that is very busy. Terminal will patiently dial the number over and over while you attend to other business. Then, Terminal will beep when it finally succeeds in connecting with the remote computer.

Terminal options

Terminal gets its name, in part, from its ability to make your computer act like or emulate a terminal when it is communicating with a remote computer. (A terminal is a single-purpose piece of hardware whose function is to communicate with another computer system.) With the appropriate terminal emulation selected, you'll be able to use the special formatting and functions normally available on dedicated terminals. You can also control line wrap (for text that runs past the right edge of the screen), the terminal font, and other preferences.

Terminal emulation

To choose the terminal you want to emulate during communications with a remote computer, select Terminal Emulation... from the Settings menu. The short list of alternatives appears in the Terminal Emulation dialog box, as shown in Figure 12-5. Select one of the emulations by clicking on its radio button and then clicking OK to confirm the choice.

Figure 12-5

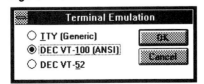

You can choose one of three terminal emulations in this dialog box.

If you select TTY (Generic), Terminal transmits only the standard alpha-numeric characters, the carriage return (the [Enter] key), backspace, and tab characters to the remote computer. Use this option if you don't know what terminal the remote system supports.

Terminal can emulate either the DEC VT-100 or the DEC VT-52 terminals, which are among the most common terminals used with large mainframe hosts. When you select one of these emulations, Terminal will be able to transmit the special formatting and control codes the remote system expects to receive from that terminal. The Windows documentation includes a table listing the functions of the terminals and how to access them from your computer keyboard. If a remote system expects an "ANSI terminal," use the VT-100 emulation. It should allow Terminal to respond to the ANSI codes that control screen colors, and so forth.

Terminal preferences

You can go beyond selecting a terminal emulation to control details of the way Terminal handles the information it receives from the remote system and how it displays the information on your screen. You'll find these controls in the Terminal Preferences dialog box, shown in Figure 12-6, which you display by selecting Terminal Preferences... from the Settings menu. The default settings will handle most situations, but Terminal allows you the flexibility to change the settings when needed. If necessary, you can even modify many of these settings while you are on-line with a remote system.

Figure 12-6

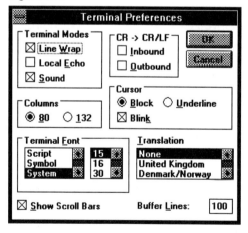

The Terminal Preferences dialog box allows you to control the way Terminal presents information on your screen.

In the Terminal Modes group box, you'll find check boxes to turn the Line Wrap, Local Echo, and Sound options on or off.

If you turn Line Wrap on, Terminal will break lines of text it receives from the host that are too long to fit on your screen and wrap them to the next line. With

Line Wrap off, you'll lose any information that runs beyond the edge of your screen. (If you run Terminal in a window that is less than the full width of the screen, you will not lose information that is wider than the window as long as it fits within the full screen. You can use the scroll bar to view long lines.)

The Local Echo option displays your keystrokes on your screen as Terminal sends them to the remote system. Oddly enough, you will normally want this option turned off. Most remote systems operate in "full duplex" mode and echo each character they receive back to your screen. Thus, if you have Local Echo turned on, each character you type will appear on your screen twice. Your screen will look something lliikkee tthhiiss! If you "see double" when you type, make sure you turn Local Echo off. If you connect to a remote system that operates at "half duplex" and doesn't echo your keystrokes, turn Local Echo on so you can see what you type.

The last option in the Terminal Modes group box is Sound. Normally, Sound is on, but you can turn it off if you don't want the remote system to be able to make your computer beep at you.

In the Columns group box, you select a radio button to tell Terminal to display information in the wide 132-column format or the standard 80 columns (80 characters per line). Normally, you would base your selection on your monitor type, but Windows can squeeze 132 columns of information onto an 80-column monitor or stretch 80 columns out to fill a 132-column monitor if you want.

Terminal can use any of the installed system fonts to display information in its work area. You can select the font you want Terminal to use from the list box in the Terminal Font group box. After you select a font, you can also specify its size. Your selection will take effect when you click on the OK button to confirm your selections in the Terminal Preferences dialog box.

The scroll bars on the Terminal window are optional. You can turn them on and off with the Show Scroll Bars check box in the lower-left corner of this dialog box. Obviously, you'll need scroll bars when you run Terminal in a small window, but they are useful even when Terminal is maximized to full-screen size. Terminal saves a certain amount of the information that scrolls off your screen in a buffer, and you can use the scroll bars to recall that information instead of having to request the remote system to retransmit it.

Terminal can automatically convert each carriage return you send or receive into a carriage return plus a line feed. (A carriage return moves the cursor to the beginning of the line; a line feed moves it down to the next line.) Some remote systems automatically add line feeds with each carriage return; others do not. The check boxes in the CR-> CR/LF group box allow you to instruct Terminal to add line feeds to either Inbound or Outbound data, or both. Your selection will depend on how the remote computer handles the end of lines. If each line you receive from the host appears on top of the previous line, you need to add line feeds to incoming data. If incoming data appears double spaced, you need to turn CR->CR/LF translation off for incoming data. The same applies to outbound data.

The Cursor group box contains two radio boxes for selecting between a Block or Underline shaped cursor. A check box lets you control whether the cursor will blink.

You can send and receive information in a foreign language by selecting a language setting from the Translation list box. Terminal will translate the information you send and receive into the International Standards Organization character set for the language you specify. Select None if you and the remote computer are both using the same language.

The last item in the Terminal Preferences dialog box is Buffer Lines. With this option, you can control how much space Terminal reserves to save information that scrolls off your screen. You can type a number between 25 and 400 in the Buffer Lines text box.

File transfer settings

One of the main reasons to establish communications with another computer is to be able to exchange files. You can transfer spreadsheets, word processor documents, programs, or electronic mail files. You can capture incoming text in a file, and you can send a text file to the remote computer instead of laboriously typing a message. But before you transfer a file, you'll need to establish the rules that will govern the exchange. You can change these settings while you are on-line with a remote computer if necessary, as long as a file transfer is not in progress.

Terminal can transfer two basic types of files: text or binary. Text files, also known as ASCII files, contain only the printable ASCII characters plus a few simple formatting codes such as carriage returns. You normally create them with a text editor, though most word processors can also create a text file by saving a document without any of the normal formatting information. Binary files, on the other hand, can include any character recognized by the computer—any of the regular or extended ASCII characters. Binary files might be created by a database application, a spreadsheet, a word processor, a graphics program, or a programming language. Any file on a personal computer could be called a binary file.

Terminal uses different rules for transferring text files and binary files. The text in text files is essentially the same as the text you type at the keyboard, and Terminal can handle it the same way. Binary files, on the other hand, require special transfer methods that check and recheck the data as it is transmitted to ensure there are no errors. You'll need to tell Terminal how to handle each type of file.

Text transfers

To specify the flow control, or pacing method, Terminal will use to transfer text files, begin by selecting Text Transfers... from the Settings menu to open the dialog box shown in Figure 12-7.

Figure 12-7

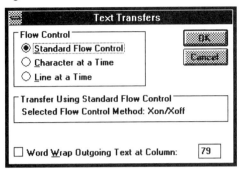

The options in the Text Transfers dialog box tell Terminal how to control the pacing of the text files you transmit.

The Flow Control group box offers three options: Standard Flow Control, Character at a Time, or Line at a Time. The default is Standard Flow Control, which allows Terminal to use the same flow control method (such as Xon/Xoff) for text file transfers that you specified in the Communications dialog box for normal text communications with the host. If you choose Character at a Time, a different group box will open in the middle of the dialog box. There, you can instruct Terminal to delay for a fixed amount of time after each character it transmits, and you can specify the exact length of the delay by changing the value in the /10 Sec text box. The other option in the Transfer a Character at a Time group box is the Wait for Character Echo radio button. If you check this option, Terminal will send one character, wait for the host to echo the character back, and then check that it is the correct character before sending the next character in the file. The Line at a Time option is similar to Character at a Time except that Terminal transmits a line of text before pausing instead of pausing after each character. With the Transfer a Line at a Time group box, you can select a fixed amount of time to delay after each line of text, or choose Wait for Prompt String. This is similar to Wait for Character Echo, except that Terminal will wait for a specific prompt from the host (usually a carriage return, which is signified by ^M) before sending the next line of text. You can specify what character or string Terminal should wait for.

You might want to use one of these slower options if you find that the remote computer's processing isn't fast enough to process all the information you transfer. You'll know when this happens because the remote computer will "drop" or lose some of the characters or lines you send.

At the bottom of the Text Transfers dialog box, you'll find the Word Wrap Outgoing Text at Column option. If you select this option, Terminal will wrap any lines of text in your outgoing files that exceed the value you type in the text box. This is a handy way to make sure you don't exceed the maximum line length of the remote system.

Binary transfers

When you select Binary Transfers... from the Settings menu, Terminal will open the dialog box shown in Figure 12-8. From the settings in this dialog box, you can choose which of the two transfer protocols you want to use for binary file transfers. Click on the appropriate radio button to make your choice, then click OK to confirm it.

Figure 12-8

The Binary Transfers dialog box allows you to choose an error-checking protocol for transferring binary files.

A transfer protocol is a set of error-checking rules the computer uses to ensure accurate reproduction of the data. To successfully transfer a binary file, both the remote computer and Terminal must use the same protocol. There are many different protocols in use in data communications today, each with its own advantages and weaknesses. Terminal includes two of the most common.

The XModem protocol uses all 8 data bits, so it is only appropriate when communicating with a remote system that operates at 8 data bits and No parity. Kermit, on the other hand, can work with any data bit setting. It is the protocol of choice for systems that require communications settings such as 7 data bits and Even parity.

Local settings

The three commands at the bottom of the Settings menu control how Terminal operates on your computer. They have no effect on communications with the remote system. All are toggle commands that you can switch on or off as needed, even in the middle of a communications session with a remote computer.

Printer Echo

Click on Printer Echo to send your dialog with the remote computer to the printer. When you enable Printer Echo, everything that appears in Terminal's work area—all the remote system's prompts and all your keystrokes—will also go to the printer. A check mark appears beside the command when Printer Echo is active. Select the command again to turn it off. You can toggle the option on and off as often as needed to control what gets printed.

Using Printer Echo usually slows the progress of your communications session noticeably as the remote system waits for the printer to catch up before sending the next line, thus increasing the cost of an on-line session.

Timer Mode

The timer that appears in the optional function key display across the bottom of the Terminal window will show either the current time according to your system clock, or the elapsed time for the current on-line session. Showing the system time is the default. Click on the Timer Mode command to time your calls.

The function keys controlled by the Show Function Keys command are Terminal's user-defined, on-screen function keys. We'll explain how to define the function keys later in this chapter. To display the function key buttons and the timer across the bottom of the Terminal window, select Show Function Keys from the Settings menu. When the function key display is on, the command changes to Hide Function Keys, and selecting it will remove the function key display.

Show Function Keys

Once you've adjusted all of Terminal's settings to conform to the remote system's requirements, you are ready to begin using Terminal for its intended purpose, going on-line to communicate with a remote computer. The three examples in this section will demonstrate Terminal's main features and how to use them to perform typical communication tasks.

GOING ON-LINE

For our first example, let's discuss the steps you'll follow to read your electronic mail on a large mainframe system. We'll use the commands and procedures for MCI Mail in this example, but the basic operations would be similar whether you need to get messages from a corporate mainframe or a local electronic bulletin board.

Reading electronic mail

Of course, the first step is to adjust Terminal's settings to match the remote computer, as we've discussed earlier in this chapter. Once the settings are established, you place the call to the remote computer by selecting Dial from the Phone menu. Terminal will display a dialog box like the one shown in Figure 12-9 while it dials the phone and waits for the remote computer to answer and establish the modem connection. You'll see the phone number Terminal is dialing and the number of seconds it will continue to wait for the connection. You can abort the call by clicking on the Cancel button.

Dial the host and log-on

Figure 12-9

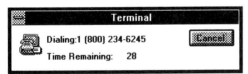

You'll see this dialog box while Terminal waits for the remote system to respond.

When Terminal makes the connection with the remote computer, the dialog box will go away and *CONNECT* will appear in Terminal's work area. This is a message from your modem informing you that it is connected to another modem. You'll often need to send a few characters from the keyboard to get the host's attention. For MCI Mail, pressing [Enter] once or twice will do the trick. When MCI prompts you to *Please enter your user name:*, type the "user name" which identifies you to the host computer, then press [Enter]. (MCI Mail user names are typically a first initial and last name with no spaces or punctuation—something like *GWASHINGTON.* Other systems might use numbers or other codes to identify individual users.) After you enter your user name, MCI Mail presents the *password* prompt. Type your password at the prompt and press [Enter], but don't be surprised when you don't see the characters on the screen as you type. As a security precaution, MCI, like most host systems, does not display your password. Identifying yourself to the host computer with a name or ID and a password is called logging on.

Reading mail on-line

As soon as you complete the log-on procedure, MCI Mail will display its welcome messages and alert you if you have electronic mail messages waiting. Then the host system will display a prompt, such as *Command:*, and wait for instructions from you. Each system will be different, but to read messages on MCI Mail, you would first type *SCAN INBOX,* then press [Enter] to see a numbered list of the messages addressed to you. At the next *Command:* prompt, you would type *READ 2* and press [Enter] if you wanted to read message number 2. MCI Mail would then send the message to your screen, and you could read it from the monitor. If you activate the Printer Echo command on the Settings menu, everything that appears on your screen will also go to your printer, giving you a printed record of your communications session. You can toggle Printer Echo off and on to selectively control how much of your dialog with the host gets printed.

Receive text file

Using Printer Echo is hardly the best way to get a copy of your messages; it's slow, and you can't edit or reformat the printout. Instead, you can capture the information in a text file. Later, you can view the files with Terminal's View Text Files command, or edit and print them with your word processor. This technique works because the data from the remote system is in the same ASCII text format as the data in a text file. Therefore, you can use Terminal's ability to send and receive text files to capture messages from the remote computer in a file.

To begin saving incoming text in a file, select Receive Text File... from the Transfers menu. As you can see in Figure 12-10, the Receive Text File dialog box is similar to the familiar File Save As dialog box. You can use the Directories list box to select the drive and directory where you want to save the file and type a name for the text file in the Filename text box.

In addition to the file name specifications, there are three check boxes in the Receive Text File dialog box for special handling options. The Append File option lets you add the incoming information to an existing file. For instance, if you have a file named MESSAGE.TXT, you could add the new messages to it instead of starting a new file. The Save Controls option instructs Terminal to keep extra formatting codes that might be in the incoming file, even if they are not "pure ASCII." The Table Format option is especially useful with spreadsheet and database files. When you select it, Terminal will translate two or more spaces in the incoming file into a tab character. You can select any combination of these options to handle a variety of file transfer needs.

Figure 12-10

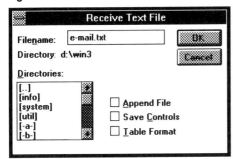

The Receive Text File dialog box includes three special handling options as well as the expected file-naming facilities.

When you click on OK in the Receive Text File dialog box, Terminal will begin sending all the incoming text it receives to the text file. With the text file open and recording data, you can issue the command to read your messages. You might want to instruct the host system to send your messages "non-stop" instead of pausing every few lines to allow you time to read the text on the screen. The text file can accept the data as fast as the host system can send it, and you'll be able to read the messages at your own pace, later after you log-off.

Terminal displays the status of the file transfer in the status bar across the bottom of the work area, as shown in Figure 12-11 on the following page. The status bar includes the name of the file and the amount of data received so far. It also includes on-screen buttons to Stop, Pause, and (alternately) Resume the file transfer. These buttons duplicate the functions of the Stop, Pause, and Resume commands on the Transfers menu.

A unique capability of Terminal's text file transfers is the ability to pause and resume sending or receiving text files. You can select the Pause command from the Transfers menu or click on the Pause button in the status bar to temporarily halt a text transfer. Click on the same button again (now labeled Resume) or select Resume from the Transfers menu to continue recording incoming text in the file. When you pause a text transfer, it stops recording text in the file; it doesn't interrupt the communications with the host system. You can pause at the end of a message, issue a series of commands to the host without the commands or prompts appearing in the text file, then resume recording to capture another group of messages. You can stop the text file transfer and close the text file by selecting Stop from the Transfers menu or by clicking on the Stop button on the status bar.

Figure 12-11

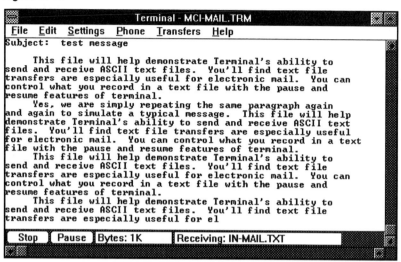

The status bar across the bottom of the Terminal work area displays the status of file transfers.

Log-off

After you've read or captured your messages, it's time to disconnect from the host system. Each system will have a log-off procedure that you should use to end the on-line session. For instance, to leave MCI Mail, you type *EXIT* and press [Enter] at the *Command:* prompt. After you log off the host system, select Hangup from the Phone menu to tell your modem to disconnect from the phone line. Following the proper log-off procedure is important. You need to tell the host system you are leaving so that it can make room for other users. But, perhaps more importantly, you want to make sure you aren't charged for extra access time. Most systems will periodically check for activity from each user that is logged on and will detect that a user has disconnected, but it may take several minutes. If you just hang up without first logging off, you may see a difference in your computer information service bill.

Save settings

After you complete your first successful communications session with a remote system, you'll want to save the Terminal settings in a file. When you want to call that host again, just open the file to re-install those settings. Select Save As... from the File menu and give the file an appropriate name in the dialog box. (MCI-MAIL might be a good choice for our example.) Windows adds the TRM extension to your Terminal files unless you explicitly supply another extension.

You can use Terminal's built-in file viewer to read text files—such as our hypothetical file of electronic mail messages we created with the Receive Text File command. When you select View Text File... from the Transfers menu, Terminal will open a dialog box like the one in Figure 12-12. As you can see, the View Text File dialog box is similar to the File Open dialog box, and you use it the same way to select a file. A pair of extra check boxes in the lower-right corner allow you to control how Terminal will handle the line feeds in the file. If the text file lacks line feeds, causing each line of text to overwrite the preceding line, you should select the Append LF check box. Choose the Strip LF check box to remove superfluous line feeds if the text file appears double spaced. Terminal's text file viewer reads the entire contents of the file into Terminal's buffer and displays the status bar as when receiving text files. Since the buffer can hold only a limited amount of text, you will need to use the Pause and Resume buttons to import the file in manageable chunks. The scroll bars will allow you to scroll through the portion of the file in Terminal's buffer.

Figure 12-12

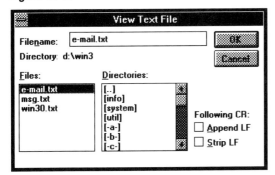

You can select a text file to view in Terminal's work-space with this View Text File dialog box.

Sending E-mail

Most host computers that offer any electronic mail services include an on-line editor to create messages. However, they are often awkward, difficult, and slow to use. Using an on-line editor can get expensive if you have to pay for the connect time while you grope for the right wording for a message. Even if there is no cost involved, it's usually more pleasant and convenient to compose your message in Notepad, Write, or your favorite word processor and save it as a text file. Then you can use Terminal to send the text file instead of typing the message into the host's on-line editor.

Let's continue the example we started above and suppose you want to send a response to one of those messages. First, jot down the electronic mail address you want to send the message to. Then, compose the message in Write and save it with the Text Only option.

Next, switch to the Terminal window. (We'll presume you left Terminal running in an inactive window.) If you've changed any of the settings, you can load the correct settings for MCI Mail from the file we saved after the last session. Select Open... from the File menu, select MCI-MAIL.TRM in the dialog box, and click OK. Terminal adjusts its settings according to the information in the file and shows the file name in the title bar at the top of the Terminal window.

Select Dial from the Phone menu and log on to MCI Mail as in the previous example. When you've successfully logged on to the host system, type the command to start creating a new message. (For MCI Mail, you would type *CREATE* and then press [Enter].) At the appropriate prompts, type the electronic mail address and subject for your message. When the host system prompts you to start entering text, you'll want to send your text file instead.

Sending a text file

When you select Send Text File... from the Transfers menu, Terminal opens the dialog box shown in Figure 12-13. Except for the Send Text File name, it is identical to the View Text File dialog box. Select the message file you created in Write and click OK. Terminal will immediately start sending the contents of the file. To the host system, it seems that you are just typing very fast. It can't tell the difference between the text coming from your keyboard, and the text Terminal transfers from a file. If the lines of text overlap, or appear double spaced, you'll need to abort the transfer, cancel the message, and try again by checking the Append LF or the Strip LF option in the Send Text File dialog box.

Figure 12-13

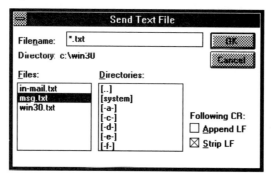

The Send Text File dialog box allows you to select a text file to transfer to the remote computer.

The status bar across the bottom of the Terminal work area will show the progress of the file transfer. When you send files, a small progress meter bar replaces the file's size counter. The Stop, Pause, and Resume commands are available both on the Transfers menu and the buttons in the status bar, just as they are when you receive text files. When Terminal reaches the end of the file, it will stop automatically.

Usually you'll need to tell the host you've reached the end of the message. (MCI Mail looks for a slash [/] on a line by itself as the instruction to switch from the message editor back to command mode.) Finish sending the message by giving the host system handling instructions and typing *YES* and pressing [Enter] at the *Send?* prompt. With the message on its way, you can log off and hang up.

Send the message and log off

Text files contain the same kind of data as the text that Terminal sends back and forth to the remote computer, and the distinction between them can be a bit fuzzy at times. The remote computer can't tell the difference between a message you type at the keyboard, and one you transfer from a text file. Terminal can't tell whether incoming text originated from a text file, a programmed system prompt, or at the keyboard typed by a human operator. All of it can go into a text file and onto your screen simultaneously.

Working with binary files

Binary files are a little different. Both Terminal and the remote computer will treat each binary file as a discrete entity and will not attempt to display its contents. Both systems must use a matching file transfer protocol to ensure that the data is transfered accurately. Typically, a host computer will have several protocols available for file transfers. You'll need to select either XModem or Kermit from the available choices, then make sure you instruct Terminal to use the same protocol. Each remote system will have its own procedures you will need to follow to prepare for a file transfer using a specific protocol.

Once the remote system is set to receive a binary file, you can select Send Binary File... from the Transfers menu. Terminal will open the Send Binary File dialog box shown in Figure 12-14, and you can select the file to send. When you click OK, Terminal and the remote computer will begin transfering data, carefully checking for errors and retransmitting any questionable sections of the file. Unlike text file transfers, you won't see the data scroll by in the Terminal work area, but the status bar will show the progress of the transfer.

Binary file transfers

Figure 12-14

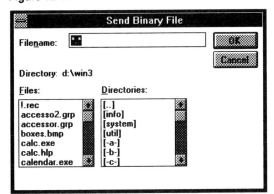

The Send Binary File dialog box lets you choose a file to transmit to the remote system.

The process of receiving a binary file is nearly the same as sending one. First, you would use the remote system's own procedures to instruct it to send a specific file using one of the protocols supported by Terminal. You would make sure Terminal is set to use the same protocol, and then you would select Receive Binary File... from the Transfers menu and supply a file name in the Receive Binary File dialog box, shown in Figure 12-15. When you click on the OK button in the dialog box, the computers will begin transferring the file.

Figure 12-15

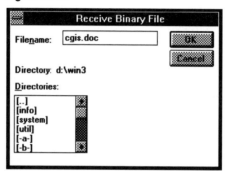

You can supply a file name and location for the incoming file in the Receive Binary File dialog box.

As you can see in Figure 12-16, the Status bar at the bottom of the work area shows the progress of the file transfer. Notice that the Pause button is missing since that option is not available during binary file transfers. You can abort the file transfer by clicking on the Stop button in the status bar, or by selecting the Stop command from the Transfers menu. However, you will not be able to resume the transfer. The Retries box at the right end of the status bar shows how many times the file transfer protocol has detected errors and retransmitted corrupted sections of the file.

Using Clipboard with Terminal

Because Terminal's work area is a little different from applications such as Write, Notepad, and Paintbrush, the Clipboard acts a little differently as well. You can copy text from the Terminal workspace to the Clipboard, but you cannot cut text from the work area. To copy text from the Terminal work area, drag the pointer across the text you want to copy to the Clipboard and then select Copy from the Edit menu. If you want to highlight all the text in Terminal's buffer, choose Select All from the Edit menu. You can switch to another application and Paste from the Clipboard in the normal manner. In Terminal, however, when you choose Paste from the Edit menu, Terminal transmits the contents of the Clipboard to the remote system.

Once you understand how the Clipboard works with Terminal, you can use it to your advantage. For example, you can copy a message from Terminal's work area to the Clipboard, and then paste the message from the Clipboard into Write or Notepad where you can edit, print, or save it in a file. If you reverse the procedure, you can use the Clipboard to send a message you composed in Notepad or Write to a remote computer without first saving it as a text file and then selecting the Send Text File command.

The Send command on the Edit menu has the same effect as copying text to the Clipboard and then selecting Paste to send it to the remote computer. It simply condenses the action into a single step. You can select the Clear Buffer command from the Edit menu to clean out the work area and Terminal's buffer.

Figure 12-16

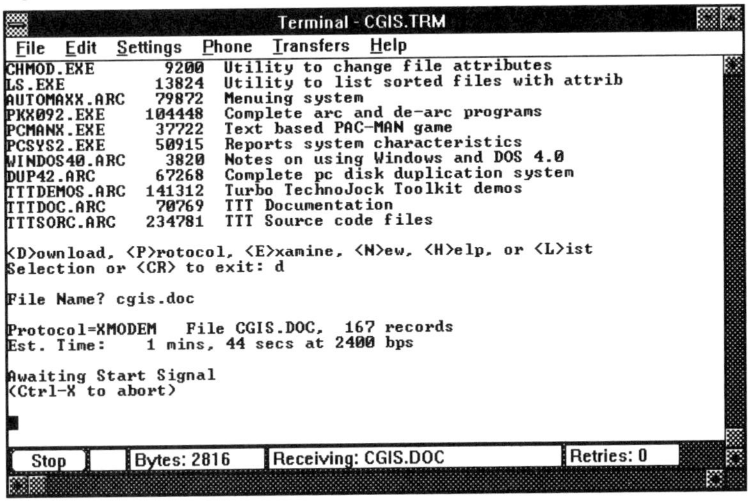

```
                    Terminal - CGIS.TRM
 File  Edit  Settings  Phone  Transfers  Help
CHMOD.EXE         9200   Utility to change file attributes
LS.EXE           13824   Utility to list sorted files with attrib
AUTOMAXX.ARC     79872   Menuing system
PKX092.EXE      104448   Complete arc and de-arc programs
PCMANX.EXE       37722   Text based PAC-MAN game
PCSYS2.EXE       50915   Reports system characteristics
WINDOS40.ARC      3820   Notes on using Windows and DOS 4.0
DUP42.ARC        67268   Complete pc disk duplication system
TTTDEMOS.ARC    141312   Turbo TechnoJock Toolkit demos
TTTDOC.ARC       70769   TTT Documentation
TTTSORC.ARC     234781   TTT Source code files

<D>ownload, <P>rotocol, <E>xamine, <N>ew, <H>elp, or <L>ist
Selection or <CR> to exit: d

File Name? cgis.doc

Protocol=XMODEM   File CGIS.DOC,  167 records
Est. Time:    1 mins, 44 secs at 2400 bps

Awaiting Start Signal
<Ctrl-X to abort>


   Stop       Bytes: 2816    Receiving: CGIS.DOC          Retries: 0
```

The status bar is missing the Pause button during a binary file transfer, but adds a Retries box to track errors.

Using function keys

Terminal provides 32 special function keys you can define to type frequently used phrases and commands for you. Terminal saves the function key definitions along with other settings when you save a Terminal file, so you can have a custom set of function keys for each remote computer you contact. During a communications session, you can access a function with a single keystroke or by clicking on an on-screen button.

Defining function keys

Figure 12-17 shows the Function Keys dialog box where you can define four sets, or "levels," of eight function keys each—a total of 32 programmable keys. For each function key, you can define a key name and a command up to 27 characters long. The commands can contain the standard alphanumeric characters, plus control codes, and special codes to program a delay, dial or hangup the modem, and send a break code. Select Function Keys... from the Settings menu to open the dialog box.

Figure 12-17

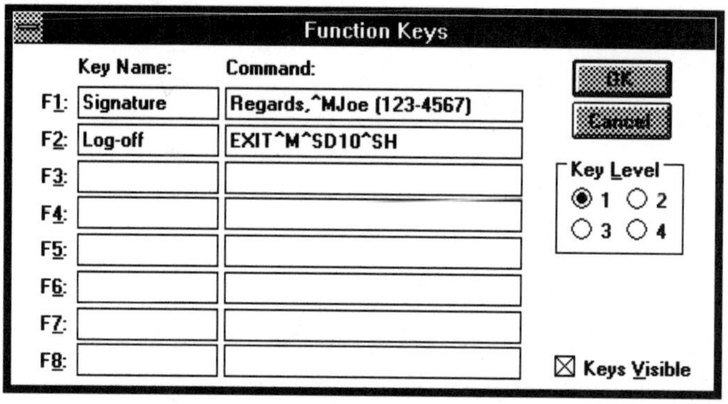

You can define up to 32 custom commands in the Function Keys dialog box.

To begin defining keys, you type a descriptive name in the Key Name text box beside the function key you want to define. As you can see in Figure 12-18, this Key Name appears on the label as the corresponding button in the function key display at the bottom of the Terminal window. In the Commands text box, type the string of characters and control codes you want Terminal to send to the remote system when you invoke this function key.

Figure 12-18

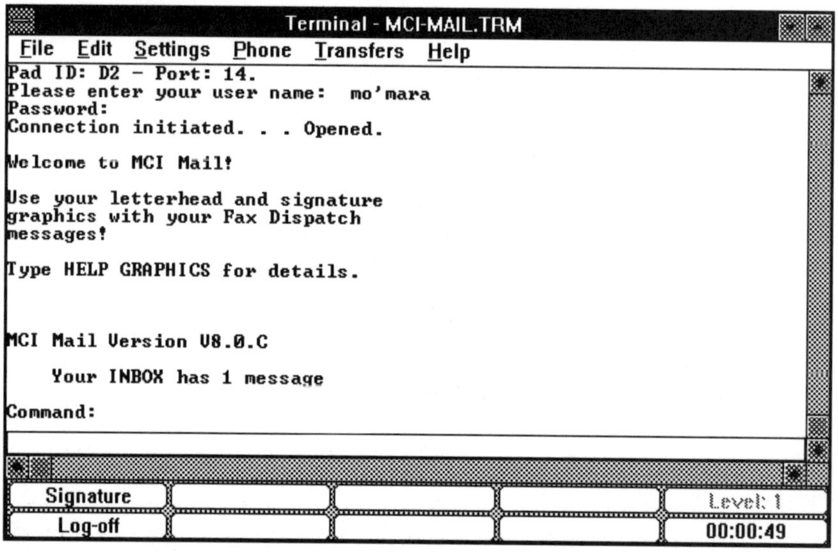

The Function Key Display at the bottom of the Terminal window makes your function key commands instantly available.

The four radio buttons in the Key Level group box of the Function Keys dialog box let you switch between the four sets of eight function keys Terminal provides. When you click on the radio button for a Key Level, the Key Name and Command text boxes in the dialog box will display the definitions for the function keys of that level. As you use Terminal, one set of eight function keys will be available at a time. Terminal will show the names of the active set of function key commands in the function key display. To use function keys from different levels, click on the Level button above the timer box in the function key display to switch to the next set of function key commands.

The Keys Visible check box in the lower-right corner of the dialog box controls whether Terminal will show the function key display at the bottom of the Terminal window automatically. Activating the option is like automatically selecting the Show Function Keys command when you open the file containing these function key definitions. You can always switch the function key display on or off by selecting the Hide/Show Function Keys command from the settings menu.

Most of your function key definitions will probably be text strings you use frequently, such as your company name, or a signature line for messages like: *Regards, Joe (123-4567)*. But, they may also include control codes (such as the commonly used codes listed in Table 12-1) that signal carriage returns or instruct Terminal to delay for a few seconds before proceeding.

Table 12-1

Code	Function
^A thru ^Z	Control code A through control code Z
^G	Bell
^H	Backspace
^J	Line Feed
^M	Carriage Return
^SD00	Delay for "00" seconds, then continue
^SC	Same as the Dial on the Phone menu
^SH	Same as the Hangup on the Phone menu
^$L0	Change to Level "0" Function Key set
^SB	Break

This table shows the control codes you're most likely to need in your function key definitions.

The following example is a function key definition that would automate the log-on sequence for MCI Mail we described earlier.

^M^SD05user^M^SD02secret^M

^M	Sends a carriage return (like pressing [Enter])—to get the remote system's attention
^SD05	Instructs Terminal to pause 5 seconds to allow time for the host system to respond with the prompt for the user name
user	Types the text *user*—just as if you typed at the keyboard
^M	Sends a carriage return
^SD02	Waits 2 seconds
secret	Types *secret*
^M	Sends a carriage return

Do as we say— not as we do!

Please note: Computer security principles, and common sense, dictate that you should *never* include your password in an automatic log-on sequence. You shouldn't even store it on disk in an unencrypted form. We do *not* recommend including your password in a function key definition! We chose a log-on as an example because the sequence is familiar to most readers and it illustrates our points. Automating the sequence of commands to read your electronic mail messages would be a better use for Terminal's function keys.

Using function keys

If the function key display is showing at the bottom of the Terminal window, you can click on a function key button and Terminal will type the text string or other command you defined for that function key. Of course, typically, you'll have to be on-line with a remote system for the command to have any effect. You can also invoke the function keys in the currently active level from the keyboard by pressing the [Ctrl] and [Alt] keys along with one of the function keys (i.e., [Ctrl][Alt][F1]). Once defined, the function keys are available from the keyboard even if the function key display is hidden. However, you'll probably want the keys to be visible, especially if you define keys on more than one level.

Background operation

You can take advantage of Windows' multitasking capability with Terminal. For instance, suppose you need to transfer a large file to another computer. You could run Terminal, log on to a remote computer, and start a binary file transfer. Once the file transfer starts, you can minimize Terminal to an icon on your desktop and run your spreadsheet, word processor, or other Windows application. As long as no other application conflicts with Terminal's use of the COM port, Terminal will continue the file transfer in the background while you attend to other business. When Terminal completes the file transfer, it will alert you by sounding a beep and the Terminal icon will blink. Then you can simply restore Terminal to a working-size window to complete the communications session.

In this chapter

Using Recorder 13

*W*indows' Recorder will record keystrokes and mouse movements and play them back at the touch of a key. With Recorder, you can automate simple, repetitive tasks or produce training demonstrations that can run continuously. Recorder operates in the Windows environment, in any of the standard Windows accessories, and in most Windows-based applications.

Microsoft chose an appropriate name for this accessory: Recorder. That is exactly what it does—records keystrokes and mouse movements. The sequence of keystrokes and mouse movements you record is called a macro. But don't confuse Recorder's macros with the kind of macros you can create with the macro commands in an application such as Microsoft Excel. Recorder is not a programming, script, or batch language. You can't pause for input, use variables, or add logic structures. You don't write and edit macros with Recorder; you simply record them.

RECORDER

Recorder may not offer all the power of a rich macro language, but it is exceptionally easy to learn and use. Recorder allows you to create your own shortcut keys for many of your routine tasks and, consequently, make your personal computer more responsive to your personal needs and working style.

To automate a procedure in Windows, you instruct Recorder to watch as you perform the task. It records each keystroke and mouse selection and even records the time between the actions. Just as a video recorder can play back a tape, Recorder can play back the recorded actions to repeat the task. You only need to select the macro's name from a list or press a special shortcut key to tell Recorder which macro you want to play. Recorder will play back the macro, reproducing your original actions, whether typing a line of text or starting another application and automatically loading a file.

Recorder allows you considerable flexibility to tailor the way you record and play back your macros. You can create macros that will work in any Windows application, or macros that work only in the application in which you recorded them. You can record mouse positions anywhere on the screen, or track mouse movement relative to the active window. For demonstrations, you can play back macros at the same pace they were recorded, or you can put Recorder into "fast forward" and send the computer commands at high speed. You can save your macros in a file and, by loading separate Recorder files, have a unique set of macros available for each type of work you do, or for each person using the computer.

Starting Recorder

To start Recorder from Windows' Program Manager, select the Accessories group window and double-click on the Recorder icon. After you create a set of macros and save them in a Recorder macro file, you may want to load that file automatically each time you start Recorder. See Chapter 5 for information on changing the properties of a Program Manager item. Normally, you will start Recorder and load the file of macros you plan to use, then immediately minimize it to an icon on your desktop. Recorder's macros will be available at the touch of a shortcut key, and you will only need to restore Recorder to the active window to load another macro file or record a new macro.

A TEXT MACRO

The best way to learn about Windows' Recorder is to use it. We'll demonstrate the principal features of Recorder, then we'll explain Recorder's other options.

In the first example, we'll create a simple text macro that will type your name in Write with a keystroke. This is the simplest of macros, but it's the sort of macro you'll use dozens (perhaps even hundreds) of times a day.

Preliminaries

First, start Recorder and minimize it to an icon on your desktop (if you haven't already done so). Unlike Clipboard, Recorder is not a built-in feature of Windows. You must run the Recorder application before you can create or use any macros.

Before you start recording a macro, you will need to configure your desktop and the application in which you'll use the macro so that everything is ready for the activity you want to record. In this case, the only applications you'll need are Recorder (which should already be on your desktop) and Write. Start Write by selecting the Accessories group window in the Program Manager and double-clicking on the Write icon. Write will open a new, untitled document with a cursor blinking on the first line. For now, resist the temptation to maximize the Write window since you'll want easy access to the Recorder icon on your desktop.

Recording

With your desktop ready and the application open, you're ready to start recording the macro. Activate Recorder by double-clicking on its icon, then select Record... from the Macro menu. The Record Macro dialog box will appear, as shown in Figure 13-1.

Figure 13-1

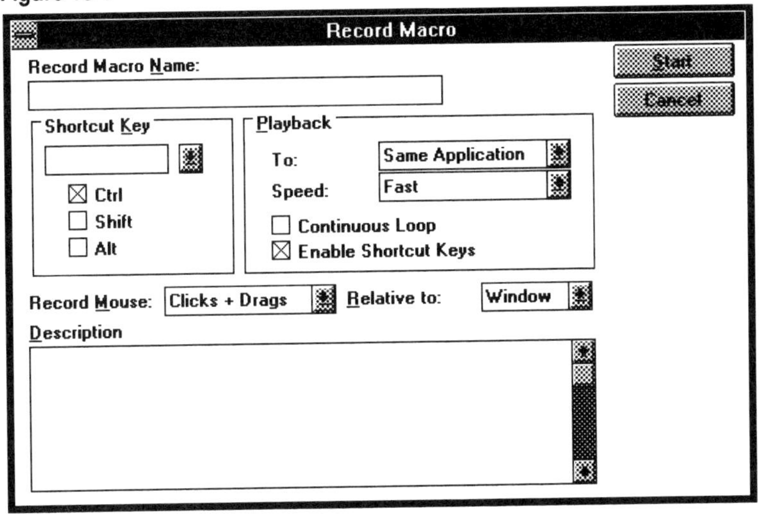

The Record Macro dialog box will allow you to specify a shortcut key and other options for your macro.

In the Record Macro dialog box, you can control most of the recording and playback options for your macro. The default settings will be suitable for most situations, including this example. Recorder requires you to fill in either a name or a shortcut key for your macro. In the Record Macro Name text box, you can give the macro a descriptive name up to 40 characters long. In our examples, we use *My Name*.

Recorder monitors the keyboard, even when it is inactive or minimized. If it detects a keystroke that matches one of the keys (or key combinations) defined in the current set of macros, Recorder steps in to execute the macro. By using shortcut keys, you can use your macros from within any Windows application without opening the Recorder window.

We'll assign the [Ctrl]N key combination as the shortcut key for this macro. Click on the text box in the Shortcut Key group box and type the letter *N*. Make sure the Ctrl check box is selected and that the Shift and Alt check boxes are not. Once the macro is recorded, you'll be able to run it by pressing [Ctrl]N.

You must give each macro either a name or a shortcut key so that Recorder can identify the macro—it is not necessary to do both. However, we recommend that you name all your macros, even the ones you execute with shortcut keys. As your list of macros grows, you'll find the names helpful, if not essential.

The rest of the Record Macro dialog box can retain the default settings. We'll explore the other options in a moment. To start recording the macro, click on the Start button. Recorder will minimize itself automatically and return you to Write. Notice that the Recorder icon will blink to indicate that it is recording.

Next, type your name the way you will want to insert it in your Write documents. Recorder will record each key you press and each mouse selection you make. If you mistype and use the [Backspace] key to make a correction, Recorder will register that as well.

Saving the macro

Once you finish performing the action you want to automate—in this case, typing your name—you need to tell Recorder to stop recording. Click on the blinking Recorder icon. Recorder will then open a dialog box that allows you to save the macro, resume recording, or cancel recording. As Figure 13-2 shows, the Save Macro radio button will be selected by default. When you click on the OK button or press [Enter], the macro will be stored in Recorder's memory (though not yet saved on disk), and the Recorder icon will stop blinking to indicate that it is no longer in record mode.

Figure 13-2

When you stop recording, this dialog box will allow you to save the macro, cancel it, or resume recording.

Testing the macro

It's always a good idea to test a new macro to make sure it was recorded properly. (Besides, you want to see your first macro work, don't you?) After saving the macro, Windows will return you to your Write document. Start a new paragraph and type some miscellaneous text to simulate creating a typical document. When you get to a place where you want to insert your name, press [Ctrl]N. Recorder will execute the macro you just recorded, playing back each keystroke just as if you were typing them—except much faster. Using the macros you create with Recorder is just that easy.

Now, double-click on the Recorder icon to bring up the Recorder application window. As you can see in Figure 13-3, Recorder's previously empty work area now lists your *ctrl+N—My Name* macro. Creating this kind of simple macro with Recorder is so fast and easy that you'll find yourself making them "on the fly" to save typing repetitive phrases in a letter or report.

**A COMMAND
MACRO**

With Recorder, you can create macros that issue commands as well as macros that play back text. In fact, command macros are often more useful than macros that reduce a long text string to a single keystroke.

Figure 13-3

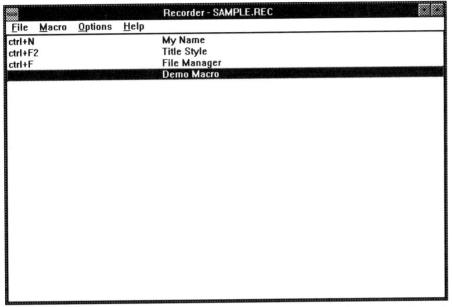

The Recorder window will display a list of the macros currently at your disposal.

To issue commands in most Windows applications, you normally use the mouse to make selections from menus. After all, that is the essence of a graphical interface. However, selecting menu items with a mouse can create potential problems in a macro.

The problem with mouse selections

Recorder registers mouse selections as position coordinates either relative to the full screen or relative to the active window. When you click the button, Recorder remembers the position of the mouse, not what is under the pointer. If you run a macro in a window whose size or position differs from when you recorded the macro, the effects can be unpredictable. A mouse click may occur on a different menu selection or fall completely outside the active window.

When you record macros, it's wise to avoid using the mouse. Instead, use keyboard equivalents to issue commands whenever possible. (That is the technique we'll use in this example.) Windows provides keyboard equivalents for essentially everything you would normally do with the mouse. It is even possible (though awkward) to use Windows without touching the mouse. You may want to review Chapter 2 for the keyboard techniques for making menu selections and accessing such Windows features as the Control menu and the Task Manager.

Fortunately, to record a macro, you'll only need to perform a task with the keyboard once. After that, Recorder will handle the playback, and you won't need to remember the keyboard or mouse selections.

Setting up the application

As an example of a macro that issues commands, we will add formatting attributes to a line of text in Write. Obviously, Recorder must be running on your desktop, either minimized or in an inactive window, and Write should be in the active window. Just to make things interesting, maximize the Write window or move it so that it obscures the Recorder icon or window on your desktop. Type a short line of text into a new document in Write, and then highlight it by dragging the pointer across the line.

This is the starting point for the macro—with the line of text already highlighted. The macro automates the process of adding formatting attributes to any text we might select. Since we might use the macro to format text anywhere in a document, selecting the text is *not* part of the macro.

Normally, you will want to make a "dry run" through the procedure you intend to automate before you start recording the macro. That way, you can make notes of the steps and commands you'll want in the macro and the keyboard alternative for each mouse selection. After the dry run, carefully return all settings to the starting configuration. Since we've already done this, you can skip the dry run and follow the instructions below.

Using Task Manager to activate Recorder

After you configure your desktop and application, it's time to activate Recorder, name the new macro, assign a shortcut key, and start recording the procedure. Since the Write window occupies the entire screen, you can't activate Recorder by double-clicking on the icon as you did in the previous example. Instead, you can use Windows' Task Manager to activate Recorder. Press [Ctrl][Esc] to open the Task List dialog box, shown in Figure 13-4, and use the mouse or arrow keys to highlight Recorder. Then, click on the Switch To button to open the Recorder window. You can use this technique to access Recorder (or any running application) when the icon or inactive window is obscured by other windows. Refer to Chapter 2 for more information on the Task Manager. You'll find many uses for this handy tool as you work with Recorder macros.

Figure 13-4

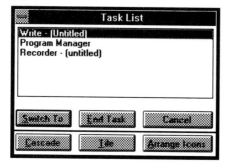

Windows' Task Manager lets you switch to any running application— even if the icon or inactive window is obscured.

Once Recorder's window appears over Write, select Record... from the Macro menu just as you did in the previous example. Then, type *Title Style* in the Record Macro Name text box.

To specify one of the standard alphanumeric keys as a shortcut key, you simply click on the text box in the Shortcut Key group box and press the key you want to use, as we did in the last example. However, to specify one of the non-alphanumeric keys, you must choose it from a drop-down list box. To use [Ctrl][F2] as the shortcut key for this macro, open the drop-down list box and scroll through the list until [F2] is visible, then click on it. Recorder will place [F2] in the text box as the shortcut key. As you can see in the list box in Figure 13-5, you can use the arrow keys, [Space], [Tab], and most of the other keys on your keyboard as shortcut keys. Make sure the Ctrl check box is selected and the Alt and Shift check boxes are not.

Selecting
non-alphanumeric
shortcut keys

Figure 13-5

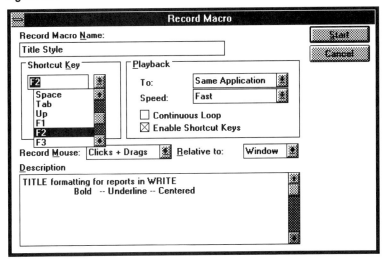

You can use non-alphanumeric keys from the drop-down list box as shortcut keys for your macros.

At the bottom of the Record Macro dialog box, you'll find a large text box entitled *Description*. You can click on this box and type several lines of text to describe your macro and its actions. As your macro collection grows and you share macros with other Windows users, you'll find this space very useful for documenting your macros.

When you finish selecting the macro recording options, click on the Start button to minimize Recorder and start recording the macro.

Using the
Description box

Recording the procedure using the keyboard

In your Write document, the line of text should be highlighted, ready to receive formatting commands. To record the procedure, first press [Alt]P to pull down the Paragraph menu. (Remember, we're using keyboard equivalents rather than selecting commands with the mouse.) Press *C* to select Centered from the menu and center the highlighted text on the page. Next, press [Alt]C to pull down the Character menu and select Bold by pressing *B*. If you would like your titles to be underlined, Press [Alt]C again to access the Character menu, then press *U* to select Underline.

Saving the macro

Once you complete the actions you want in the macro, press [Ctrl][Break] to stop recording. Pressing [Ctrl][Break] has the same effect as clicking on the Recorder icon. The same dialog box shown in Figure 13-2 appears, giving you the choice of saving the macro, resuming recording, or canceling what you've recorded. Click on the Save Macro radio button and then click on the OK button. Instead of using [Ctrl][Break], you could also stop recording by selecting Recorder from the Task Manager. If you use this second method to stop recording, you'll sacrifice speed since Recorder will add these steps at the end of the macro.

Using the macro

To use this macro in Write, you must first highlight an appropriate line of text. In this case, you'll probably need to type a new, short line of text to serve as a candidate for a title. Drag the pointer across the text to highlight the entire line, then press [Ctrl][F2]. Recorder will recognize the shortcut key for the macro you just recorded and repeat the procedure on the new text.

Saving the macro file

The macros you create with Recorder exist only in your computer's memory until you save them on your hard disk in a Recorder file. Only the macros that appear on the list in Recorder's work area are available for you to use. You can load a set of macros by opening a Recorder file or add to the list by recording new macros. Recorder doesn't limit the number of macros in a single file, but you'll probably want to organize macros you use as sets into separate files.

Recorder's File menu supplies the usual complement of file management commands to save, open, and start files, plus a Merge command we'll discuss later.

To save your macros in a file, activate Recorder and select Save As... from the File menu. In the familiar File Save As dialog box, type a file name in the Filename text box, and select the appropriate drive and directory in which you want to save the file. When you click OK, Recorder will save the file and (unless you included your own extension) add the .REC extension to the file name you supplied.

AN "ANY APPLICATION" MACRO

In the preceding examples we recorded two macros that we intend to use only in Write. The commands to format text in the Title Style macro would be inappropriate in another application. At best, there would be no equivalent menus or commands, and the application would sound an error beep when it received unrecognizable instructions. If another application has menus and commands that use the same keyboard equivalents, the macro would invoke those commands, and the results would be unpredictable. For this reason, Recorder notes which application was active when you recorded a macro, and by default restricts the macro to running in only that application.

You can change Recorder's default and specify that a macro can run in all applications. When used carefully, the Any Application option is a very powerful feature. The following example creates a macro that will activate File Manager from your desktop or from within any Windows application (except Program Manager) with a single keystroke.

Of course, the first step is to set up your desktop with the applications you will use in the macro. In addition to having Recorder available on your desktop, you'll need File Manager running as an icon or inactive window plus any other application running in the active window.

Recording

To start recording the macro, activate Recorder and select Record... from the Macro menu. In the Record Macro dialog box, name the macro *File Manager* and specify [Ctrl]F as the shortcut key. In the Playback group box, activate the drop-down list box for the To option by clicking on the button. Then, click on Any Application. After you make these selections, you can click on the Start button to begin recording the macro.

Next, access File Manager from the Task Manager by pressing [Ctrl][Esc]. If you use the mouse to select File Manager from the Task List, the macro will probably select the wrong application if you play it back when a different task occupies that position in the list. Instead, press *F* to jump the highlight to the first task starting with an *F*, and then press [Alt]S or [Enter] to switch to File Manager. Since none of the other standard Windows applications begin with *F*, this technique has a much better chance of reliably selecting File Manager each time you run the macro.

To stop recording, click on the Recorder icon, then select the Save Macro option from the dialog box and click OK.

Using the macro

The sole purpose of this macro is to create a fast, easy way to get to File Manager from anywhere in the Windows environment—even when the File Manager icon or window is not readily accessible. To demonstrate the macro's usefulness, activate another application, such as Write or Terminal, and maximize it to occupy the full screen. When you press [Ctrl]F, the macro will bring up File Manager, even though you recorded it in another application.

A "DEMO" MACRO

As a final example, we'll create a macro that will show off several other Recorder features. This macro will play back continuously at the same speed it was recorded, and will repeat indefinitely. Both features are well-suited to training and product demonstrations. This macro is another example of one that plays back in Any Application, and it also illustrates nesting macros within other macros.

Preparation

As always, you need to have the appropriate tools available before you begin recording (or playing back) a macro. For this macro, you'll need Recorder, File Manager, and Write on your desktop. After you minimize the applications, drag each icon into position on the desktop. If you manually position an icon on your desktop, it will return to that position each time you minimize it during this Windows session. If you allow Windows to position the icons, it will place them on a grid in first-come first-serve fashion, which may shuffle their positions. If the icons change positions, your macro may select File Manager when it was supposed to activate Write.

The other example macros described in this chapter must be available in Recorder, and Write should start with a new, untitled document.

Since this macro will play back at the same speed you record it—complete with all your pauses and hesitations—you may want to practice the sequence of actions before you record them. In this mode, recording a macro is akin to recording a performance.

First, activate Recorder by double-clicking on its icon, then select Record... from the Macro menu. In the Record Macro dialog box, name the macro *Demo Macro,* but do not assign any shortcut key.

Any Application

Now turn your attention to the Playback group box. Open the drop-down list box for the To option, then highlight the Any Application option. This will allow the macro to function in the various applications you'll use.

Playback speed

Using the same process, select Recorded Speed for the Speed option to direct Recorder to replay your actions at the same pace you use when you record them, rather than dumping the commands to the computer as fast as possible. In addition to the obvious implications for training and demonstrations, you may find this option useful when you automate procedures that require time to complete one step before starting the next. Recorder always registers the timing of your actions as you record a macro regardless of how the Speed option is set. Later, you can switch between Fast and Recorded Speed playback modes.

Continuous playback

To have Recorder automatically repeat the macro until you stop it, click on the Continuous Loop check box. This is another feature you can activate or deactivate, after you record the macro. The Continuous Loop option is especially helpful for creating self-running product demonstrations.

Enable Shortcut Keys

The Enable Shortcut Keys check box allows you to nest other macros within this macro. You can select this check box in order to include another macro's shortcut key as part of this macro. You can disable this feature when necessary, such as when you have created a macro that uses the same shortcut key as a command in an application and you want to issue the application's command rather than run the macro.

The Record Mouse text box lets you adjust the way Recorder registers mouse movements and selections. For this example, you can use the default setting, Clicks + Drags. Recorder will capture the position of the mouse each time you press the mouse button and track its movement during drags. The Ignore Mouse and Everything options are to ignore the mouse completely or to record all mouse movements (even when no mouse button is pressed). You'll rarely need to change these options.

Mouse settings

The Relative To drop-down list box controls whether Recorder tracks mouse movements relative to the entire screen or to the active window. Select Screen from the drop-down list box to record mouse movements anywhere on the desktop. Generally, mouse actions relative to the active window are more reliable—especially actions within fixed-size windows, such as dialog boxes. However, we want to demonstrate Recorder's full-screen mouse-sensing capability, and this macro will create a controlled situation that minimizes the chances of an unexpectedly resized window causing problems.

When you have properly set all the options, press [Enter] or click on the Start button to begin recording the macro.

You're ready to start recording the demonstration. Recorder will register each key you press and each mouse selection you make. It will also record the speed at which you type and make selections. When you're playing the macro, the actions will be repeated at exactly the speed you recorded them.

Conducting the demo

First, activate Write by double-clicking on the icon. Type a short headline in Write and then press [Enter] twice. Below the title, type a paragraph of miscellaneous text. The content isn't important, as long as you include your name so that you'll have a chance to demonstrate the My Name macro.

At the appropriate place in the paragraph, press [Ctrl]N to insert your name. Recorder will then run the My Name macro and register the shortcut key in the macro you are recording. It won't record the contents of the nested macro. If you replace the My Name macro with a new macro using [Ctrl]N as its shortcut key, Recorder will use the new [Ctrl]N macro the next time you run this macro.

Nesting macros

Next, use the mouse to drag the pointer across the top line of text, the one you typed as a headline or title. With the line of text highlighted, press [Ctrl][F2]. Again, Recorder will play back the Title Style macro that adds formatting to the text, but will record only the shortcut key in this macro.

Your demo isn't confined to a single application. For example, you can press [Ctrl]F to activate File Manager and then use the mouse or keyboard to browse through a couple of directories on your hard disk.

Since you want this macro to repeat itself in a continuous loop, you need to return the desktop to its starting configuration before ending the macro. First, you'll need to minimize File Manager. Next, select New from the File menu in

Returning to starting configuration

Write, and then click on the No button in the warning dialog box to dispose of the untitled sample document you were using for this demonstration. Finally, minimize Write by clicking on the minimize button.

Stop recording and save the macro

As soon as you return the desktop to its original state, press [Ctrl][Break] to stop recording the macro. When the dialog box appears, as shown in Figure 13-2, select the Save Macro radio button and then click on the OK button. If you want to save the macro on disk, activate Recorder by double-clicking on its icon, then select Save from the File menu.

Starting the Demo macro

You've run the other macros by pressing shortcut keys, but this macro isn't assigned to a shortcut key. So how will you run it? You can select and run any of your macros from the Recorder window. This procedure is handy for less frequently used macros that you don't assign shortcut keys, or for those times you simply forget the shortcut key that activates a certain macro. When you activate Recorder, you'll find the Demo macro listed in the Recorder window along with your other macros. You can execute the Demo macro by clicking on the line containing its name and then selecting Run from the Macro menu (or simply double-clicking on the macro name). Recorder will minimize itself and execute the macro you recorded.

A continuously running demo

Because we selected the Continuous Loop playback option, this macro won't stop. When it ends, it will return to the beginning and start over, repeating until you halt it. When you want to stop the macro, just press [Ctrl][Break] and confirm your action by clicking on the OK button in the dialog box Recorder presents.

OTHER OPTIONS

In addition to the features that our four example macros illustrate, Recorder includes tools to manage your macro files and control many of the macro recording and playback options.

Merging files

The Merge... command on Recorder's File menu is similar to the Open... command. When you choose Merge..., you'll see the File Merge dialog box shown in Figure 13-6. You can select a Recorder file from your disk and load the macros from that file into memory. The difference between the Open... and Merge... commands is that Open... removes all the existing macros from the list in Recorder's work area and replaces them with the macros from the file you select. Merge..., on the other hand, doesn't remove the existing macros. It adds the macros from the file you select to the macros that are already active, thereby "merging" the two sets of macros. If Recorder encounters two macros with duplicate shortcut key assignments, it will alert you to the problem with a dialog box and erase the offending shortcut key from the newly imported macro. After the merge operation, you can use the Properties... command on the Macro menu to assign a new shortcut key to the problem macro.

Figure 13-6

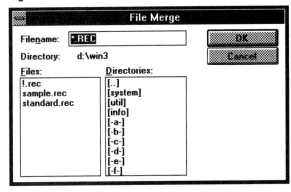

The File Merge dialog box will let you select a file of macros to add to the macros already in memory.

Deleting macros

The Delete command on the Macro menu allows you to remove a macro from Recorder's macro list. To get rid of an unneeded macro, simply highlight the macro in the macro list by clicking on the macro name with the mouse or by moving the highlight with the arrow keys, then select Delete. Recorder will prompt you for confirmation that you want to delete the macro. When you click on the OK button, Recorder will erase the macro from memory. However, if the macro is in a Recorder file on disk, the disk version will not be changed until you save the altered file.

Changing a macro's properties

Selecting the Properties... command from the Macro menu will display the properties of the currently highlighted macro in the Macro Properties dialog box. You can change nearly all the options you set when you originally recorded the macro. In fact, as Figure 13-7 on the following page shows, the Macro Properties dialog box is nearly identical to the Record Macro dialog box. The Macro Name, Shortcut Key, Playback, and Description areas are the same in appearance and operation. The significant difference is in the mouse options. You cannot change the way Recorder sees mouse selections once they are recorded. The Macro Properties dialog box shows information on whether mouse coordinates were recorded relative to the screen or active window and on what type of display. This information can be essential in determining whether you will be able to share a macro with someone working on another system.

Temporarily disabling Recorder

Occasionally, you may want to disable Recorder temporarily without removing it from your desktop. At least, you may need to disable Recorder's reaction to shortcut keys to avoid conflict with the shortcut keys in an application. The Shortcut Keys command on the Options menu is a toggle that will allow you to switch Recorder's ability to sense shortcut keys on and off. The default is for shortcut key sensing to be active, as indicated by a check beside the command on the menu. Simply click on the command to force Recorder to ignore shortcut keys. Repeat the same action to reinstate shortcut key sensing. While shortcut keys are disabled, you will still be able to run macros by opening the Recorder window, highlighting a macro in Recorder's list, and selecting the Run command from the Macro menu.

Figure 13-7

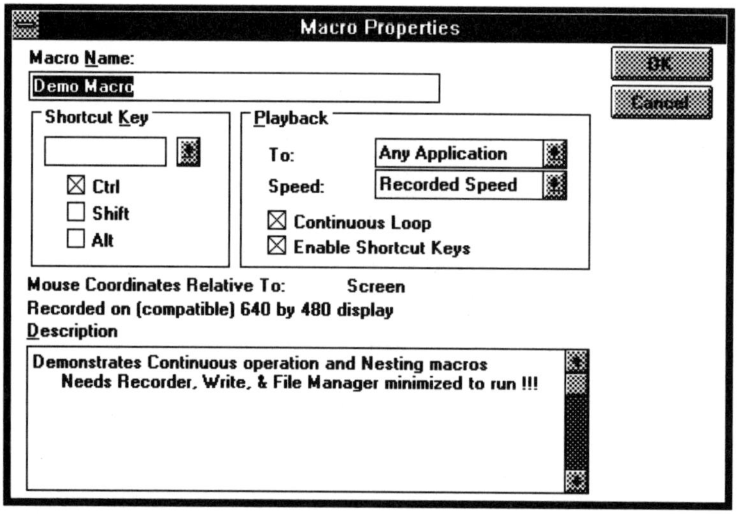

The Macro Properties dialog box will allow you to change nearly all original macro settings and will display the mouse recording options used in this macro.

Minimize On Use

Normally, Recorder minimizes itself automatically when you start recording a macro, stop recording a macro, or select and run a macro from the Recorder window. If you would rather have Recorder remain on your desktop as an inactive window instead of an icon, select Minimize On Use from the Options menu. This command switches the feature on or off, and a check mark will indicate whether it is active.

The uninterruptable demo

Pressing [Ctrl][Break] will normally stop recording a macro or halt execution of a running macro. You also press [Ctrl][Break] to stop a macro that you have set to play back repeatedly in a continuous loop. You can create a "bullet-proof" demo that will run with no possibility of interruption from random keyboard input by disabling Control+Break Checking. You can select Control+Break Checking from the Options menu to tell Recorder to ignore [Ctrl][Break]. If you run a continuous loop macro with Control+Break Checking disabled, the macro will continue to repeat itself until you reboot the computer. Like Shortcut Keys and Minimize On Use, Control+Break Checking is a toggle command with a check mark to indicate when it is active.

If you find yourself changing Playback To or Speed settings, or the Record Mouse and Relative To options nearly every time you start to record a macro, you can save time by changing the defaults. Select Preferences... from the Options menu to bring up the Default Preferences dialog box, as shown in Figure 13-8. If you change the settings here and then click on the OK button, Recorder will use your selections instead of the original defaults in the Record Macro dialog box.

Changing defaults

Figure 13-8

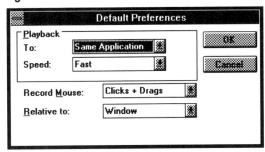

You can change the default settings that appear in the Record Macro dialog box from this Default Preferences dialog box.

With Recorder, it's easy to create macros that will help with many of your routine tasks. However, there are a few things you should keep in mind as you record and use macros so that your macros will be reliable and trouble-free.

CARE AND FEEDING OF YOUR MACRO

Pay attention to your Windows environment when you record your macros and when you use them. What applications are running? Which are minimized and which are inactive windows? What is the size and position of each open window? When you run a macro, any of these factors that differ from your Windows environment when you recorded the macro might cause unpredictable results. For example, our File Manager macro discussed earlier in this chapter assumes that File Manager is available on the desktop and that it is the only application available in Task Manager that begins with *F*. The macro will not have the intended effect if either assumption is not true. Macros that play back in any application, and macros that use the mouse (especially relative to the full screen) are especially vulnerable to changes in the Windows environment.

A good place for notes about a macro's environment requirements is in the Description box at the bottom of the Macro Properties dialog box.

Preparing the environment for macros

When you select shortcut keys for your macros, you'll want to avoid selecting keys and key combinations that your applications will need for normal operations. Obviously, you wouldn't use one of the standard typewriter keys alone or combined with [Shift] as a shortcut key. If you did, you couldn't use that key to type text while Recorder was active. You'll also want to avoid most [Alt] letter combinations since they are used extensively to access Windows' menus. Combinations that use the [Ctrl] key are generally safer selections for shortcut keys.

Selecting shortcut keys

It's important to note that combinations such as [Ctrl][Shift]S that use more than one of the "shift" keys ([Shift], [Ctrl], [Alt]) will almost never conflict with an application's predefined shortcuts.

Mousing about

Use your mouse sparingly when you record macros! Remember that Recorder registers the position of the pointer when you click the mouse button. It does not record the effect of the mouse action. The macro will have the same effect when you play it back only if the window, menu, or command you selected with the mouse is in the same position as when you recorded the macro. Remember also that Windows is a dynamic environment with windows that may be different sizes and in different positions each time you use a macro. Mouse movements relative to the active window are generally more reliable than movements relative to the entire screen area (especially within fixed-size windows, such as dialog boxes).

Use the keyboard equivalents instead of the mouse to issue commands and make menu selections in your macros. Windows allows you to duplicate essentially every mouse action with the keyboard. Chapter 2 covers using the keyboard with Windows. You can also select Keyboard from the Help menu in most Windows applications for a brief listing of the keys used specifically by that application. If you must use the mouse in a macro, you may want to first maximize the window to help ensure more predictable positioning by standardizing the window size and position.

Sharing macros

Sharing your Recorder macros with someone else using Windows 3 is as simple as giving your friend a copy of the Recorder file containing your macros— provided they have the same applications and use similar settings and hardware.

If you record macros on one computer and attempt to play them back on a different computer, you may encounter problems if both systems don't use the same display adapter and keyboard. Recorder senses mouse movements relative to the screen resolution of your system. If you record a macro that includes mouse selections on one system, it will seldom work on a system that uses a different display adapter.

A similar but less severe problem occurs when you record a macro on a system with one type of keyboard and play it back on a system with a different kind of keyboard or a different Country setting. While most keystrokes may be the same on both systems, you should be alert to the potential for some problems arising from the keyboard differences.

Using Recorder with non-Windows applications

Recorder was designed to work with Windows and Windows-based applications. If you are running Windows in the standard or real modes, Recorder might work with some non-Windows applications. However, the reliability of your macros will be questionable, at best. We don't recommend the practice.

Macros will *not* work with non-Windows applications if you use Windows 386 enhanced mode. The same technology that allows Windows to perform multi-tasking and advanced memory management also insulates applications in a DOS session from its Windows parent too thoroughly to allow Recorder to work.

In this chapter

Using Desktop Accessories 14

Windows provides important time-management tools in its desktop applications. Notepad, Calendar, Cardfile, Calculator, and Clock are applications that will help you with schedules, appointments, phone numbers, and the countless details that must be managed to maintain the efficient daily operation of your office. Because you can minimize these applications into icons on your desktop, they are available at any time, from any Windows-based application. By using these icons, you won't have to take much time away from a project to add a note in your calendar or write a message to a colleague. You can find all these application icons in the Accessories group window in the Program Manager, as shown in Figure 14-1. In this chapter, we'll show you how to use the desktop applications to enhance efficiency and creativity, and how to exchange data between them.

Figure 14-1

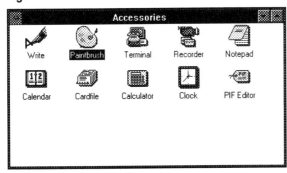

You can start these applications from the Accessories group window.

NOTEPAD

Jotting down a quick idea for later use is an important part of the creative process. The Notepad application will help you keep track of your ideas, great and small. You also can use Notepad to keep a phone call log, a things-to-do list, a time log, or even a diary. The Notepad is a simple word processor whose built-in search functions enable you to gain access to your notes for a particular date, phrase, or idea.

Notepad creates an ASCII text file that has no hidden character formatting like Write's invisible paragraph markers. Chapter 9 provides more about data formats.

Starting Notepad

To start Notepad, double-click on the Notepad icon in the Accessories group window (which you'll find in the Program Manager window) to view a Notepad window like the one in Figure 14-2. As you can see, the window contains all the standard elements (Control menu, title bar, frame, scroll bars, etc.). Aside from the standard File, Edit, and Help menus, Notepad offers an additional menu, the Search menu. The flashing cursor is automatically positioned in the upper-left corner of the work area. When you move the pointer into the work area from the desktop, it will change from an arrow into an I-beam.

Figure 14-2

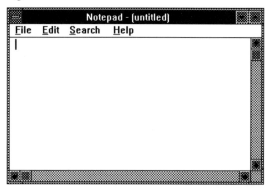

Notepad's window has search capabilities.

Exiting Notepad

To exit Notepad, choose the Exit command from the File menu. For more about exiting an application, refer to Chapter 9.

Entering text

As you've seen, Notepad starts with an untitled notepad. To make an entry in your active notepad, simply begin typing. Your text will appear to the left of the flashing cursor. If you want to open and enter text in an existing notepad, choose the Open... command from the File menu and Notepad will display the File Open dialog box. As you can see in Figure 14-3, this dialog box will display all the available Notepad files. You can either select one of the files in the Files list box or type a file name in the Filename text box. For more about opening files, refer to Chapter 9.

Figure 14-3

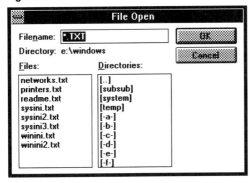

The File Open dialog box will display all available Notepad files.

Sometimes you may need to refer to information in one notepad while you're working in another. You can do this easily because Windows lets you open multiple notepads. If you have a notepad open and want to create another one, you need to resize or move the first window to gain access to the Notepad application icon in the Program Manager. When you double-click the Notepad icon again, an untitled notepad will appear and you'll be ready to start typing additional information.

Applying Word Wrap

To tell Notepad where you want your lines of text to end, you can use two techniques. One way is to press [Enter] to add a carriage return manually. If you don't want to keep pressing [Enter], you can use the Word Wrap command on the Edit menu to tell Notepad to automatically wrap the lines. However, you'll still need to press [Enter] to start a new paragraph.

Word Wrap is a toggle command. When it is active, a check mark will appear beside it on the Edit menu. Because Word Wrap isn't active by default, you'll need to select it every time you start Notepad. You can also tell that Word Wrap is on when the horizontal scroll bar disappears. The horizontal scroll bar isn't necessary with Word Wrap since Notepad confines the text to the left and right boundaries of the window. If you make your window smaller in order to accommodate other Windows on the desktop, the text will conform to the new space. As you add text, the slider on the vertical scroll bar will move down. Notepad imposes a limit of 50,000 characters per file. You can see how many characters are in the file you're working with by issuing the About Notepad... command on the Help menu. If you need to create a file larger than Notepad can accommodate, you'll need to purchase another application that specializes in ASCII text editing. We used the Word Wrap feature to type the text in Figure 14-4.

Figure 14-4

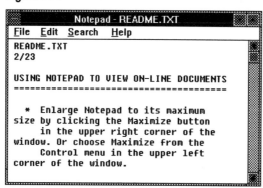

```
┌─────────────────────────────────────────────┐
│         Notepad - README.TXT                  │
│  File  Edit  Search  Help                     │
│ README.TXT                                  ▲ │
│ 2/23                                          │
│                                               │
│ USING NOTEPAD TO VIEW ON-LINE DOCUMENTS       │
│ ============================================  │
│                                               │
│    * Enlarge Notepad to its maximum           │
│ size by clicking the Maximize button          │
│    in the upper right corner of the           │
│ window. Or choose Maximize from the           │
│    Control menu in the upper left             │
│ corner of the window.                         │
│                                             ▼ │
└─────────────────────────────────────────────┘
```

The size of the window determines how Word Wrap will wrap text in the work area.

Editing text

If you make mistakes or want to change anything in your document, you'll need to use Notepad's editing features. Notepad lets you insert and delete characters; cut, copy, and paste words; and insert spaces for a limited form of formatting. You can delete a character by backspacing to remove the character to the left of the cursor, or by pressing [Delete] to remove the character to the right of the cursor. You can delete a series of characters by dragging the pointer over the characters to highlight them and then pressing [Backspace] or [Delete]. You can also delete highlighted characters by choosing the Delete command from the Edit menu. The Cut command removes any highlighted text and puts it on Clipboard. The Copy command copies highlighted text and places it on Clipboard. The Paste command takes text from Clipboard and inserts it at the position of the cursor. For more details on editing text, refer to Chapters 2, 9, and 10.

Besides deleting or adding text, you can format it by using tabs or spaces. Notepad tabs are predefined as eight spaces in the system font, 10-point Helvetica (about $\frac{1}{2}$"), and you can't change or set additional tabs. If you need more control over spacing, you need to copy the file into Write.

Searching for words and phrases

Notepad's search functions let you look for particular characters, words, or phrases in your text. For example, if you want to copy a name and phone number, but can't find it, select Find... from the Search menu. In the Find dialog box shown in Figure 14-5, enter the character, word, or phrase you want to find in the Find What text box. If case is important, as it would be in a person's name, select the Match Upper/Lowercase check box. Since punctuation makes a difference, be sure to include any spaces, slashes, hyphens, or other punctuation in your search text. Notepad will start its search from the location of your cursor. You can control the direction of the search, either forward from the cursor or backward, by using the Forward or Backward radio buttons. After you enter the search text and select the appropriate buttons, press [Enter] or click on OK. Notepad will find the text and highlight it. If it can't find the text, Notepad will present an information dialog box like the one in Figure 14-6, with the message *Cannot find* and the search text. Click on OK to return to your document.

Figure 14-5

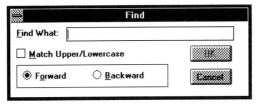

The Find dialog box will help you search for text.

Figure 14-6

This information dialog box lets you know when Notepad can't find a match to your search text.

You can repeat a search for a string of characters (93 East Street) or a word (Bruce). Instead of reissuing a Find... command, you can just select Find Next from the Search menu or press the accelerator key [F3]. If Notepad can't find additional matches, it will present the same type of information dialog box that the Find... command does. The Find Next command is handy if you have misspelled a word the same way throughout your notepad, and you need to correct each occurrence.

Your notepad entries can be a valuable resource if you design them with a plan for retrieving the information they contain. For example, if you want to be able to track phone calls by time and date, you should incorporate that information into the text of the messages. To add the time and date, select the Time/Date command from the Edit menu or use the accelerator key ([F5]). As you can see in Figure 14-7 on the following page, Windows inserts the time and date at the position of the cursor. (Remember, you can change the format of the time and date as well as the actual time and date through the Control Panel.) Next, add the caller's name, phone number, and message. Later, you can easily copy the name and phone number into a Rolodex card file.

Another way to insert the time and date is to use an embedded .LOG command. Windows will insert the time and date at the end of your Notepad session if you save Notepad before you exit. You can use Notepad's time and date capability to keep a time log for a project. For instance, open a notepad and type *.LOG* as the first entry on the first line of your notepad. Then, you can insert the

Using Time/Date

time you started working by pressing [F5] and perhaps type the project name. You can then minimize the notepad time log into an icon and open the application containing your project. When you complete the work on your project, maximize the Notepad icon, save it, and then exit from Notepad. When you reopen your time log notepad, there will be a register of time started and finished plus any notes you may have included. As a result, you'll have a history of start and finish times for your project.

Figure 14-7

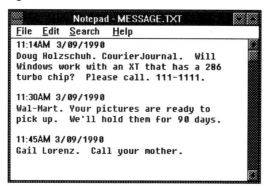

You can insert a time and date line into your notepad entry.

Accelerator keys

After you become familiar with the basic operations of Notepad, you can use accelerator keys as shortcuts for commands. The accelerator key for finding the next item in a search is [F3]. The accelerator key for inserting the date and time is [F5]. You can read Chapter 2 for more about accelerator keys and common functions.

Saving the notepad

After you have made all the entries into Notepad, you need to save them in a Notepad file. As we showed you in Chapter 9, you can save your file with the Save command on the File menu. To save a new file, enter the file name (which can be up to eight characters) in the Filename text box in the File Save As dialog box, shown in Figure 14-8. Click on OK to save the file. When you save the file again, Notepad won't present a dialog box and prompt you for a file name. It will simply save your file with the same name. To save the file under a different name, use the Save As... command on the File menu.

The file name you choose for your notepad is important. Since the file name appears on Notepad's title bar and on its minimized icon, you'll want to use a name that describes your notepad. Notepad will need to recognize the file too. Notepad will add a .TXT extension so it can find its files from among all the other Windows data files created in other applications. Figure 14-9 demonstrates the value of naming your Notepad files so you can distinguish between multiple Notepad icons.

Figure 14-8

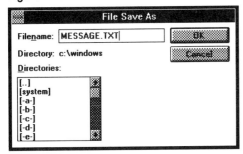

The File Save As dialog box will save your file under any eight-character name and in any directory.

Figure 14-9

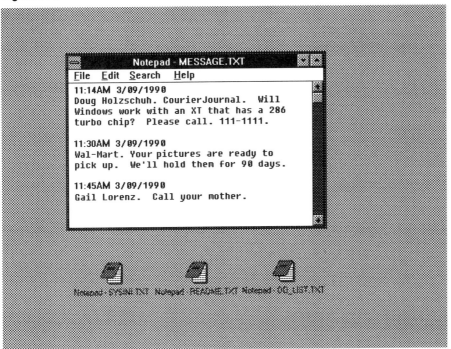

File names are essential when more than one notepad is open.

You'll probably want to print some of your Notepad files, but before you send a file to the printer, you need to define your margins, specify any header or footer information, and choose a printer. The Page Setup... command on the File menu lets you define the margins, headers, and footers, while the Printer Setup... command lets you set up your printer. Let's look at the Page Setup... command.

Printing a notepad

Setting margins,
headers, and footers

To set up margins, headers, and footers, issue the Page Setup... command to bring up the Page Setup dialog box shown in Figure 14-10. As you can see, settings for the left, right, top, and bottom margins are expressed in inches. To change a margin setting, click on the appropriate text box, then type the new measurement. The default margins are 1" for top and bottom and .75" for left and right. The header and footer are printed in the 1" top and bottom margins, respectively. You can enter codes in the header and footer that will align the header/footer or add system information. For example, if you want today's date left-aligned at the top of every page, enter &d &l in the Header text box. If you want the word *DATE* to appear next to the current date, type *DATE &d &l* in the Header text box. Chapter 9 provides a table listing these codes. By default, Notepad prints the file name as the header and the page number as the footer.

Figure 14-10

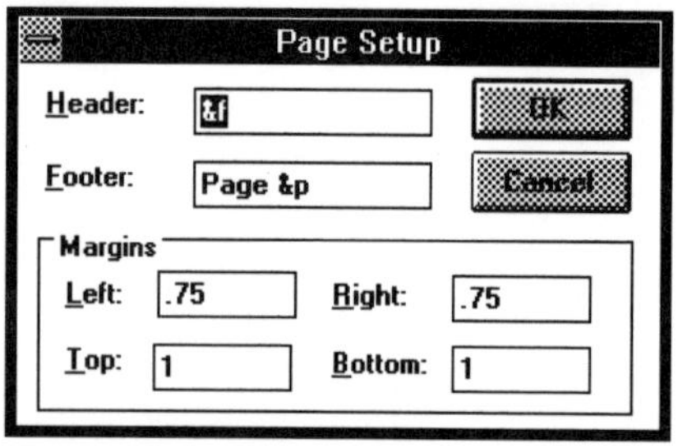

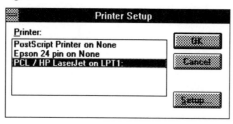

You can use the Page Setup dialog box to set the margins and header and footer text.

Printer setup

After the page is set up, you need to set any printer options before you can print your document. To set these options, use the Printer Setup... command on the File menu. (We cover printer settings in more detail in Chapters 3 and 9.) When you see a Printer Setup dialog box like the one shown in Figure 14-11, click on OK if you want to accept the default settings. If you need to modify the settings, click on the Setup... button to access a setup dialog box for your printer.

Figure 14-11

The Printer Setup dialog box lists the installed printers.

Once you've established the page and printer settings, you're ready to print your file. To do this, select the Print command from the File menu. The Print Manager icon will appear at the bottom of the desktop, and a dialog box like the one shown in Figure 14-12 will tell you Notepad is printing your text and will let you cancel the printing.

Figure 14-12

A Notepad dialog box provides a Cancel button to let you stop printing a notepad.

Your printed document will look exactly like the entry on your screen because Notepad creates an ASCII text file that has no formatting. If you used Word Wrap, then the printout will have the same appearance as the wrapped text on your screen. If you need a higher quality printout, you'll have to copy your notepad into Write before you print it.

Now that you have mastered the basics, you're ready to try some of Notepad's complex features. You can use the Copy and Paste commands to move data between Notepad and other applications, such as Write and Cardfile. For example, if you want to transfer the names and phone numbers from a notepad to your Rolodex card file, just highlight the name and phone number from an entry, then select Copy from the Edit menu. Notepad will copy the text onto Clipboard. Next, open the Cardfile application and then open your phone number card file and select Paste from the Edit menu. (We'll discuss Cardfile in greater detail later in this chapter.) You'll want to size the Cardfile application window so you can see the Notepad window too. Both the Notepad and Cardfile applications now will be visible on the desktop. To repeat the process, just move the pointer to the Notepad, select a new name and phone number, and copy it. Then, you can move the pointer to the Cardfile window, add a new card, and paste the information.

Although you can copy and paste text from other applications into Notepad, you can't copy and paste graphics. Notepad, as an ASCII editor, uses only characters, each of which is represented by an ASCII code. Graphics are not based on ASCII codes and, therefore, can't be pasted into Notepad. If you need to combine text and graphics, use Write.

Using Notepad files with other applications

You can use Notepad files with applications other than those running under Windows. Communication programs can send Notepad ASCII text files over a modem. You can create program files that any compiler will accept since there are no formatting characters in the file to disrupt compiling. Notepad also can edit or create DOS batch files and other system files such as AUTOEXEC.BAT and CONFIG.SYS DOS files.

CALENDAR

You can use Windows' Calendar to keep a record of appointments and important events. Between Calendar and Notepad's time-logging capabilities, you can keep an accurate record of how you spend your time. Calendar's alarm will help you keep track of important appointments.

Before we explain how Calendar works, we need to introduce a couple of terms. We call Calendar's files *books,* but you need to determine the time frame for the book and your use for the book. We call one day's appointments a *page.*

Windows permits you to keep more than one calendar book. For example, an administrative assistant can keep a calendar book on the desktop for each of several managers in a company. The calendar book can be assigned a specific manager's name, but remember the primary objective is to label files distinctively so you can find them easily. The administrative assistant can also print the day's appointments and distribute them. If the company uses a network, each manager could make changes to the calendar books on-line. Since the calendar books are shared, the administrative assistant could work with the same file so all the changes occur in one place.

Starting Calendar

To start Calendar, double-click the Calendar icon in the Accessories group window. An untitled calendar book, like the one in Figure 14-13, will appear. The Calendar window has all the standard window controls plus a few new ones for the Calendar appointment area. As you can see in the figure, the top of the window has a standard Control menu, title bar (with file name), Minimize box, Maximize box, and menu bar. The status bar beneath the menu bar gives the time and date. The increment arrows on the status bar let you scroll through the different appointment pages by date. Below the status bar, you see an appointment page where you can enter text at the cursor beside the 24-hour stack of time slots. You can use the vertical scroll bar to move through the different time slot entries on the page. Below the appointment page is the scratch pad space for your notes.

Exiting Calendar

After you have finished using the Calendar, choose the Exit command from the File menu. For more about exiting an application, see Chapter 9.

Opening an existing book

If you've already begun a calendar book and want to work on it, select the Open... command from the File menu. When you do, the File Open dialog box, shown in Figure 14-14, will appear. Calendar will look for all files with the .CAL extension, then list them in the Files list box. If the file you're looking for isn't there, you can use the Directories list box to look in another directory. Chapter 9 explains more about using the Directories list box. To open the file, click on a file name, then click on OK.

Figure 14-13

file name (book)

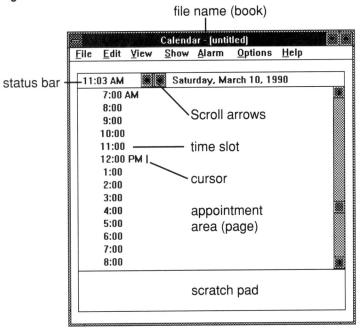

status bar

The Calendar application window features a status bar, appointment page, and scratch pad.

Figure 14-14

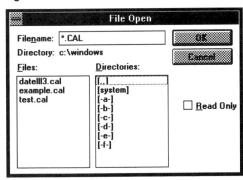

The File Open dialog box lists Calendar's files.

Notice that there is a Read Only check box in the File Open dialog box. If you select this option, you won't be able to make changes to the file. The Read Only option prevents you from making accidental changes to your book or to someone else's.

Starting a new book

If you are working on one calendar book but want to start a new one, you can choose New from the File menu to create an untitled calendar book. For instance, you can start a new book for each fiscal year.

Accelerator keys

After you've learned to use Calendar's commands and features, you may want to speed up some of the processes with the accelerator keys. Table 14-1 lists Calendar's accelerator keys and their command equivalents.

Table 14-1

Accelerator keys	Command
[F4]	Show Date
[F5]	Alarm Set
[F6]	Mark
[F7]	Special Time
[F8]	View Day
[F9]	View Month
[Ctrl][Page Up]	Show Previous
[Ctrl][Page Down]	Show Next

Accelerator keys can improve Calendar's performance by speeding up your access to various functions.

Making an entry

To make an entry in one of the time slots in a calendar book, click on it to position the cursor. The pointer in the appointment area is an I-beam that indicates you can enter text there. You can enter up to 80 characters in your message. If you exceed that limit, Calendar will beep and you will see a *Text truncated* message like the one in Figure 14-15. To scroll to the beginning of a long message, click on the numbers that identify the time slot.

Setting up time slots

As you are making entries into your calendar book, you might have an appointment at a time other than the ones listed on the page. You can add a new time slot or restructure the page to add more time slots at smaller time increments.

Figure 14-15

If you exceed the 80-character limit for a time slot, you'll get a message like this one.

To add a new time slot, select Special Time... from the Options menu or press [F7]. The Special Time dialog box, shown in Figure 14-16, contains a text box for your time entry. For example, you would have to add a new time slot for a 10:05 AM appointment. First, enter the time 10:05 and then choose the AM radio button. Next, click on Insert to add the new time slot to the appointment page.

Adding a special time

Figure 14-16

The Special Time dialog box lets you add a time slot to your appointment page.

Calendar has a feature that will let you divide your day into time slots of hour, half-hour, or quarter-hour segments, which we'll explain in a moment. It's important to note that Calendar will insist on your use of the correct time format. If you should slip and enter a semicolon for a colon or add too many numbers, Calendar will display a message dialog box reminding you that it was an incorrect entry.

After you've created a special time slot, it will be necessary on occasion to delete your new time slots. To delete a special time slot, issue the Special Time... command on the Options menu. Simply enter the time you want to remove in the Special Time text box and then click on Delete. Calendar will automatically insert your newly created time in the Special Time text box if you place the cursor beside the offending time slot before opening the Special Time dialog box. Note that you can't delete a regular time slot, only ones you added with the Special Time... command.

Deleting a time slot

If you want to restructure and reformat a page in smaller time increments, choose Day Settings... from the Options menu. As you can see in Figure 14-17, the Day Settings dialog box lets you set the appointment page's hour format and the starting time slot. The three Interval options let you format the page in quarter, half, or whole hour increments. Just choose the appropriate radio button. The

Formatting time slots

Hour Format's default setting is a 12-hour system that uses AM and PM notation. The 24-hour format is used for military or European time. The Starting Time text box lets you specify the first entry on the appointment page. The default Starting Time option is 7:00 AM.

Figure 14-17

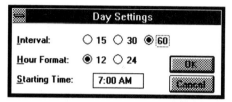

The Day Settings dialog box lets you set up time-slot intervals and determine the time of the first time slot on the appointment page.

Editing an entry

To edit a Calendar entry, move the pointer to its time slot, point to the part of the message you want to edit, then click on it. Now you can use [Backspace] or [Delete] to remove text at the cursor, or you can simply insert new text. You can make more sophisticated changes by using the Cut, Copy, Paste, or Remove... commands on the Edit menu.

Cutting text

You can cut characters or blocks of text and paste them in another time slot or application. For instance, if you need to reschedule a meeting, you could cut the message from the original time slot and paste it into a new one. To do this, you would highlight the message, then select Cut from the Edit menu. (As we mentioned earlier, cutting text places it on Clipboard.) Then, find the new time slot, click there, and select Paste from the Edit menu. If you make a things-to-do list in Notepad (and name the file DO_LIST), you could also add the appointment to that list. After you paste the appointment in the new time in your Calendar, open or activate the DO_LIST notepad (it would be handy to have it minimized on your desktop), and paste the message into the list.

Copying text

If you want to repeat a message, you can use the Copy command. For instance, if you have a weekly Wednesday staff meeting at the same place and time, you can copy the appointment to each Wednesday of the month. To do this, highlight the message and select Copy from the Edit menu. You can then paste the message to other Wednesdays several months in advance. Copying and pasting the information is another way to get the message to your DO_LIST notepad.

Removing a page's appointments

Remove..., one of the more powerful commands on the Edit menu, lets you delete an entire page of appointments. Unlike the Cut command that removes only one entry or part of an entry and then allows you to retrieve the entry with the Paste command, Remove... deletes the appointments for a set block of time. The

page won't go to Clipboard. The only way to retrieve data if you removed it accidentally with the Remove... command is to exit the calendar book without saving your changes and then reopen it.

To use the Remove... command, select it from the Edit menu. The Remove dialog box, shown in Figure 14-18, provides two text boxes in which you can type the time frame of the appointments you want to delete. You enter the beginning date in the From text box and the ending date in the To text box. When you click OK, Calendar will remove all the appointments between and including the dates you selected. If you want to remove only one page of appointments, make the From and To dates the same.

Figure 14-18

You can delete pages of appointments within a range of dates by using the Remove dialog box.

Using the scratchpad

You also can use the scratchpad, the empty box below the appointment area, to remind yourself of important events. For example, you can use the scratchpad for a short things-to-do list or to jot down notes that can be copied or cut, then pasted into your calendar. Calendar automatically wraps the text in the scratchpad but won't scroll text to let you add more text than one box will hold.

Setting the alarm

Another interesting Calendar feature is the alarm. You can set the alarm to sound when the system time matches any one of the time slots on your appointment page. For example, you can set the alarm to alert you for your 10:05 meeting by first selecting the 10:05 time slot and then choosing the Set command on the Alarm menu. In Figure 14-19 on the following page, notice that a bell symbol appears next to the 10:05 appointment. If you select Set again, the alarm will toggle off. The Alarm menu places a check mark beside the Set command to show that it is active. When you select it again, the check marks goes away.

When the system time matches the marked time slot, your PC will beep and an information box will appear. In Figure 14-20 on the next page, the information dialog box tells you to remember your appointment and displays the message you typed in that time slot. If Calendar is an inactive window, its title bar will flash and the computer will beep. If Calendar is a minimized icon, the icon will flash and the computer will beep to alert you. You need to click on either the flashing icon or the flashing title bar to read the message. When you click on it, Calendar will display only the information dialog box and not the entire Calendar window.

Figure 14-19

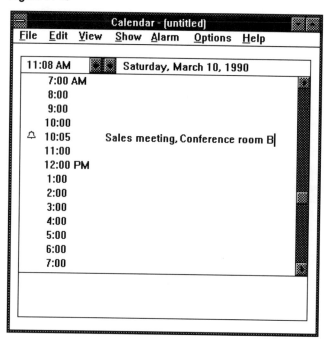

The Alarm symbol appears next to the time slot of the selected entry when you choose the Set command from the Alarm menu.

Figure 14-20

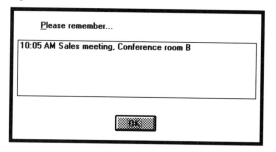

When the alarm sounds, Calendar will display your message and the PC will beep.

Controlling the alarm

You can control how early the alarm sounds and whether the PC will beep by selecting the Controls... command from the Alarm menu. The Alarm Controls dialog box in Figure 14-21 shows a text box for Early Ring. If you want the alarm to sound at the exact time indicated by the time slot, set Early Ring to 0. If, however, you want a 10-minute warning before an actual appointment time, set Early Ring to 10. The Sound check box will let you toggle the beep on and off. The beep is on by default.

Figure 14-21

The Alarm Controls dialog box lets you set an alarm and specify whether it will use the PC beep.

You can page through your calendar book quickly with the Show menu commands and the status bar. If you want to look at an appointment just a couple of days away, you can use the increment arrows on the status bar. The right arrow will advance you one day at a time, while the left arrow will scroll the page to the previous day's appointments.

Moving between pages

The Next and Previous commands on the Show menu perform the same actions as the right and left increment arrows, respectively. Alternatively, you can use the accelerator keys [Ctrl][Page Down] for Next and [Ctrl][Page Up] for Previous. If you hold the keys down, you'll scroll continuously until you release the keys.

The Date... command on the Show menu will let you open the Show Date dialog box and enter the destination date, as shown in Figure 14-22. After you've entered the destination date, click OK and Calendar will move to the day you selected. You can use hyphens or slashes to separate the date elements. For example 4-12-90 or 4/12/90 is acceptable. If you use any other marks as separators, a Calendar information dialog box, like the one shown in Figure 14-23, will remind you of the correct format.

Figure 14-22

The Show Date dialog box offers a text box for entering the destination date.

Figure 14-23

A Calendar information dialog box will remind you of the correct date format if you enter the wrong one in the Show Date dialog box.

After you have moved through your calendar book for a while, you may find yourself far from the starting point, the current date. Instead of entering the current date in the Show Date dialog box to return to the page of appointments for the current date, simply choose the Today command from the Show menu. Calendar will then bring up the page that matches your system date. If your system date is correct, the page will be the current date.

Viewing months

Another quick way to move between dates is to select them from a month view. If you select the Month command from the View menu, or press [F9], the calendar book's dates will appear in month view, as shown in Figure 14-24. Calendar changes only the appointment area of the window. The status bar and scratchpad are unchanged. Since the scratchpad is still available, you can display daily information for the highlighted date. If you double-click on a date in the month view, the appointment page for that date will appear in the window. You can use [F8] or the Day command to move back to day view.

Figure 14-24

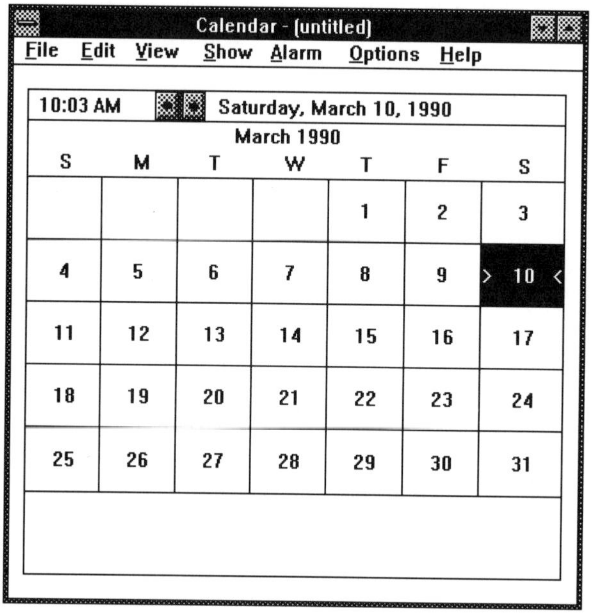

	Calendar - (untitled)	
File Edit View Show Alarm Options Help		
10:03 AM	Saturday, March 10, 1990	

March 1990

S	M	T	W	T	F	S
				1	2	3
4	5	6	7	8	9	> 10 <
11	12	13	14	15	16	17
18	19	20	21	22	23	24
25	26	27	28	29	30	31

You can view your calendar by month.

You can move between months using the same techniques you used to move between days. In month view, the right and left arrows page through months at a time. The Next and Previous commands on the Show menu will also scroll the display a month at a time.

Marking days of the month

If you want to be able to track activities by month, you can add symbols to, or mark, the days in month view. The Month view always marks the current date. For example, the tenth day of the month would be marked > 10 <. If you click on a date, it becomes active or selected. You can add other marks to month view, such as X's for vacation days, boxes for birthdays, or dots for project deadlines. To mark a date, first select it by clicking on it. Calendar will then highlight the date and add a blinking cursor. Now, choose the Mark... command from the Options menu or press the accelerator key ([F6]) to display a Day Markings dialog box, as shown in Figure 14-25. You can mark a day more than once, checking as many different marks as are listed for any single day. If you want to track your vacation days, you can use the X to consistently mark your vacations over the year. You could also mark birthdays, anniversaries, pay days, doctor's appointments, and so forth. The calendar in Figure 14-26 marks vacation days with X's, birthdays with boxes, and project due dates with dots.

Figure 14-25

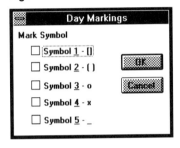

The Day Markings dialog box provides an assortment of Calendar marks you can use to flag special dates.

Figure 14-26

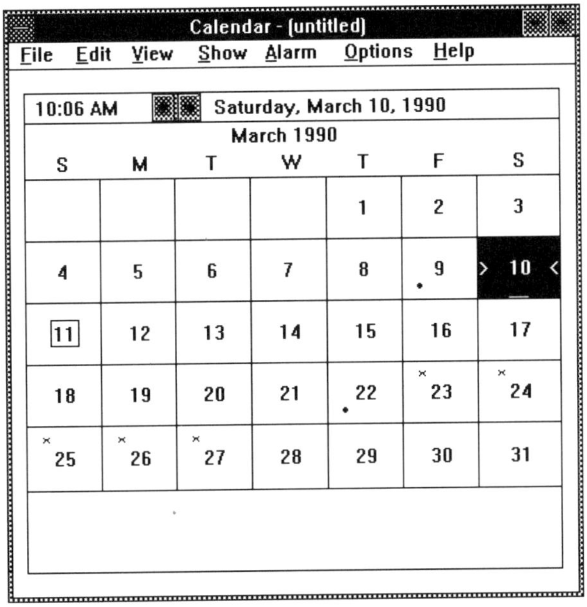

			Calendar - (untitled)			
File	Edit	View	Show	Alarm	Options	Help

10:06 AM			Saturday, March 10, 1990			
			March 1990			
S	M	T	W	T	F	S
				1	2	3
4	5	6	7	8	9 •	> 10 <
[11]	12	13	14	15	16	17
18	19	20	21	22 •	ˣ23	ˣ24
ˣ25	ˣ26	ˣ27	28	29	30	31

In this sample calendar, X's represent vacation days; boxes, birthdays; and dots, project due dates.

Saving a book

It's always a good idea to save the calendar book before you print and after you have made changes or added entries. That way, if the printer has trouble and Calendar locks up, you won't lose the work you've completed so far. To save your work, select Save from the File menu. If you are working on an untitled calendar book, Calendar will prompt you for a name with the File Save As dialog box. Type a distinctive name the Filename text box and click on OK.

Saving a copy

If you want to save a copy of a book, choose the Save As... command from the File menu. When you do, you'll see the File Save As dialog box. Enter the new file name. If you save the book with a different file name, you will have two identical books named differently. You can use the new one for a template for another calendar or as a backup copy. In general, it's a good idea to keep all your appointments in one place to limit confusion.

**Printing a
calendar book**

You can print the appointments in your calendar book. Calendar prints only the daily log, not the Month view. Before you print your appointment pages, you need to set up the margins, headers, and footers. Then, you need to verify which printer you're going to use and define its settings. After all the preparation, you're ready to print. Let's go over page setup first.

Page setup

If you want to use headers and footers on your report, choose Page Setup... from the File menu. The Page Setup dialog box has text boxes for the header and footer codes. Along with the code, you can include text. (Refer to Chapter 9 for a list of the assorted codes.)

You set the left, right, top, and bottom margins in the Margins section of the dialog box. To change a margin, click on its text box and the cursor will appear in the box. Delete the old number and then type the new margin size.

Setting printer options

After the page is set up satisfactorily, you need to choose printer options. Select the Printer Setup... command from the File menu. Next, click on the Setup... button to access the printer options so you can set the number of copies or page orientation.

Printing a
range of dates

After you've specified the page setup and printer setup, you're ready to print. When you select Print... from the File menu, you'll see the Print dialog box shown in Figure 14-27. In this dialog box, you can enter the dates of the appointment page or pages you would like to print. You can specify one page or a range of pages by entering dates in the From and To text boxes. Remember that you need to enter the dates with hyphens or slashes. If you fail to use the correct punctuation, an *Invalid range of dates* message will appear. You'll also need to enter a date in each text box or you'll get the same error message. If you want to print only one day's appointments, enter the same date in each text box.

Figure 14-27

In this dialog box, you can enter the dates of appointment pages you want to print.

When you select OK, Windows will call on the Print Manager to control the printer and print your pages. While the Print Manager is in use, the icon in Figure 14-28 will appear in the area at the bottom of the desktop. The Print Manager will keep your appointment pages in a list called a queue until the printer is ready for them. After the pages are printed, the Print Manager icon will disappear from the desktop. While the icon is on the desktop, however, you can use it to stop the printer or change the priority of printing. For more on the Print Manager, see Chapter 7.

Figure 14-28

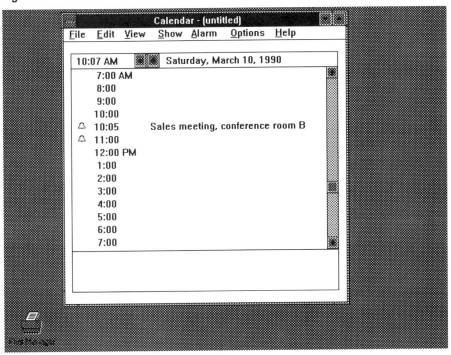

The Print Manager icon will appear on the desktop whenever you are printing an appointment page.

When Calendar prints the pages you've selected, it will print only those time slots and scratchpads that contain messages. Figure 14-29 shows a sample printout with an appointment and a scratchpad entry.

Figure 14-29

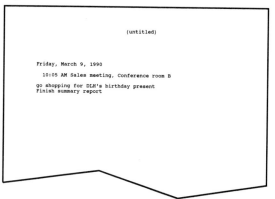

Friday, March 9, 1990

10:05 AM Sales meeting, Conference room B

go shopping for DLH's birthday present
Finish summary report

We printed a calendar book appointment page.

CARDFILE

Cardfile is another Windows accessory application. You can think of Cardfile as a sophisticated box of index cards that you can use to keep a list of names, birthdays, phone numbers, or even a price catalog. If you keep your phone messages in Notepad, you can copy the names and phone numbers from that file and paste them onto cards in your Cardfile to create an electronic Rolodex phone number file. Then, you can print your cards on perforated card stock and create a traditional Rolodex file system. For now, let's look at how you would make a phone number Cardfile from scratch.

Starting Cardfile

To start Cardfile, double-click on Cardfile's icon in the Accessories group window at the Program Manager. Cardfile's application window, shown in Figure 14-30, will open a new untitled file.

Exiting Cardfile

Once you finish using Cardfile, choose the Exit command on the File menu to return to the Program Manager. Read Chapter 9 for more about exiting or leaving an application.

What you'll see

Let's look at the anatomy of Cardfile. Cardfile's workspace displays an empty card with two places to enter information. The index line holds the word or phrase that Cardfile uses when it sorts your cards, while the information area stores all the details. You can have more than one card in the workspace, but the active card (the one you're working with) will always be in front of the others. You can maximize the Cardfile application window to display more cards. You can call this series of cards a stack. The index lines are always visible in the stack of cards so you can choose the one you want to work on.

Figure 14-30

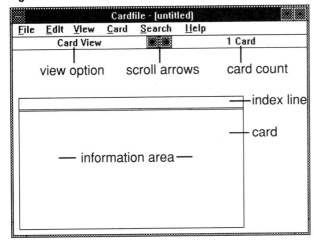

When you first open Cardfile, the application window presents a new file containing one empty card.

The status bar above the workspace has three display areas: scroll arrows, card count, and the view option. You can use the scroll arrows in the status bar to move through the stack of cards one at a time. The card count tells you how many cards are in your stack. The view option can be card view or list view. Card view is the default setting and displays each card. List view displays only the index line of each card. Either the List or Card command will be checked on your View menu to indicate the view setting.

Notice that you can change the size of the Cardfile window, but you can't change the size of a card. Cardfile shows as much of the active card as possible despite the window's size.

When you select the List command, the status bar and workspace change. As you can see in Figure 14-31 on the following page, the status bar displays the words *List View* instead of *Card View*. The workspace displays just the index lines in alphabetical order. If you double-click on an index line or choose the Index… command from the Edit menu, the Index dialog box comes up. You can change the index line in the text box, as shown in Figure 14-32.

Listing the index lines

Figure 14-31

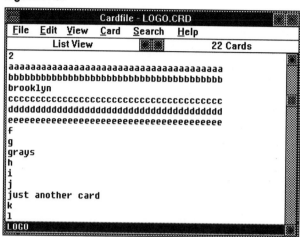

The status bar and the workspace change when you select the List command on the View menu.

Figure 14-32

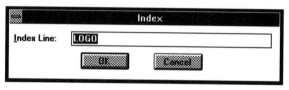

The Index dialog box lets you change the index line.

Accelerator keys

Cardfile uses accelerator keys just like Notepad and Calendar. Table 14-2 summarizes Cardfile's accelerator keys and can serve as a handy reference as you use Cardfile.

Table 14-2

Accelerator keys	Command
[F3]	Find Next
[F4]	Go To...
[F5]	Autodial...
[F6]	Index...
[F7]	Add...

These are Cardfile's accelerator keys.

Adding information to the card

You can add text to two parts of a card: the index line and the information area of the card. By default, the index line and the information area of the card are blank. When you start a new stack or open Cardfile for the first time, a blank card appears in the workspace.

To add text to the index line, choose the Index... command from the Edit menu. You can enter the index line information in the Index Line text box. Remember that Cardfile uses the index line to sort the cards, so put the key word first on the index line. Next, click on OK to place the text on the card's index line.

To add text to the body of the card, simply begin typing. Cardfile automatically wraps your text to fit the card. To end a line early, press [Enter]. You can also use spaces or tabs to format your text. Cardfile uses a five-space tab, which you cannot change.

If you didn't put the key word first on the index line, you can use the Index... command to edit the text. First, click on the card you want to edit to bring it to the front. Next, choose the Index... command from the Edit menu. Now click in the Index Line text box to place the cursor where you want to change the text. When you open the Index dialog box, you'll notice the index line is highlighted, so if you want to completely reword the text, simply begin typing. After you correct the text, click on OK to place your changes on the card.

Adding a card

When you add a new card with the Add... command on the Card menu, Cardfile gives you a shortcut for adding text to the index line. Instead of issuing the Index... command and entering the text, Cardfile immediately presents a similar dialog box, the Add dialog box shown in Figure 14-33, so you can enter the text in one step. After you click on OK, Cardfile adds the card to the front of the stack. Now the cursor is in the information area of the new card so you can enter the body text.

Figure 14-33

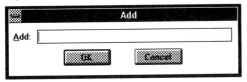

The Add dialog box prompts you for the text for a card's index line.

Entering text in the body of the card

Now you can enter text into the body, or information area, of the card. Since Cardfile automatically wraps lines of text, you don't have to press [Enter] at the end of each one. If you want to end a line early, press [Enter] to go to the next line. Calendar uses the system font (proportional 10-point Helvetica) for text. Because the font is proportional, you'll have trouble lining up text with spaces. You'll get better alignment with tabs. As we mentioned, the tabs are set five spaces apart. Unfortunately, you can't change the tab spacing or the font that Cardfile uses. If you want to print your information in a different font, you will have to copy the information to Write and change the font there.

Editing the card

You can use the same editing commands you used in Notepad and in Calendar when you edit in Cardfile. You can delete characters and tabs with the [Delete] or [Backspace] key. When you want to work with more than one character, you can cut or copy text and then repeatedly paste it on any card or in any Windows application. All you have to do is highlight the text you want to cut or copy, issue the Cut or Copy command, click at the spot in which you want that text to appear, then issue the Paste command from the Edit menu. You can even cut text from the information area of a card and paste it into the index line and vice versa.

Restoring a card

One of the editing commands unique to Cardfile is the Restore command, a more powerful version of the Undo command. While a card is active and is at the front of the stack, you have the option of using the Restore command. If you don't like any of the changes you made to a card since you made it active, you could restore it to the condition it was in when you first brought it to the front of the stack. Once you make another card active, you can't use the Restore command to undo editing changes to the first card.

Deleting a card

If a card is no longer valid or useful, you can simply delete it by moving it to the front of the stack, then choosing the Delete command from the Card menu. When you choose the Delete command, a message dialog box appears to verify your actions. If you delete the wrong card, the only way you can retrieve it is to quit Cardfile without saving the changes and then restart with the old file. This means that all your changes from that work session are gone too.

Editing the index line

You need to use a procedure other than adding a card in order to add text to the default card's index line. Since the default index line is blank, you'll have to add text to it. To add the text, click on that card and then choose the Index... command from the Edit menu or double-click in the index line. The Index dialog box will appear, in which you can add up to 39 characters in the Index Line text box.

You can also use the Index... command to edit the index lines of existing cards. First, click on the card you want to edit and choose the Index... command. When the Index dialog box appears, the characters in the Index Line text box will be highlighted so you can type in new text.

Adding graphics to a card

Once you've mastered the basics of Cardfile, you can move on to one of its more advanced features: adding graphics. The only limitation is that the graphic must be Clipboard compatible so it can be pasted onto your card. (All of Windows' applications are Clipboard compatible.) The easiest way to copy a graphic is to generate it in Paintbrush, then use the Paintbrush Edit menu to copy it. For example, you can open a graphic of a logo in Paintbrush, copy the image to Clipboard, then paste it onto a card. You can also create a graph in Excel and copy it onto Clipboard with Excel's editing commands.

Before you can paste the graphic on the card, you need to tell Cardfile that you want to use graphics with the active card. To do this, select the Picture command on the Edit menu. A rectangle will appear on the active card. Now you can paste the graphic onto the card with the Paste command. The rectangle resizes to fit around the graphic after you paste it onto the card. Figure 14-34 shows a card before and after we pasted the graphic. You can move the graphic around by dragging it with the mouse or by using the direction keys on the keyboard.

Figure 14-34

 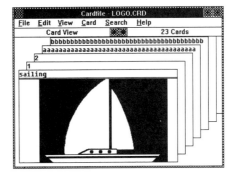

The card on the left shows the graphic rectangle before we pasted the graphic, and the card on the right shows the pasted graphic.

The graphic you paste into a card can be larger than the dimensions of the card. However, when you print the card, only the displayed part of the graphic will be printed. Although you can have only one graphic per card, you can overcome this limitation by selecting two graphics in one Paintbrush file, then copying them both into Clipboard with the same Copy command.

Mixing text and graphics

After you paste a graphic on a card, you can add text to the card. Before you can add text, you need to swap the rectangle for a cursor. To do this, choose the Text command on the Edit menu. As you type, you'll notice that Cardfile won't wrap the text around the graphic. The text will overwrite the graphic. You'll need to use the [Enter], [Tab], and [Spacebar] keys to manually wrap the text around the graphic. Figure 14-35 on the following page shows a finished card with both text and a graphic.

Duplicating a card

If you find that you are using the same basic card information over and over, you can save some time by duplicating the card. To do this, activate the card to bring it to the front of the stack and then select the Duplicate command from the Card menu. Cardfile will insert a duplicate, which will become the active card, at the front of the stack.

Figure 14-35

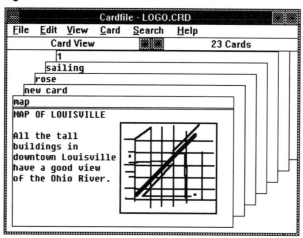

You can put both text and a graphic on the same card.

Moving between cards

The easiest way to move between cards in the workspace is to click on the card's index line, causing Cardfile to move that card to the front of the stack. Another way is to use the scroll arrows on the status bar. The left arrow will bring the last card in the stack to the front. The right arrow will bring the first card under the active card to the front. If you continue selecting a scroll arrow, you will eventually return to the top of the card stack.

You can also use the list view to move to a card. After you display the list of cards with the List command, click on an index line. The list view method of selecting the active card is especially useful with large stacks. You also can use a shortcut to move to a card. Simply press [Ctrl]*n*, where *n* is the first letter of the index line.

Dialing a phone number from a card

Cardfile has a perk for frequent phone users. You can get your PC to dial the phone for you! You need a modem that shares the phone line with your phone set. All you do is highlight a phone number on one of the cards in your card file. Next, select Autodial... from the Card menu. In the Autodial dialog box, shown in Figure 14-36, select the Use Prefix check box if your phone system uses a prefix and then click OK. The PC will dial the phone through your modem.

Figure 14-36

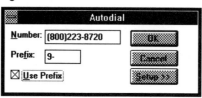

The Autodial dialog box will dial your phone through a modem.

If you haven't configured your modem port from Control Panel, you can set it up from the Autodial dialog box. Click on the Setup>> push button to expand the Autodial dialog box. The expanded dialog box shown in Figure 14-37 has settings for Dial Type, Port, and Baud Rate. The most common settings are a Tone Dial Type using COM2 at 2400 baud. If you have a rotary dial phone, you have a pulse telephone line and need to use the Pulse Dial Type. The Port and Baud Rate depend on your PC hardware and modem hardware. Check your modem manual for its baud rate.

Setting up the modem

Figure 14-37

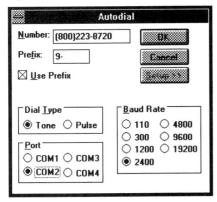

The expanded Autodial dialog box will let you establish settings for Dial Type, Port, and Baud Rate.

If you inherit a phone number list from someone who also uses Cardfile, you can merge the two files into one stack without copying each new card. To merge two files, choose the Merge... command from the File menu. The File Merge dialog box, shown in Figure 14-38, lists all available Cardfile files. You can double-click on a file from the Files list to choose it and issue the Merge... command. To look at other volumes (or drives) for a file, you can use the Directories list box.

Merging files

Figure 14-38

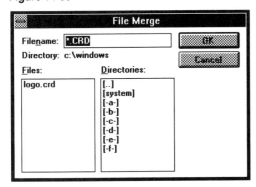

The File Merge dialog box displays available Cardfile files.

After you select a file, Cardfile adds all the cards from the selected file to the one you're working on. It automatically re-indexes the stack to put the new cards in alphabetical order. Now you can save the merged stack under a new file name. This way, both the source and target files will not be changed permanently.

Saving the stack

Before you print your cards or exit Cardfile, you should always save your work. You can save your stack of cards by choosing the Save or Save As... command from the File menu, as you did with Notepad and Calendar. Refer to Chapter 9 for more about saving your work.

Cardfile does have a limitation to the number of cards you can save in a file. It's determined by the size of the media on which you're storing the file. You can review the memory used by issuing the About Cardfile... command on the Help menu. You won't encounter a storage problem as often when you use a hard drive as when you use a floppy disk.

Printing with Cardfile

Printing the cards in your stack is similar to printing a Notepad file or a Calendar appointment page. You'll need to define the page setup and the printer setup before you print. If you want to enter the headers and footers for your page setup, refer to Table 9-1 in Chapter 9 for a list of codes.

Cardfile separates printing into two commands: Print and Print All. You can print one card or all of them. The Print command prints the front or active card of your stack. The Print All command prints the entire stack with three cards per page. Cardfile prints the card as you see it on your monitor, as shown in Figure 14-39, with an index line and a frame around the card.

Figure 14-39

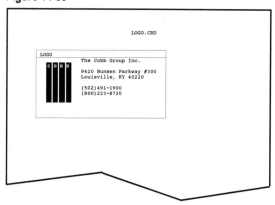

Cardfile prints a card exactly as you see it on the monitor.

Windows' Calculator is another desktop accessory that can interact with your other applications. You can't print from Calculator, but you can paste any number you generate with Calculator into another application. In this section, we'll show you how to use the standard and scientific modes of Calculator. We'll explain the functions, calculator buttons, and keyboard equivalents.

CALCULATOR

As with other applications, to open Calculator, you simply double-click the icon. A calculator like the one in Figure 14-40 will appear. See Appendix 2 for a color version of Figure 14-40. The Calculator window, like the Control Panel window, cannot be sized, only minimized. In the two modes of Calculator, scientific and standard, the keys are color-coded according to their function. Calculator will always open in the mode in which you closed it.

Starting Calculator

Figure 14-40

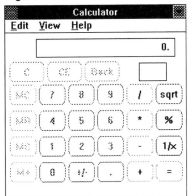

The standard mode is the default view when you start Calculator for the first time.

The standard and scientific modes both use the same title bar, menu bar, and number display of the Calculator window, but their functions and related buttons differ. You can select the mode you want with the View menu. A check mark will appear next to the selected command. The Standard command will display the standard mode calculator, and the Scientific command will display the scientific mode calculator.

To exit Calculator, you must close the window. There is no Exit command. Calculator doesn't need an Exit command since you don't use data files that have to be put away.

Exiting Calculator

The standard mode of Calculator performs basic mathematical functions for quick calculations. For instance, you can use it when you want to determine a discount for a customer or balance your checkbook.

Standard mode

The easiest way we found to use Calculator is to use your keyboard's numeric keypad to enter numbers and then use your mouse to click on function keys. In order to use the numeric keypad, you need to have [Num Lock] on.

Calculator has buttons framed in color that are grouped by function. The blue buttons are numbers or letters that enter information into the display; the red buttons are mathematical or logical operators; the pink buttons are memory functions; and the green buttons are advanced mathematical functions. The display areas are black-framed boxes.

Starting a calculation

All you have to do to start a calculation is to enter a number by either clicking on a key or typing on the numeric keypad. For example, if you want to make a 15% discount on a customer purchase of $495, you would type *495*, click on * for multiplication, type *.85 (100%-15%=85%),* and then either click on = or press the [Enter] key on the numeric keypad. The display would then change to 420.75, the discounted price.

If you make a mistake in your calculation, you can erase just the current entry or clear the entire calculation and start over. To clear just the current entry, click on the CE button. If you want to clear the entire calculation, click the C button. If you use a keyboard instead of a mouse, use [Delete] for CE and [Esc] for C.

Table 14-3 lists the functions in the standard mode, the calculator button and its keyboard substitution, and a description of the function performed by each. You can use either a period or a comma for the decimal point, depending on which format you chose in the International dialog box from Control Panel (which we explained in Chapter 3).

Using memory functions

The memory buttons (the pink ones) on the standard mode Calculator let you put a number in a safe place until you want to use it again. When you put a number in memory, an *M* will appear in the display box just under the number display, as shown in Figure 14-41 on page 368. To put a number in memory, type or click the number in the display and then click on the M+ button to store it. (All the keyboard equivalents for the memory buttons are in Table 14-3.) If you want to store a number that is a result of a calculation, complete your calculation and, when the result is displayed, click on the MS button. Suppose you want to display the number you stored. All you have to do is click on the MR button to recall the number from memory at any time. You can use this technique to reuse a number during a calculation. Instead of re-entering the number, just click on MR when you would normally enter the number in your calculation.

Table 14-3

Button	Keyboard	Function
+	[+]	Add
-	[-]	Subtract
*	[*]	Multiply
/	[/]	Divide
+/-	[F9]	Apply positive or negative sign
.	[.]or [,]	Insert decimal point
%	[%]	Calculate percent
=	[=] or [Enter]	Calculate or Equals
1/x	R	Calculate reciprocal
Back	[Backspace] or ←	Delete last number entered
C	[Esc]	Clear calculation
CE	[Delete]	Clear last function or displayed number
M+	[Ctrl]P	Add displayed number to value in memory
MC	[Ctrl]C	Clear memory
MR	[Ctrl]R	Recall value from memory
MS	[Ctrl]M	Store value in memory
sqrt	@	Take square root of displayed number

This table describes each function of the standard mode, its related button, and the keyboard substitution for the button.

Figure 14-41

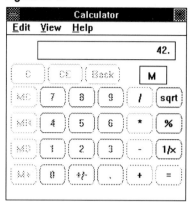

Calculator uses an M *to tell you if there is a number in memory.*

Keeping a running total is easy with the M+ button. If you click on M+, the number in the display will be added to the value in memory. If you click on M+ each time you complete an equation, then the value in memory is the running total.

If you don't want the number in memory anymore, you can clear it with the MC button. After you clear the memory, notice that the M in the display box disappears. Once the value is gone, the M will be gone too.

Using the Clipboard with Calculator

Besides storing a displayed number, you can copy the number to Clipboard for use in another application. Just select Copy from the Edit menu when the number you want is in the display. For example, if you are keeping customer history cards with Cardfile and need to record their discounted purchases, after you calculate the discounts, you can copy and paste them to their card in Cardfile.

You can also paste a number or equation from Clipboard to Calculator's display. To copy the number from another application, select Paste from the Edit menu, and Clipboard will enter the number into the display.

Calculator also accepts letters from Clipboard. Any letters are interpreted as command shortcuts. For example, 84m tells Calculator to store the value 84 into memory where *m* is the equivalent to a [Ctrl]M. Table 14-4 lists the letters and their related commands.

Scientific mode

To change from standard to scientific mode, select the Scientific command from the View menu. As you can see in Figure 14-42, the Calculator window has expanded to include new display areas and buttons. A color version of Figure 14-42 appears in Appendix 2.

Table 14-4

Character	Command
c	Clear memory. ([Ctrl]C)
e	In decimal mode, specifies scientific notation. You can use plus and minus signs after the *e* for the exponent. In hexidecimal mode, specifies the number E.
m	Store displayed number in memory ([Ctrl]M).
p	Add displayed number to value in memory ([Ctrl]P).
q	Clear the current calculation ([Esc]).
r	Display value in memory without removing it from memory. ([Ctrl]R)
: (colon)	If used with letters, it is interpreted as a [Ctrl] key. If the colon precedes a letter, then the colon and the letter form a control key sequence. (For example :C means [Ctrl]C.) If used with numbers, it's interpreted as a function key. (For example, :8 means [F8].)
\ (backslash)	Represents the Data key ([Insert]).

You can paste letters from Clipboard that Calculator will interpret as commands.

Figure 14-42

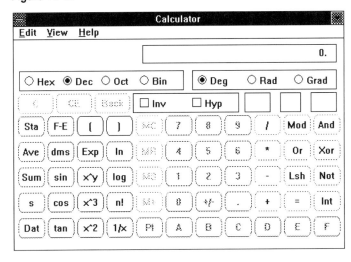

The scientific mode provides sophisticated settings and increases the number of function buttons.

Let's examine the additions to Calculator in scientific mode. The title bar, menu bar, and number display didn't change. The two number system settings boxes appear below the number display. The second-level function settings (inverse and hyperbolic) are centered below the number system section. The three status boxes to the right tell you if statistics, memory, or parentheses are active, respectively. Figure 14-43 shows the display boxes with samples.

Figure 14-43

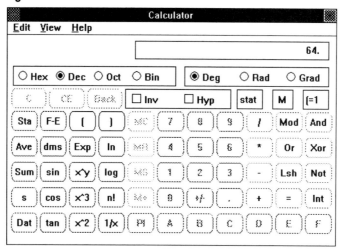

Calculator uses three status boxes to show the status of statistics, memory, or parentheses options.

Choosing a number system

When you first bring up scientific mode, Calculator uses the decimal (base 10) numbering system as the default. The number, system settings area lets you choose between hexadecimal (base 16), decimal, octal (base 8), and binary (base 2) number systems with the Hex, Dec, Oct, and Bin radio buttons. Table 14-5 lists the number system functions and their keyboard equivalents.

Table 14-5

Button	Keyboard	Function
Bin	[F8]	Use binary number system
Dec	[F6]	Use decimal number system
Hex	[F5]	Use hexadecimal number system
Oct	[F7]	Use octal number system

This table lists the buttons, keyboard equivalents, and related number system functions.

When you are using the default decimal system, the settings area on the right will provide choices between degree (Deg), radian (Rad), and gradians (Grad) for trigonometric calculations. When you use the hexadecimal, octal, or binary systems, the radio buttons change so you can choose between Dword (full 32-bit version of the displayed number), Word (16-bit version), or Byte (8-bit version).

Calculator will convert the displayed number if you need to change number systems after you enter or calculate a number. It will convert decimals to integers if you are converting from the decimal number system. A conversion to the decimal number system will also result in an integer.

Calculator also knows if the number you typed fits into the selected number system. It will let you use the letter buttons with hexadecimal but not with any other number system. If you press the 9 key on your numeric keypad while using the binary system, Calculator won't accept the entry; instead, it will beep at you.

For example, if you wanted to convert the hex value to binary, you need to click on the Hex radio button to change the number system from decimal to hexadecimal. Next, enter the value 300. Now click on the Bin radio button. Calculator will convert the 300h into 1100000000.

Using logical operators

If you look on the far right side of the Calculator, you'll see more red buttons besides the standard mathematical operators. These are the logical operators. The black framed parentheses buttons to the left of the memory buttons are also considered logical operators. You can use up to 25 nested parentheses. Table 14-6 on the next page lists the logical operator buttons and their functions.

Applying statistics

Calculator has advanced function statistics waiting inconspicuously under the Sta button. When you click on the Sta button, a Statistics Box, like the one in Figure 14-44 on the next page, will appear. It has a large list display area with four buttons and a population value (n=0) at the bottom. Calculator adds a scroll bar to the list display after you enter enough numbers. You can't use any of the statistics buttons in the scientific mode without having the Statistics Box open. Table 14-7 on page 373 summarizes all the scientific mode statistic functions, calculator buttons, and keyboard equivalents. You can move the Statistics Box to a corner of the desktop to make the rest of the Calculator more accessible.

Table 14-6

Button	Keyboard	Function	Inverse Function (Inv + button) (i + key)
(	[(]	Start a new level of calculation	none
)	[)]	Close level of calculation	none
And	[&]	Calculate bitwise and	none
Int	[;]	Display numbers to the left of decimal point (integer)	Display numbers to the right of decimal point (fraction)
Lsh	[<]	Shift bit register left one bit	Shift bit register right one bit
Mod	[%]	Display modulus or remainder of x/y	none
Not	[~]	Calculate bitwise inverse	none
Or	[|]	Calculate bitwise or	none
Xor	[^]	Calculate bitwise exclusive or	none

The logical operators can be used with numbers or letters across number systems.

Figure 14-44

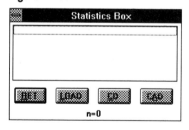

The Statistics Box has a list display area and four buttons.

Table 14-7

Button	Keyboard	Function	Inverse Function (Inv + button) (i + key)
Ave	[Ctrl]A	Calculate mean or average	Calculate mean or average of the squares
Dat	[Insert]	Enter displayed number into Statistics Box	none
s	[Ctrl]D	Calculate standard deviation, population=n-1	Calculate standard deviation, population=n
Sta	[Ctrl]S	Open Statistics Box	none
Sum	[Ctrl]T	Calculate sum or total	Calculate sum of squares

This table summarizes all the calculator buttons, keyboard equivalents, and the scientific mode statistic functions.

To begin a statistics calculation, you enter the numbers you're going to work with. For instance, if you were trying to find the average of several test scores, you would enter all the students' scores into the Statistics Box. To enter a number, first click anywhere on Calculator's window to make it active. Next, type the number into Calculator's display with the numeric keypad, or click on the calculator keys, then click on the Dat button to enter the number into the list. After you've entered all the scores, you'll notice that the population value at the bottom has changed to match the number of scores you entered (n=28). Now click on Ave to display the average or mean. You can immediately click on the s button to get the standard deviation based on the population value (n-1).

Sum is another statistical function you can use with the Statistics Box number list. After you've entered the numbers, click on Sum to display the total of all the numbers. To clear the numbers, highlight them and delete them, or exit from the Statistics Box. When you reopen the Statistics Box, the display will be clear.

You can also use the Inv check box on the scientific mode Calculator with the statistics buttons to get a variation on the function. If you use inverse with average, Calculator will compute the mean using the squared values from the Statistics Box. If you use inverse with sum, you will get the sum of the squares. Inverse with the s button will find the standard deviation using a population of *n* instead of *n-1*. After you finish using inverse, remember to toggle off the Inv check box, or the rest of your calculations will not work the way you planned.

The list of numbers in the Statistics Box appear in one column with one number highlighted at a time. Although you can click on another number to highlight it, Calculator won't let you select more than one number at a time. Click on the scroll arrows or use the arrow keys to move up and down the list.

Three of the four buttons at the bottom of the Statistics Box work with the numbers in the list. LOAD copies the highlighted number to the Calculator's display; CD removes the highlighted number from the list; and CAD removes all the numbers from the list. The fourth button, RET, will return the pointer to the Calculator window. You can simply click on the Calculator window to do the same thing. To return to the Statistics Box, you can click on the box or click the Sta button again. After you finish using statistics, you can close the dialog box by double-clicking on the Statistics Box Control menu or choosing the Close command on the Control menu.

Other functions

The scientific mode has many more function buttons besides the statistical ones, including trigonometric functions and scientific notation. Table 14-8 lists the remaining scientific mode functions. There is also a number button for the value of pi, which is located below the column of memory function buttons.

If you are using the trigonometric functions, remember that there are a couple of check boxes that will affect the sin, cos, and tan buttons and the number display. If you check Hyp, the hyperbolic of the function or, in other words, its inverse will be calculated. The group of three radio buttons on the right (Deg, Rad, and Grad) determine the unit of measurement for degrees, radians, or gradians. The dms button changes the number display to degree-minute-second format. All trigonometric functions must use the decimal number system.

When you use exponents or scientific notation, you must work within Calculator's limits. When you use the Exp button, the exponent can be as large as 307. When you use the F-E button, the scientific notation can be as large as 10^15. You can use exponents and scientific notation only with the decimal number system.

CLOCK

The Clock is a useful Windows application. Clock displays the time whether you keep the application open or minimize it into an icon. Clock uses your PC's system time so, if you change the system time with the Date/Time icon on the Control Panel or with a DOS command, the clock will change too.

Starting the Clock

To start Clock, go to the Program Manager window and click on the Accessories group window. Double-click on the Clock icon to start the application. Clock always appears as you left it when you closed it last.

Exiting Clock

To exit Clock, you must close the window. There is no Exit command. You can close the window by double-clicking on its Control menu.

Table 14-8

Button	Keyboard	Function	Inverse Function (Inv + button) (i + key)
sin	S	Calculate sine	Calculate arc sine
cos	O	Calculate cosine	Calculate arc cosine
tan	T	Calculate tangent	Calculate arc tangent
dms	M	Display number in degree-minute-second format	Display number in decimal format
Exp	X	Enter exponent for scientific notation	none
F-E	V	Toggle scientific notation on or off	none
ln	N	Calculate natural logarithm (base e)	Calculate e raised to the xth (displayed number) power
log	L	Calculate common logarithm (base 10)	Calculate 10 raised to the xth (displayed number) power
n!	!	Calculate factorial	none
PI	P	Display pi	Display (2Xpi)
x^y	Y	Calculate x raised to the yth power	Calculate the yth root of x.
x^2	@	Calculate square	Calculate the square root
x^3	#	Calculate cube	Calculate the cube root

The remaining scientific mode functions are listed here.

Clock faces

Clock has two faces: analog and digital. Figure 14-45 shows both choices. Both faces use predefined system colors and aren't affected by the colors you set with Control Panel. The first time you use Clock, it has the analog face. To change the face, open the Settings menu and click on Analog or Digital.

Figure 14-45

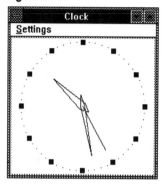 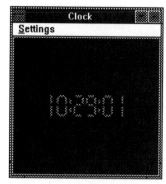

Clock has an analog face with hands and a digital face with numbers.

Sizing Clock

Unlike Calculator or Control Panel, you can size Clock's window to any dimension. Clock can be maximized to fill the screen or minimized into an icon. The face will change to fit the window. The face with hands will expand to fit the entire window, but the digital numbers will not get any larger than $5/_{8}$" tall. You can size the clock so you can see it while you are working with another application. You'll discover that the digital face is easier to read while Clock is a minimized icon.

In this chapter

Playing Games 15

A wise man once said: "There is a time for work, and a time for play."

Most of Windows is devoted to giving you the tools you need for serious work. But when it comes time for play, Windows doesn't let you down. Windows supplies two excellent games. Users of previous versions of Windows will remember Reversi; Solitaire is a new addition. Whether you're looking for a leisure activity or a stress-reducing break from more serious pursuits, you'll enjoy playing both of these games.

The new Windows Setup program automatically installs both Reversi and Solitaire on your hard drive and creates a group window called Games. You can select the Games application in the Program Manager, then launch either game by double-clicking on its icon.

Reversi, a computer version of the popular board game, is a two-player strategy game derived from the classic Oriental game of Go, and it retains a distinctly Eastern flavor. In this version, the computer is your opponent; there is no provision for play between two human opponents.

The game board is composed of 64 squares in an eight-by-eight grid. Figure 15-1 shows the game board in the starting configuration with four circular markers in the center of the board, two of each color, positioned diagonally. (See Appendix 2 for a color version.) On a color monitor, your markers are red and the computer's are blue. On a monochrome system, yours will be white and the computer's will be black. (The light gray markers in this section's figures represent your markers.)

Figure 15-1

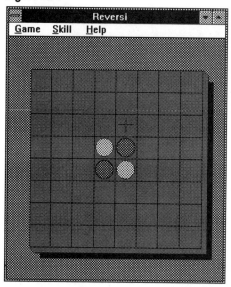

Reversi starts with four markers in the center of the board. In this example, the human player is about to make the first move.

**The object
of the game**

The object of Reversi is to have more game pieces of your color on the board at the end of the game (usually defined as filling all the spaces on the board). Players take turns placing markers on the board to surround and capture their opponent's markers. Captured pieces reverse color and become part of the captor's inventory. With each move, markers reverse color, the board changes, the advantage shifts. There is no score for capturing an individual piece; only the final count at the end of the game determines the winner. Even a sizable temporary advantage may be fleeting, and games can be won or lost on the last move.

Starting a game

When you launch the Reversi game, the board appears in the starting position ready to begin play. The New command on the Game menu allows you to begin a new game at any time. Simply pull down the Game menu and click on New to return the game board to the starting configuration. You will use this option at the conclusion of a game, or if you like, you can abort an ongoing game and start over.

Pausing a game

You can also pause a game in progress, perform tasks in other windows, then return to Reversi and resume play. As in other Windows applications, you can click on the Minimize icon or select the Minimize command from the Control menu to suspend play at the end of the computer's move and reduce Reversi to an icon on your desktop. (This can be a handy feature for those times when the the boss suddenly walks in.) To return to the game, double-click on the Reversi icon. The game board returns to the screen ready for your next move.

Playing Reversi

You and the computer take turns placing markers on the board to reverse the color of at least one of the opposing pieces. To capture a piece, place your marker so that your opponent's piece is trapped between your new marker and another marker of your color. You can trap pieces in a horizontal, vertical, or diagonal line. In other words, you want to place your marker to create an unbroken horizontal, vertical, or diagonal line of your opponent's markers with one of your markers at each end. Once captured, your opponent's markers change to your color and are played and scored the same as the markers you place on the board. But beware: Any advantage you gain may be short-lived. The computer will capture and reverse the color of some of your pieces on its next move.

Each move must capture at least one of your opponent's pieces. A move may capture several pieces in a row or pieces radiating in several directions from your newly placed marker. As long as the pieces are bracketed between an existing marker of your color and the marker you place on the board, they are captured and reversed to your color.

You should note that you can capture your opponent's piece only during your move. One of the markers enclosing a row of opposing pieces must be the one you are playing. Conversely, if your opponent moves into a square between two of your markers, that piece is not captured. On the contrary, it is relatively safe, since the adjoining squares in at least one of the potential capture angles are already occupied. Of course the same rules apply to both you and the computer.

X marks the spot

Making a move is simple. Just use the mouse or arrow keys to position the pointer on the square to which you want to move. Reversi makes it easy to find a legal move. The pointer changes from an arrow to a cross on squares that are valid (but not necessarily good) moves. Figure 15-2 on the following page shows the cross-shaped pointer on a square representing a valid move. If you press the [Tab] key, the pointer will jump to a square where you have a valid move. By pressing the [Tab] key repeatedly, you can see all your potential moves.

To make your move, simply position the pointer on a square where the pointer changes to a cross, then click the mouse (or press [Spacebar]). Reversi will not accept an illegal move. If you try to click on a space where the pointer remains in its arrow shape, a dialog box will appear with an error message. You'll need to click on OK to dispose of the dialog box, then select a valid move.

As soon as you click on a square to place your marker, Reversi will complete your move by automatically reversing the color of any pieces you capture. Figure 15-3 on the next page shows the results of this move.

Figure 15-2

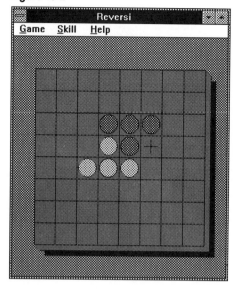

This is Reversi's game board before a move. Note the cross-shaped pointer positioned on the chosen square.

Figure 15-3

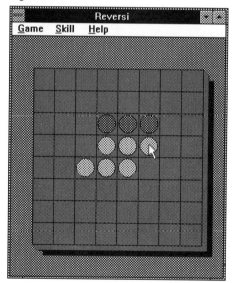

This is how the board would look as a result of the move in Figure 15-2.

The computer's turn

Immediately after you complete your move, the computer will make its move. It can happen fast, so don't blink! Figure 15-4 shows our game at this point.

Figure 15-4

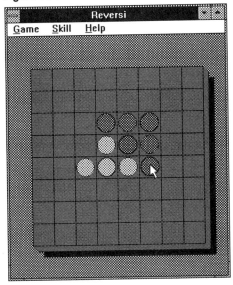

This is how the game board looks after the computer moved into the square with the pointer.

The computer's speed in making its moves poses the greatest problem for beginners trying to learn the game. Reversi will reverse the colors of the pieces captured in your move, the computer will make its own move, and reverse the color of its captured pieces, all so quickly that the entire sequence seems to be one action. You may click on a space to make your move, only to see it change to blue as your computer opponent captures the marker you just played. This can be very confusing. (Sometimes it even seems like Reversi is cheating!)

The Skill menu allows you to select Reversi's (not your) playing level. Lower skill levels force the computer to respond faster. At higher skill levels, Reversi allows the computer longer to consider its next move. The longer the computer has to search its memory banks, the better chance it has of finding a scenario that leads to victory from its current situation. By selecting the appropriate skill level, a beginning player should have a sporting chance of winning, while a seasoned Reversi player can find a challenging adversary.

The Skill menu offers four skill level commands: Beginner, Novice, Expert, and Master. Reversi's default setting on the Skill menu is the Beginner level. To select another skill level, choose the appropriate command from the Skill menu. You can change skill levels at any time, even in the middle of a game.

The Beginner level forces the computer to respond in the shortest time, thus limiting the number of options it can explore. On faster hardware, the computer's response may seem instantaneous.

Setting the skill level

The Novice level allows the computer slightly more time to consider each move. Depending on the speed of your system, you may not notice a difference in how fast the computer makes its move, but you'll probably find it harder to beat.

At the Expert level, most systems show a noticeable delay before the computer makes its move. There's a corresponding improvement in the computer's play.

The Master setting allows the computer to search for the best possible move. It may take well over a minute for each move, even on very fast computers. At this level, Reversi proceeds at a slow, chess-like pace, enabling the computer to challenge—and beat—even the best players.

Slowing Reversi

As we noted earlier, Reversi's almost instantaneous response can be disconcerting and often confusing for beginning players. Slowing Reversi may allow you to see the consequences of your own move before the computer's move changes the board. This, in turn, may help you learn the game; even though allowing your opponent more time to make each move may reduce your chance of winning.

Try playing your first few games at the Expert level so you will have time to see the effect of each of your moves. (Depending on the speed of your system, the Novice level may provide enough delay between moves.) After you gain experience visualizing the outcome of your moves and learn to recognize the effects of your opponent's moves, you can return to the Beginner or Novice setting.

Don't get discouraged

The computer is very good at this sort of game and makes a formidable opponent. It will regularly beat most human opponents, at least until they gain some experience with the game. After all, this is exactly the kind of activity that computers are designed for. To win a Reversi game—even at the lower skill levels—is quite an accomplishment. Fortunately, a losing game is still a pleasantly diverting mental exercise, and with concentration and experience you'll begin to win your share.

Pass

Occasionally, one player will not have a legal move available. When this happens, the player (you or the computer) must pass and allow the opponent to make the next move. Reversi will alert you to situations where you must pass, with a message in a bar under the menu. When you see the message *You must pass,* open the Game menu and select the Pass command. If your opponent must pass, the message will just say *Pass,* and Reversi will wait for you to make your move.

At times, doing nothing may seem preferable to making the only move you see open. You'll be tempted to pass, but don't try it! If you do, Reversi responds with a dialog box that admonishes you: *You may not pass. Move where the cursor is a cross.* You will have to click on OK to remove the dialog box and get on with your move. Remember, you cannot pass if there is any legal move available on the board.

The only exception to this rule occurs at the beginning of a new game. You can select Pass before making any move to allow the computer to make the opening move of the game. (You can force Reversi to make the first move by passing at the beginning of a new game, even though the Help text explicitly states that you must make the first move.)

Winning the game

Play continues until neither you nor your opponent can make another legal move. Usually, that does not occur until the game board is completely filled. However, one or more spaces may remain open if neither player can capture an opponent's piece by moving there.

Scoring Reversi is simple. The player with the most markers wins. At the conclusion of a game, Reversi will count the pieces of each color and announce the winner, as shown in Figure 15-5. We won this game, but Reversi's *You lost by...* message may look more familiar at first.

Figure 15-5

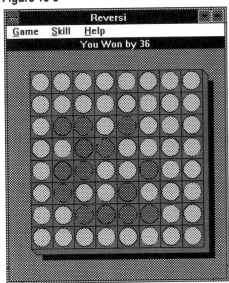

The message bar shows that we won this game.

Getting hints

If you find yourself stumped, you can ask Reversi to offer a suggestion for your next move. If you select Hint from the Game menu, Reversi will place the cross-shaped pointer in the square that it considers your best move. You can accept the suggested move or move elsewhere. To accept the hint, simply click the mouse button (or press the [Spacebar]). By asking for a hint on each turn and accepting Reversi's suggestions, you can force Reversi to play (and occasionally beat) itself.

When you use the Hint command, Reversi will change the title bar at the top of the window to read *Reversi Practice Game*, as shown in Figure 15-6. It makes no difference whether you accept or reject the offered suggestion. If you ask for help, Reversi labels your game *Practice*. If you want help locating valid moves without labeling the game *Practice*, you can press the [Tab] key repeatedly to jump the pointer to each of your valid moves. You can then decide which of those moves you wish to make.

Figure 15-6

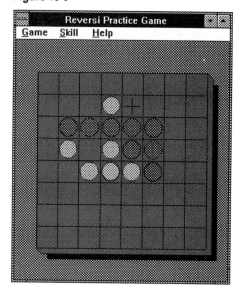

When you select Hint from the Game menu, Reversi will suggest your next move and label the game Practice.

Exiting Reversi

To exit Reversi, you select Exit from the Game menu. Note that the Exit command is located on the Game menu since Reversi has no File menu.

Tips and strategies

In this section, we'll share a few tips and strategies we've found useful in playing—and occasionally winning—Reversi. We hope they help.

Taking the long view

It's impossible to overemphasize the importance of taking the long view as you play Reversi. Only the final count of pieces at the end of the game is significant. The game board constantly changes as pieces are captured and reverse color. A temporary advantage may not last past your opponent's next move. In fact, it may hurt in the long run if it creates long strings of markers in your color that are vulnerable to mass capture.

As in chess, you must think several moves ahead and consider how your opponent will respond to the results of each move. You need to ask yourself, "Can

I gain a strategic advantage while minimizing my exposure?" Remember that your opponent must make a legal move if one is available. Can you create a situation that will force the computer into making moves that help you? Plan your moves. Anticipate the response. Adapt to the changing situation, but always keep long-range goals in mind.

Positions along the edges of the board are harder to capture than those in the middle. In fact, while most other markers can be captured in a horizontal, vertical, or diagonal row, markers along the edge are vulnerable in only one direction: along the edge of the board. Thanks to their relatively secure status, markers at the edge of the board often serve as anchors for moves that repeatedly reverse markers in the middle of the board.

Edges are important

If the edges are important, the corners are crucial! Once occupied, the corners are invulnerable to capture because there is no way for an opponent to get pieces on two sides of a corner. They are the only positions on the Reversi board where the color of the markers cannot be changed.

Corners are crucial

Much of the strategy of Reversi revolves around maneuvering for position to occupy those four coveted corners. As a result, the corners are usually played late in the game, which further exaggerates their importance. Often, an entire outside row will change when you play into a corner, which can change the complexion of a game.

The critical importance of the corners, and the strategies involved in capturing them, lends added significance to some other squares on the Reversi board as well. You will want to avoid occupying the spaces adjacent to an unoccupied corner and try to maneuver your opponent into them instead. If you can occupy the square two spaces from a corner, you will be poised to move into the corner if your opponent is forced into the square between your position and that corner.

Leverage points

In addition to Reversi, Windows now includes a Solitaire game. Solitaire is an automated version of Klondike, one of the most popular of the many single-player card games. The graphics of the card faces and backs are stunning, especially on a VGA monitor. Solitaire is not only pretty, it's relaxing to play.

SOLITAIRE

The computer serves as dealer and scorekeeper rather than as your opponent. It takes over all the tedious details of dealing and keeping the rows of cards neatly arranged. It will even keep score using either a point system or a casino-style betting model, leaving you free to concentrate on just playing the game.

You'll find Solitaire in the Games group windows in Windows' Program Manager. Double-click on the Solitaire icon to start the game. In addition to the usual menu bars at the top of the Solitaire window, a status bar at the bottom will show your score (if you activate one of the scoring options).

**The rules
of the game**

Almost anyone who has picked up a deck of cards has played some kind of Solitaire game. Solitaire actually encompasses a whole class of card games, but the game of Klondike (also known as Fascination, Demon, and Patience) is the one most people think of first; and it's the one included with this version of Windows. This computer implementation of Solitaire is faithful to the original card game, and playing it will soon feel completely natural. We'll briefly review the rules. If you are already familiar with the game, you may want to skip this section.

The initial deal

Solitaire uses a single deck of 52 playing cards and deals 28 of those cards into seven piles, arranged in a row across the playing area, as shown in Figure 15-7. Starting from the left, the first pile contains one card; the second pile, two cards; and so on, to the last pile, which contains seven cards. The top card in each pile is face-up and the rest are face-down. We'll refer to these as the row piles.

The remaining 24 cards of the deck go face-down in the upper-left corner of the window. This is called the stock. You'll draw from the stock and place the cards you draw face-up in a pile beside it. Then you can play the top card from this stock pile. The four empty rectangles across the top of the playing area are reserved for the suit stacks. (See Appendix 2 for a color view of the cards.)

Figure 15-7

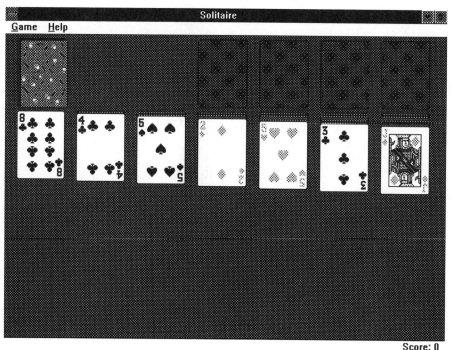

Solitaire deals 28 cards into the seven row piles to start the game.

Most plays in Solitaire take place on the seven row piles. You build each pile in descending order, alternating red cards (Hearts or Diamonds) and black cards (Spades or Clubs). For instance, if the face-up card on one of the piles is a 10 of Hearts, you could play either the 9 of Spades or the 9 of Clubs on it, followed by the 8 of either Hearts or Diamonds. The face-up cards in a row pile are fanned (staggered) down so that all the cards are visible at all times.

You can play face-up cards from one pile onto the top face-up card of any other pile. For example, in Figure 15-8, the black 7 in the second pile from the left will play on the red 8 in the first pile, and all the cards in the fourth pile will move over to the sixth pile since the red 5 (and the rest of the face-up cards in that pile) will play on the black 6. Figure 15-9 on the next page shows the results of these moves. When you move the face-up cards from a pile, you'll expose the next face-down card. You can then turn that card face-up so it is available for play.

Building the row piles

Figure 15-8

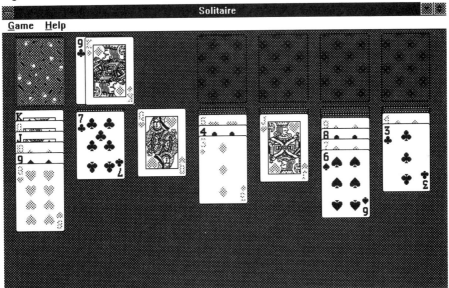

In this example, there are several available plays.

If your play creates an empty pile with no more face-down cards, you can move a King into the vacant position. Only a King can fill an empty pile. If you don't have a King in one of the other piles, the space must remain vacant until a King appears in the draw or you turn one up in another pile.

Filling empty row piles

Figure 15-9

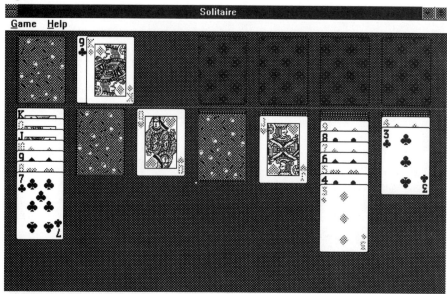

This screen shows the game from the preceding figure after we made the plays described in the text.

Drawing from the stock

When there are no more plays available in the row piles, you draw from the stock. Normally, you would draw three cards at a time, place them face-up in a pile to the right of the stock, and then play the top card. You can always play any exposed, face-up card. A variation of the game allows you to draw cards from the stock one at a time (see the "Options" section later in this chapter).

Once you reach the bottom of the stock, you can turn it over and go through the deck again. You can make multiple passes through the stock if you are not playing a scored game. We'll explain the restrictions imposed by the scoring systems later.

Building the suit stacks

The four empty rectangles across the top of the playing area are the suit stacks. Each suit stack must start with an Ace and build in ascending order, by suit. When you expose your first Ace, you can move it to one of the four rectangles to start a suit stack. For example, if you turned up the Ace of Diamonds, you could move it to one of the four rectangles to begin the stack of diamonds as shown in Figure 15-10. Then you would play the 2 of Diamonds (when it appears) on the Ace. You can play cards from the row piles or from the stock pile onto the suit stacks.

Figure 15-10

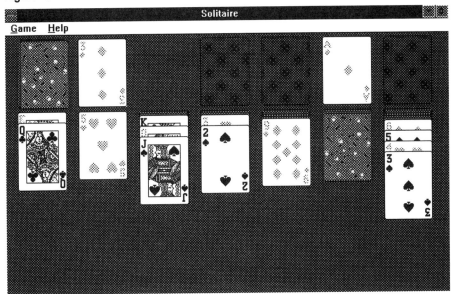

When you expose an Ace, you can move it up to the suit stacks.

The object of the game

The object of Solitaire is to move all the cards from the stock and row piles to the suit stacks. At the completion of a game, the entire deck is arranged into four stacks, each containing the Ace through King of a suit. Unfortunately the luck of the deal often blocks this kind of absolute win. Crucial cards are often buried, face-down, in the row piles. As an alternative to an all-out win, Solitaire offers two styles of scoring, which we will discuss later in this chapter.

Beginning play

When you start the program, Solitaire automatically deals the cards and is ready to play. However, you will probably want to maximize the window before you begin moving any cards. (The default window for Solitaire sometimes crops the piles on the right side of the screen and can render the game unplayable.) The Solitaire window lacks scroll bars, so maximizing or sizing it is the only way to ensure that all the cards in a long pile will remain fully visible.

Starting a new game

You can re-deal the cards and start a new game at any time—even if the current game isn't complete. Select Deal from the Game menu for an immediate re-deal.

Pausing a game

You can pause a Solitaire game at any point by minimizing the window. Click on the Minimize box or select Minimize from the Control menu to reduce Solitaire to an icon on your desktop. Then, to return to your game, simply double-click on the Solitaire icon. Of course, like all Windows applications, you can just open another window over your Solitaire game if you need to perform some other task. Your game will be waiting when you return.

Playing Solitaire

Most plays in Solitaire involve moving a card from one pile or stack to another. You can play any face-up card, whether it is in the row piles, the stock pile, or the suit stacks. When you expose a face-down card in a pile, you turn it face-up so that it can be played. You can draw from the stock pile. If you inadvertently make the wrong move, you can undo it. You accomplish all these plays with a few simple moves of the mouse.

**Moving cards —
click and drag**

You move cards with the click and drag technique—the same technique you use to reposition and resize windows, select a range of text in Write, or draw in Paintbrush. Begin by positioning the pointer on the card you want to move, then press the mouse button to pick up the card, and hold the button down while you move the mouse to drag the card to its destination. Release the mouse button to deposit the card at the end of the move.

You will often need to move all the face-up cards in a pile as a single unit. To move a group of cards, position the pointer on the bottom card you want to move. When you click and drag that card, all the cards on top of it will also move.

You can move cards between piles, from the stock pile to any of the row piles, or from either the stock or row piles to the suit stacks. As you move a card over the empty suit stacks, the empty rectangles change color to indicate a valid move.

Solitaire will accept only legal moves. If you click and drag a card to a new position, only to have it pop back to its original position when you release the mouse button, you'll know the move you attempted was not valid and Solitaire refused it. If this happens often, or if your display is jumpy as you make moves, try activating the Outline Dragging option (which we'll discuss in a moment).

Turning cards face-up

When you move the face-up cards from one pile to another pile, you'll expose the next card in the pile, which is face-down. To turn a card face-up, simply click on it. Solitaire will reveal the face of the card and make it available for play.

**Drawing from
the stock**

To draw from the stock, simply click the mouse on the face-down cards of the stock pile. Solitaire will draw three cards and turn them face-up in a pile just to the right of the stock. You can then move the top face-up card to play it on any of the row piles or suit stacks. The next face-up card in the stock pile then becomes available for play. The Draw command, which we will elaborate on later, allows you to set Solitaire to draw one card at a time instead of three.

Turning the stock pile

After several draws, you will deplete the face-down stock, and all the cards will be in the face-up pile. To continue playing with a traditional deck of cards, you would turn the stock pile over and make another pass through the deck. To turn the deck over, click on the rectangle to the left of the face-up stock pile.

If you use the Vegas scoring option, which we'll discuss in a moment, the rules restrict the number of passes you can make through the stock. Solitaire will put a red X in the stock rectangle to indicate that you may not turn the deck over when you've exhausted your allowed number of passes.

Sometimes you'll make a mistake. You may draw a card from the stock before you play the top card on the stock pile. Or you'll mistakenly move a card to the wrong pile. For those occasions, Solitaire can reverse the effect of your last draw or move with the Undo command. If you need to use this feature, just select Undo from the Game menu. The computer will cancel your last action.

Undo

You win a game of Solitaire when you are able to move all 52 cards to the suit stacks. When you move the final King from the stock or row pile onto its suit stack, Solitaire signals your win by starting a rather flamboyant graphic display. The cards spring from the suit stacks and bounce off the screen one by one, leaving a trail behind them, as shown in Figure 15-11. It's fun to watch for a moment, but you will probably get tired of it long before the Aces finally bounce away. Click the mouse button or press any key to abort the display.

Winning the game

Figure 15-11

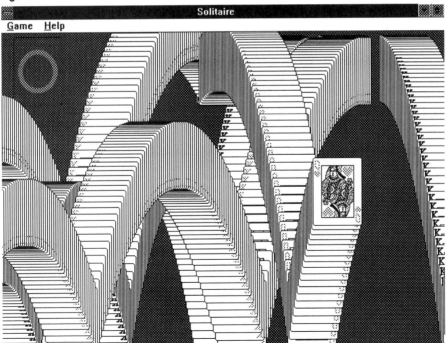

To signal a win, Solitaire puts on a graphics show, bouncing the cards off the screen one by one.

Scored games

In Solitaire, an outright win, where you manage to move all the cards to the suit stacks, is unusual. It requires skill and concentration, plus a lot of luck. (Perhaps that's why the programmers created such an elaborate display to reward the winner.) To make the game more interesting, even if it doesn't end in a win, Solitaire includes two methods of scoring games—Standard and Vegas scoring.

Standard scoring awards points for each card you move to the suit stacks and for moving cards from the stock to the row piles. Vegas scoring simulates casino-style wagering on Solitaire. You start with an ante and get winnings for each card you move to the suit stacks. The object is to win more than you wager.

Options

The Game menu includes commands to let you start a new game, undo a move, choose a deck, or select scoring and other options.

Starting a new game

If you see that a game is hopeless, you can give up and start a new game that may be more interesting. Select Deal from the Game menu to force an immediate re-deal. You can select the Deal command at any time, whether or not the current game is over. Unlike gathering and shuffling a deck of cards by hand, Solitaire will re-deal in seconds.

Oops!

As we pointed out earlier, the Undo command can come to the rescue when you make a mistake. Just select Undo from the Game menu to reverse the effect of your last draw or move. Undo will change only your most recent action. It's intended to cancel the effects of a single mistake, not step back to an earlier move that turned out to be unwise.

Selecting the deck

Solitaire includes 12 different designs for the back of the cards. Initially, Solitaire will randomly choose one of the designs each time it deals. You can choose your favorite design by selecting Decks... from the Game menu. Solitaire will open a window showing the 12 card back designs with the current selection highlighted by an extra outline. Click on the deck you want to use, then on the OK button. Once you choose a deck, Solitaire will remember your preference and use it exclusively. Of course, you can always use this procedure to select another deck any time you like. You can even change decks in mid-game, since only the backs of the cards are affected. The programmers hid a few surprises for the sharp-eyed player in some of the deck designs.

The playing options

Select the Options... command from the Game menu to open Solitaire's Options dialog box, as shown in Figure 15-12. There you can designate the draw and scoring options, hide the status bar, or invoke Outline Dragging.

Figure 15-12

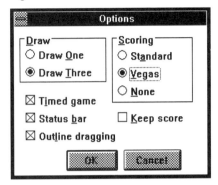

Solitaire's Options dialog box allows you to select the style of draw and scoring, hide the status bar, and activate Outline Dragging.

Draw

Solitaire allows you to choose from two variations in the way you draw from the stock. The default is the more traditional method of drawing three cards at a time from the stock and turning them face-up in a pile to the right of the stock. As you work through the stock, you see every third card in the deck, and you are allowed at least three passes through the stock. Alternately, you may choose to draw one card at a time. This way you see every card in the deck in a single pass. Traditionally, the rules dictate only one pass through the stock if you are using a single card draw. However, Solitaire does not enforce these limits unless you choose the Vegas scoring option.

The draw options appear in the Draw area in the upper-left portion of the Options dialog box. Click on the radio button beside the option of your choice. If you change the draw option, Solitaire will re-deal and start a new game when you press the OK button and return to the playing window.

Scoring

Since the luck of the deal makes an outright win rare in Solitaire, the program offers two ways to keep score that can add interest to otherwise "unwinnable" games. The Scoring section in the upper right-portion of the Options dialog box, shown in Figure 15-12, allows you to choose between the Standard and Vegas scoring modes or to disable scoring completely.

Standard scoring assigns point values to the significant moves as you play Solitaire. You score points for moving cards from the stock to the row piles and for moving cards to the suit stacks. Solitaire penalizes you for moving cards from the suit stacks down to the row piles and for excessive passes through the stock.

In Solitaire's Vegas scoring mode, you ante $52 at the outset of each game. Solitaire automatically assesses the initial wager at the start of the game and gives you an opening score of -$52. The "house" pays $5 for each card you move onto the suit stacks. You'll need to get 11 cards onto the suit stacks before you reach a positive score.

The radio buttons will indicate which scoring mode is active in the Scoring section. To choose another mode, click on its radio button.

The Keep Score check box below the Scoring section works with the Vegas scoring mode. Instead of zeroing the score at the end of each game, if you activate the Keep Score check box, Solitaire will keep a running total of your winnings (or losses) until you close the Solitaire window.

You can't change scoring modes in the middle of a game. Any change you make in the scoring options will force Solitaire to re-deal when you return to the playing window.

Standard

In Standard scoring, Solitaire assigns the following point values:

- +10 points for each card played onto the suit stacks from either the stock or the row piles

- +5 points for each card played from the stock to any of the row piles

- -15 points penalty for each card played from the suit stacks down to piles

- -20 points penalty for each pass through the stock after three passes with the Draw Three option checked

- -100 points penalty for each pass through the stock after one pass with the Draw One option checked

Vegas

The Vegas scoring rules are simple:

- Ante (initial wager) $52 — you start with a score of -$52

- Win $5 for each card you play to the suit stacks

- Only one pass through the stock with the Draw One option checked

- Only three passes through the stock with the Draw Three option checked

None

If you select None in the Scoring section, Solitaire will not display any score in the status bar at the bottom of the screen. Except for the score display, there is no difference between Standard scoring and None. Remember, any change in scoring selections forces a re-deal. Consequently, we suggest that you avoid this option since you can achieve essentially the same effect by hiding the status bar when you don't want to see your score. If you choose to hide the Status bar, you can change your mind in mid-game and decide to display your score without aborting the game with a re-deal.

The Outline Dragging check box allows the system to use a simplified outline to represent the cards you click and drag. There are two reasons you may want to enable Outline Dragging.

Dragging a fully detailed graphic of the card across the screen in real time places significant demands on your computer. Fast computers with high speed displays may handle those demands with ease, but on slower systems, your screen may jump and flicker. Moving a simple outline on the screen as you click and drag a card lightens the computer's load, resulting in a smoother, faster display.

In addition to faster operation, Outline Dragging contains a built-in Help feature. As you can see in Figure 15-13, when you drag the outline to a valid destination, the top card in the pile (or the empty rectangle) will change color, making it very easy to recognize legal moves. By dragging the outline across all the piles and suit stacks on the screen and noting which piles change color as the outline passes, you can force Solitaire to identify all the potential moves for you.

Figure 15-13

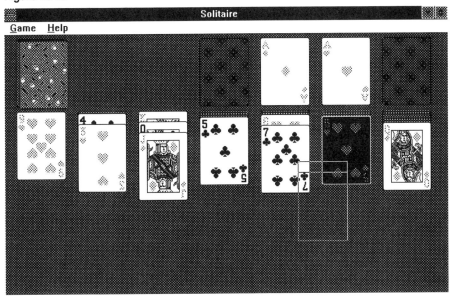

In this example of Outline Dragging in action, notice that the row pile under the outline changes color to indicate a valid potential move.

An *X* in the check box indicates that the Outline Dragging option is active. Click anywhere on the box or its text to change it.

Other options

The Keep Score check box tells Solitaire to keep a running total of your winnings under the Vegas scoring mode instead of resetting the score at the beginning of each game. This check box is is dimmed and unavailable when you select either the Standard or None scoring options.

The Status Bar check box controls the status bar at the bottom of the screen with the score display. Turn it off to remove the status bar.

The Timed Game check box adds a time display to the status bar. The timer starts with your first move and counts in seconds. In the Standard scoring mode, Solitaire reduces your score as time passes, to encourage faster play. Selecting this option in the middle of a game will force a re-deal.

Exiting Solitaire

You'll find the Exit command for Solitaire on the Game menu since Solitaire has no File menu. To exit from the game and close its window, choose Exit from the Game menu.

Using the keyboard

Like most Windows applications, Solitaire was designed for use with a mouse. In fact it's one application that you can use without ever touching the keyboard. Pointing and clicking the mouse to draw or turn cards face-up, and clicking and dragging to move cards, will soon become second nature, even to people who have not used a mouse before.

However, if you are one of those unfortunate few who are struggling along in a graphical user interface minus the requisite supported pointing device (i.e., using Windows without a mouse), you can still play Solitaire. You can make all the essential moves with the keyboard. The keyboard equivalents are also a boon to those of you who develop a nervous twitch in your fingers if you don't peck at the keys every few seconds (or just prefer to use the keyboard).

The [Tab] key moves the pointer among the main playing areas: the stock pile, the suit stacks, and the row of piles. It automatically skips over any stack or pile that is not applicable to the next move.

Press the ← or → keys to move the pointer to the next stack or pile to the left or right. Use the ↑ and ↓ keys in the row piles to select more than the top card in a pile.

Pressing the [Spacebar] is roughly equivalent to pressing the mouse button, except you won't have to hold it down to simulate click and drag moves. To move a card or group of cards, first you would press the [Spacebar] to pick up the card at the pointer. Next, press [Tab], or the ← and → keys to move to your destination. Then press the [Spacebar] again to release the card and complete the move. To turn a card face-up, position the pointer on the card, and press the [Spacebar]. To draw, press the [Spacebar] while the pointer is on the stock pile.

The other keys and key combinations that access menus and select menu options are the same as in other Windows applications.

Here are a few tips to help you play Solitaire and improve your score, although you may find the score is immaterial. Solitaire is fun to play, regardless of scores and winners.

One principle of playing Solitaire is never to miss a play. That goes double when you play with Standard scoring. When you draw a card from the stock that will play directly on a suit stack, look first to see if you can play it on one of the row piles. If you can, Solitaire will award you 5 points for moving the card from the stock to the row pile, then another 10 points for moving it from the row pile to the suit stack, a total of 15 points. Moving the same card directly from the stock to the suit stacks earns only 10 points. Breaking the move into two parts won't help your chances of getting all the cards to the suit stacks, but it will increase your score under the Standard scoring rules.

Many of the common ways to cheat at Solitaire (such as shuffling the deck) are simply not allowed by the Solitaire program. However, there are a few loopholes that let you improve your odds of winning or increasing your score.

Traditionally, the rules allow only one pass through the stock if you are drawing one card at a time. As we mentioned, Solitaire does not enforce this rule unless you choose the Vegas scoring option. Making multiple passes through the stock with the Draw One option checked is not strictly legal, but it greatly enhances your chances of winning. Keep in mind that Solitaire discourages the practice by penalizing you 100 points for each extra pass through the deck if Standard scoring is active. In Draw Three mode, Solitaire allows you three passes through the deck before it deducts a smaller penalty of 20 points for each additional pass.

Furthermore, it is customary when you move the face-up cards from one pile to another to move all the face-up cards together in a pile. Solitaire allows you to move any face-up card or cards in a pile. Occasionally, moving a partial pile will help you expose a card of a particular suit that you can then move into the suit stacks.

Tradition dictates that once a card has been moved to the suit stacks, you can't move it back down to the row piles. Windows' implementation of the game permits the move, but it imposes a penalty of 15 points in the Standard scoring mode and subtracts from your winnings in Vegas scoring.

Beyond the Basics

In this chapter

Of Modes and Memory 16

*W*indows offers three operating modes, each with its own capabilities and limitations, to accommodate various computer and memory configurations and the demands of different applications. To facilitate a better understanding of Windows' operating modes and how Windows uses the different kinds of computer memory, this chapter will offer brief explanations of some of these often confusing concepts.

Most people understand the difference between the kind of memory provided by a hard drive and the computer's temporary, working memory or RAM (Random Access Memory). But when it comes to sorting out the different kinds of RAM, many PC users get lost in the maze of conventional memory, DOS memory, extended, expanded, and virtual memory. To make matters worse, much of the computer jargon we must decipher seems to be an alphabet soup of acronyms (DOS, RAM, ROM, EMS, XMS, LIM 3.2, LIM 4.0). Let's start our examination of memory by looking at how memory has evolved in MS-DOS-based computers.

A BRIEF HISTORY OF PC MEMORY

In the beginning, there was conventional memory. Conventional memory is the name given to the RAM available for applications running under the MS-DOS operating system on computers based on the 8086 and 8088 processors (IBM PC, IBM XT, and compatibles). The 8088 chip can actually address up to 1Mb (1024Kb) of memory, but 384Kb of that is reserved for various hardware and system requirements, leaving 640Kb available for applications. Originally, conventional memory was simply called memory; the term "conventional memory" was coined to differentiate it from the other forms of memory that were subsequently introduced. Conventional memory is also sometimes called DOS memory since it is the memory MS-DOS and DOS-based applications can address directly.

Conventional memory

Initially, 640Kb of memory seemed like more than anyone would ever need in a "personal" computer. Most computers were sold with only about 256Kb installed, and most software ran with room to spare. However, as software grew more complex, machines faster and more powerful, and users more sophisticated and demanding, the "huge" 640Kb capacity of DOS became the "640K barrier." New generations of applications offering powerful new features, ease of use, and the ability to manipulate large amounts of data could barely shoehorn themselves into 640Kb of memory. Nevertheless, the need to maintain compatibility with the installed base of DOS computers dictated working within the confines of conventional memory, and the 640Kb barrier became an albatross around the necks of PC programmers and users alike.

Expanded memory (EMS RAM)

The inevitable eventually happened, and applications grew to use all the available conventional memory and still needed more—much more! Enter the LIM (Lotus-Intel-Microsoft) Expanded Memory Specification (EMS). EMS memory evolved when hardware and software engineers devised a way to put extra memory on an add-in board and address it by shuffling data back and forth into a special section of conventional memory a "page" at a time. EMS requires special hardware plus a special device driver in your CONFIG.SYS file to tell your system how to find the extra memory. Since DOS can't recognize expanded memory, your applications must request data from the expanded memory manager, which must then locate the data on the EMS memory board and move it into a section of conventional memory where your application can use it.

Expanded memory is an afterthought—an add-on patch designed to allow an 8088-based computer to go beyond its original design specifications and address more memory than is otherwise possible. (286- and 386-based computers can also use EMS memory, but they have a better option available in extended memory.) Furthermore, applications must be written specifically to take advantage of EMS, and there are major limitations on its usefulness. For instance, under the widely accepted LIM EMS 3.2 specification, applications can store data in EMS memory, but the application itself (its program code) must remain in conventional memory. Consequently, you can create a monstrously large spreadsheet or database file with an application that uses EMS memory, while the 640Kb barrier continues to be an obstacle to multitasking. After all, some larger applications barely fit in 640Kb of memory themselves, much less allow room for another application to simultaneously reside in conventional memory. The LIM EMS 4.0 standard, however, allows newer EMS cards to move programs as well as data into EMS memory. As a result, EMS memory becomes available for multitasking, but it is much slower than directly addressing conventional or extended memory. Still, EMS has been around for years and many applications will use it to their advantage if it is available.

With the introduction of the 80286 processor (the IBM PC AT and compatibles) came extended memory (XMS). (Yes, the terms exPAnded and exTEnded are confusingly similar.) The 80286 chip can address up to 16Mb of RAM, and there is no physical difference between what we call conventional and extended memory. Some of the memory (usually 1-4Mb) will be on the computer's motherboard. The rest may be installed on an add-in board similar to expanded memory, but unlike EMS memory, the computer addresses all XMS memory directly with no special hardware needed to move "pages" of data in and out of conventional memory. You do need an extended memory manager (such as HIMEM.SYS, which is supplied with Windows) to assign blocks of extended memory to different applications since DOS can't handle this job.

Extended memory (XMS)

The only difference between conventional and extended memory is a conceptual one imposed by the architecture of MS-DOS. On a 286-based computer, DOS uses the first 640Kb of memory—the conventional memory—just as it does on an 8088-based machine. Any memory past 1Mb in a 286-based machine is called extended memory. While MS-DOS (and therefore normal DOS-based applications) cannot directly access more than 640Kb of memory for applications and data, there is not a similar limitation on the amount of memory that can be physically installed in a system running MS-DOS. In other words, your computer can have more memory installed than DOS can use.

Prior to Windows 3, the chief limitation on using XMS memory has been the availability of applications that could effectively use extended memory. Typically, XMS memory is home to a RAM disk and perhaps a disk cache, but not much else—hardly optimal use of a vital system resource. Often, XMS memory sits idle while "RAM cram" in conventional memory severely limits your productivity.

An 80386-based computer can do everything a 286 machine can do—and more. The 386 chip, with its 32-bit architecture, dramatically expands the maximum amount of extended memory. The 386 chip also has a few more tricks up its sleeve, such as the ability to emulate conventional or expanded memory in extended memory, create virtual machines, and even support virtual memory.

Virtual memory

The 386 virtual memory manager uses a special section of your hard drive that allows the processor to treat it as additional RAM. To an application, the virtual memory on the hard drive appears identical to extended memory. The 386 processor can swap large blocks of information between the hard drive and XMS memory to make more memory available for data and run more applications concurrently than would normally fit within your system's combined conventional and extended memory.

As with extended memory, MS-DOS cannot access and control the special features of 386-based computers without help. Prior to Windows 3, only a few 386 control programs and specially written applications could take advantage of these powerful features.

**REAL MODE vs.
PROTECTED MODE**

Life with an 8088-based computer is simple, if confining. The 8088 chip has only one operating mode and only addresses conventional memory. If you need more than 640Kb of RAM, an expanded memory board is the only option.

Things get a little more interesting with the newer processor chips that have distinct operating modes. The 80286, 80386, and 80486 all maintain full backward compatibility with older computers and MS-DOS software with their "real mode." Real mode simulates the operation of an 8088 processor chip, complete with its limitations. Nearly all MS-DOS-based applications (including previous versions of Windows) were designed to operate in real mode and consequently can't use many of the advanced features of 286-, 386-, and 486-based computers.

The added features of the newer processors are available only in "protected mode." In 286 (16 bit) protected mode, they can address XMS memory; and, in the 386 and 486 processors' 32-bit protected mode, they can play their virtual memory and virtual machine tricks. However, accessing protected mode requires special software. MS-DOS alone can't do it, but Windows 3 can.

**WINDOWS'
OPERATING
MODES**

To accommodate the memory configurations of various systems, Windows can run in three operating modes. Real mode is compatible with essentially all MS-DOS computers and previous versions of Windows. The two new operating modes—standard and 386 enhanced—take advantage of the protected modes of 286, 386, and 486 chips to add extended memory management and improved multitasking capabilities to Windows 3. Windows no longer comes in different versions for different computers. All three operating modes are integrated into a single package, and Windows will automatically sense which mode to use.

Real mode

Windows' real mode is the default operating mode on 8088-based computers. (In fact, it's the only mode available on 8088- and 8086-based computers.) You can also use Windows' real mode on a 286- or 386-based computer to force the processor into its real mode, which simulates the operation of an 8088 computer and does not address extended memory (even if it is available). In real mode, your applications will be confined to the 640Kb of conventional memory, thus sacrificing most of the advanced memory management capabilities of Windows 3.

One of the greatest advantages of the Windows environment is the ability to open various applications in different windows, then switch between them quickly without the need to exit one application and load the next, as you would have to do under DOS. Windows allows you to open as many Windows applications as your memory capacity permits. In real mode, Windows provides a limited degree of multitasking for your Windows-based applications. Windows also detects and uses the idle time while your foreground application waits for input to run the background applications. For example, your spreadsheet could be recalculating in one window while you edit a report with your word processor in another window. Of course, this presumes that both applications fit into conventional memory along with Windows.

Windows extends your ability to switch tasks from Windows to the DOS applications you run from Windows. When you execute a DOS application from within Windows, Windows swaps your Windows applications out of memory to your hard drive, thus freeing memory for the DOS application. If you switch back to Windows from the DOS application, Windows will suspend the DOS application and swap it to disk. You can switch back and forth between your Windows tasks and one or more DOS tasks without exiting one program and loading another. However, Windows can't multitask the applications it swaps to disk, so your Windows applications will be suspended while you run a DOS application and vice versa.

If the memory on your system meets the LIM EMS 4.0 standard, Windows will automatically attempt to use it as efficiently as possible. Windows can use EMS memory to allow you to open more Windows applications simultaneously. Although Windows can't use expanded memory that conforms to the older LIM EMS 3.2 standard, your applications will still be able to use it to store data.

Unless your equipment restricts you to Windows' real mode, you'll probably want to take advantage of the advanced features available in one of the other operating modes. However, real mode does provide backward compatibility with the widest possible range of hardware and software. Previous versions of Windows operated only in real mode. You may need to use Windows' real mode for compatibility with some older Windows-based applications (at least until you get upgrades) and perhaps with some DOS-based applications.

Standard mode

In standard mode, Windows applications can break the DOS 640Kb barrier and make full use of XMS memory on 286- and 386-based computers. Access to extended memory is especially significant for multitasking since it makes XMS memory as well as conventional memory available for running applications. With enough extended memory installed on your system, you can run several large Windows applications simultaneously. In standard mode, you can multitask Windows applications, but Windows still must suspend DOS applications while you are working in the Windows environment, as well as Windows applications while a DOS application is active.

Windows' standard mode is the default on 286 computers and on 386- and 486-based computers with less than 2Mb of memory. It's an optional operating mode for 386- and 486-based computers with more than 2Mb of memory. Since their processors have no protected mode, Windows' standard mode is not available on 8088- or 8086-based computers. In standard mode, Windows can use your computer's full complement of conventional and extended memory, but will not use any expanded memory you might have installed. Although Windows itself won't use EMS memory while operating in standard mode, Windows won't interfere with your applications (either Windows-based or DOS-based) using expanded memory if it is available on your system.

Some developers of DOS applications have found ways to break the DOS 640Kb barrier on machines with extended memory by using "DOS extender" technology to access that memory through the processors' protected mode. For example, Lotus 1-2-3 release 3.0 is a DOS application that uses a DOS extender to access extended memory. In standard mode, Windows is compatible with other programs that strictly conform to the VCPI specification for extended memory access. Even if your computer can support Windows' 386 enhanced mode with its advanced features, you'll probably find yourself using standard mode much of the time because of its speed and compatibility with applications that use DOS extender technology.

386 enhanced mode

Windows packs real memory management and multitasking muscle into its 386 enhanced mode. You'll need a 386- or 486-based computer with at least 2Mb of memory to use Windows' 386 enhanced mode. With it, you'll finally be able to realize the potential of your sophisticated system—and do it easily.

In 386 enhanced mode, Windows can use all your system's conventional memory and extended memory, and optionally use a swap file (which we'll explain in the next section) on your hard drive as virtual memory to simulate even more memory for your applications. Windows will not use expanded memory when it operates in 386 enhanced mode, although your expanded memory remains available for applications that request it. If you have applications that need EMS memory but do not have an expanded memory board installed on your system, Windows can convert a block of extended memory into what appears to be expanded memory. Your DOS applications can then access this simulated EMS memory when you run them from Windows.

Windows provides its most powerful multitasking capabilities when it's operating in 386 enhanced mode. In addition to multitasking Windows applications, as it does in standard mode, Windows also can run DOS applications simultaneously with Windows applications or other DOS applications. In 386 enhanced mode, Windows can divide your system's processing power between the various running applications and manage contention between the applications for shared resources, such as printers and COM ports. Since 386 enhanced mode uses alternate methods of multitasking from real and standard modes, you'll have the flexibility to fine-tune the way Windows allocates your system resources to each DOS application during multitasking. Windows can allocate a separate section of memory to each application that you launch from Windows in 386 enhanced mode. While the actual location of this memory will likely be in XMS memory, above the 640Kb normally accessed by DOS, Windows takes advantage of the 80386 CPU's virtual 8086 mode to make the memory appear to be conventional memory. The 386 chip's virtual machine emulation also builds a simulated display and provides a separate copy of the operating system and device drivers for each application so it can function as if it were running on a separate computer.

Windows provides more sophisticated memory management than you'll find in the traditional DOS environment. In the appropriate mode, Windows makes optimal use of your system's memory—in all its various forms. Windows can even create virtual memory out of hard drive space by creating a swap file when you use its 386 enhanced mode. In real or standard mode, Windows automatically creates application swap files to facilitate switching between Windows applications and DOS applications. Although this kind of swapping is available within a few DOS applications and separate utility programs, Windows provides it automatically for all Windows applications and even for the DOS-based applications you run from Windows.

MANAGING SWAP FILES

When you launch a DOS application while Windows is operating in real or standard mode, Windows automatically creates a temporary file on your hard drive. When you switch back to Windows or to another application, Windows moves (or "swaps") some of the first application out of RAM and stores it in the application swap file on your hard drive. Swapping allows you to open more DOS applications from Windows than would normally fit within your available memory. This swapping ensures that the maximum amount of memory is available for the next active application. When you exit an application, Windows deletes the associated application swap file.

Application swap files

In 386 enhanced mode, Windows doesn't use temporary application swap files. Instead, it uses a single swap file on your hard drive that the 386 processor can treat as virtual memory, thus effectively increasing your system's RAM resources by the size of the swap file—a far more powerful arrangement than application swap files. For example, on a 386-based system with 2Mb of XMS and a 5Mb swap file, 386 enhanced mode allows Windows to function as if the computer has 7Mb of extended memory available.

Swap files in 386 enhanced mode

When it operates in 386 enhanced mode, Windows will automatically create a temporary swap file and adjust its size as needed, unless you have created a permanent swap file for Windows' use. The permanent swap file is more efficient but occupies hard drive space even when Windows is not running, or is running in another mode. When you install Windows on a 386 or 486 computer that can use 386 enhanced mode, Setup offers to create a permanent swap file during the installation process. Windows also includes a separate utility program—SWAPFILE.EXE—to create, remove, or change the size of a permanent swap file. We'll explain more about the Swapfile utility in Appendix 1.

In this chapter

PIFs—Working with Non-Windows Applications 17

*W*indows provides a number of important services to the applications that are designed to run in its environment. In addition to the common user interface, Windows supplies memory management, and display and printer interfaces. More importantly, Windows creates and administers a multitasking environment, making sure each application gets its fair share of system resources and mediating contention between applications for items such as the printer or a COM port. As a result, you can run multiple applications simultaneously, switch quickly between running applications, and share information via Clipboard because Windows-based applications follow certain rules in the way they request and use system resources. DOS-based applications don't follow the same rules and weren't designed to share system resources in a multitasking environment.

The more Windows knows about the way a program operates and what it needs and expects from the computer system, the better job Windows can do of integrating that application into the Windows environment with the rest of your applications. Windows-based applications supply Windows with the information automatically—DOS-based applications do not. To run a DOS-based application, Windows must make certain assumptions about the application's requirements. If the assumptions are correct, the application should run normally. But, if they aren't, the application may run poorly or not at all. There could be problems with such details as memory requirements or the display—especially when you switch between the DOS application and your Windows applications.

Fortunately, there is a way to provide Windows with the information it needs to optimize its interaction with your non-Windows applications. You can create a PIF—a Program Information File—for a non-Windows application to inform Windows how it should run that application. Whenever you start a DOS appli-

WHAT IS A PIF?

cation under Windows, Windows will look for that application's PIF and use the information in the PIF instead of its default assumptions about how the application operates. For instance, when you start a DOS application under Windows' 386 enhanced mode, that application's PIF will tell Windows how much memory the application requires, whether to run the application full-screen or in a window, whether to continue running the application in the background when you switch to other applications, and so forth. In other words, a PIF is a file of technical information about a non-Windows application that enables Windows to optimize the way it runs and interacts with that application.

In this chapter, we'll cover PIFs in great detail. We'll explain how to install a PIF and show you how to use the PIF Editor to create and modify PIFs. We'll also explain all the settings you'll find in the PIF Editor for both standard mode and 386 enhanced mode and examine the impact they will have on your applications running under Windows.

INSTALLING A PIF

Microsoft includes in your Windows package predefined PIFs for several popular DOS applications. As Windows' Setup finds and installs applications during your Windows installation, it automatically installs the predefined PIFs for the non-Windows applications it finds in your Windows directory.

Unfortunately, Windows can't provide predefined PIFs for every DOS application that exists. However, many software manufacturers provide a PIF for their application on the application's program disks (or they will make the PIF available on request). If you're using an application for which the manufacturer has supplied a PIF, you can install that PIF simply by copying it from your program disk into your Windows directory. (See Chapter 6 for an explanation of how to copy files.) Once you've copied the PIF into your Windows directory, you can use Windows Setup to install the application, or add the application to the Program Manager yourself. Chapter 5 covers adding applications to the Program Manager. Then, when you start the application from the Program Manager, Windows will automatically look for and use the PIF you've copied. You can also explicitly instruct Windows to use a PIF for an application by installing the PIF in the Program Manager instead of the application's executable file.

If neither Windows nor your software manufacturer provides a predefined PIF for your application, don't worry. If Windows can't find a PIF for an application, it will start the application using a set of default PIF settings. For the vast majority of DOS applications, the default PIF settings will work just fine. However, if your application doesn't run properly, or if it doesn't run as you prefer, you might need to create a custom PIF for your application. Similarly, if an application with a predefined PIF isn't working properly, you might need to change some of the settings in that application's PIF—especially if you want to make use of some of the new capabilities of Windows' 386 enhanced mode. When you need to create or modify the settings in a PIF, you'll need to use one of Windows' most important accessories—the PIF Editor.

To start the PIF Editor, use the Program Manager to open the Accessories group window and double-click on the PIF Editor icon. Immediately, Windows will open the PIF Editor window. The PIF Editor is sensitive to Windows' operating mode and presents the appropriate settings for the current mode. If you're running Windows in real or standard mode, the PIF Editor window will include only the settings that apply to standard mode, as shown in Figure 17-1. If you're running Windows in 386 enhanced mode, the PIF Editor window will have a slightly different set of basic options and will add settings to control the advanced options available only in 386 enhanced mode. Like most Windows applications, you select Exit from the File menu to close the window and leave the PIF Editor.

PIF EDITOR

Figure 17-1

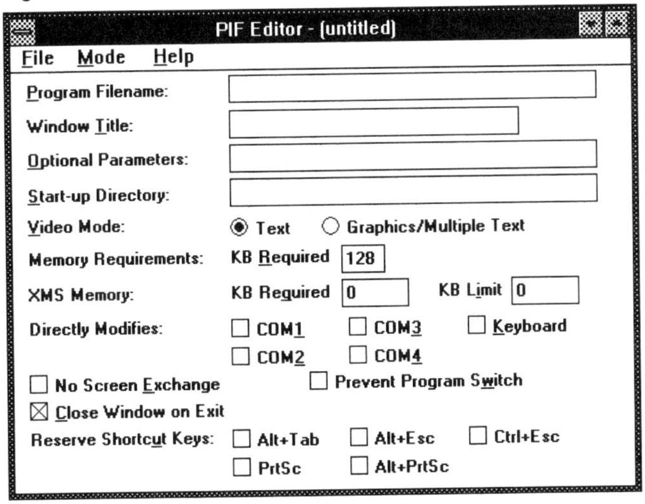

```
┌──────────────────────────────────────────────────────┐
│ ▓▓         PIF Editor - (untitled)          ▓▓ ▓▓     │
├──────────────────────────────────────────────────────┤
│ File   Mode   Help                                    │
│ Program Filename:  ┌────────────────────────────┐     │
│ Window Title:      ┌────────────────────────────┐     │
│ Optional Parameters: ┌──────────────────────────┐     │
│ Start-up Directory:  ┌──────────────────────────┐     │
│ Video Mode:         ◉ Text   ○ Graphics/Multiple Text │
│ Memory Requirements:  KB Required  │128│              │
│ XMS Memory:          KB Required │0│   KB Limit │0│   │
│ Directly Modifies:   □ COM1   □ COM3   □ Keyboard     │
│                      □ COM2   □ COM4                  │
│ □ No Screen Exchange       □ Prevent Program Switch   │
│ ⊠ Close Window on Exit                                │
│ Reserve Shortcut Keys:  □ Alt+Tab  □ Alt+Esc  □ Ctrl+Esc │
│                         □ PrtSc    □ Alt+PrtSc        │
└──────────────────────────────────────────────────────┘
```

If you're running Windows in real or standard mode, the PIF Editor window initially opens with these defaults.

Each PIF contains two sets of options: one for standard and real modes, and one for 386 enhanced mode. The PIF Editor also has two modes—standard and 386 enhanced—for editing the two sets of options. If you plan to run your application either under Windows' real mode or standard mode, you'll want to run the PIF Editor in standard mode so you can specify standard mode options. On the other hand, if you plan to run your application under Windows' 386 enhanced mode, you'll want to run the PIF Editor in 386 enhanced mode so you can specify 386 enhanced mode options. Notice the difference between the PIF Editor in standard mode, as shown in Figure 17-1, and in 386 enhanced mode, as shown in Figure 17-2.

Changing PIF modes

Figure 17-2

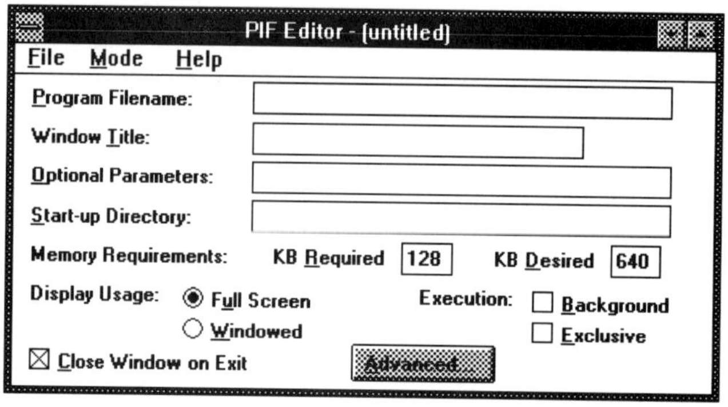

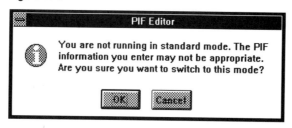

In 386 enhanced mode, the PIF Editor window offers a slightly different set of basic options, plus a button to access a dialog box of Advanced settings.

By default, the PIF Editor displays the options for the mode in which Windows is currently running. Although this is typically what you'll want, you can use the Mode menu to toggle the PIF options between standard and 386 enhanced modes. For example, if you're running Windows in 386 enhanced mode, and you want to create a PIF for a DOS application that will run in real mode, you'll need to choose the Standard command on the Mode menu before editing that application's PIF. Whenever you use the Mode menu to switch to a mode that differs from Windows' current operating mode, the PIF Editor will display a message box like the one shown in Figure 17-3. When you choose OK in this message box, the PIF Editor will bring up the options for the new mode you selected.

Figure 17-3

> **PIF Editor**
>
> (i) You are not running in standard mode. The PIF information you enter may not be appropriate. Are you sure you want to switch to this mode?
>
> [OK]   [Cancel]

The PIF Editor asks for confirmation when you switch between standard and 386 enhanced modes.

Creating new PIFs

When you first start the PIF Editor, it will create a new, untitled PIF with all the PIF Editor's default settings. At this point, you can change any of the settings that appear in the PIF Editor window. When you're ready to save the settings to disk, choose the Save command from the File menu to bring up the familiar File Save As dialog box, then type into the Filename text box the name of the executable file that starts the application. You don't need to supply a file name extension—Windows will automatically append the extension .PIF. Make sure you save the PIF either in your Windows directory or in the same directory as the application whose PIF you're creating. If you use a different name for your PIF file, or store it in another directory, Windows will not automatically find and use the PIF settings when you launch the application. However, you can always launch an application by installing its PIF file in the Program Manager instead of the executable file. This technique is handy when you want to use different PIFs to run an application with different configurations.

You can create a new, untitled PIF whenever you want simply by choosing the New command from the PIF Editor's File menu. Remember, each time you issue the New command, Windows will display the default settings in the PIF Editor window.

Opening PIFs

To open an existing PIF, choose the Open... command from the PIF Editor's File menu. The File Open dialog box will appear with the file descriptor *.PIF in the Filename text box, and Windows will display the names of all PIF files in the Files list box.

If the name of the PIF you want to open appears in the Files list box, simply select its name and click on OK. Or, if necessary, use the Directories list box to activate the PIF's directory, then choose its name in the Files list box. As soon as you click on OK, Windows will display the selected file's settings in the PIF Editor window and place the PIF's name in the PIF Editor title bar.

Once you open an existing PIF, you can modify its settings, then use the Save command to save those changes. If you want, you can select the Save As... command from the File menu and supply a new name in the Filename text box to save your changes as a new PIF.

STANDARD OPTIONS

The PIF Editor offers several options for running DOS applications under real or standard mode. Most of these options will appear in 386 enhanced mode as well. In this section, we'll explain each of the PIF Editor's standard options and how they affect your DOS applications.

By the way, you'll need to be familiar with several technical terms and concepts in order to understand much of the discussion in the rest of this chapter. You can refer to Chapter 16 for help with these technical terms.

Program Filename

The Program Filename text box in the PIF Editor stores the full path name of the file that starts your DOS application. This file will have either a .COM, .EXE, or .BAT file name extension. Make sure you include the drive and directory path when you specify the Program Filename entry.

For example, suppose you're creating a PIF for the DOS application Microsoft Word. You've installed Word in the directory C:\WORD, and the name of the file that starts the application is WORD.COM. In this example, you would enter *C:\WORD\WORD.COM* in the Program Filename text box.

Window Title

The Window Title text box stores the name you want to appear in the application window's title bar and under its icon when it is minimized in the Program Manager. If you leave this text box empty, Windows will use the file name you've entered in the Program Filename text box for the icon name and window title (without the extension).

For instance, returning to our Microsoft Word example, if you leave the Window Title text box empty, Windows will use the name *Word* to label the Microsoft Word icon. If you prefer to label the icon with the name *Microsoft Word*, just type that name into the Window Title text box.

Optional Parameters

If you usually type some parameters after the application's file name when you start the application from the DOS prompt, you'll want to type those parameters into the Optional Parameters text box. If you don't need to supply any parameters, just leave this text box empty.

For example, if you normally type *WORD /L* to start Microsoft Word and automatically load the last file you worked on, you'll want to type */L* into the Optional Parameters text box. You can specify as many parameters as you like, as long as the total number of characters does not exceed 62. Depending on your application, you might insert a file name for a file you want the application to open automatically, or command line switches that instruct the application to start in a particular mode or perform some automatic function.

If you want, you can ask Windows to prompt you for parameters when you start the application. To do this, simply type a question mark (?) into the Optional Parameters text box.

By the way, if you specify optional parameters in an application's PIF, and later want to start that application with a different set of parameters, you can do so by choosing Run... from the File menu in the File Manager or Program Manager. When you use the Run... command to start an application, the parameters you supply in the Run dialog box will override those you've entered with the PIF Editor.

Start-up Directory

If you want Windows to make a particular directory the current directory when it starts an application, simply enter the name of that directory into the Start-up Directory text box. This procedure is roughly equivalent to issuing the CD command at the DOS prompt to change directories before starting an application. Although you can leave this text box empty, you'll probably want to enter the name of the directory containing the application's program files. In this way, you can ensure that the application has access to all the files it will need while running.

For example, if you're creating a PIF for Microsoft Word, and you've installed Word in the directory C:\WORD, you'll want to enter *C:\WORD* into the Start-up Directory text box.

The Video mode options—Text and Graphics/Multiple Text—determine how much memory Windows reserves for your application's display. If your application runs only in text mode, you'll want to choose the Text option, since this mode will leave more memory available for your application. However, if your application takes advantage of your display's graphics mode, you'll need to choose the Graphics/Multiple Text option, which will set aside more memory for storing your application's display. You'll also want to choose this option if your application requires more than one text screen's worth of display memory.

Video Mode

If you aren't sure which video mode your application uses, choose the Graphics/Multiple Text option. Although this option requires more memory, it is the safest option. It will ensure that Windows reserves enough display memory to save the application's display when you switch back to the Program Manager.

The Memory Requirements setting allows you to tell Windows how much memory your application requires to run. Keep in mind that this setting does not restrict the amount of memory Windows provides for the application—Windows will suspend its own applications and give this application all available conventional memory when you are operating in standard mode. The Memory Requirements setting simply tells Windows the minimum amount of memory that must be available before it should even attempt to start the application.

Memory Requirements

If Windows can't provide the application with at least as much memory as you've specified in the KB Required text box, Windows will display a message dialog box warning that the memory available is insufficient when you attempt to start the application.

The XMS Memory options let you provide extended memory to DOS applications that conform to the Lotus/Intel/Microsoft eXtended Memory Specification standard. Although only a few DOS applications use extended memory, one of the most popular applications—Lotus 1-2-3 version 3—does. Let's consider the two options that relate to XMS memory.

XMS Memory

The KB Required setting tells Windows how much memory your application requires. The operative word here is "required." Although some applications might be able to use extended memory, very few will *require* it. You'll probably want to leave this setting at 0 since any other KB Required setting will significantly increase the amount of time required to switch to and from that application. Use this setting to tell Windows the application will not operate without at least the specified amount of XMS memory.

KB Required

KB Limit

The KB Limit setting specifies the maximum amount of memory that Windows should permit the application to use. If you want to prevent the application from using any extended memory, enter 0 into the KB Limit text box. If you want to grant the application a specific amount of extended memory, enter the appropriate value into the text box. Strangely enough, a value of -1 permits the application to use all the available extended memory.

Directly Modifies

Remember that DOS applications were created assuming that they would be the sole application operating on a computer and not sharing the computer with other applications. Consequently, DOS applications often presume they have exclusive use of the computer resources and manipulate them directly instead of allowing Windows to act as a central clearinghouse.

The check boxes that appear in the Directly Modifies area of the PIF Editor window allow you to tell Windows that the application monopolizes certain resources. If you select any of these options, Windows will prevent other applications from using the selected resource, and prevent you from switching to other applications without first quitting from that application.

As you might expect, you'll use the COM1, COM2, COM3, and COM4 check boxes to tell Windows which communications port(s) the application will monopolize. You'll want to select the Keyboard check box if the application takes direct control of the keyboard. If you choose this option, you will not be able to use the keyboard shortcut that allows you to copy the screen's contents to the Clipboard. By the way, selecting the Keyboard check box will provide some additional memory for the application—memory that Windows would otherwise reserve for storing the current state of the application.

No Screen Exchange

Selecting the No Screen Exchange check box prevents you from using the [Print Screen] or [Alt][Print Screen] keys to copy the application's screen to the Clipboard. The only reason you would want to select this option is if you want to provide a small amount of additional memory to the application. As you'll see in a moment, the effect of selecting this option is similar to selecting the PrtSc and Alt+PrtSc check boxes in the Reserve Shortcut Keys area of the PIF Editor.

Prevent Program Switch

Selecting the Prevent Program Switch option prevents you from switching from an application and returning to the Windows desktop. Once you've started an application with the Prevent Program Switch option selected, the only way you can use another application is to quit from that application as you would in DOS. The benefit of selecting this option is that it provides a small amount of additional memory to the application.

As you'll see in a moment, selecting the Prevent Program Switch check box is similar to selecting all the check boxes in the Reserve Shortcut Keys area of the PIF Editor. Selecting the Prevent Program Switch check box is also similar to selecting any of the Directly Modifies check boxes.

By default, the PIF Editor selects the Close Window on Exit check box, which tells Windows to automatically close the application's window when you exit the application. If you want Windows to leave the application's window on the screen even after you exit, deselect the Close Window on Exit check box.

Close Window on Exit

You'll want to use the Reserve Shortcut Keys options if your application uses any of the shortcut keys that Windows normally uses for its own functions. By selecting any of the check boxes in this section of the PIF Editor, you can allow your application to respond normally to the selected key combination and prevent Windows from intercepting and acting on those keystrokes.

Reserve Shortcut Keys

For instance, suppose your application inserts a tab marker when you press the [Alt][Tab] key combination, but Windows uses the same key combination as a shortcut key to switch to the next application—a conflict in which Windows will win. Windows will intercept the [Alt][Tab] key combination and switch to the next application instead of allowing your application to insert a tab marker. However, if you select the Alt+Tab check box in the application's PIF, Windows will ignore that key combination, reserving it for the application instead. Then, pressing [Alt][Tab] while your application is in the foreground will insert a tab marker instead of telling Windows to switch to the next application.

Keep in mind that the Reserve Shortcut Keys options affect only the application with which that PIF is associated. You can still use all of Windows' built-in shortcuts when another application is in the foreground.

For a description of the normal functions of Windows' shortcut keys, refer to Chapter 2 or the Reference section.

In 386 enhanced mode, Windows uses the ability of the 80386 or 80486 processor to create a virtual machine for each DOS application you run from Windows. You can exercise considerable control over this simulated machine environment by changing the PIF settings for an application. In 386 enhanced mode, Windows can run some DOS applications in a window alongside the Windows applications on your desktop. It can multitask DOS applications with Windows applications rather than suspending the Windows applications while each DOS application runs and vice versa. Windows can simulate conventional or EMS memory in a block of XMS memory to provide the appropriate environment for each application and then, when you exit from the application, reallocate that memory in a different configuration for the next application. Of course, as you might expect, more control and more options means more settings to adjust.

386 ENHANCED MODE OPTIONS

If you intend to run your DOS application under Windows' 386 enhanced mode, you'll want to supply the appropriate settings to take advantage of the special capabilities of the 386 enhanced mode. If you open the PIF Editor when you are operating in 386 enhanced mode, it will automatically present the 386 enhanced mode options shown in Figure 17-2. If, on the other hand, you are currently running Windows under real or standard mode, you can bring up the 386 enhanced settings by choosing the 386 Enhanced command from the PIF Editor's Mode menu. When you switch to 386 enhanced mode, Windows will present a message box notifying you that your PIF settings are not appropriate for the current mode. If you choose OK in this message box, the PIF Editor will display the 386 enhanced mode settings.

The standard options

Most of the basic PIF settings in 386 enhanced mode are the same as their counterparts in standard mode. The Program Filename, Window Title, Optional Parameters, and Start-up Directory text boxes are all duplicated from the standard mode PIF settings, as is the Close Window on Exit check box. Along with the similarities come a few changes. Several standard mode options are missing—notably the Directly Modifies, No Screen Exchange, and Prevent Program Switch check boxes. They are not necessary in 386 enhanced mode. The XMS Memory and Reserve Shortcut Keys settings are also missing from the PIF Editor window in 386 enhanced mode, but will reappear in the Advanced Options dialog box reached by clicking on the Advanced... button.

Memory Requirements

The Memory Requirements options are slightly different from those in standard mode. The Memory Requirements options let you control the amount of *conventional* memory Windows will provide to the application. In the Advanced Options dialog box, other settings control EMS and XMS memory.

KB Required

The KB Required setting is equivalent to the KB Required option in standard and real modes. This setting does not limit the amount of memory available to the application—it merely tells Windows to make sure the specified minimum amount of memory is available before trying to start the application.

KB Desired

The KB Desired setting specifies the maximum amount of memory that Windows will permit the application to use. By default, PIF Editor supplies a KB Desired setting of 640—the maximum amount of conventional memory any DOS application can use. If you want to limit the amount of conventional memory Windows will provide for the application, simply enter the desired amount into the KB Desired text box. The only time you might want to enter a value less than 640 is if you want to reserve more memory for other applications.

Display Usage

The PIF Editor's Display Usage options let you tell Windows whether you want to run the application full-screen or in a window. This is one of the powerful new capabilities of the 386 enhanced mode. You can run many of your DOS applications in a window on your desktop similar to your Windows applications. Not all applications can run in a window, and those that do require more memory than full-screen applications. However, windowed applications make it easier to switch between multiple applications and to copy and paste information.

By the way, after you start a DOS application, you can easily toggle between full-screen and a window by pressing [Alt][Enter].

Execution

The two check boxes in the Execution area of the PIF Editor determine how the application cooperates with other applications for multitasking. In real and standard modes, Windows suspends its own applications while a DOS application is running, and suspends the DOS application when you switch back to Windows. In 386 enhanced mode, this is no longer necessary—at least not for all DOS applications. Under Windows' control, many DOS applications can multitask with Windows applications and even other DOS applications.

Let's consider each of these check box options. (Notice these are two independent check box options—not mutually exclusive option buttons.)

Background

If you select the Background check box, Windows will allow an application to run in the background while you use another application in the foreground. If you deselect the Background check box, Windows will stop running an application when you switch to another application.

The Background option comes in handy for communications programs. By selecting the Background check box in your communications program's PIF, that program can exchange data with another computer while you use a spreadsheet or word processing application in the foreground.

Exclusive

Selecting the Exclusive check box option tells Windows to suspend execution of all other applications while the application controlled by the PIF is running in the foreground—even if the other applications have their Background option selected. The advantage to selecting this option is that it gives the application more memory and processor time.

If you choose to select the Exclusive option for an application, you might as well select the Full Screen option in the Display Usage section. It normally isn't productive to run an exclusive application in a window, since windows are designed to let you load and run multiple applications simultaneously.

**ADVANCED 386
ENHANCED MODE
OPTIONS**

In addition to the basic PIF options we've covered so far, you can control a number of other details in the virtual machine environment Windows creates for each DOS application it runs in 386 enhanced mode. If you click on the Advanced... button in the PIF Editor window, Windows will open the Advanced Options dialog box, which contains advanced 386 enhanced mode options, as shown in Figure 17-4.

Figure 17-4

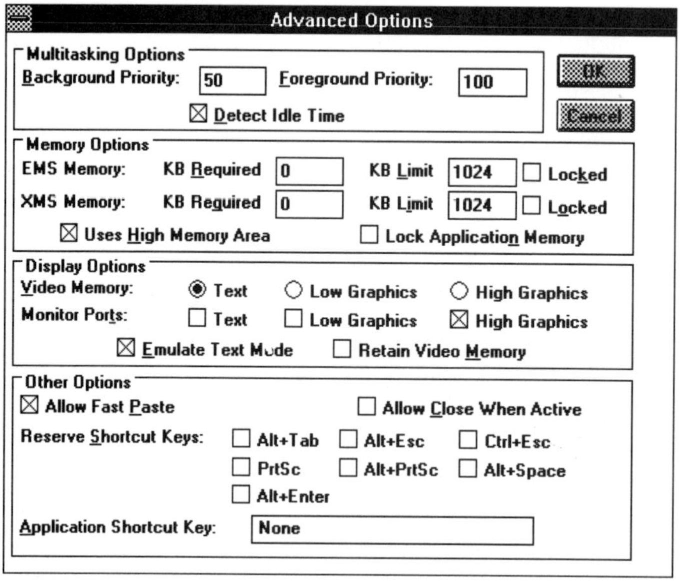

Choosing the Advanced... button in the PIF Editor window opens the Advanced Options dialog box.

You probably won't need to modify any of the options in the Advanced Options dialog box. However, we'll briefly discuss how each of these options will affect your DOS application.

Multitasking Options

The Multitasking Options section of the Advanced Options dialog box determines how an application will share processor time with other applications. The values in the Background Priority and Foreground Priority text boxes determine how much processor time the application will receive when it is running in the background or foreground, respectively. The Control Panel sets the default Background Priority at 50 and the Foreground Priority at 100. These values, which can range from 0 to 10,000, are meaningful only when compared to the corresponding values for other applications. Let's consider an example.

Suppose you're running three applications with the PIF Editor's default Priority settings. The application in the foreground has a Foreground Priority of 100, while the two applications in the background each have a Background Priority of 50. The total Priority values for all three applications is 100 (for the foreground application) plus 2 times 50 (for the background applications), which equals 200. Now, each application will get the percentage of processor time equal to its Priority value divided by the total Priority value. Consequently, the foreground application will get 100/200, or 50 percent of the processor's time. Similarly, each background application will get 50/200, or 25 percent of the processor's time.

The Detect Idle Time check box tells Windows to give processor time to other applications while an application is idle. In other words, if an application is waiting for your input, Windows will let other applications use its share of the processor's time.

Typically, you'll want to leave this option selected, since it will usually enhance overall system performance. However, if you notice that an application is running unusually slowly, you might deselect that application's Detect Idle Time check box to see if it improves the application's performance.

Detect Idle Time

The Memory Options settings, along with the Memory Requirements settings in the basic PIF options, control the way your application uses the computer's memory when running under Windows' 386 enhanced mode. The Memory Requirements setting controls conventional memory, while the Memory Options control expanded and extended memory.

Memory Options

As you know, Windows is designed to take advantage of the extended memory you've installed in your machine. Unfortunately, many DOS applications can take advantage of expanded—but not extended—memory. If your DOS application uses expanded memory, you can use the EMS Memory options to tell Windows to simulate expanded memory for that application. (See Chapter 16 for an explanation of the difference between extended and expanded memory.)

EMS Memory

The KB Required setting tells Windows the *minimum* amount of expanded memory your application requires. Although many applications can use expanded memory, very few actually *require* it. For this reason, you will probably want to leave this setting at 0.

Like the similar setting for conventional memory, this setting does not limit the amount of expanded memory an application receives—it merely tells Windows to make sure this amount of expanded memory is available before it attempts to start the application. Once Windows starts the application, that application will receive as much expanded memory as it requests, up to the amount specified by the KB Limit settings.

KB Required

The KB Limit setting specifies the *maximum* amount of expanded memory that Windows will permit the application to use. By default, the PIF Editor supplies a KB Limit setting of 1024 (1Mb). If you want to prevent the application from using any expanded memory, enter 0 into the KB Limit text box. If you want to grant the application a specific amount of expanded memory, enter the appropriate value into the KB Limit text box.

KB Limit

Selecting the Locked check box tells Windows not to swap to disk the contents of the expanded memory used by an application. Although selecting the Locked check box will improve the performance of a particular application, it will decrease the overall performance of the system.

Locked

XMS Memory

The XMS Memory settings are essentially the same as the XMS Memory settings in standard mode. It lets Windows provide extended memory to DOS applications that conform to the Lotus/Intel/Microsoft eXtended Memory Specification standard. Because very few DOS applications use extended memory, you will probably not want to change these default settings.

Like the other memory settings, the KB Required setting controls the *minimum* extended memory that must be available for Windows to start the application. The KB Limit setting specifies the *maximum* extended memory Windows will allow the application to use, and selecting the Locked check box prevents swapping the extended memory to disk.

Uses High Memory Area

Selecting the Uses High Memory Area check box tells Windows that this application can use your computer's high memory area (HMA), which is the first 64K of extended memory. You'll want to keep this option selected for most applications, since it will give your application access to additional memory. To prevent the application from using the HMA, deselect this check box.

Keep in mind that in order for an application to use the HMA, the HMA must be available when you start Windows. If you run a memory-resident program that uses the HMA before you start Windows, none of your applications will be able to use the HMA.

Lock Application Memory

Selecting the Lock Application Memory check box tells Windows to keep the application running in memory and not to swap it out of RAM and onto disk. Selecting this option will speed up the application at the expense of slowing down the rest of the system.

Display Options

The Display Options area of the Advanced Options dialog box lets you control how Windows displays your applications and how it manages your display memory. We'll discuss each option in this area.

Video Memory

The Video Memory option buttons tell Windows how much memory to initially set aside for the application's display. The Text option tells Windows to reserve enough memory to display the application in text mode, which requires the least amount of memory (less than 16Kb).

The Low Graphics option tells Windows to reserve enough memory to display the application in low-resolution graphics mode, which roughly corresponds to CGA-quality graphics. For most video adapters, CGA graphics require about 32Kb of memory.

The High Graphics option tells Windows to reserve enough memory to display the application in high-resolution graphics mode, which corresponds to EGA- or VGA-quality graphics. High-resolution graphics mode typically requires about 128Kb of memory—the most memory of the three available modes.

It's important to remember that the Video Memory options specify only how much memory is *initially* reserved for displaying the application. Once the application is running, Windows can adjust the amount of memory used for the application's display. For example, if you start an application in text mode, then invoke a function that shifts the application into graphics mode, Windows will provide additional display memory automatically (assuming the additional memory is available). Similarly, if you're using an application in graphics mode, then switch to text mode, Windows will free up the extra display memory, thus making it available for other applications.

If, while running an application, you switch to a video mode that requires more memory than Windows can provide, you might lose some or all of your display. To avoid this, choose the High Graphics option button and select the Retain Video Memory check box, which we'll discuss in a moment.

Monitor Ports

The Monitor Ports check boxes help prevent problems that can occur when an application directly interacts with your computer's display adapter. If your application's display functions normally, you should not modify these settings, since they will probably slow down the application significantly.

However, if the application's display doesn't appear as it should, select the check box that corresponds with the display mode in which the application was running when the problem occurred. If that doesn't correct the problem, try selecting another Monitor Ports check box until the display functions normally.

Emulate Text Mode

Selecting the Emulate Text Mode check box typically allows the application to display text very quickly. Consequently, you'll want to make sure this check box is selected for most applications. However, if the text in the application's display doesn't appear properly, or if the cursor appears in the wrong place, deselect this option and restart the application.

Retain Video Memory

As we explained a moment ago, Windows can adjust the amount of memory used for the application's display while the application is running. This dynamic memory management works fine as long as you don't run out of memory. However, if, while running an application, you switch to a video mode that requires more memory than Windows can provide, you might lose some or all of your display. To prevent this situation from occurring, choose the Video Memory option button that corresponds to the highest video mode your application will use, then select the Retain Video Memory check box. Once you've done this, Windows will not allow any other applications to use the memory reserved for your application's display, even if the application isn't using all of that memory.

Other Options

As you can see at the bottom of the Advanced Options dialog box in Figure 17-4, Windows offers several other PIF options that let you customize the way an application runs under Windows' 386 enhanced mode. We'll explain the Allow Fast Paste, Allow Close When Active, Reserve Shortcut Keys, and Application Shortcut Key options next.

Allow Fast Paste

Selecting the Allow Fast Paste option lets Windows paste text as fast as possible from Clipboard into the application. Because most applications can accept fast pasting, Windows selects this option by default. If an application cannot accept information at maximum speed, Windows will usually detect this and automatically slow down.

Occasionally, Windows may not be able to detect that an application has difficulty with its fast paste. If you're having problems pasting text into an application, deselect the Allow Fast Paste check box and restart the application.

Allow Close When Active •

The Allow Close When Active check box affects the way Windows responds when you attempt to exit Windows while the application is running. If you do not select this check box, Windows will not allow you to end your Windows session until you issue the application's Exit command. If you select this check box, however, you can exit your Windows session without having to activate the application and issue its Exit command.

If you want to select the Allow Close When Active check box for your application, first make sure that the application uses standard MS-DOS file handles. If it doesn't, allowing Windows to exit the application automatically could result in data loss.

Reserve Shortcut Keys

The Reserve Shortcut Keys options operate in the same manner as those in standard mode. In 386 enhanced mode, they appear in the Other Options group box, rather than in the main PIF Editor window.

Application Shortcut Key

The last option in the Advanced Options dialog box, Application Shortcut Key, allows you to define a special shortcut key combination for your application. Once you've defined a shortcut key combination for an application, you can press that key combination whenever you want to immediately switch to that application from any other application.

To define a shortcut key for your application, first click on the Application Shortcut Key text box to activate it. Next, press the key combination you want to define as the shortcut key combination. Acceptable key combinations must include either the [Alt] or [Ctrl] key, but cannot include the [Esc], [Enter], [Tab], [Spacebar], [Print Screen], or [Backspace] keys. For example, some acceptable key combinations include [Alt]L, [Ctrl][F8], [Alt][Shift]Y, and [Ctrl][Alt]G.

Whenever you press a key while the Application Shortcut Key text box is activated, the name of that key will appear in the text box. If you accidentally press the wrong key, simply use the [Backspace] key to remove it from the definition.

To completely remove a shortcut key definition, activate the Application Shortcut Key text box and press [Shift][Backspace]. As soon as you do this, Windows will remove the previous shortcut key definition and display *None* in the text box.

Keep in mind that once you've started an application with a defined shortcut key, that shortcut key can serve no purpose except to activate the associated application. This means that no other application will recognize that shortcut key, including Windows, Windows applications, other DOS applications, or even the application itself. For this reason, you should choose your shortcut keys carefully.

For example, imagine you're editing the PIF for Microsoft Works and that you want to assign the shortcut key combination [Alt][Shift]W to this application. To do this, activate the Application Shortcut Key text box and press [Alt][Shift]W. Windows will then display *Alt+Shift+W* in the Application Shortcut Key text box. Now, the next time you start Microsoft Works, then switch to another application, you can immediately bring Works back to the foreground simply by pressing [Alt][Shift]W.

CREATING A PIF FOR A BATCH FILE

If you've created a DOS batch file that you want to run under Windows, you'll need to create a PIF for that batch file. To do this, first start PIF Editor and supply the name of the batch file (including the .BAT extension) in the Program Filename text box. Next, specify the appropriate settings in the PIF Editor window. Keep in mind that the PIF settings you specify will be in effect for all applications and utilities that the batch file starts.

Once you've created a PIF for your batch file, you can run that batch file just as you would any other application. Specifically, you can add the batch file's PIF to a Program Manager group, then select it from that group, or you can start the File Manager, then double-click on the PIF's file name.

Section  4

Appendices

In this appendix

Installing Windows *A1*

*I*nstalling Windows 3 is a much simpler task than installing previous versions of Microsoft Windows. The new Setup utility program goes beyond simply copying files onto your hard drive; it configures your computer and Windows to work together, installs printer drivers, and even installs most of your existing applications into Windows. Setup does most of its work automatically, but doesn't rob you of control. Instead, it keeps you informed of its progress and allows you to make key choices that affect how it installs Windows on your system. The on-screen instructions are generally clear and complete, but if you need more information, Setup provides its own Help system.

DECISIONS, DECISIONS

You will need to make a few decisions about how you want Windows installed on your system. The first few questions Setup asks pertain to your hardware and system configuration. In most cases, the defaults that Setup offers will be appropriate and you will only need to confirm them. In addition to installing Windows, Setup will allow you to set up printers and applications, and read on-line documentation. Exercising these options may require you to supply some additional information. Before you run Setup, be sure you have the information you'll need to complete the installation. The following list will enable you to anticipate the decisions you'll need to make and the information Setup will request.

- Set the drive and path—Before Setup can copy files to your hard drive, you'll need to specify the drive and directory where you want Windows installed. The default is C:\WINDOWS.

- Identify hardware—Setup automatically tests your hardware and presents, for your approval or editing, a list of what it found. It checks the computer type, display, keyboard (including foreign language keyboard layouts), mouse, and network adapter.

- Modify AUTOEXEC & CONFIG—Setup will propose some changes in your AUTOEXEC.BAT and CONFIG.SYS files. You'll have the opportunity to accept, reject, or edit the suggested changes.

- Set up printers—Setup allows you to specify the printers you'll use with Windows during installation. Printer set up is the most complicated part of installing Windows, primarily due to the variety of printers Windows supports. It isn't difficult, but you'll need to answer several questions about the printer. You can always add and modify printer settings later. Whether you do it now or later, you'll need to provide information on the brand and model of your printer, the port to which it's attached to the computer, plus specifics such as font cartridges, memory, resolution, and paper trays. If you choose to wait until later to add printers, be sure to keep your Windows disks handy. You'll need them when you load printer drivers and fonts.

- Install applications—You can ask Setup to scan your hard drive(s) and list the applications it finds. Then, you can choose items from the list and have Setup install them in Windows' Program Manager for you. You can easily change things later if you don't like the way Setup groups your applications in Program Manager. This step is optional and, like setting up printers, you can do it later from within Windows. Setup may not recognize every application you've installed on your system, but it's a good start toward configuring your computer for operation under Windows.

- Read on-line documents—Reading the on-line documentation is essential! Setup makes it easy by offering to automatically display the files on the screen during installation. These documentation files will contain important information about Windows 3, such as any last-minute changes or updates since the manual was printed. The only reason to disable this option is if you are re-installing Windows and have already read these files.

- Reserve a disk swap file—You can tell Setup whether you want it to create a special file on your hard drive for Windows to use in 386 enhanced mode. This swap file can improve Windows' performance, but it requires considerable space on your hard drive.

INSTALLING WINDOWS

Setup is actually two separate programs that share the task of installing Windows. First, the DOS portion of Setup verifies your hardware components, creates a directory on your hard drive for Windows, and copies files from the installation disk. Then, the Windows portion of Setup takes over to complete the installation. It copies more files, modifies your AUTOEXEC.BAT and CONFIG.SYS, and automatically goes through the steps needed to configure your Windows environment. To set up printers, install applications in Program

Manager, and read the on-line documentation, Setup uses the same tools that will be available to you within Windows—Setup simply automates the procedures involved and adds helpful instructions.

To begin installing Windows on your computer, insert disk 1 from your Windows package into your disk drive. Make the drive with the Windows disk the active drive by typing *A:* at the DOS prompt and pressing [Enter]. (If you inserted the Windows disk into another drive, substitute its drive designation for *A:* in these instructions.) At the A> prompt, type *SETUP* and press [Enter]. This will start the DOS portion of Windows' Setup program.

From this point on, you will simply follow the instructions on the screen. We won't attempt to recount every step of the installation in this appendix. Instead, we'll outline the major decision points so you can change the way Setup installs Windows on your computer.

If you need more information than the on-screen instructions provide, press [F1] to activate Setup's built-in Help feature. If you decide to abort your Windows installation before it is complete, you can press [F3] to exit from Setup.

Setup's first question will ask you for the drive and directory in which you want Windows installed. Setup supplies C:\WINDOWS as the default. To accept the default, just press [Enter]. If you want to install Windows in a different drive or directory, use the [Backspace] key to erase Setup's suggestion, type any valid path name, then press [Enter]. If the directory doesn't exist, Setup will create it for you and then copy files from Windows' disks to your hard drive.

Next, Setup tests your computer system to evaluate your hardware and its configuration. It will show you a list of its findings and ask for confirmation. The items Setup checks are:

- Computer type—Basically the choice is between a generic MS-DOS/PC-DOS computer, such as IBM PC AT or IBM PS/2, and certain other near compatibles. You don't need to distinguish between 286 and 386 models. Windows will do that automatically each time you run it.

- Display—Is your monitor and display adapter a VGA, an EGA, or one of the other supported displays?

- Mouse—Which type mouse do you have? (You do have a one, don't you?)

- Keyboard—Do you have an 84-key or 101-key keyboard?

- Keyboard layout—The Standard US keyboard is the default and most people won't need to change it. If you are using a keyboard with a language-specific layout, you'll need to tell Windows so it can properly interpret your keystrokes.

- Language—Windows applications that perform language-specific tasks, such as spell-checking and sorting, will refer to the Language setting. The default is American English. If you work in another language, you'll need to change this setting. You can also change this setting later within Windows by using the International dialog box in Control Panel.

- Network—If your computer is attached to a network, make sure this setting is correct so that Windows will be able to address network drives and share files. Otherwise, select No Network Installed.

Below the list of configuration items, the line *The above list matches my computer* will be highlighted in inverse video. If the statement is true, you can simply press [Enter] to confirm the settings.

If you need to change one of the settings, use the ↑ and ↓ arrow keys to move the inverse video highlight bar to the item you want to change and press [Enter]. Setup will switch to a screen that lists the options available for that setting. Some of the lists are long, and you'll need to scroll down through them with the arrow keys to see all the options. To make your selection, move the highlight to the proper item on the list and press [Enter]. You can return to the main hardware list without changing the selection by pressing [Esc]. Once you confirm that the list is correct, Setup copies more files onto your hard drive and then automatically runs the Windows portion of Setup.

Running Setup (Windows)

Because the Windows portion of Setup starts automatically, you won't need to run it as a separate step. Once you have entered Windows, you will be using standard Windows mouse and keyboard techniques to interact with Setup. We'll assume you are using a mouse in our instructions. However, if you don't have a mouse installed, you can move the pointer on the screen with the arrow keys and press the [Spacebar] instead of the mouse button. To "click on" something, position the pointer on it and press the main (left) mouse button. See Chapter 2 for more on mouse and keyboard techniques in Windows.

The Windows Setup screen

The Windows Setup screen has three main components. The main window in the center of the screen is where Setup will ask you questions and keep you informed of its progress. At the bottom of the screen, you'll find another window where Setup will display more complete instructions for each step of the installation process. To the right of the Instructions window are two buttons for the Help and Exit commands. You can position your pointer on one of these buttons and click the mouse button, or use the keyboard by pressing the [F1] key for Help or the [F3] key to exit.

The first dialog box you will see allows you to select three optional functions for Setup to perform as part of your Windows installation. You can choose Set Up Printers, Set Up Applications Already on your Hard Disk (add them to the Windows Program Manager), or Read On-Line Documentation. An *X* in the check box beside each option indicates that the option is selected. You can select and deselect an option by clicking on its check box. Normally, you'll want to go ahead and set up your printer and applications, and read the on-line documents while you are installing Windows. After you select the installation options, click on the Continue button on the screen, or press [Enter] to proceed.

Setup will start copying more files from the Windows' disks to your hard drive. It will inform you of its progress by showing the file names as it copies each one and also posts the progress of the copy procedure on a bar chart.

When Setup needs another disk, it will ask you to place the disk in a drive—usually A. If the disk is in another drive, or if the files are available elsewhere on your system, you can edit the path name. To do so, move the pointer into the text box and click the mouse button. Next, use the [Backspace] key to erase the default drive designation *A:* and type in the appropriate drive and path name. After you place the requested disk in the proper drive, press [Enter] or click on the OK button. Continue to supply disks when Setup requests them.

After Setup copies the Windows files to your hard drive, it will automatically open the Program Manager and build group windows containing the standard Windows accessories and applications so they will be available when you enter Windows. Chapter 5 covers launching applications from the Program Manager.

Setup proposes modifications to your AUTOEXEC.BAT and CONFIG.SYS files and offers you a choice of three ways to implement them. Setup can modify the files automatically, let you edit the proposed changes before it records them, or save the suggested modifications in separate files for you to edit later. When Setup modifies the files, it saves your existing AUTOEXEC and CONFIG files with the extension OLD.

In most cases, you'll want to review and edit the modifications. Setup will open two text boxes with your existing AUTOEXEC.BAT file in the lower box and its proposed changes in the top box. You'll see that Setup inserts the new Windows directory into your PATH statement, and assigns an environment variable: *SET TEMP = C:\WINDOWS\TEMP*. You can edit the proposed file by moving the pointer to the appropriate position on the text and clicking the mouse button, then using the traditional editing keys to make your changes. As a convenience, when you use the scroll bars to navigate through the file, the text in both boxes move together. After you edit the proposed AUTOEXEC.BAT, click on the Continue button.

Your CONFIG.SYS will undergo a few more changes. Setup assigns a value of 30 to FILES and sets BUFFERS to 20, unless your configuration was already set to a higher value. It adds device drivers such as HIMEM.SYS and SMARTDRV.SYS, and may disable your existing device drivers by modifying those lines of your CONFIG.SYS to begin with REM (Remark). Setup does this because your existing device drivers may conflict with Windows 3. Later, we'll explain more about these device drivers and other measures for optimizing Windows.

Setting up printers

If you chose to set up printers during installation, Setup will open Control Panel and select the Printers command. From the Printer Setup dialog box, you can install printer drivers, configure port assignments, install fonts, and establish printer-specific preferences. See Chapter 3 for an explanation of setting up printers to work with Windows.

Setting up applications

Setup will search your hard drive for applications to install in Program Manager (assuming you chose that option on the opening screen). This is the same tool that is available as part of the Windows Setup application within Windows. For more information on Windows Setup, refer to Chapter 3.

Reading on-line documents

If you chose to read the on-line documentation, Setup will automatically run Windows' Notepad and open a text file. This file will contain important information, such as late news of additions and modifications to Windows since the manuals were printed. You can use the scroll bars on the side of the Notepad window to move through the document. After you read the on-line documentation, select Exit from Notepad's File menu to close Notepad and continue your Windows installation.

Creating a disk swapping file

On a 386 computer with 2Mb or more of total memory, Setup opens a dialog box and proposes creating a section of your hard drive for Windows' exclusive use. In 386 enhanced mode, Windows can use this disk swapping file as additional RAM, noticeably improving Windows' performance—but the price in disk space is high. Depending on your system, the swap file may require several megabytes of hard drive storage space. If you have a large, fast hard drive or expect to work with multiple, large applications, you may want to use the disk swap file. Otherwise, you may prefer to live with lower performance from Windows rather than give up so much hard drive space. Your decision doesn't have to be irrevocable; Windows includes a utility for adding, deleting, or changing the size of the disk swapping file. (There is more information on the SWAPFILE utility later in this appendix, and Chapter 16 explains how Windows' 386 enhanced mode uses the disk swapping file as virtual memory.)

Click on the Yes button in the dialog box to have Setup create the disk-swapping file for Windows. If you opt not to create a permanent disk-swapping file, click on the No button.

Once you've completed the basic installation, you'll need to restart Windows before your newly installed options can take effect. The Exit Windows Setup dialog box gives you the option to reboot the computer, restart Windows, or return to DOS. If you changed your AUTOEXEC.BAT or CONFIG.SYS files, you'll want to select Reboot. Click on the appropriate button to end the Windows installation. After you reboot, you should be able to start Windows by typing *WIN* at the DOS prompt. See Chapter 1 for other Windows startup options.

Exiting Windows Setup

Once Setup has done its job, Windows should be ready to run—at least in its basic configuration. If you opted *not* to allow Setup to modify your AUTOEXEC.BAT and CONFIG.SYS files, you will need to edit them before you reboot your computer and start Windows. And, if you didn't set up a printer during installation, you'll need to do so before you can print from Windows, or any Windows-based application. Refer to Chapter 3 for details on working with your printer from Windows.

TWEAKING YOUR INSTALLATION

Windows is a very powerful operating environment with many features and capabilities. However, its power is not without a price. Windows makes significant demands on your computer hardware. And, since Windows interacts directly with your computer to deliver its impressive performance, it may conflict with third-party software such as RAM disks, disk caching, memory management, and some Terminate-and-Stay-Resident programs.

Optimizing your system

Windows can't perform at its best if your system isn't performing at its best. You'll need to take a few steps to optimize the speed, capacity, and available disk space of your system. Although the steps we outline below are not normally required to get Windows up and running, they often can improve performance significantly. These steps require varying degrees of technical knowledge about your computer system. Don't feel intimidated. Remember, the steps are optional performance enhancements, not required parts of the installation. (For the technically adept, there are several more suggested performance enhancements in the Optimizing chapter of the Windows User's Guide.)

The first step in optimizing your system is cleaning up your hard drive. Get rid of those old, unneeded files cluttering up your drive. If the files are obsolete, delete them. If they are still valuable but infrequently used, save them on floppy disks where they'll be available when you need them, but don't tie up valuable space on your hard drive. If you don't plan to use all the Windows' accessories, you can delete the program and help files for the applications you won't need. The Windows User's Guide even includes a list of the most likely candidates to be deleted in the Optimizing chapter.

Hard drive housecleaning

If your system crashes, locks up, or otherwise exits applications unexpectedly, you may find temporary files left on your disk that would normally be deleted automatically. It's a good idea to check for and delete any orphaned temporary files after an application aborts unexpectedly.

The DOS command—CHKDSK—is a valuable tool for hard drive maintenance. You should use it regularly, in addition to running it after any system crash. But, do *not* run CHKDSK from within Windows! Exit from Windows first, then type *CHKDSK /F* at the DOS prompt and press [Enter]. CHKDSK will scan your disk for lost chunks of data that it can't identify as part of a file. If it finds any, CHKDSK will offer to convert the lost data to files. Unless you are highly skilled in these matters, you should answer N at the prompt allowing CHKDSK to simply delete the lost data. Reconstructing files from lost data chains is a job best left to experts. Others must rely on backup files or resort to re-installing applications and re-entering information (depending on what files were damaged).

As you create, delete, and modify files, DOS stores the data in the first available space it finds on your hard drive. It doesn't necessarily save a file in one contiguous string—a single file may be fragmented into bits and pieces scattered across your disk. DOS keeps track of where it puts all the pieces of a file and can reassemble the file on demand. However, hard drive performance suffers noticeably when the disk heads must move to multiple locations to read each file.

Several good utility programs on the market will restore order to the disjointed files on your hard drive. They are called de-fragmentation utilities, disk compression, or disk compaction programs, and the major brands all work well. We recommend you purchase one, and use it regularly. Just don't attempt to use it from within Windows and, for safety, always have a current backup.

Running "lean-and-mean"

Conventional memory is your most precious system resource, especially if you must run Windows in real mode. The small device drivers and memory-resident utilities that need only "a couple of Kb" each can add up and consume memory that your applications desperately need.

You'll want to examine your AUTOEXEC.BAT and CONFIG.SYS files and strip out anything that might unnecessarily eat up RAM. (Use Windows' Notepad to edit the files, then reboot your system to use the edited version of the system files.) You can deactivate a device driver in your CONFIG.SYS or a command in your AUTOEXEC.BAT by typing *REM* at the beginning of the line containing the device driver. This causes DOS to treat that line as a remark. (It may also cause a harmless error message like *Unrecognized command in CONFIG.SYS.*)

Windows incorporates a built-in mouse interface and doesn't require a separate device driver (at least for the Microsoft Mouse and most compatibles). Windows includes a new version of the MOUSE.SYS device driver that you should use instead of your old device driver for the Microsoft Mouse. (This is one of the changes Setup automatically makes in your CONFIG.SYS.) If you don't expect to use your mouse with DOS applications outside Windows, you can save some memory by removing the mouse driver from your CONFIG.SYS or

AUTOEXEC.BAT. In your CONFIG.SYS, the mouse driver might appear as *device = c:\windows\mouse.sys.* To disable the mouse driver, edit the line to read *REM device = c:\windows\mouse.sys.* In your AUTOEXEC.BAT, the mouse might appear as *MOUSE.COM, C:\DOS\MOUSE.COM* or simply MOUSE. Typing *REM* at the beginning of the line will also disable a command in the AUTOEXEC.BAT file.

There are other device drivers commonly found in your CONFIG.SYS that you should remove or replace with the drivers supplied with Windows. We'll outline the purpose of each of Windows' device drivers in a moment. Setup automatically installs most, but it's a good idea to check for yourself. Generally, you should use the driver supplied with Windows if one is available. If there is none, consider removing the device driver if it's not essential to your system.

In addition to device drivers, Country settings, and the like, your CONFIG.SYS will contain FILES and BUFFERS statements. FILES should be set at 30 unless you expect to run applications that require more. A lower setting won't save any memory and may cause problems for Windows, while a higher setting will use more RAM. A setting of 20 is normally adequate for BUFFERS, and you can often save some memory by reducing it to 10 if you use the SMARTDrive disk cache driver supplied with Windows.

After you've scrutinized your CONFIG.SYS for unnecessary uses of memory, it's time to turn your attention to your AUTOEXEC.BAT file. The AUTOEXEC.BAT is often home to many small Terminate-and-Stay-Resident utilities (TSRs) and pop-up accessories. Because these are installed in memory when you start your system, they will be available at any time. Some, such as network interfaces, are vital parts of your system and should remain. Others are unnecessary and inappropriate on a system operating under Windows. They may conflict with Windows and create serious problems or simply be useless in the Windows environment and represent a waste of precious system memory. Be ruthlessly objective in evaluating TSRs and remove any that are not essential to your system.

If a particular application requires a TSR to run, consider moving the TSR to a batch file that loads the TSR, runs the application, and then removes the TSR when you exit the application. See Chapter 17 for more information on using batch files to run DOS applications from within Windows. If the application that needs a TSR is a Windows application, one option is to put the commands in a file called WINSTART.BAT, as we'll explain in a moment.

During installation, Setup adds a line to your AUOTEXEC.BAT file that tells Windows where to store temporary files. Usually the line reads *Set TEMP = C:\.* You might change it to any convenient directory, such as C:\TEMP. If you have a RAM disk installed in extended or expanded memory, you can use it for the temporary files. For example, if your RAM drive is E, change the line in your AUTOEXEC.BAT to read *Set TEMP = E:.* Reading and writing temporary files into fast memory instead of a slow disk drive noticeably improves the performance of applications that use temporary files extensively.

**Windows'
device drivers**

Device drivers are a special class of memory-resident programs that, once installed, effectively become extensions to your computer's operating system. Device drivers provide an interface between your computer and a peripheral device or another feature (such as extended memory management) not included in the MS-DOS operating system. You install device drivers by including a statement in your CONFIG.SYS file such as DEVICE = PATHNAME\DRIVER.SYS.

Microsoft provides several device drivers with Windows that were created especially to maximize Windows' capabilities. Whenever possible, you should use the device drivers supplied with Windows since other device drivers intended to perform similar functions may conflict with Windows (especially in standard mode and 386 enhanced mode). You may need some, none, or all the device drivers supplied with Windows depending on your computer hardware, Windows' operating mode, and the applications you use. The Windows User's Guide includes a full explanation of each device driver with its options and syntax in the Optimizing Windows chapter and again in the CONFIG.SYS appendix.

HIMEM.SYS

HIMEM.SYS, Windows' extended (XMS) memory manager assigns blocks of extended memory to your various applications and makes sure one application doesn't usurp another application's memory during multitasking operations. DOS performs similar functions within conventional memory, but can't manage the extended memory addressed by your 286 or 386 computer's protected mode. (You don't need HIMEM on an 8088- or 8086-based computer since those processors don't have a protected mode or support extended memory.)

HIMEM adds one unusual capability to its repertoire. In addition to managing extended memory, HIMEM can effectively increase your conventional memory by making the first 64Kb of extended memory available for use as conventional memory. It's like having 704Kb of conventional memory.

On a 286- or 386-based computer, Setup automatically copies I IMEM.SYS to your hard drive and installs it in your CONFIG.SYS. Be sure you use the new version of HIMEM.SYS supplied with Windows 3 rather than an older version from a previous Windows installation. Microsoft created HIMEM.SYS specifically to work with Windows. As this book goes to press, we know of no other extended memory manager that is fully compatible with Windows 3.

SMARTDRV.SYS

SMARTDrive is a disk-cache utility that uses extended or expanded memory to improve your system's speed. SMARTDrive, like other disk-cache programs, stores in memory a copy of the latest information read from your hard drive. Then, when your application requests the same information again (as often happens), SMARTDrive can supply the information from memory much faster than reading it from disk again. Unlike other disk-cache programs, this version of SMARTDrive allows Windows to automatically reduce the memory allocated to the disk-cache and use that memory for applications.

If Setup detects the necessary memory available on your system, it automatically copies SMARTDRV.SYS to your hard drive and installs it in your CONFIG.SYS during installation. You may want to experiment with different settings for the maximum and minimum cache sizes to find the optimum settings for your system and the applications you use.

RAMDRIVE.SYS

A RAM disk is a section of memory that your computer system can use as a hard drive. The advantage of a RAM disk is that moving information to and from memory is much faster than reading and writing the same information to a physical disk. The disadvantage of a RAM disk is that you will lose the information when you turn the computer off since it is stored in volatile RAM instead of on the magnetic media of a physical disk.

A RAM disk has many uses, but perhaps the most appropriate is to store temporary files. Applications that create and use temporary files extensively will benefit greatly from the speed of the RAM disk, and the impermanent nature of the RAM disk is not a negative factor since temporary files are normally deleted when you exit an application.

RAMDrive is the RAM disk supplied with Windows. Setup copies the RAMDRIVE.SYS file to your Windows directory during installation but does not install RAMDrive in your CONFIG.SYS. You can configure a RAM disk of any size in conventional memory (not recommended), expanded memory, or extended memory. However, you should remember that any memory devoted to a RAM disk will not be available for your applications.

EMM386.SYS

EMM386 is an expanded memory emulator for 386-based systems. It can configure a block of extended memory on a 386- or 486-based computer to simulate LIM EMS 4.0 expanded memory. In 386 enhanced mode, Windows can simulate EMS memory for the applications that need it without any help from a separate EMS emulator. You'll need EMM386 only if you expect to run applications that require EMS memory outside Windows or with Windows in real mode. In many cases, the new capabilities of Windows' 386 enhanced mode will eliminate the need for any other expanded memory manager. You can simply run your DOS applications that need EMS memory from Windows.

Previously, you may have used Quarterdeck's QEMM, 386MAX from Qualitas, or another utility to perform similar functions. However, as this book goes to press, those programs conflict with Windows (although future versions may be Windows-compatible). Setup copies EMM386.SYS to your Windows directory but does not install it in your CONFIG.SYS.

EGA.SYS

If you have an EGA display, Windows needs EGA.SYS to help manage the video display for DOS applications you run from Windows in real or standard mode. If your system includes an EGA monitor, make sure your CONFIG.SYS includes the line *device = c:\windows\EGA.SYS*.

MOUSE.SYS

For mouse users (Microsoft Mouse and compatibles), Microsoft includes an updated version of the MOUSE.SYS device driver with Windows. This new version is specially modified to be compatible with Windows and the other Windows device drivers. Be sure to use the new version of MOUSE.SYS in your Windows directory rather than your original mouse driver. If you use your mouse only in Windows, you may not need a mouse driver at all. Windows includes a built-in mouse interface (at least for the Microsoft Mouse and compatibles) that doesn't require a separate mouse driver or MOUSE.COM program.

Managing swap files

Windows creates and uses three kinds of swap files. In real and standard modes, Windows uses application swap files to store the inactive application when it switches between Windows and a DOS application. In 386 enhanced mode, Windows uses a swap file on your hard drive as virtual memory. Windows can create a temporary swap file each time you enter 386 enhanced mode, or you can create a permanent swap file for Windows to use as virtual memory.

Application swap files

In real and standard modes, Windows uses application swap files to facilitate task switching between Windows and DOS applications. When you execute a DOS application from within Windows, Windows first suspends your Windows applications and swaps them from memory to a file on your hard drive thus freeing your memory for the DOS application. At the same time, Windows creates a temporary application swap file for the DOS application. If you switch back to Windows (or another DOS application) without first exiting the DOS application, Windows will suspend the DOS application, swap it to its application swap file on disk, and restore Windows to memory from the swap file. When you exit an application, Windows deletes the application swap file it created for that application.

Application swap files are temporary files that Windows automatically creates and deletes. They are hidden files, normally stored in your Windows directory, and the names begin with ~WOA. If you suspect that an abnormal exit from an application or from Windows left application swap files lingering on your disk, use the File Manager to find and delete them. See Chapter 6 for instructions on how to view hidden files with the File Manager.

386 enhanced mode swap files

In 386 enhanced mode, Windows doesn't use application swap files; it uses a different kind of swap file as virtual memory. Virtual memory is a special section of your hard drive the 386 processor can treat as additional RAM. The processor can swap large blocks of information between your hard drive and extended memory to make more memory available for data and to run more applications concurrently than would normally fit within your system's combined conventional and extended memory.

Windows can create a temporary swap file each time you start Windows in 386 enhanced mode and automatically adjust its size depending on the applications you run and your available disk space. Windows names the temporary swap file WIN386.SWP and normally creates it in your Windows directory. The temporary swap file has the advantage of being only as large as needed under the current circumstances and, since Windows automatically deletes it at the end of your Windows session, the swap file doesn't tie up hard drive space when you use Windows in real or standard mode or work outside the Windows environment entirely. The disadvantages of a temporary swap file are that it is slower than a permanent swap file, it doesn't work well if your disk is fragmented, and it doesn't offer large contiguous blocks of disk space.

As an alternative to a temporary swap file, you can create a permanent swap file on your hard drive for Windows to use as virtual memory. Using a permanent swap file is faster and more efficient than a temporary swap file. The permanent swap file creates a section of your hard drive for Windows' exclusive use, but that space is unavailable when you use Windows in real or standard mode or work outside the Windows environment.

Setup automatically offers to create a permanent swap file on your hard drive if your system will support it (a 386-based computer with 2Mb and sufficient hard drive space). You can also create, delete, or change the size of your permanent swap file at a later time with the Swapfile utility.

Swapfile

Swapfile is a utility program that will allow you to manipulate a permanent swap file Windows can use as virtual memory when it operates in 386 enhanced mode. With Swapfile, you can create a new permanent swap file, change its size, or delete it. Setup copies SWAPFILE.EXE to your hard drive during installation, but since you will rarely need Swapfile, Setup puts it in the SYSTEM subdirectory of your Windows directory (usually C:\WINDOWS\SYSTEM).

You'll need a large contiguous block of hard drive space for the permanent swap file, so you should compact your hard drive before attempting to create a permanent swap file. To use Swapfile, you'll first need to start Windows in real mode. Then, you can run the Swapfile utility from the File Manager by double-clicking on its file name (SWAPFILE.EXE). The Swapfile utility has only a few options and is fairly easy to use. For more about Swapfile, refer to the Optimizing Windows chapter of the Windows User's Guide.

A word of warning: Be sure to use only the Swapfile utility to manipulate your permanent swap file. Do not attempt to manipulate the 386SPART.PAR and SPART.PAR files with the File Manager or with DOS commands.

Windows startup files

Each time you start Windows, it refers to its initialization files for information about your system configuration and preferences. It finds this information in the WIN.INI, SYSTEM.INI, and WINSTART.BAT files, as we'll explain in this section.

WINSTART.BAT

Just as DOS automatically executes the AUTOEXEC.BAT file each time you boot your computer, Windows automatically executes its own startup batch file each time you start Windows in 386 enhanced mode. The WINSTART.BAT file is a normal DOS batch file that Windows will automatically execute if the file exists in the Windows directory or any directory in your DOS search path. WINSTART.BAT functions only with Windows in 386 enhanced mode, where it serves to separate commands and memory-resident programs (such as a 3270 terminal emulator) that are needed only by Windows applications from commands in your AUTOEXEC.BAT that both DOS and Windows applications need. By placing commands that apply only to Windows applications in the WINSTART.BAT file, Windows will know not to duplicate those commands for each DOS application it runs in 386 enhanced mode.

WIN.INI

The WIN.INI file contains a wealth of information about your Windows environment and how you have customized it for your own system and working preferences. The WIN.INI file records your preferences for everything from the color of your desktop, and the file name extensions associated with certain applications, to the deck design you selected the last time you played Solitaire. Although you often had to edit the WIN.INI to exercise various options in previous versions of Windows, that is no longer the case. Now, you can control nearly every aspect of your Windows environment with Control Panel, and the built-in control features of the other Windows applications. Windows will record your changes in the WIN.INI file; you won't need to edit it yourself.

Even though it isn't usually necessary, you can edit the WIN.INI file with Windows' Notepad accessory (or any ASCII text editor). You can also use Notepad to read the WININI.TXT file, which lists the purpose and correct syntax for each setting in the WIN.INI file.

The LOAD and RUN settings

The LOAD and RUN settings in the WIN.INI file are worth mentioning despite the fact that using them requires manually editing the WIN.INI file. With the LOAD and RUN settings you can instruct Windows to set up your desktop automatically with the applications and files you normally use.

By default, the *LOAD=* and *RUN=* lines at the top of the WIN.INI file are blank, and Windows starts with the Program Manager in the active window. You can add a list of applications and files to these lines to have Windows automatically start the applications and open the specified files when you start Windows. The LOAD and RUN settings are very similar in that both automatically start the applications you list. The difference is that LOAD minimizes each application to an icon on your desktop, while RUN runs the application in a window. If you use the RUN setting, Windows will reduce Program Manager to an icon as well.

For example, consider the following lines from a WIN.INI file:

```
load=winfile.exe    mci-mail.trm
run=schedule.cal
```

As you can see in the first line, you can list more than one item for Windows to load—each separated by a space. If you list the file name for an application, Windows will load that application as an icon on the desktop (WINFILE.EXE is the executable file for the File Manager). If you list a data file that is associated with an application (in this case, MCI-MAIL.TRM is a file that contains the settings for Terminal to use with MCI Mail), Windows will load the associated application and open the file. The RUN setting on the next line causes Windows to minimize the Program Manager to an icon, run Calendar in the active window, and load the Calendar data file SCHEDULE.CAL.

SYSTEM.INI

The SYSTEM.INI file is Windows' other major file of initialization information. It contains hardware configuration information, such as the display and keyboard drivers, and the location of the temporary swap file. Like the WIN.INI file, you can control nearly all the SYSTEM.INI options from within Windows with Windows Setup and Control Panel. You can edit the SYSTEM.INI with Notepad (or any ASCII text editor), although it should rarely be necessary. The SYSINI.TXT file contains a list of the SYSTEM.INI settings and their correct syntax. Study the information in the SYSINI.TXT file carefully before attempting to edit the SYSTEM.INI file.

Customizing Windows

The true power of a product such as Windows lies in its ability to help you work in a more natural, intuitive fashion. To take full advantage of Windows, you need to customize it to reflect *your* preferences and style. Chapter 3 discusses Control Panel, where you'll learn to change everything from printers and ports to the color and pattern of Windows' desktop and window borders.

To use Windows as a true operating environment from which you launch applications, you'll need to add your applications to the Program Manager as icons. If you instructed Setup to search your hard drive, you should be well on your way. Although it will find most major Windows-based applications and many others as well, Setup probably won't recognize all your applications. You'll need to add some of them to the Program Manager yourself. Chapter 5 discusses the Program Manager. You may need to create or edit PIF files for some of your DOS applications before they will run optimally with Windows 3. See Chapter 17 for information on using the PIF Editor. And don't forget the Associate... command in the File Manager. With it, you can instruct Windows to automatically open an application when you double-click on a file name with a given extension; see Chapter 8 for the details.

SPECIAL CASES

The standard installation procedure we've described assumes that you are installing Windows for the first time on a single, stand-alone computer. There are some additional considerations if you are upgrading to Windows 3 from a previous version of Windows, or installing Windows on a computer that is part of a network.

Upgrading previous versions of Windows

Windows 3 is an entirely new product with exciting capabilities and demanding requirements. Windows 3 adds two new operating modes—standard and 386 enhanced—that take advantage of the protected modes of 286 and 386 chips to add extended memory management and improved multitasking capabilities. Windows' user interface has been revamped completely, with proportional fonts and three-dimensional buttons. The revised and expanded Control Panel allows you to control your Windows environment with unprecedented ease. The Program Manager and the File Manager replace the aging MS-DOS Executive with powerful, graphically oriented tools. In many ways, switching to Windows 3 will be more like setting up a new environment than making an incremental upgrade to an existing one.

You cannot assume that because something worked with Windows 2.x that it will also work with Windows 3. Windows' new standard and 386 enhanced operating modes supplant other protected mode control programs, such as 386Max and DESQview. Although these programs worked with Windows 2.x (and may work with Windows 3 in real mode), two programs cannot simultaneously control your processor's protected mode and you can expect conflicts. Fortunately, thanks to the added capabilities of Windows 3, you no longer need another program to realize the potential of the protected mode of your 286- or 386-based computer.

You'll need to update your current Windows applications to take advantage of the new features of Windows' standard and 386 enhanced modes. Existing Windows-based applications must be modified to work with the advanced memory management. Check with the manufacturer of your software about upgrade procedures. Until your updates arrive, real mode is your ticket to compatibility with older software.

Despite the significant differences in Windows 3, you won't have to discard *all* your previous work establishing a Windows environment. Setup will preserve as much of your existing Windows configuration as possible. If you have been using a previous version of Windows, you have already gone through the process of installing various Windows applications and often modifying the WIN.INI file for each one. You won't have to start over and re-install every Windows application from scratch when you upgrade to Windows 3. Setup will recognize most Windows applications and install them in the Program Manager for you if you choose the Setup Applications option. Setup will also transfer the WIN.INI modifications to your new Windows 3 WIN.INI file.

To upgrade from a previous version of Windows, simply specify your existing Windows directory when Setup prompts you for the directory in which you want to install Windows 3. Setup will install Windows 3 over your older Windows files and maintain as much of your existing set up, environment preferences, and application-specific settings as possible.

If you are installing Windows in a network environment, first you'll need to decide whether to install it on an individual work station or as a shared resource on the network server. The installation procedures for these two situations are quite different; we discuss both in Chapter 8. Chapter 8 also covers using Windows' network features, such as how to use network printers with the Print Manager and how to address network disk volumes with the File Manager.

Networking Windows

Color Figures $A2$

*T*his appendix provides color versions of the black and white figures you saw in several chapters throughout this book. We grouped all the figures by chapter and used the same figure numbers.

Figure 3-6

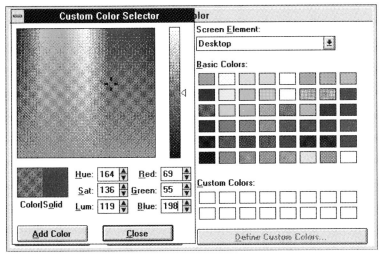

You can use the Custom Color Selector dialog box to define a new color scheme.

Table 3-2a

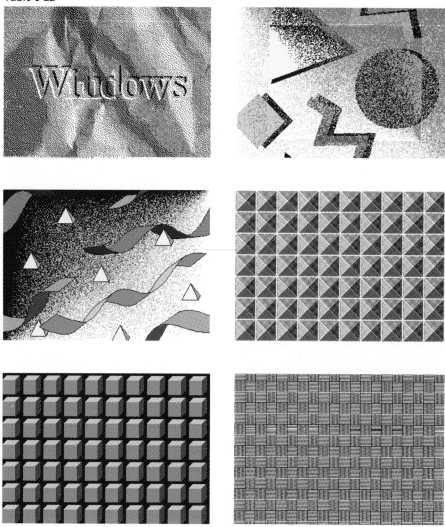

Windows offers a variety of wallpaper images.

Table 3-2b

The Chess wallpaper fills the desktop.

Figure 11-1

This poster presents a variety of images that you can create with Paintbrush.

Figure 11-18

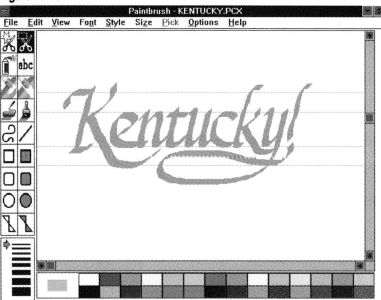

You can use the diagonal brush shape to pen calligraphy letters.

Figure 11-25

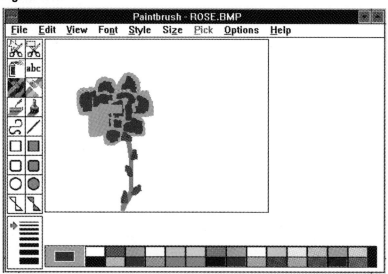

The color eraser changes only one color and leaves the other colors alone.

Figure 11-36

The View Picture command shows all the balloons.

Figure 11-52

You can leave messages on your desktop with wallpaper.

Figure 14-40

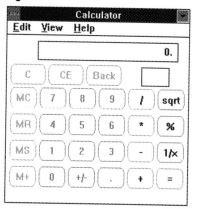

(Note: These color figures are somewhat different from your screen version. The purple buttons in the figures are blue on your screen, the blue buttons are green, and the orange buttons are red.)

The standard mode is the default view when you start Calculator for the first time.

Figure 14-42

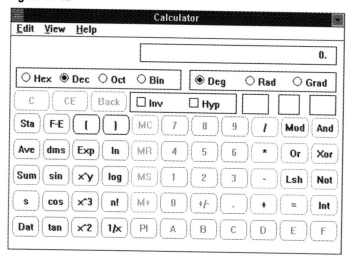

The scientific mode provides sophisticated settings and increases the number of function buttons.

Figure 15-1

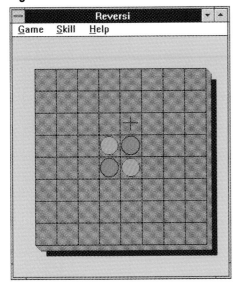

Reversi starts with four markers in the center of the board. In this example, the human player is about to make the first move.

Figure A2-1

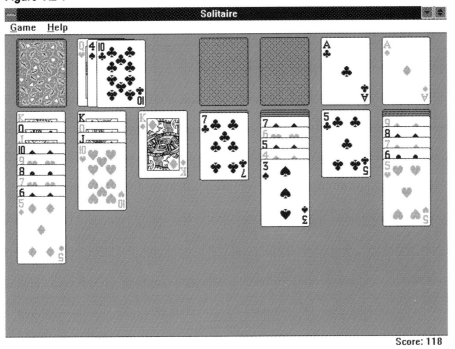

Solitaire is a computerized version of the popular single-player card game, featuring excellent graphics.

Section

Glossary
Window Maps
Index
Quick Reference

Glossary

386 enhanced mode   386 enhanced mode is one of Windows' three operating modes. It takes advantage of a 386 computer's protected mode to offer advanced memory management and multitasking. See Chapter 16 for a more complete explanation.

accelerator key   An accelerator key, a keyboard shortcut for a command, is commonly a function key, like [F5], or a combination of [Alt] or [Ctrl] with another typing or function key.

active window   Active refers to the window on the desktop currently operating in the foreground. It's the one currently selected or the one in which you're working.

active printer   An active printer is the one currently selected on Control Panel for a particular port. You can have only one active printer per port.

alert message   An alert message is a dialog box with a graphic and a message. Critical, warning, confirmation, and information messages are alert messages, which are also called message dialog boxes.

alignment icons   In Write, the alignment icons (Left-align, Centered-align, Right-align, and Justified) allow you to change a paragraph's formatting.

ANSI   ANSI, which stands for the American National Standards Institute, is the set of codes Windows uses to define characters you enter into documents and other types of files. The ANSI character set is the standard across all DOS applications and includes the 128 characters in the ASCII (American Standard Code for Information Interchange) set. The ASCII character set defines all the letters, numbers, punctuation marks, and symbols on your keyboard, as well as special instructions like paragraph breaks, page breaks, and tabs. In addition to the ASCII characters, the ANSI set also includes foreign language characters for Western European countries.

application window	An application window is a type of window that furnishes menus of commands and a work area for your data. All Windows applications run in application windows.
arrow pointer	The arrow pointer, the "mouse pointer" for all Windows applications, is used for selecting commands, activating applications, and moving windows.
arrow keys	The arrow keys consist of ↑,↓, ←,→ and typically control cursor movement.
background operation	A background operation refers to a task performed by one application while another application is running in the active window (foreground). For example, while you are editing a document in Write, the Print Manager can print a Paintbrush drawing in the background.
Calculator	Calculator is an application packaged with Windows to provide standard and scientific versions of a calculator.
Calendar	Calendar, packaged with Windows, is a tailored database that keeps track of your appointments by date and time.
Cardfile	Cardfile, a Windows package, is a simple database that has two fields and sorts on one of them (the index line).
cascade	Cascade is a process in which Windows stack windows diagonally so their title bars show.
cascading menus	Cascading menus branch from a command on a superior menu. Windows indicates that an entry on a menu is attached to a cascading menu by displaying a triangle next to the menu selection. When you click on a cascading menu command, another menu of commands appears next to the current drop-down menu.
check box	A check box lets you turn a particular dialog box option on or off. When selected (option on), a check box will contain an X.
clicking	Clicking is a mouse action that selects an item or activates a command. To click, you press the primary mouse button (the left button of a Microsoft mouse) once and immediately release it.
Clipboard	Clipboard is a Windows utility that provides a conduit to transport data between applications running in Windows. The Cut, Copy, and Paste commands found in all Windows applications use Clipboard to store and retrieve data.
Clock	Clock is an application packaged with Windows that displays the time of day either with a traditional clock face or a digital number face.
color pattern	A color pattern is a color in Paintbrush's Color Palette that uses a composite of two colors to form a third color. For example, light yellow is a combination of yellow and white.

color scheme A color scheme is a set of colors for the desktop. Windows comes with a set of preformatted color schemes including Designer, Arizona, and Fluorescent.

command buttons Command buttons are the large, gray, rectangular, 3-D buttons that appear in dialog boxes. The command associated with the button appears in black letters in the center of the button.

Control menu When you click on the box containing the dash in the upper-left corner of a window (or press [Ctrl][Esc]), Windows displays the Control menu of that window. The Control menu provides keyboard access to many window manipulations that otherwise require a mouse (for example, moving or sizing the window).

Control Panel Control Panel is a built-in Windows application that modifies your WIN.INI file to customize your Windows environment. For example, you can use the Control Panel to change screen colors and install printers.

Copy Copy is a command that duplicates selected text or graphics in the work area and places the copy in Clipboard. You can retrieve the text or graphics with the Paste command.

critical message Windows presents a dialog box with a red stop sign and a message to tell you that a critical error has occurred. Some critical messages also suggest a way to recover from the error.

crosshair pointer Whenever you work with graphics, you'll see the crosshair pointer or a variation of it. This pointer is often found in Windows' drawing application, Paintbrush.

cursor The cursor is a blinking vertical line that appears in an active desktop element in which you can enter text. The cursor is sometimes referred to as the insertion point marker.

Cut Cut is a command that removes selected text or a graphic from the work area and places it in Clipboard. You can retrieve the text or graphic with the Paste command.

DDE DDE, Dynamic Data Exchange, is a protocol that enables Windows to dynamically update data in one application with data from another application. The two applications issue the commands, and Windows provides the path for the flow of data.

desktop The desktop is the screen area on which all Windows operations take place. As the graphical representation of the memory that Windows utilizes to perform its functions, the desktop fills the entire screen, and all windows and icons appear on top of it.

desktop pattern A desktop pattern is a bit map that fills your desktop, adding a decorative accent to Windows. Windows comes with several patterns, including Weave, Scotties, and Diamonds.

dialog box	A dialog box is a Windows element that you use to define parameters or options before implementing a command. A dialog box is made up of a framed box, a title bar, a Control menu, and various option-setting elements like radio buttons and text boxes. A command or command button with an ellipsis (...) after its name indicates that a dialog box will appear before Windows processes the command.
Directory Tree	The Directory Tree, a document window of the File Manager, displays a visual representation of the directories on a floppy disk, hard drive, or network drive.
directory window	A directory window is a document window of the File Manager that displays the subdirectories and files located in a selected directory. When you activate a directory icon in the Directory Tree or in an open directory window, the File Manager opens a directory window.
display box	A display box provides a picture of the results from one or more options in a dialog box.
document window	A document window is a type of window that partitions an application window's work area so you can display and work with more than one data file at once. However, not all Windows applications are designed to use document windows.
double-clicking	A double-click refers to pressing the primary button on your mouse twice in quick succession. Double-clicking activates icons, chooses items from lists, and can even open a file.
draft quality	If you print a file with draft quality, Windows will print the file quickly (faster than proof quality) but won't include all the details that the advanced features of your printer provides.
dragging	Dragging is a mouse technique in which you point to a desktop element (such as an icon), click to select the element, then hold down the mouse button while you move the mouse. As long as you hold down the mouse button, Windows will move the desktop element in accordance with your mouse movement. When you want to release the element, release the mouse button.
drop-down list box	Drop-down list boxes allow you to choose a single option from a large list. Their lists are not immediately visible in dialog boxes. When you open a dialog box, you see only a text box containing the drop-down list box's current setting. To display the options, click on the drop-down arrow. After you make a selection, the list will disappear.
drop-down menu	A drop-down menu refers to a menu that appears below its title on a menu bar. When you click on the title of the menu, a list of options drops down.
File Manager	The File Manager is a built-in Windows application that you can use to manage all your DOS files. The File Manager creates a multiple-window environment that provides file management capabilities based on, but exceeding, those of DOS.
font	Fonts are typefaces that determine the shape, size, and spacing of characters both on your screen and on the printed page.

full-screen window
By default, Windows sets up a full-screen window for a non-Windows application when you launch it from the Program Manager or the File Manager. A full-screen window looks like a DOS screen but lacks a Control menu and a title bar.

global memory
Global memory is RAM on your PC that Windows sets aside to store files that multiple applications need to access (such as printer drivers, fonts, Clipboard, and DDE).

granularity
Granularity refers to the invisible guidelines on the desktop that Windows uses to arrange windows and icons. You can use Control Panel to vary the spacing of this invisible grid.

graphics mode
Graphics mode is a setting in an application's PIF that informs Windows that it can display images as well as text. (The opposite of graphics mode is text mode, where an application can display only text.)

group box
A group box organizes dialog box elements by function so an option is easier to find. The group box doesn't set an option itself but simply frames a number of different options under one main heading.

group window
A group window, a variant of a document window, groups icons inside the Program Manager.

guideline
Windows uses guidelines to represent the outline of a window or graphic when you resize or move it. The guidelines are tiny dashed lines that appear only as you drag the pointer.

hand pointer
While in the Help application, you use the hand pointer to jump between Help topics.

Help
Help is an on-line information application packaged with Windows. You can use Help from any application packaged with Windows to find out more about that application's keyboard, menu, and procedures. You can also get help for Help.

HIMEM.SYS
HIMEM.SYS is an extended memory manager (actually a device driver for memory) in Windows that assigns blocks of extended memory to different applications.

hot link
A hot link is a dynamic relationship created with DDE commands between two files in different applications. In a hot link, the source application automatically updates data in the receiving application whenever linked data changes.

hourglass pointer
The hourglass pointer indicates that Windows is working to complete the command you issued. While the hourglass is on the desktop, you can't issue any other commands or select desktop elements. When the pointer returns to its previous shape, you can go on to the next task.

I-beam pointer   The default arrow pointer changes into an I-beam shape whenever you point to an area in which you can enter text.

icon   An icon is a graphic with a title that represents an application, directory, file, or minimized window. You can usually select an icon by clicking on it. Double-clicking on it causes the action associated with that icon to occur. For example, double-clicking on an application icon will launch the application, while double-clicking on a minimized window icon will restore the window to its original size.

inactive   Inactive refers to the window on the desktop currently operating in the background.

increment arrows   Increment arrows are the arrows that appear on an increment box. When you click on one of the increment arrows, the number in the increment box increases or decreases.

increment box   An increment box is a text box that will accept numbers only. Windows adds a pair of arrows to the increment box so you can scroll through the range of values for an option.

information message   An information message appears in a dialog box with a lowercase *i* in a purple circle and informs you about an aspect of the command you just issued.

key repeat rate   The key repeat rate is the speed at which a key will type or repeat characters while you hold down the key.

Line Wrap   Windows' Terminal application uses the Line Wrap option to break long lines of incoming data into shorter lines that will fit on your screen, like Word Wrap does in word processors.

list box   List boxes let you choose a single option from a group of options. List boxes use scroll bars when a long list of options is available.

macro   A macro is a sequence of keystrokes and mouse movements you can have Windows repeat when you issue a command or type a key combination. You use the Recorder application packaged with Windows to record and play macros.

maximize   Maximizing an application window expands it to fill the desktop. To maximize a window, click on the Maximize box in the window's upper-right corner or issue the Maximize command on the window's Control menu. To restore a maximized window to its original size, click on the box displaying up and down arrows (the Restore box) in the window's upper-right corner or issue the Restore command on the window's Control menu.

menu bar   The menu bar, located below the title bar, is an application window that contains a series of menus listed by title (for example, the File menu).

minimize   Minimizing an application window reduces the window to an icon on the desktop. To minimize a window, click on the Minimize box in the window's upper-right corner or issue the Minimize command on the window's Control menu. To restore a minimized window to its original size, select the window's icon, then choose the Restore command from its Control menu, or simply double-click on the window's icon.

move pointer   The move pointer appears when you issue the Move command from a window's Control menu. After you see the move pointer, which includes arrows pointing in all four directions, you can use the arrow keys on your keyboard to move the window on the desktop. As you press arrow keys, Windows will move an outline of the window, but will not reposition the actual window until you press [Enter].

MS-DOS Executive   The MS-DOS Executive is the file manager for Windows 2.X.

Notepad   Notepad is a simple word processor that works only with ASCII-based text and is packaged with Windows. Notepad is handy for creating and editing DOS batch files and electronic mail messages.

Owner Display   Owner Display is a data format that uses a unique screen font supplied by an application.

Paintbrush   Paintbrush is a graphics application for "paint"-style drawing (bit map editing) which is packaged with Windows.

palette   A palette refers to a range of colors provided by Windows. Control Panel's Color dialog box and Paintbrush both provide palettes.

PIF   A PIF (short for Program Information File) contains technical information about a non-Windows application that enables Windows to optimize the way the application runs when you launch it from Windows. You can modify or create your own PIF's with the PIF Editor.

PIF Editor   PIF Editor is an application packaged with Windows that helps you customize the way an application launches and how it utilizes Windows capabilities and features, including memory and multitasking processing.

pixel   A pixel is one dot of an image that Windows displays on your screen or sends to your printer. The detail of the image depends on the number of pixels your monitor or printer can display in an area.

pointer   The pointer is a floating graphic on your screen that represents the actions of your mouse. It changes shape to reflect changes in your mouse's capabilities. For example, when you move the default arrow pointer over a word processor's document, the pointer turns into an I-beam, indicating that you can work with text.

prevent pointer   The prevent pointer, which looks like a circle with a slanted line through it, indicates that you can't relocate a desktop element where you're pointing.

466 ────────── Windows 3 Companion ──────────────────

primary mouse button

The primary mouse button is the one you use to make all your selections and perform all mouse actions. By default, it's the left button on a Microsoft mouse. You can use the Control Panel to make the right button the primary button.

Print Manager

The Print Manager is a Windows application that controls printing for all Windows applications. The Print Manager, Windows' print spooler, allows you to work with applications while you print.

printer driver

A printer driver is a device driver that tells Windows how to format data for a particular type of printer.

processor time

Processor time refers to the way the computer processor splits its time between different applications running simultaneously. If you're running Windows in 386 enhanced mode, you can define the size of the timeslice (the processor's basic time unit) with Control Panel.

Program Manager

The Program Manager is a built-in Windows application that is a program execution shell. That is, it's an application devoted to launching other programs. The Program Manager presents each application as an icon, which you can launch by double-clicking on it.

proof quality

If you print your file with proof quality, Windows will use all the advanced features of your printer to produce the highest quality image.

protected mode

Protected mode is the operating mode of the computer's 80286, 80386, or 80486 processor chip that enables extended memory management and other advanced features—as opposed to the chip's real mode. See Chapter 16 for more information.

push button

A command button with two chevrons (>>) next to the command is called a push button. Push buttons expand the dialog box to include more options.

queue

A queue is a list or a waiting line. In Windows, a queue keeps track of which file is next in line for a printer in the Print Manager.

radio button

Radio buttons allow you to choose a single option from a group of options, much as you'd choose one answer to a question on a multiple-choice exam. A radio button looks like a small circle, and when selected, looks like a circle with a dot in it.

real mode

Real mode is one of Windows' three operating modes. It provides maximum compatibility with nearly all computers and software since it operates within the capabilities of the 8088 processor chip—the brains of the original IBM-PC and compatibles. The 80286, 80386, and 80486 processor chips also have a "real mode" for compatibility with the 8088 and the software designed for that chip. See Chapter 16 for more information.

Recorder

The Recorder is a Windows application that records keystrokes and mouse movements as a macro and plays them back when you issue a key combination such as [Ctrl]*n,* where *n* is a letter you assign.

restore	When you restore a window, you return it to its original size. You can restore an icon representing a minimized window or restore a maximized window to its smaller, original size on the desktop.

Reversi	Reversi is a board game packaged with Windows. It's a version of the classic game of Othello.

scaling	Scaling refers to enlarging or reducing an image. You can vary scaling when you set up certain types of printers.

screen capture	A screen capture is a graphic image (bit map) of your PC's screen. In Windows, you can capture the entire desktop by pressing [Print Screen] and copying it into Clipboard. If you press [Alt][Print Screen], you'll capture only the active desktop element such as a window or dialog box. You can retrieve and manipulate the image in Paintbrush. (We captured some of the figures in this book using this technique.)

scroll bar	A scroll bar lets you navigate within a window by using the vertical or horizontal bars located at the right and bottom of a window, respectively. If you click on the arrows at the ends of a scroll bar, you'll move one line at a time. You can drag the slider to move more quickly.

shell	A shell is a variation of an application window from which you can launch other applications. The Program Manager and File Manager are both shells.

shortcut key	A shortcut key is a keystroke or sequence of keystrokes that activate a command or Recorder macro. Accelerator keys are also shortcut keys.

Sizing pointers	These pointers let you adjust the size of a window on the desktop by dragging a window's frame.

slider	A slider is the square on a scroll bar that indicates the cursor's or selection's current location in a document or in a list. You can drag the slider to change position.

SMARTDrive	SMARTDrive is a disk-cache utility that uses extended or expanded memory to improve your system's speed by storing, in RAM, the latest information read from your hard drive.

Solitaire	Solitaire is a card game packaged with Windows. Its rules follow the traditional game of Klondike.

standard mode	Standard mode is one of Windows' three operating modes. It uses a 286 computer's protected mode to address extended memory up tp 16Mb. See Chapter 16 for more information.

swap file	A swap file is a portion of your hard drive that Windows sets aside when it installs its files. Windows uses this part of your hard drive for temporary storage when RAM fills up. In 386 enhanced mode, Windows can treat the swap as if it was RAM (virtual memory). You can use the Swapfile utility to make changes to the swap file as described in Appendix 1.

system font   The system font for Windows is Helvetica (10-point proportional). All the desktop elements use the system font for text appearing on the title bar, menu bar, status bars, dialog boxes, list boxes, text boxes, message boxes, etc.

system message   Windows informs you of an error that occurs at the system level with a system message in an unnamed special dialog box. These messages usually concern devices like disk drives or major programming bugs.

SYSTEM.INI   SYSTEM.INI stores your Windows system information, some of which is supplied with the Windows Setup application. This information includes type of monitor, keyboard, mouse, PC, network, and others.

Task Manager   Task Manager is a Windows utility that manages the multiple applications on the desktop and provides access to them with the Task List dialog box. You can open the Task List dialog box by pressing [Ctrl][Esc] or by double-clicking on the desktop.

Terminal   Terminal is a communications application packaged with Windows.

text box   Text boxes allow you to answer a dialog box's "fill in the blank" questions. You type any character you want into a text box.

text mode   If your non-Windows application runs only in text mode (as specified in its PIF), then it displays only character information and doesn't display any graphic images.

tile   If you use the Tile command on the Window menu to tile a series of windows, Windows will divide the available space for windows (either the desktop or a shell's work area) among all the windows so you can see the work area of each window. You can also press [Shift][F4] to tile windows.

title bar   The title bar, a line of information appearing at the top of every window, presents the name of the application and the file it's working with (if applicable). The color of the title bar tells you if the window is active or inactive. By default, an active window has a blue title bar and an inactive one has a white title bar.

tracking speed   Tracking speed refers to the pace of Windows' effort to keep up with you when you drag the mouse.

wallpaper   Wallpaper is a Paintbrush image that you can use to decorate your desktop. It can fill all or part of your screen. Windows comes with wallpaper images, such as Chess, Paper, and Pyramid.

warm link   DDE links data between between applications. In a warm link, the source application updates data in the receiving applications only when the receiving application (or user) approves the transfer.

warning message

A warning message appears in a dialog box containing an exclamation mark in a yellow circle and cautions you that a command will permanently change the status of a file. For example, the File Manager will present a warning message before it lets you delete a file. If Windows needs more information to complete the operation you began, it will present a dialog box with a question mark inside a green circle and a message to warn you and ask for additional information.

WIN.INI

WIN.INI stores your Windows environment preferences, such as screen colors or installed printers, most of which are set with the Control Panel.

window

A window is a framed area in which Windows runs an application, displays a document, or performs a task. Windows provides several types of windows, but the two you will use most are application and document windows.

Windows Setup

Windows Setup is an application packaged with Windows that lets you change your installed hardware specifications and stores your settings in SYSTEM.INI and WIN.INI.

WinPopup

WinPopup is an application supplied as part of Microsoft LAN Manager that allows you to send messages to other Windows users on the network.

work area

The work area is the space in a window in which you can enter and manipulate information. For example, when you use Cardfile, you can open multiple cards, each of which has its own work area for data. In the File Manager, you can open multiple directory windows that each has its own work area.

workspace

The workspace is the part of an application window in which you can place additional windows and icons representing data. For example, the workspace for Cardfile displays windows and icons representing cards, and the File Manager's workspace displays various directory windows. Each window you open on the workspace has its own work area in which you can manipulate data.

Write

Write is a word processing application packaged with Windows.

Window Maps

The menu maps on the following pages show you all the commands available in an application with their shortcut keys and display the options and parameters in the dialog boxes. We've organized the maps by application. Each section starts with the top portion of the application's window showing the title bar and the menu bar to provide some context for the menus that appear below.

An ellipsis following a command, such as Save As..., indicates there is a dialog box associated with the command. We included most, but not all, of the dialog boxes in the menu maps. Due to space limitations, we left out many that contain only a single text box or list box and the inevitable OK and Cancel buttons. In cases where a push button (e.g., Color Pallette >>) expands a dialog box to display additional options, we show the expanded version in the menu maps. Please note: Depending on your hardware and installed options, you may notice slight differences between the menus and dialog boxes we show and the ones on your system.

The first set of menus are from the Program Manager. Included with the Program Manager's menus are the Control Menu and Task Manager. Following the Program Manager, you will find the menus for the File Manager, Control Panel, and Windows Setup, and the menu maps for the standard applications included with Windows. To avoid repetition, we show the dialog boxes for a typical File menu first since nearly all applications have the same basic File menu commands.

Program Manager

Program Manager
Menus

Control Menu

386 Settings/
Task List

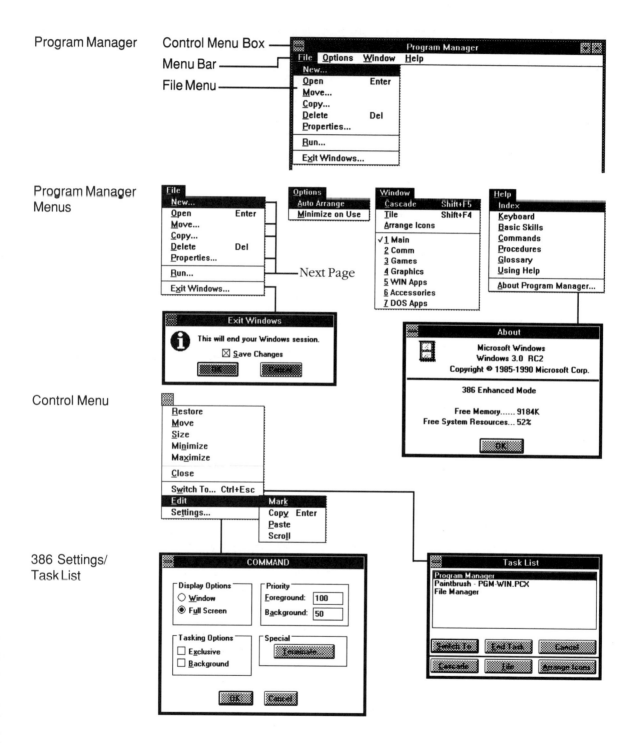

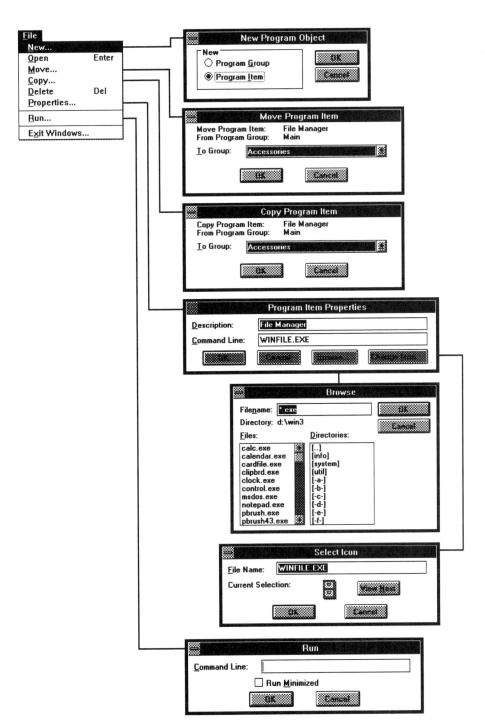

Program Manager
File Menu

File Manager

File Menu

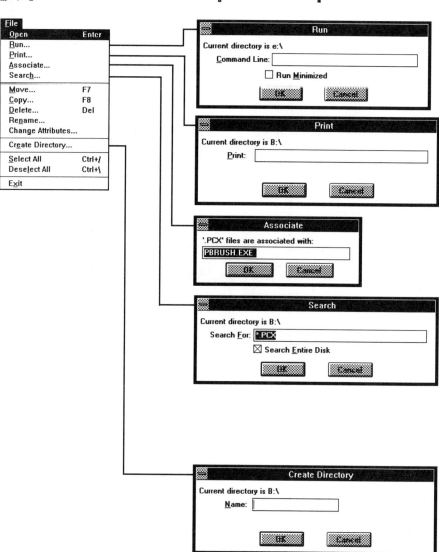

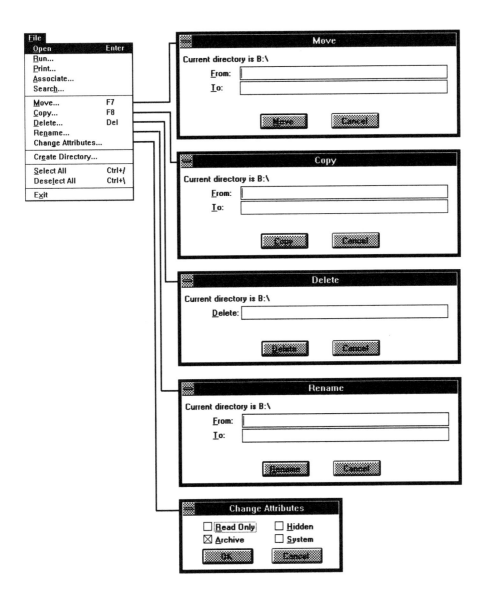

File Manager
File Menu

File Manager
Disk Menu

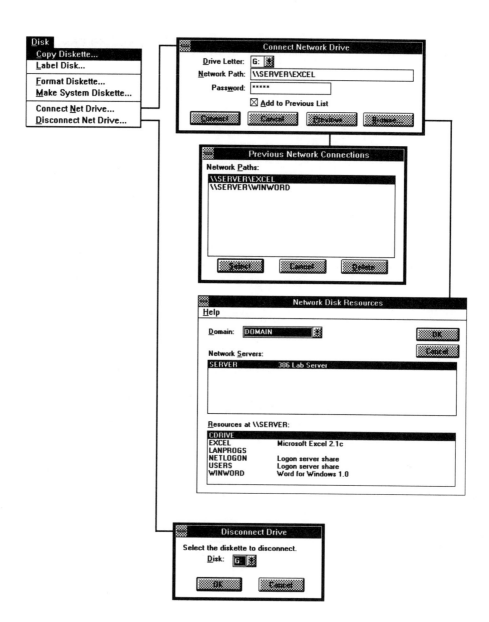

Disk
Copy Diskette...
Label Disk...

Format Diskette...
Make System Diskette...

Connect Net Drive...
Disconnect Net Drive...

Connect Network Drive
Drive Letter: G:
Network Path: \\SERVER\EXCEL
Password: *****
☒ Add to Previous List

Previous Network Connections
Network Paths:
\\SERVER\EXCEL
\\SERVER\WINWORD

Network Disk Resources
Help

Domain: DOMAIN

Network Servers:
SERVER   386 Lab Server

Resources at \\SERVER:
CDRIVE
EXCEL   Microsoft Excel 2.1c
LANPROGS
NETLOGON   Logon server share
USERS   Logon server share
WINWORD   Word for Windows 1.0

Disconnect Drive
Select the diskette to disconnect.
Disk: G:

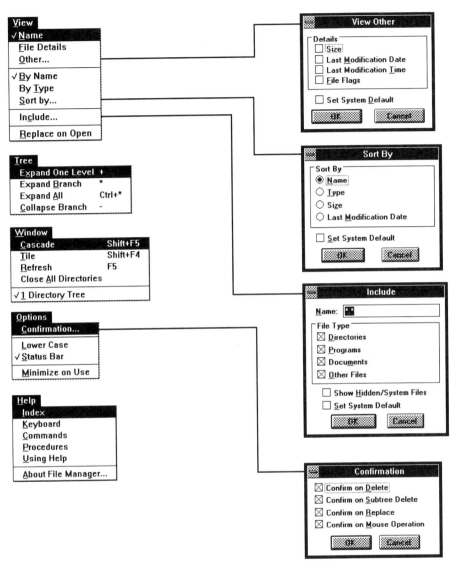

File Manager

Control Panel

Settings Menu

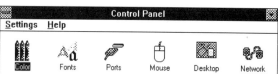

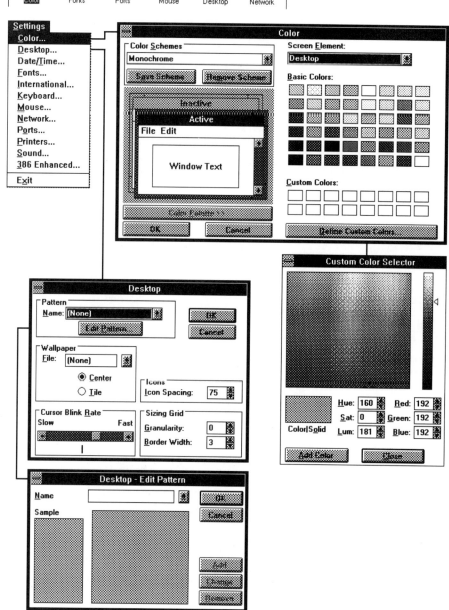

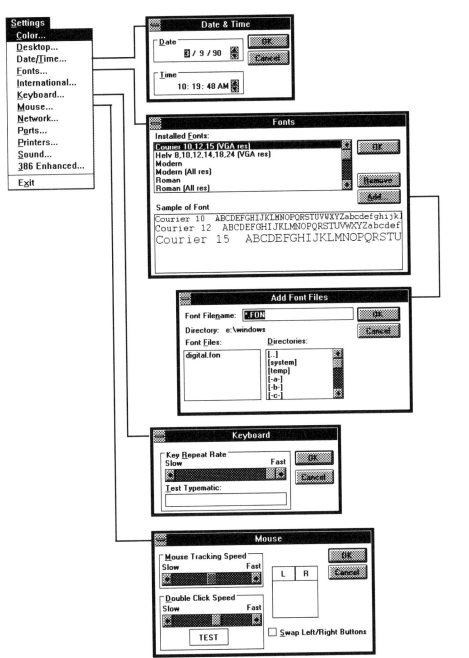

Control Panel
Settings Menu

Control Panel
Settings Menu

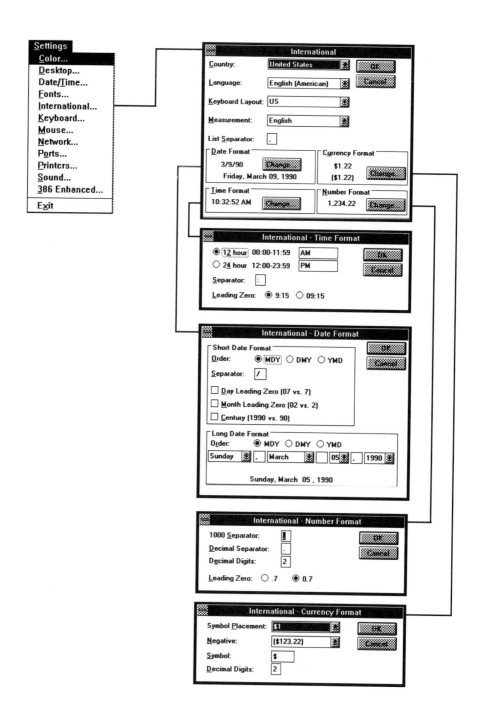

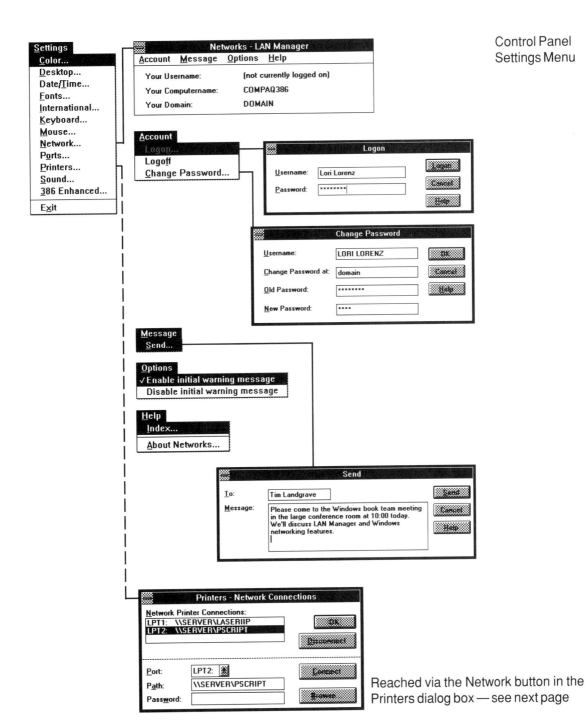

Control Panel
Settings Menu

Reached via the Network button in the
Printers dialog box — see next page

Control Panel
Settings Menu

Also available by
selecting Printer Setup...
from most File menus

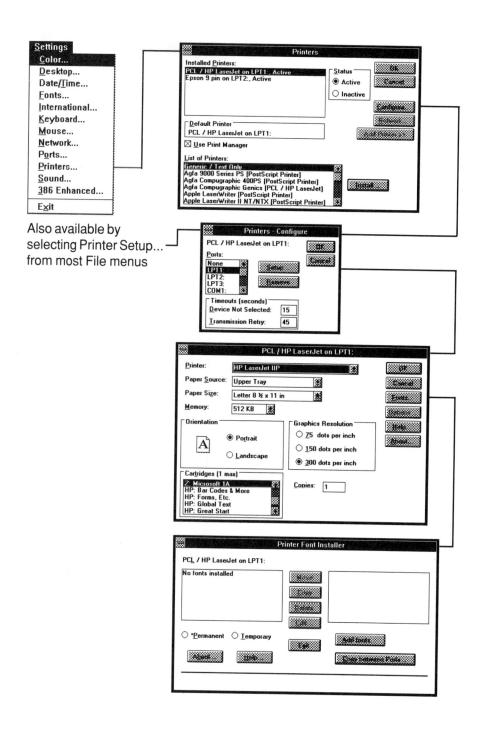

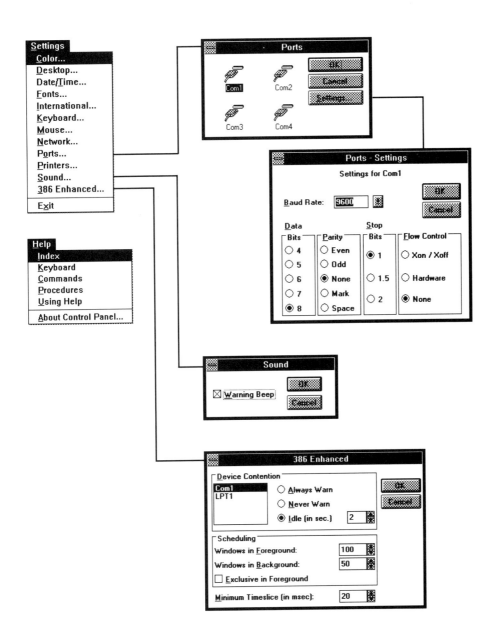

Windows Setup

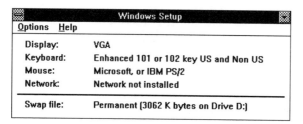

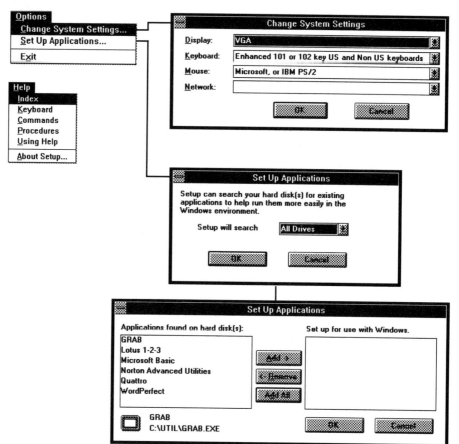

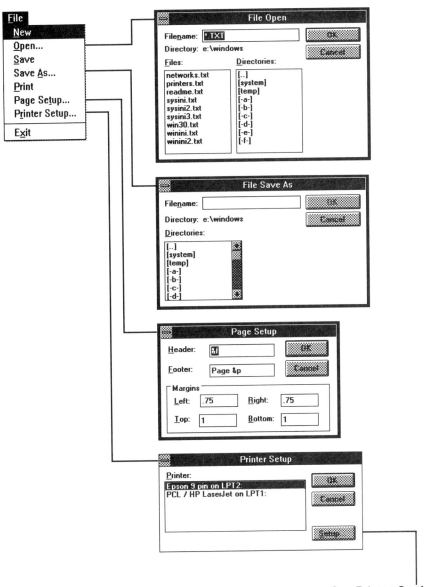

Typical File Menu

See Printer-Configure
in Control Panel

Print Manager

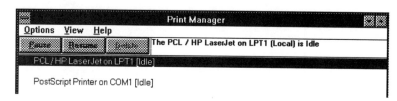

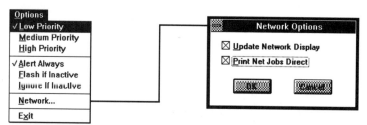

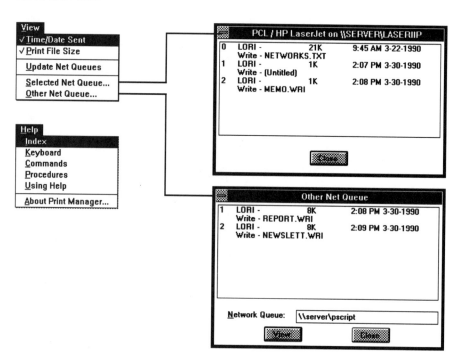

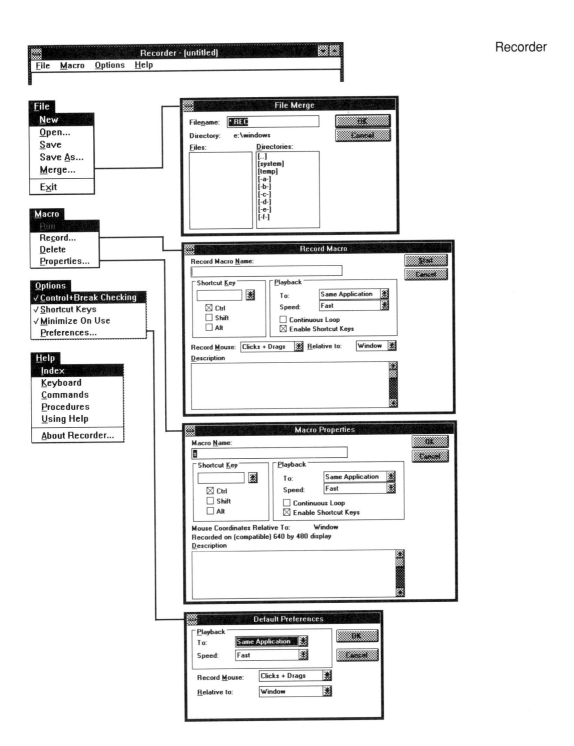

Recorder

Terminal

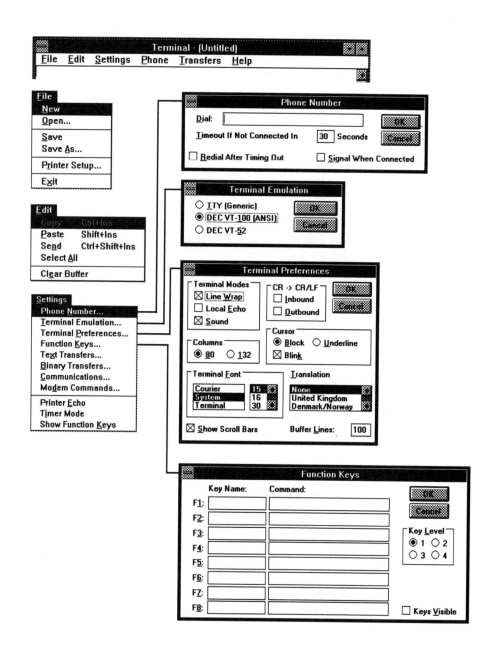

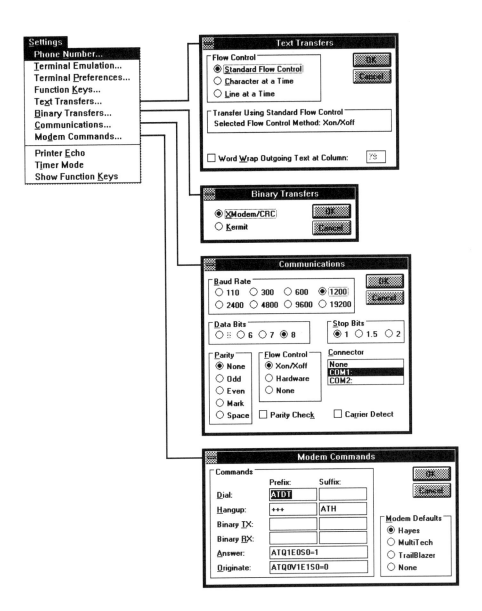

Terminal
Settings Menu

Terminal

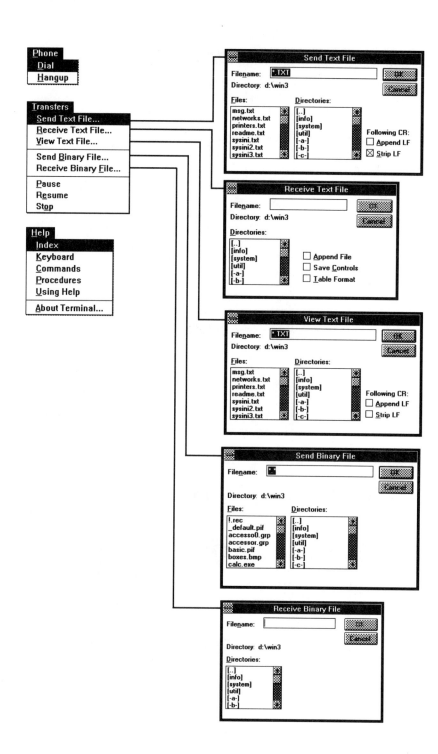

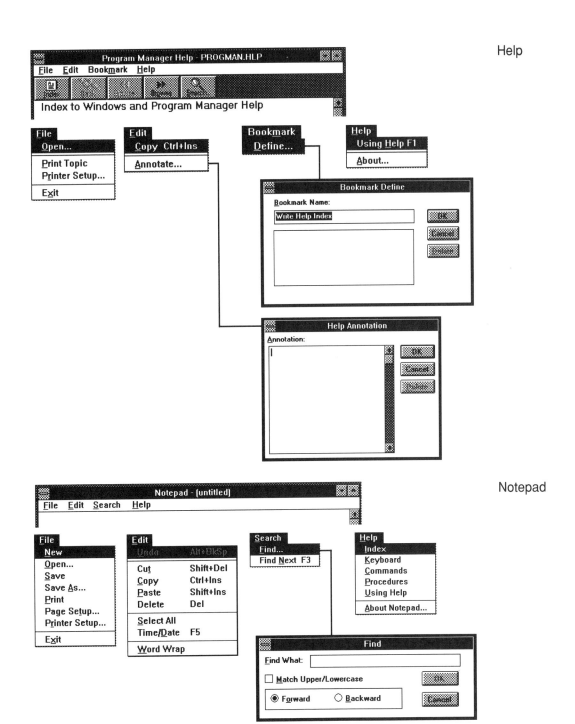

Help

Notepad

Paintbrush

File Menu

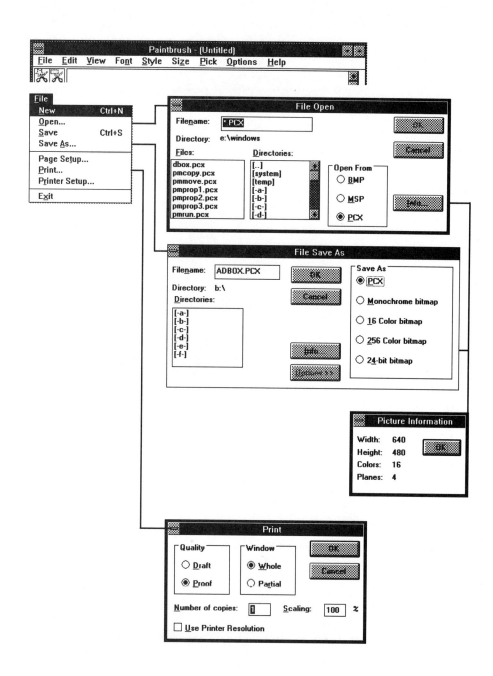

Paintbrush

Edit

Undo	Alt+BackSpace
Cut	Shift+Del
Copy	Ctrl+Ins
Paste	Shift+Ins
Copy To...	
Paste From...	

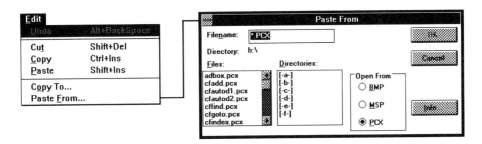

Paste From

Filename: *.PCX

Directory: b:\

Files:
adbox.pcx
cfadd.pcx
cfautod1.pcx
cfautod2.pcx
cffind.pcx
cfgoto.pcx
cfindex.pcx

Directories:
[-a-]
[-b-]
[-c-]
[-d-]
[-e-]
[-f-]

Open From
○ BMP
○ MSP
◉ PCX

OK
Cancel
Info

View

Zoom In	Ctrl+Z
Zoom Out	Ctrl+O
View Picture	Ctrl+C
√ Tools and Linesize	
√ Palette	
Cursor Position	

Font

Terminal
Helv
Courier
Tms Rmn
Symbol
Roman
Script
Modern
√ System

Style

√ Normal

Bold	Ctrl+B
Italic	Ctrl+I
Underline	Ctrl+U
Outline	
Shadow	

Size

6	24	44	66
8	26	45	70
10	28	48	72
12	30	50	74
√ 15 *	32	52	75
16 *	36	54	76
18	37	56	78
19	38	57	80
20	40	60	84
22	42	64	

Pick

Flip Horizontal
Flip Vertical
Inverse
Shrink + Grow
Tilt
Clear

Options

Image Attributes...
Brush Shapes...
Edit Colors...
Get Colors...
Save Colors...

Next Page

Help

Index
Keyboard
Commands
Procedures
Tools
Using Help
About Paintbrush...

Paintbrush
Options Menu

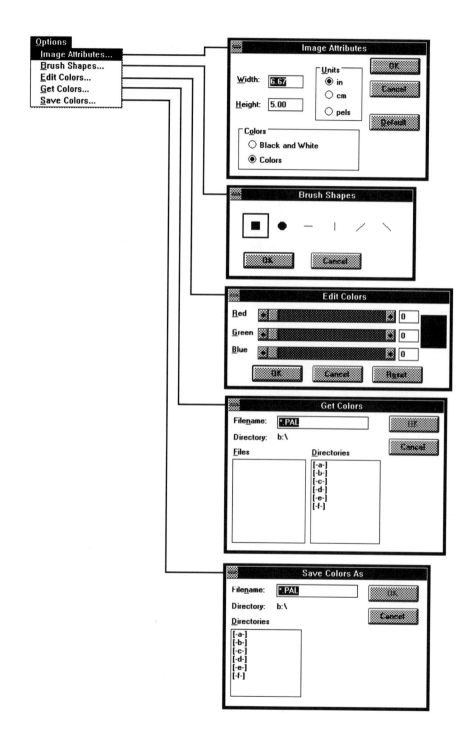

Calendar

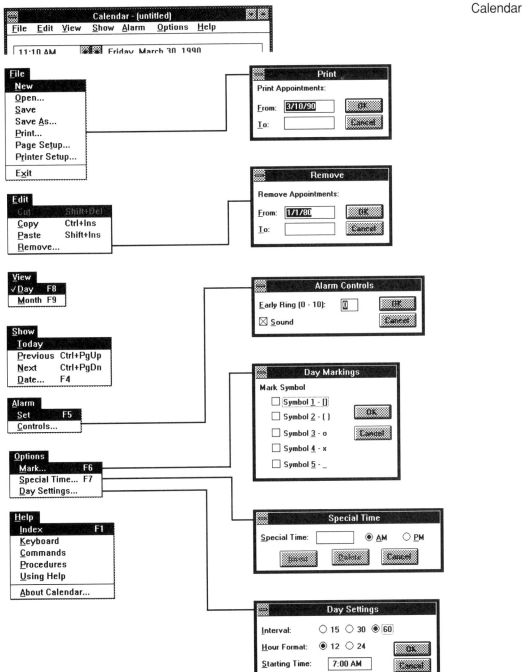

Write

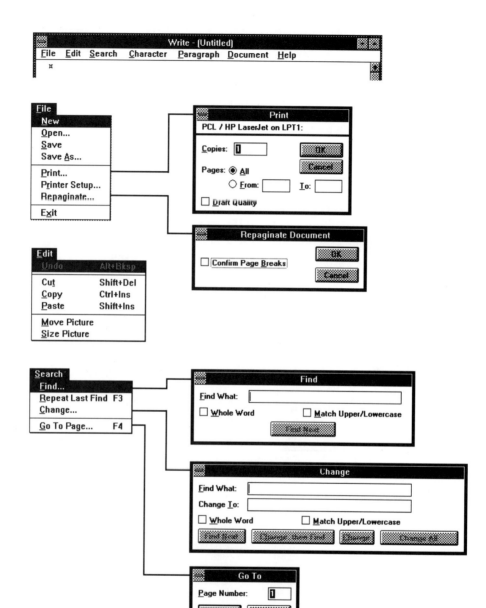

Write

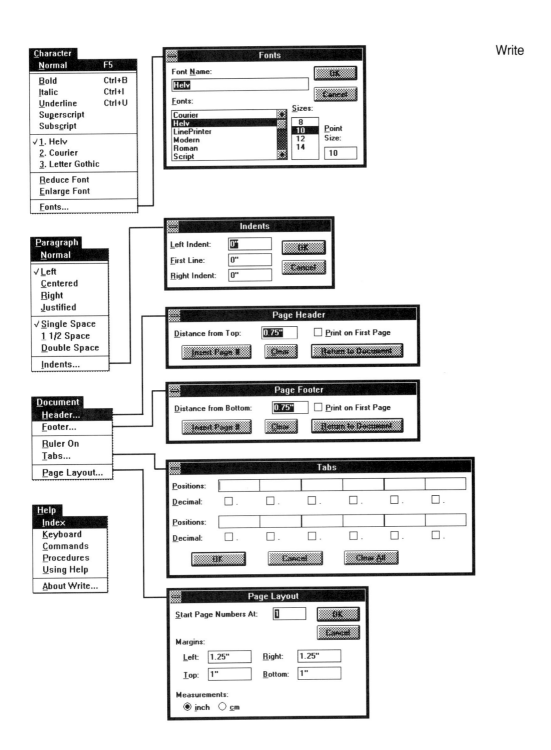

Cardfile

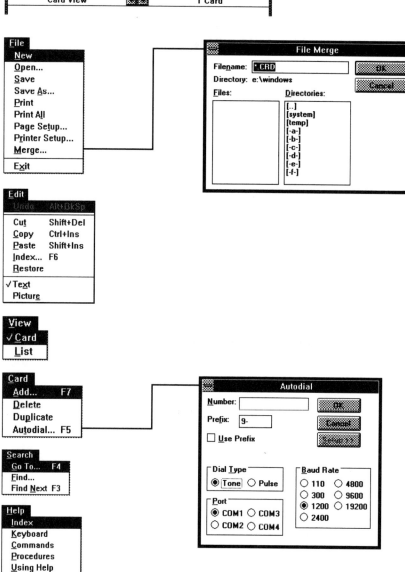

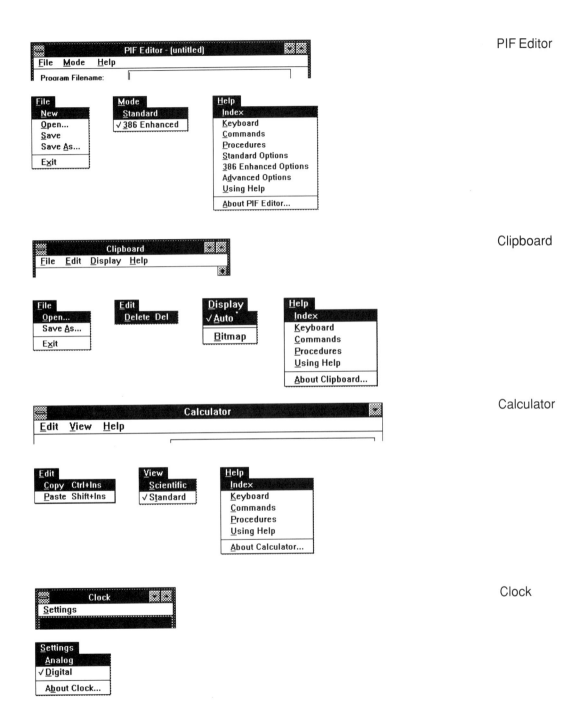

PIF Editor

Clipboard

Calculator

Clock

Solitaire

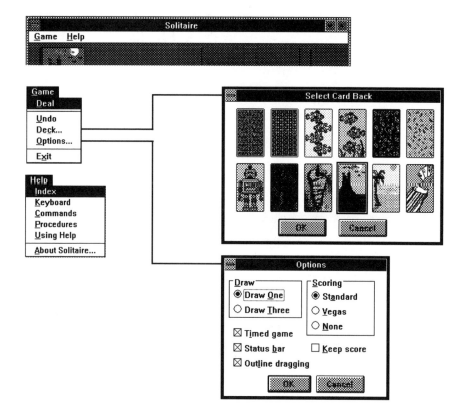

Reversi

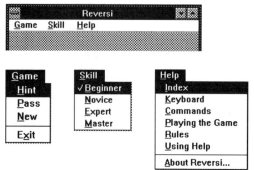

INDEX

X

Windows 3 Companion Quick Reference

Windows Keys

Keystroke(s)	Function
[Alt][Spacebar]	Opens the Control menu for an application window
[Alt][Hyphen]	Opens the Control menu for a document window
[Alt][F4]	Closes a window
[Alt][Escape]	Cycles through application windows and icons
[Alt][Tab]	Switches to the next application window, restoring applications that are running as icons
[Alt][Enter]	Switches a non-Windows application between running in a window and running full screen
↓ ↑ ← →	Move a window when you have chosen the Move command from the Control menu, or change the size of a window when you have chosen Size
[Ctrl][Tab]	Cycles through document windows and icons
[Ctrl][Esc]	Switches to Task List dialog box
[PrintScreen]	Copies an image of the screen contents into Clipboard
[Alt][PrintScreen]	Copies an image of the active window into Clipboard
[Ctrl][F4]	Closes the active document window
[F1]	Displays the Help Index for an application; displays Index to Using Help when Help window is open
[Shift][F1]	Changes the pointer to a question mark to access Help on a specific command, screen element, or key

Menu Keys

Keystroke(s)	Function
[Alt] or [F10]	Selects first menu on the menu bar
[Alt]n	Opens the menu whose underlined letter matches n
n	Chooses the menu or command whose underlined letter matches n

Menu Keys continued

← →	Move among menus
↑ ↓	Move among menu items
[Enter]	Chooses the selected menu item
[Escape]	Cancels the selected menu

Dialog Box Keys

Keystroke(s)	Function
[Tab]	Moves to the next item
[Shift][Tab]	Moves to the previous item
[Alt]n	Moves to the item with a title that has underlined letter n
↑ ↓ ← →	Move between options in a group, or move the cursor up or down in a list or left or right in a text box
[Home]	Moves to the top item in a list box, or the first character in a text box
[End]	Moves to the last item in a list box, or the last character in a text box
[Page Up] [Page Down]	Scrolls up or down one boxful of data at a time in a list box
[Alt] ↓	Opens a drop-down list box
[Alt] ↓ or [Alt] ↑	Selects item in a drop-down list box
[Spacebar]	Selects or cancels a highlighted item in a list box or a check box
[Ctrl]/ (slash)	Selects all items in a list box
[Ctrl]\ (backslash)	Cancels all selections except the active item in a list box
[Shift] ↑, ↓	Extends the list box highlight in the direction of the arrow
[Shift][Home]	Extends the text box highlight to the first character
[Shift][End]	Extends the text box highlight to the last character
[Backspace]	Deletes one character at a time from left of cursor
[Enter]	Selects the highlighted item (if any) and executes active command button
[Esc] or [Alt][F4]	Closes or exits a dialog box without completing any commands

File Manager Keys

Keystroke(s)	Function
In the Directory Tree:	
[Home]	Selects root directory
[End]	Selects last listed directory
→	Selects first subdirectory of selected directory
←	Selects directory in the previous directory level
[Page Up]	Selects directory one window up from current one
[Page Down]	Selects directory one window down from current one
[Ctrl] ↑	Selects previous directory in same level
[Ctrl] ↓	Selects next directory in same level
n	Selects directory whose name starts with n
[Ctrl]n	Selects and activates disk drive called n
- (hyphen)	Collapses highlighted directory
+ (plus)	Expands highlighted directory
* (asterisk)	Expands entire branch of highlighted directory
[Ctrl]* (asterisk)	Expands all directory branches
[Tab]	Selects current disk drive
In directory windows:	
↑	Selects file or directory above current one
↓	Selects file or directory below current one
[End]	Selects last file or directory in list
[Home]	Selects first file or directory in list
[Page Up]	Selects first file or directory in previous window
[Page Down]	Selects last file or directory in next window
n	Selects file or directory whose name starts with n
[Ctrl]/ (slash)	Selects all files in list
[Ctrl]\ (backslash)	Deselects all files in list
[Shift][F8]	Begins selecting files or directories out of sequence and ends selection

File Manager Keys continued

In the File Manager:	
[Enter]	Opens directory or file
[F7]	Issues Move... command
[F8]	Issues Copy... command
[Delete]	Issues Delete... command
[Shift][F5]	Cascades all document windows
[Shift][F4]	Tiles all document windows
[F5]	Issues Refresh command
[Ctrl][Tab] or [Ctrl][F6]	Moves between document windows
[Alt] drag	Moves the highlighted file or directory to destination on different drive
[Ctrl] drag	Copies the highlighted file or directory to destination on same drive

Program Manager Keys

Keystroke(s)	Function
↑ ↓ → ←	Move among items within group window
[Ctrl][F6] or [Ctrl][Tab]	Moves among group windows and icons
[Alt][Spacebar]	Opens Control menu
[Alt]	Closes Control menu
[Enter]	Starts highlighted program
[Shift][F4]	Tiles open windows
[Shift][F5]	Cascades open windows
[Ctrl][F4]	Closes active group window
[Alt][F4]	Exits Windows

Print Manager Keys

Keystroke(s)	Function
[Ctrl] ↑	Moves selected file up in print queue
[Ctrl] ↓	Moves selected file down in print queue
[Alt]D	Deletes file from print queue
[Alt]P	Pauses printing
[Alt]R	Resumes printing

CUT HERE

Windows 3 Companion Quick Reference

Cursor Movement Keys

Press this	To move
↑	Up one line
↓	Down one line
←	Left one character
→	Right one character
[Ctrl] →	Right one word
[Ctrl] ←	Left one word
[Home]	To beginning of line
[End]	To end of line
[Page Up]	Up one window
[Page Down]	Down one window
[Goto] →	To next sentence
[Goto] ←	To previous sentence
[Goto] ↓	To next paragraph
[Goto] ↑	To previous paragraph
[Goto][Page Up]	To previous page
[Goto][Page Down]	To next page
[Ctrl][Home]	To beginning of document
[Ctrl][End]	To end of document
[Ctrl][Page Up]	To top of window
[Ctrl][Page Down]	To bottom of window

Clipboard Keys

Keystroke(s)	Function
[Shift][Delete]	Cuts highlighted selection and places it on Clipboard
[Ctrl][Insert]	Copies highlighted selection and places it on Clipboard
[Shift][Insert]	Pastes selection from Clipboard into document at cursor
[Delete]	Clears the contents of Clipboard
[PrintScreen]	Copies entire screen onto Clipboard
[Alt][PrintScreen]	Copies active window onto Clipboard

Text Selection Keys

Press this	To select
[Shift] ← [Shift] →	One character to the left or right; or if the character is selected and you move back over it, to cancel selection
[Shift] ↑ , [Shift] ↓	One line of text up or down; or if the line is selected, to cancel selection
[Shift][Page Up]	Text up one window; repeat to cancel selection
[Shift][Page Down]	Text down one window; repeat to cancel selection
[Shift][Home]	Text to beginning of line
[Shift][End]	Text to end of line
[Ctrl][Shift] ←	Previous word
[Ctrl][Shift] →	Next word
[Ctrl][Shift][Home]	Text to beginning of document
[Ctrl][Shift][End]	Text to end of document

Editing Keys

Keystroke(s)	Function
[Backspace]	Deletes a character to the left of the cursor; also deletes selected text
[Delete]	Deletes a character to the right of the cursor; also deletes selected text
[Alt][Backspace]	Undoes the previous editing command or function
[Shift][Delete]	Deletes selected text and places it on Clipboard
[Ctrl][Insert]	Copies selected text on Clipboard
[Shift][Insert]	Inserts, or pastes, text from Clipboard into document at cursor

Recorder Keys

Keystroke(s)	Function
[Ctrl][Break]	Halts recording or replaying macro

CUT HERE

Calculator Keys

Keystroke(s)	Function
+, -, *, /	Adds, Subtracts, Multiplies, Divides
[F9]	Applies positive or negative sign
. (period) or , (comma)	Inserts decimal point
%	Calculates percent
= or [Enter]	Calculates or Equals
R	Calculates reciprocal
[Backspace] or ←	Deletes last number entered
[Esc]	Clears calculation
[Delete]	Clears last function or displayed number
[Ctrl]P	Adds displayed number to value in memory
[Ctrl]C	Clears memory
[Ctrl]R	Recalls value from memory
[Ctrl]M	Stores value in memory
@	Takes square root of displayed number

Paintbrush Keys

Keystroke(s)	Function
[Insert]	Equivalent to clicking left mouse button
[Delete]	Equivalent to clicking right mouse button
[F9][Insert]	Same as double-clicking left mouse button
[F9][Delete]	Same as double-clicking right mouse button
[Shift][Page Up]	Moves left one screen
[Shift][Page Down]	Moves right one screen
[Tab]	Moves pointer counterclockwise among Toolbox, Linesize, Palette, & drawing areas
[Shift][Tab]	Moves pointer clockwise among Toolbox, Linesize, Palette, and drawing areas

Notepad Keys

Keystroke(s)	Function
[F3]	Issues Find Next command
[F5]	Issues Time/Date command

Terminal Keys

Keystroke(s)	Function
[Ctrl][Insert]	Copies selection onto Clipboard
[Shift][Insert]	Sends Clipboard contents to remote system
[Ctrl][Shift][Insert]	Sends selected text to remote system
[Ctrl][Alt][F1]-[F8]	Executes one of 32 user-defined commands

Calendar Keys

Keystroke(s)	Function
In Day view:	
↑	Moves to the time above
↓ or [Enter]	Moves to the time below
[Page Up]	Moves to the previous screen
[Page Down]	Moves to the next screen
[Ctrl][Home]	Moves to the starting time
[Ctrl][End]	Moves to 12 hours after starting time
[Tab]	Moves between appointment area and scratch pad
[Ctrl][Page Up]	Issues Next command
[Ctrl][Page Down]	Issues Previous command
In Month view:	
↑, ↓	Moves to week above/below
[Page Up]	Moves to previous month
[Page Down]	Moves to next month
[Tab]	Moves between date and scratch pad
[Enter]	Changes to Day view
[Ctrl][Page Up]	Issues Next command
[Ctrl][Page Down]	Issues Previous command

Write Keys

Keystroke(s)	Function
[Ctrl][Shift]-(hyphen)	Inserts optional hyphen
[Ctrl][Enter]	Inserts manual page break
[F3]	Issues Repeat Last Find command
[Alt][F6]	Switches between document and Page Header or Page Footer dialog box
[F5]	Selects Normal style
[Ctrl]B	Selects Bold style
[Ctrl]I	Selects Italic style
[Ctrl]U	Selects Underline style

Cardfile Keys

Keystroke(s)	Function
[Page Down]	Scrolls forward one card
[Page Up]	Scrolls backward one card
[Ctrl][Home]	Brings first card in file to front
[Ctrl][End]	Brings last card in file to front
[Ctrl]n	Displays first card whose index line begins with n
↓, ↑	Scrolls forward/backward one card

CUT HERE

Microsoft*University***

Training That Makes Sense

At Microsoft University, we believe the proof of excellent training is in a student's ability to **apply** it. That's not a complicated philosophy. And, it's not a new idea. But it does represent an uncommon approach to training in the microcomputer industry, mainly because it requires extensive technical and educational resources, as well as leading-edge programming expertise.

When you attend Microsoft University, our courses take you to the heart of our microcomputer software architecture. Lab sessions provide practical, hands-on experience and show you how to develop and debug software more efficiently. Our qualified instructors explain the philosophy and principles that drive our systems designs.

OUR LAB-BASED DISTINCTION

Because our courses are lab-based, when you graduate from Microsoft University, you'll begin applying what you've learned immediately. Throughout our courses, you'll be designing a software application that demonstrates the principles you've just learned in class.

The power of our sheepskin pays off in the increased knowledge and time savings as soon as you begin your next development project.

PLOT YOUR OWN COURSE

Our curriculum allows you to customize your course of study from timely, fundamental courses for support personnel to highly focused, technical courses for sophisticated developers. We offer courses on Microsoft Windows,™ Microsoft OS/2, Microsoft OS/2 Presentation Manager, Microsoft LAN Manager, Microsoft SQL Server, and Microsoft C.

TIME IS OF THE ESSENCE

To find out more about Microsoft University, call our registrar at (206) 867-5507, extension 604. We'll send you our current course schedule, which describes our courses in detail and provides complete registration information for our campus facilities in Seattle, Boston, and Baltimore, as well as our growing, nationwide network of Microsoft University Authorized Training Centers.

Microsoft University also offers our courses on-site at your location, when it's convenient for you and your staff. To find out more about hosting an on-site course, contact the Microsoft University Sales Manager at (206) 867-5507, extension 604.

Our courses fill up quickly—so don't delay.

▬▬ ▬▬ ▬▬ ▬▬ ▬▬ ▬▬ ▬▬ ▬▬ ▬▬ ▬▬ ▬▬ ▬▬ ▬▬ ▬▬ ▬▬ ▬▬ ▬▬ ▬▬

I'D LIKE TO KNOW MORE!

☐ Please send me the most current course schedule.

☐ Please send me the Microsoft University catalog.

☐ Please have a representative call me regarding an on-site course for

_____
Course / Topic

☐ Please send me more information on the Authorized Training Center program.

☐ Please send me the latest information on The Lecture Series.™ *

☐ Please send me more information on the following Microsoft University courses:

  ☐ MS® OS/2   ☐ Microsoft SQL Server

  ☐ MS OS/2 Presentation Manager   ☐ Microsoft Windows™

  ☐ MS LAN Manager   ☐ Microsoft C

When it's available, please send me information on:

☐ Microsoft University Technical Training Video Courses

_____
Course / Topic

* Seminars and lectures on highly focused topics

PLEASE PRINT

_____
Name:

_____
Job Title/Function:

_____
Company (if applicable):

_____
Street Address:

_____

_____
City: *State:*   *Zip*

_____
Daytime Phone:

Please clip along dotted line and mail to:

Microsoft*University***

One Microsoft Way, Redmond, WA 98052-6399

Microsoft, the Microsoft logo, and MS are registered trademarks, and Windows and The Lecture Series are trademarks of Microsoft Corporation.

X604

Other Titles from Microsoft Press

WORD FOR WINDOWS™ COMPANION
Mark W. Crane

WORD FOR WINDOWS COMPANION will make Word for Windows easier to learn and use. Regardless of your level of expertise, you'll find a wealth of useful information in this comprehensive resource. It's both an exceptional tutorial for new Word users and a master reference guide for experienced users. You'll learn basic concepts of word processing, typography, and design so that you'll be able to create professional-looking documents with confidence and ease. In addition to detailed explanations, the book offers scores of illustrations, examples, and tips to enhance your productivity. An extensive index and side-margin headings make information readily accessible.

896 pages, softcover   7 $1/2$ x 9 $1/4$ $26.95   Order Code WOWICO

WORKING WITH WORD FOR WINDOWS™
Russell Borland

WORKING WITH WORD FOR WINDOWS is the most comprehensive book available for intermediate users of Microsoft Word for Windows. Written by a member of the Word for Windows development team, this example-packed book will be your primary reference to all the exciting document processing, desktop publishing, and WYSIWYG features of Microsoft Word for Windows. In-depth information, advice, and hands-on examples show you how to customize the user interface, use a variety of fonts and type sizes, insert graphics into documents, use macros to automate routine editing, position text and graphics, link text and graphics within documents, and more.

656 pages, softcover   7 $3/8$ x 9 $1/4$ $22.95   Order Code WOWOWI

MICROSOFT® WORD TECHNICAL REFERENCE
For Windows™ and OS/2 Presentation Manager
Microsoft Corporation

The extraordinary power of Microsoft Word for Windows and Word for OS/2 Presentation Manager places them far ahead of conventional word processors and document processors—even desktop-publishing software. They are an ideal platform for developing sophisticated business applications for individual, work-group, or company-wide needs. The MICROSOFT WORD TECHNICAL REFERENCE is the single source of detailed, authoritative information for advanced users and corporate developers creating applications and document-processing systems with Microsoft Word in the PC environment. This guide includes in-depth coverage on macros and fields, WordBASIC, external file converters, Rich Text Format (RTF), Dynamic Data Exchange (DDE), and Dynamic Link Libraries (DLL).

450 pages, softcover   7 $3/8$ x 9 $1/4$ $22.95   Order Code WOTERE

RUNNING MICROSOFT® EXCEL
The Complete Reference to Microsoft Excel on the IBM® PC, PS/2,® and Compatibles
The Cobb Group: Douglas Cobb and Judy Mynhier

Here is the most complete and authoritative guide to Microsoft Excel available anywhere. No matter what your level of expertise—seasoned spreadsheet user, beginning or occasional Microsoft Excel user, or longtime Lotus 1-2-3 user—RUNNING MICROSOFT EXCEL will be your primary source of information, advice, and tutorials. It's packed with step-by-step instructions, scores of examples and tips, and dozens of illustrations, and it covers every significant function and command of the spreadsheet, database, and charting environments. The easy-to-follow tutorial will help you quickly learn both the basics and most advanced features of Microsoft Excel.

736 pages, softcover   7 $3/8$ x 9 $1/4$ $24.95   Order Code RUEX

TOOLBOOK® COMPANION
Joseph R. Pierce

The first and definitive book on using and understanding ToolBook—the software construction set that makes it possible for users to "desktop program" in the Windows environment. This authoritative tutorial is for anyone—regardless of Windows programming experience—who wants to create Windows applications with ToolBook. Along with step-by-step instructions are dozens of practical examples that show how to create buttons, fields, and other elements in the typical Windows application. Most importantly, there is a special section on using OpenScript, ToolBook's built-in programming language.

720 pages, softcover $7^{1}/_{2}$ x $9^{1}/_{4}$ **$27.95**   **Order Code TOCO**

MICROSOFT® WINDOWS™ GUIDE TO PROGRAMMING
Microsoft Corporation

MICROSOFT WINDOWS GUIDE TO PROGRAMMING is an example-packed introduction—for experienced C programmers—using the Microsoft Windows version 3 Application Programming Interface (API). You'll discover how to use Windows' functions, messages, and data structures to build efficient and reliable programs. If you've never programmed in Windows before, you'll appreciate the step-by-step instructions accompanied by dozens of sample applications you can compile and run under Windows. Some of the topics include using the Graphics Device Interface (GDI) to create your own output, processing input from the keyboard and mouse, using push buttons and list boxes, using the Clipboard, working with printers, displaying bitmaps, and more. You'll also find introductory information on advanced topics including memory management, dynamic data exchange, and printer initialization.

560 pages, softcover $7^{3}/_{8}$ x $9^{1}/_{4}$ **$29.95**   **Order Code WIGUPR**

MICROSOFT® WINDOWS™ PROGRAMMER'S REFERENCE
Microsoft Corporation

If you are a Windows programmer, you need this up-to-date, comprehensive reference to each component in the Windows Application Programming Interface (API). Included is detailed information on every Windows version 3 function, message, data type, resource-compiler statement, assembly-language macro, and file format. This information is the foundation for any program that takes advantage of Windows' special capabilities: data interchange with other applications; device-independent graphics; multitasking; dynamic linking and shared display; memory, keyboard, mouse, and system timer resources.

1136 pages, softcover $7^{3}/_{8}$ x $9^{1}/_{4}$ **$39.95**   **Order Code WIPRRE**

MICROSOFT® WINDOWS™ PROGRAMMING TOOLS
Microsoft Corporation

MICROSOFT WINDOWS PROGRAMMING TOOLS provides detailed information on using the C Compiler and the linker to compile and link source files and the Resource Compiler to compile application resources. In addition, you'll find details on debugging and on using the Resource Editors and optimizing tools (including CodeView) that come with the Microsoft Windows Software Development Kit. Of special importance is the section on the Windows Help system, its design, and its programming guidelines.

384 pages, softcover $7^{3}/_{8}$ x $9^{1}/_{4}$ **$24.95**   **Order Code WIPRTO**

Microsoft Press® books are available wherever quality computer books are sold,
or credit card orders can be placed by calling 1-800-MSPRESS.
Please refer to BBK.